High culture and tall chimneys

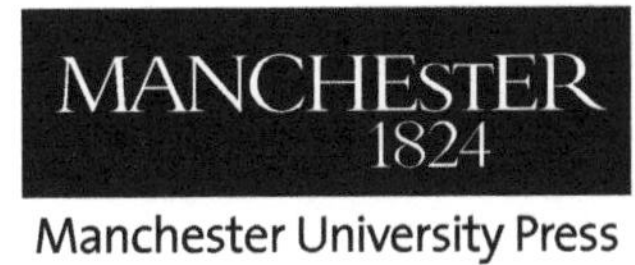

Manchester University Press

High culture and tall chimneys

Art institutions and urban society in Lancashire, 1780–1914

James Moore

Manchester University Press

Published by Manchester University Press
Oxford Road, Manchester M13 9PL
www.manchesteruniversitypress.co.uk

British Library Cataloguing-in-Publication Data
A catalogue record for this book is available from the British Library

ISBN   978 1 7849 9147 0   hardback
ISBN   978 1 5261 6699 9   paperback

First published 2018
Paperback published 2022

Typeset
by Toppan Best-set Premedia Limited

CONTENTS

FIGURES

ACKNOWLEDGEMENTS

The author would like to thank friends and former colleagues at the University of Manchester who provided advice and support during the research for this book. He would particularly like to acknowledge the assistance of Professor Marcia Pointon, Dr Helen Rees Leahy, Dr Colin Trodd, Dr Dongho Chun and Dr Catherine Tite, from the School of Art History and Archaeology, and the late Dr Peter Lowe, from the School of History, who offered encouragement and critical support. This book began as part of an Arts and Humanities Research Board project at the University of Manchester, and thanks are particularly due to members of the project's advisory board, especially Edward Morris, Dr Julian Treuherz, formerly of the Walker Art Gallery, and Terry Wyke of Manchester Metropolitan University. This is a work that has been more than ten years in development, and the author would also like to acknowledge the support and fellowship of colleagues at the University of Lancaster, the Institute of Historical Research, the British University in Egypt and the University of Leicester who have commented on aspects of the book. The author would also like to thank the archivists and staff at the many gallery archives and local record offices consulted during the course of this research. Omissions and errors in this work are solely the responsibility of the author.

Some of the material from Chapter 8 has been previously published in the journal *Northern History*. See J. Moore, 'Periclean Preston, Public Art and the Classical Tradition in Late-Nineteenth-Century Lancashire', *Northern History*, 40 (2003), 299–323.

ABBREVIATIONS

AGC	Art Gallery Committee
APFA	Association for the Patronage of the Fine Arts
BL	British Library (London)
CGM	Council General Meeting
CM	Council Minute Book
FLM	Free Library and Museum (Oldham)
GM	General Meeting
LC	Liverpool Corporation
LRI	Liverpool Royal Institution
LRO	Liverpool Record Office
MCC	Manchester City Council
MCL	Manchester Central Library
ORO	Oldham Record Office
PLS	Preston Local Studies Library
RMI	Royal Manchester Institution
SRML	Salford Royal Museum and Library
UMSC	University of Manchester Special Collections

1

Introduction: art in the first industrial society

The 1857 Manchester Art Treasures Exhibition was a landmark in British cultural life.[1] It marked the emergence of the industrialist and merchant as a key force in the patronage of British art in the same way that the 1832 Reform Act heralded the arrival of that same social class in British politics.[2] The exhibition was organised by a largely middle-class network of patrons, and many of the most celebrated exhibits came from the homes of those who had made their wealth through trade, finance and industrial production (see Figure 1).[3] Yet while studies have been undertaken on the great private collections of these industrial and commercial leaders, less systematic attention has been paid to the contribution they made to the formation of the art institutions that grew up alongside this extensive pattern of private collecting.[4] Where urban art institutions have received attention, interest has often been focused on capital cities, with one influential essay all but ignoring regional institutions.[5] Where art historians have taken an interest in the English regions, the focus has often been on the role of voluntary bodies and local corporations as the sponsors of individual artistic projects, such as the famous Ford Madox Brown murals at Manchester's town hall, with less attention paid to the emergence of art institutions and the role they played in the wider cultural economy of industrial centres.[6] Waterfield's recent national survey was an important landmark but it suffers from a London-centric perspective, contrasting London to what are described as the 'provinces' while offering little on the smaller towns, the dynamics of urban processes or questions of regionality.[7] Hill has made important contributions to our understanding of the class dimensions of late nineteenth-century city art museums, while Woodson-Boulton has highlighted the influence of Ruskinian agendas on major municipal art galleries.[8] The present study takes a broader perspective, informed by a detailed understanding of the nature of industrial Britain. Rather than

1

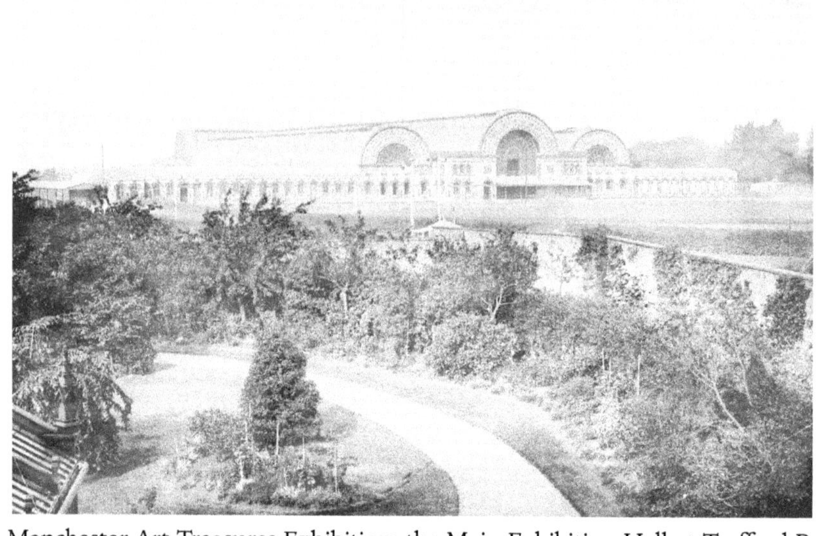

1 Manchester Art Treasures Exhibition: the Main Exhibition Hall at Trafford Park

seeing art institutions as primarily a late Victorian phenomenon, this book seeks to explore their development from their origins in the late eighteenth century. In particular, it will reject the view that one particular set of cultural ideas ever came to dominate the public art movement. By focusing on the world's 'first industrial region', the county of Lancashire and its hinterland, it is possible to develop a more thorough understanding of the roots of these institutions, the new urban elites that created them and the different values that they promoted and celebrated. This detailed regional approach will allow for an understanding of the complex cultural politics surrounding art institutions, the ways in which they were used as a platform for a range of social reform agendas and the reasons why their role came to be questioned in the early twentieth century. This volume will explore art institutions as key elements of the urban public sphere, as agents for social inclusion and, eventually, as cultural democratisation. Although managed largely by a small segment of the urban middle class, art institutions could exercise influence only if they were public bodies, promoting a public purpose. By the 1850s this meant advancing the interests of all classes, through the spread of cultural knowledge and visual literacy. Sometimes this was to be done for narrow instrumental purposes; sometimes a 'higher' objective was postulated. Sometimes this was primarily to serve the civic community, sometimes to advance the self-improving aspirations of the individual.

This is a study of institutions, networks and decisions as much as of art production and display. Understanding how institutions evolved in response to the changing society around them is the focus of this work. The ecological concentrations of population, urbanisation and capital surpluses created by proto-industrialisation were important preconditions for the evolution of cultural institutions, but they do not in themselves provide a sufficiently powerful explanation for why particular types of institutions emerged.[9] Although middle-class cultural leaders promoted a vision of cultural life that reflected bourgeois and largely liberal values, there was, in practice, a great deal of disagreement about the function and role of art institutions. Sometimes this could reflect the political fissures in the urban middle class.[10] However, the disagreement could reflect more profound differences about the type of cultural education that was required in the modern liberal state, the quality or otherwise of modern British art or the role of modern capitalism in facilitating or undermining cultural production. By the time Edwardian Lancashire had inherited vast public collections of Victorian art, it had begun to question the cultural insularity that had inspired them and even the cultural value of the art galleries in which they were housed.

The growing wealth of Lancashire in the late eighteenth century is the starting point for this study. The early part of the book explores the processes through which private capital was converted into social and public institutions, often building on pre-existing urban networks. Adopting a regional perspective offers a number of advantages over approaches that focus on the locality or nation, especially when one is attempting to assess processes of long-term historical transformation. Most importantly, it provides a useful strategic perspective for understanding how a variety of cultural and geographical identities can be expressed through artistic patronage and production. Gunn has shown how the specificities of locality and region could be expressed by newly emergent cultural practice and how cultural performances reshaped those identities.[11] Although London institutions exercised a powerful influence over the national art market, regional art activity, particularly that in Lancashire, did much to shape the taste for modern British paintings – a trend well established by the early Victorian period. Perhaps the most influential British art trader of all, Thomas Agnew and Sons, began business in Lancashire and continued to have strong associations with Liverpool and Manchester throughout the nineteenth century. The advice of Agnews was to shape private collections across Britain and was very influential in the formation of the major municipal art galleries in Manchester, Salford, Liverpool and other towns of the region.[12]

A regional perspective, then, allows for a deeper analysis of the landscape of cultural formations. Since Langton's influential article on the emergence of regional cultures, historians have begun to see industrialisation as a factor in the formation and reformation of distinctive cultural outlooks.[13] This approach does not deny the importance of national narratives and agendas or the significance of individual taste and personal influences. However, it shows how sub-national cultural communities are formed and helps us to understand how those communities are sustained, whether that be through personal friendships, commercial inter-urban networks, civic projects or new cultural institutions such as art galleries and schools. As this study will illustrate, the growth in support for modern British art, often seen as a 'national' movement, was frequently driven by regional art markets and regional art institutions in industrial towns far distant from London. Much of the expansion of this market was due to the surpluses created by industry, with a rising middle class eschewing many of the artistic canons celebrated by the aristocracy for new cultural forms appropriate to their own interests and identities. It was profits from regional industry that allowed for the formation of a genuinely national market, creating new opportunities not only for collectors but also for artists who could often exploit civic and regional networks and loyalties to establish remunerative careers. These loyalties were complex and often overlapped, sometimes stretching overseas. Lancashire was the first industrial region and a key hub in a global economic network. Its worldwide commercial networks eventually provided new international dimensions to its regional identity and, unsurprisingly, its cultural life.[14]

While the networks of collectors stretched across the world, civic and regional networks provided the immediate framework for a stable and predictable art market. Early nineteenth-century collectors such as William Roscoe, William Hardman, Henry McConnel and Thomas Agnew often drew upon their local civic networks among the emerging middle-class citizenry to institutionalise the practices of art collecting and appreciation within the region and their own cities. Art museums, galleries, academies and schools were the mechanisms for bringing new cultural groupings together, establishing practices of cultural display and exchange and, ultimately, forging new artistic canons and approaches. It was through these institutions that the cultural politics of the new middle class were fought out, as competing elements sought to institutionalise their own practices through public display and validation. While these organisations often began as private societies or clubs, by the end of the century many had received official recognition, either by being absorbed by the local state or by becoming the recipients of official, and sometimes royal, patronage. Therefore this book will explore how private activity and private networks came together in institutional forms. It will examine the political relationships inherent in the development of institutional art, the power of institutional culture and the tensions between different, sometimes competing, institutional models.

While almost all cultural actors saw the institutionalisation of art as a public good, there was frequent disagreement about the objectives of such institutions – disagreement that became, if anything, more intense as cultural critics accused art institutions of 'failing' to meet the educative and intellectual agendas of wider society. Conservative critics questioned the utility of art as a specifically 'public' commodity as independently minded artists, collectors and social theorists refused to subsume their activities within dominant civic, regional and national agendas. Radical critics, meanwhile, accused artists and collectors of becoming subservient to oppressive national, institutional and commercial norms. By the end of the nineteenth century the city and the region were seen as key artistic communities, but for different reasons. For some, they were promulgators of distinctive socially improving cultural forms, promoting civic virtue and guarding against anarchy; for others the region and the city were a refuge where independent schools could flourish free from the authority of the dominant cultural institutions of the Royal Academy and the commercialism of the auction room.

This study will focus on Lancashire and towns in its immediate industrial hinterland, including Warrington and Stockport, that, while nominally in Cheshire, were closely integrated into Lancashire's industrial economy. This immediately raises the issue of whether Lancashire as a region possessed a cohesive identity. This is not a straightforward question. Regional stereotypes have influenced not only popular discourse but also academic historiography. Traditionally seen as the world's first industrial region, Lancashire has often been characterised as fostering a race of men 'independent, practical, rough, calculating and enterprising', with little interest in the genteel or liberal arts.[15] Charles Dickens's Thomas Gradgrind and Josiah Bounderby, unimaginative men obsessed with facts and unable to think creatively, became widely perceived as typical examples of Lancastrian industrialists.[16] Yet this is an unbalanced characterisation. Lancashire represented the 'leading sector' of British industrialisation, with economic growth and productivity gains driven by creativity and innovation.[17] The county developed a vibrant cultural economy, played a central role in the revival of British contemporary art, created a network of art institutions and produced some of the most distinctive public buildings of the nineteenth century. By 1914, even relatively small industrial towns such as Bury, Oldham and Rochdale each had a public art gallery, an art school and a strong network of local painters. Around the region, public buildings manifested the taste and identity of the local citizenry. Manchester's Gothic town hall, Liverpool's neo-classical St George's Hall and Preston's Periclean temple of art, the Harris Art Gallery, all served as monuments to a governing class prepared to express their new-found wealth through the canons of visual culture.

Lancashire was the first industrial region, but it was not solely an industrial region. Although it had only a small landed aristocracy, there were some important landed estates in Lancashire's hinterland, especially around the county town of Chester, most notably those of the Grosvenor family. Some members of the rural gentry, such as John Fleming Leicester of Tabley House, had important connections with Lancashire's elite urban society and supported cultural institutions, such as the Royal Manchester Institution (RMI).[18] Even in Lancashire itself, a county often thought to be dominated by the cotton trade and its associated industries, a resident gentry remained both politically and culturally influential. Henry Blundell of Ince was an important supporter of the early Liverpool Academy, while his friend and fellow collector Charles Townley provided the collection that led to the foundation of the Department of Greek and Roman Antiquities at the British Museum.[19] Agriculture continued to dominate the economy of south Cheshire and north Lancashire until the twentieth century, and even the cotton districts were not as homogeneous as one might expect. The cotton industry was internally divided between those towns which specialised in spinning and those associated with weaving, and as the century progressed larger towns tended to focus on the distribution trades.[20] The cotton district itself was really limited to only a small part of the region, south-east Lancashire.[21] Manchester may have been 'Cottonopolis', but by the second half of the nineteenth century it was more a centre of trade, storage and distribution than of production. The region's largest city, at least in 1800, was Liverpool, a city that generated most of its wealth from sea-borne trade and commerce. The towns between Liverpool and Manchester, such as Warrington and Wigan, came to be associated with the chemical industry, while the north Lancashire centres of Preston and Lancaster were the county's traditional administrative centres. There was no single primary economic centre but two economically dominant cities, Manchester and Liverpool. Although in some respects their economic functions were complementary, their rivalry grew as the nineteenth century progressed. The phrase 'Manchester men, Liverpool gentlemen' highlighted the popular perception that Manchester was the centre of industrial production, while Liverpool represented the gentrified commercial marketplace. In reality, the development of the railways ensured that Manchester would soon become an important marketplace itself, and the construction of the Manchester Ship Canal was a direct and audacious challenge to Liverpool's dominance of the sea-borne trade. It was a move that highlighted the increasingly bitter commercial rivalry between the two centres.[22]

If a shared sense of regional identity did exist, it tended to find its expression through the preservation of pre-urban forms of popular culture, the transmission of 'traditional' folk tales and different manifestations of the Lancashire dialect. The pioneering Liverpool collector Roscoe was well known for his broad Liverpudlian accent in metropolitan artistic circles and this formed an important component of his public persona.[23] The wide dissemination of the works of John Collier and Tim Bobbin in the eighteenth century suggests that there was a significant middle-class literary public who saw them as an important expression of their own identity.[24] Throughout the nineteenth century, the genre of Lancashire dialect writing continued to be influential.[25] Benjamin Brierley and Edwin Waugh were compared with Burns and Tennyson and often republished by middle-class sponsors.[26] Yet it is doubtful whether the dialect and folk tales of Lancashire ever became the basis of a firm and coherent cultural identity for the region. First, they tended to be rooted in an anti-urban localism of imagined village life that had only passing antiquarian relevance for the industrial worker.[27] Secondly, the most famous folk and dialect tales were associated with a particular part of Lancashire, the villages around Rochdale, where Tim Bobbin first collected his elements of local dialect.[28] In reality, Lancashire embraced a variety of linguistic traditions and, of course, even today Mancunian and Liverpudlian accents and dialect are widely divergent. As the nineteenth century passed processes of migration, most particularly the Irish diaspora, produced a cosmopolitan community in which linguistic uniformity was impossible to imagine as an element of regional cohesion.

The political fragmentation and ideological diversity of Lancashire also made it difficult for a distinctive sense of regional identity to emerge. The administration of Lancashire county government was divided between the old county town of Lancaster, which housed the county assizes, and the port and gentry town of Preston, which had the benefit of a more geographically central location and was home to the duchy courts. Politically, the region's two major cities, Liverpool and Manchester, sat at the opposite points of the ideological spectrum.[29] Manchester was a bastion of liberalism; it led the way in the parliamentary reform movement and acted as the headquarters of free trade, through the activities of the Anti-Corn Law League.[30] Manchester local government was dominated by the Liberal party until the early 1880s, and in the Edwardian period the city became a strong supporter of progressive or social democratic Liberalism, through the work of C. P. Scott of the *Manchester Guardian*.[31] Liverpool, in contrast, developed a reputation for political conservatism. Its associations with the slave trade meant that many of its merchants were reluctant to support Abolition.[32] Large-scale Irish immigration caused widespread working-class hostility that manifested itself in the formation of a strong Orange movement, allied to the Conservative party.[33] For much of the nineteenth century, the political leaderships of the two cities sat in outright opposition, a rivalry that was to be enhanced by economic competition and mutual cultural emulation. Thus, while regional identity remained weak, civic identity tended to be articulated more widely.

Identification with the town or city was not, of course, simply a reflection of partisan competition, or even of the economic processes associated with mass urbanisation. It was often a process fostered by emerging political elites who saw the local urban centre as both their political power base and a platform for projecting their status within the region.[34] The enfranchisement of large towns and cities by the 1832 Reform Act and the creation of representative urban government following the 1835 Municipal Corporations Act not only shifted the basis of political power: it encouraged the citizenry to see the town or city as the primary unit of local political organisation. As urban government took more powers, building city halls, libraries, art galleries and public infrastructure, civic identity was increasingly expressed and legitimised through these very processes of public improvements.[35] The town and city, not the region, became the focus of local political authority and local identity. However, economic processes drew towns and cities together into wider inter-urban networks. Cultural links were important too, with networks of libraries, museums, art galleries and exhibitions creating distinctive communities of cultural interest. The very fact that Lancashire was not centred on any single urban centre may have fostered a greater willingness, on the part of cultural patrons and agents, to visit neighbouring towns and cities, reciprocating social invitations and sharing innovations. The sense of region therefore lay more in its networks, public events and shared experience than in a focus on a single geographical location or place of authority.

Although it is difficult to locate a regional identity in geographical terms, the towns and cities of Lancashire undoubtedly enjoyed the common experience of rapid economic expansion that is traditionally described as industrial revolution.[36] This rapid economic expansion is clearly crucial in explaining the creation of so much cultural capital in the region. However, while many economists have traditionally sought supply-side explanations for the processes of industrial transformation, it is also important to explore the demand side of the economy if long-term cultural change is to be understood. The consumer revolution has been described as 'the necessary analogue to the industrial revolution', with demand for new goods coming not merely as a response to productivity savings, but as a result of increased propensity to consume.[37] This increased propensity was not merely a product of the general growth in disposable income, but rather a cultural change fostered by emulation and social competition and encouraged by the growth of the commercial media. It also exploited Romanticist notions of self-expression and self-realisation, providing consumption with an ethical dimension.[38] The purchase of luxury goods, including art and works of culture, allowed citizens to aspire to higher social and cultural status and, in this view, helped to make eighteenth-century urban society more open, increasing opportunities for social mobility. Of course, this now 'traditional' historical interpretation of the consumer revolution needs to be treated with some caution; Fine and Leopold are probably right to suggest that it both underestimates the levels of social inequality and overestimates the contribution of luxury goods to industrial transformation.[39] However, the growth of the luxury goods market, with its focus on creative material products, did have important implications for the nature of cultural life and associated social institutions. It was a consumer revolution predicated on visible, material, personal competition. Since Veblen, historians have seen consumption as an inherently public act, with material possessions gaining meaning through actions of social display.[40] In order to maximise the impact of this visual performance, much of the display of consumption took place in urban locations where influential social groups were ecologically concentrated: on promenades, in meeting rooms, during concerts or as part of associative public functions. Without the city, the public display of consumption – and culture – was difficult and its impact more limited.

The English 'urban renaissance' was the product of the broadening of the distribution of wealth and the desire for status in a rapidly changing social climate. Borsay is particularly emphatic in linking this consumer revolution with the development of the city and, in particular, the sophisticated public amenities where wealth could be put on display.[41] While some, notably McInnes, have suggested that the geographical distribution of this urban renaissance may have been more limited than Borsay suggests, there can be little doubt that those towns that exhibited the greatest expansion of the consumer economy were among those who developed the earliest public and cultural institutions.[42] Detailed empirical research would seem to indicate that it was indeed the urban middle classes who were the economic engines of this urban renaissance and not the traditional gentry.[43] Certainly, the expansion of urban public and cultural institutions in the mid-eighteenth century would suggest a considerable broadening in those who had sufficient disposable income and sufficient inclination to support activities associated with the public sphere. Innovations, such as the development of the provincial printing press, the newspaper and the subscription library, had become almost universal in major towns by the end of the century. An important part of this consumerist expansion of the public sphere was associated with the market for literature. The lapse of the restrictive Licensing Act of 1695 marked a period of rapid literary expansion. By 1760 around 150 newspapers had been established in over fifty towns.[44] The creation of a literary public served to form a public space of political and social engagement that went beyond the traditional ties of family, locality and kinship. In an era of a highly restricted urban franchise and limited organs of local administration, the press created a forum for public intercourse and debate. Above all, it gave citizens, in a world that was rapidly becoming urbanised, personal visibility to advertise not only their products, but also their common cultural interests.[45] Associations no longer needed to be left to personal introduction, the public meeting or chance, but could be forged through the agency of print. It is, then, unsurprising that so many of the pioneering art institutions, such as the Liverpool Academy and the RMI, used the print media to create visibility, credibility and legitimacy.

The urban renaissance fostered a range of new spaces where people gathered to conduct cultural business, and not all were elitist. Coffee dens, inns and alehouses were important social institutions for all classes. Even the gentry were happy to frequent the eighteenth-century alehouse. The Earl of Derby, for example, made the Albion Inn in Manchester his long-term residence during his annual visit to the city.[46] Magistrates were known to meet in inns, especially when formal public buildings were unavailable locally.[47] However, by the end of the eighteenth century, there was an increasing tendency for larger urban centres to develop higher-class cultural facilities, often with restrictive access, that were aimed at an emerging elite element of the bourgeoisie. Some urban improvements, especially those associated with key infrastructure projects, were financed by public loans raised through local state-appointed Improvement Commissioners. Cultural institutions, however, were usually financed by a system of subscription or share ownership.[48] Improvement Commissioners rarely had powers to fund public buildings, and there were few opportunities to raise them through private credit. Private subscription associations were notoriously unstable and difficult to sustain, especially those without a distinct commercial function, such as art institutions.[49] Even the irascible William Roscoe in Liverpool encountered difficulties, and the modern Liverpool Academy succeeded only after several earlier manifestations collapsed through lack of sustained support.[50] There was little prospect, therefore, of banks providing substantial support to new cultural societies, and even in 1815 credit facilities were limited and restrictive.[51] Public institutions therefore depended on private patronage and subscription income to provide the necessary capital.[52]

Cultural institutions should be viewed as part of a consumer revolution that was closely associated with a new public sphere of display and emulation. Regions such as Lancashire, which became urbanised and industrialised most quickly, enjoyed particularly rapid growth of a consumerist public sphere. This broadening of consumer culture undermined some of the traditional tenets of visual authority. If a merchant of wealth could dress as well as a duke, he could obtain the same visual status. Similarly, if poorer classes could obtain cheap imitation fancy goods they could both aspire to, and undermine, the value of the consumer products of the middle class. A more open, consumer society allowed cultural goods to be obtained outside the usual processes of elite socialisation; access to financial resources was the only significant limitation.[53] Mass consumption threatened not only the status of certain luxury goods but also the aristocracy's claim to be the guardians of cultural wealth.[54] The mass copying of old masters, often for middle-class collectors, was to fundamentally devalue old master works and eventually led to a rise in the relative value of contemporary British art.[55] For some, the 'mass production' of artists in public art schools threatened the status of art itself. Consumerism and the creation of new social spaces changed the nature of group activity and socialisation to one that prized abstract liberal principles of inclusivity over traditional patterns of elite sociability. Habermas's work on the public sphere has shown how rational and critical values often lay behind the establishment of group activity, providing an objectively legitimised public space of identity and discourse free from traditional forms of authority.[56] Ultimately, the creation of a more open, universal public sphere also created universal insecurities. The fear of the mass-produced 'commodity public' saw its most vivid expression in Arnold's *Culture and Anarchy* in 1869, where culture was seen as the only defence against a commodified and debased mass 'anarchy'.[57]

The emergence of a powerful cultural life in industrial towns, such as those in Lancashire, coincided with the rise of the middle class to urban political dominance. This has led some authors to see 'culture' as the outgrowth of an essentially materialist struggle. Bermingham, for example, has argued that culture emerged as an exclusive category to enshrine power, protect value and validate authority, the product of distinct phases of capitalist consumerism.[58] Bermingham's view of the history of culture clearly owes much to that of Bourdieu, who sees the notion of culture and taste as a way of both creating and maintaining social distinctions. This notion of culture, or more specifically 'high culture', is often associated with the capitalist desire to maintain the economic value of specific accumulated assets, such as picture collections. Art institutions often played an important role in this process of promoting specific schools and thus maintaining the value of particular collections. There are certainly early examples of cultural institutions adding to the reputations of particular artists and, consequently, the commercial value of their paintings.[59] However, this approach to studying culture is not necessarily useful in understanding the motivations for all cultural action, such as those inherent in the formation of civic art institutions. First, a civic institution was a collective effort which emphasised the production of an external, specifically public good – an exhibition, a lecture or a programme of education. Although cultural achievements often enhanced the social status of the leaders of the organising institution, the focus of that institution's work was the creation of an externality that would be beneficial to a much broader group of citizens. This was essential in providing the public justification for, and legitimisation of, art institutions. To limit the benefits of the externality too narrowly damaged both the reputation of the institution and its constituent membership. Therefore there was inherent tension between the supposed pressure for exclusivity and the absolute necessity for broader public validation.[60] Secondly, empirical evidence suggests that the semi-private and exclusive nature of art institutions was an embarrassment in an emerging liberal community obsessed by the public visibility and accountability of its leaders. The problems of the late nineteenth-century Royal Academy demonstrate both the tension between commercial and academic pressures and the difficulty inherent in a semi-private body claiming national cultural authority.[61] Similar tendencies can be observed in Lancashire; it is notable that both the Liverpool Royal Institution (LRI) and the RMI eventually surrendered their private status and were brought under representative civic control. Finally, Bermingham's type of approach makes little reference to the specific intellectual problems with which cultural institutions attempted to engage, viewing their activities as an effort to sustain a subjective category (taste or culture) for the purpose of a subjective grouping (usually the middle class). This approach neglects the complex cultural preoccupations of the period and fails to engage with the ways in which these preoccupations themselves shaped the category of culture. In order to understand why cultural institutions are created, why they have such purchase and why they have so much prominence in the field of visual art, it is necessary to examine something of the broader intellectual trends of the eighteenth century and the tensions that lay within them.

The power of 'culture' was in its ability to command wide public acknowledgment and recognition, or, in other words, to have a demonstrable social or civic purpose. Within public cultural activity, the notion of taste took on particular importance and was often used to mark out differential status.[62] In an era of uncertainty and instability, the notion of taste was gradually established to create a category of citizenry who had discriminatory ability.[63] Taste was associated with particular forms of social training that were traditionally limited to certain landed social classes. However, the growth of a consumer society broadened access to that training, such that by 1766 Oliver Goldsmith's *Vicar of Wakefield* was able to argue that it was 'in this middle order of mankind are generally to be found all the arts, wisdom and virtues of society'.[64] Some went beyond this, arguing that the traditional aristocracy lived an essentially debased, idle and uncultured life, cut off from the broader social intercourse and cosmopolitanism of the city. Cultural politics thus reflected the spatial politics of early nineteenth-century social conflict. The city of the urban middle class was increasingly seen as the centre of culture, taste and virtue. Taste was a quality to be cultivated, and it could be effectively cultivated only in the social environment of the city, where it would develop for the benefit of the wider community.[65]

This association between the city and the development of sophisticated cultural tastes reflects not only contemporary social debate, but also Renaissance and Enlightenment interpretations of the classical and Renaissance past, when the arts were at their supposed zenith.[66] The whole notion of 'civility' was, of course, intimately tied to the city.[67] Ancient civilisations saw culture as unthinkable outside cities, and the term 'barbarian' was used to describe any foreigner unassociated with a city or recognised urban colony. Pausanias, writing in the second century AD, declined to describe a settlement as a city unless it possessed certain key cultural features, such as a theatre, an agora or public buildings.[68] In other words, cities were defined in terms of their function as cultural, as well as administrative or economic, centres. The great artistic civilisations of the past were associated with specific city states, and the models of Periclean Athens and Medici Florence were to appear repeatedly in debates about contemporary culture and taste. In Lancashire, Roscoe became famous for his historical writings on the Medici family and self-consciously saw his home city of Liverpool as a latter-day Florence.[69] Manchester's urban topography soon became littered with Florentine-style architecture, with modern cotton warehouses aping the appearance of their Renaissance predecessors. However, it was classical models that had the most widespread application and most enduring legacy. The RMI of Charles Barry is the best-known early 'neo-Grec' building in Lancashire, but it was only one instance of a more widespread attempt to transform the Manchester skyline. Nearby buildings, such as the Portico Library, reflect a similar preoccupation, as do early municipal buildings such as the city's original town hall.[70] William Fairbairn's attempt to reconstruct the entire city centre around Piccadilly Square was perhaps the most audacious attempt to impose a neo-classical vision on a modern city. Under Fairbairn's plan the whole central square would have been reconstructed into a grand classical gateway, with a new public university, baths, infirmary and columnar arcades.[71] Although this visionary classical reinterpretation of urban space never found enough financial support to be realised, Manchester's rival, Liverpool, did reconstruct much of its key urban core in a neo-classical style. The magnificent St George's Hall came to dominate the city's central square and was gradually joined by similar emulative classical buildings, including the public library, museum and Walker Art Gallery. Significantly, other major British industrial cities, such as Birmingham and Glasgow, adopted similar styles.[72] The enduring success of neo-classical, and particularly Greek, forms was reflective of the civic virtues associated with the ancient city.[73] Similar cultural reference points and values lay behind the construction of the Portico Library, Manchester, in 1808 (Figure 2), St George's Hall, Liverpool, in the 1850s (Figure 3) and the Harris Art Gallery, Preston, in the 1880s. In a world of consumerism and debased public taste,

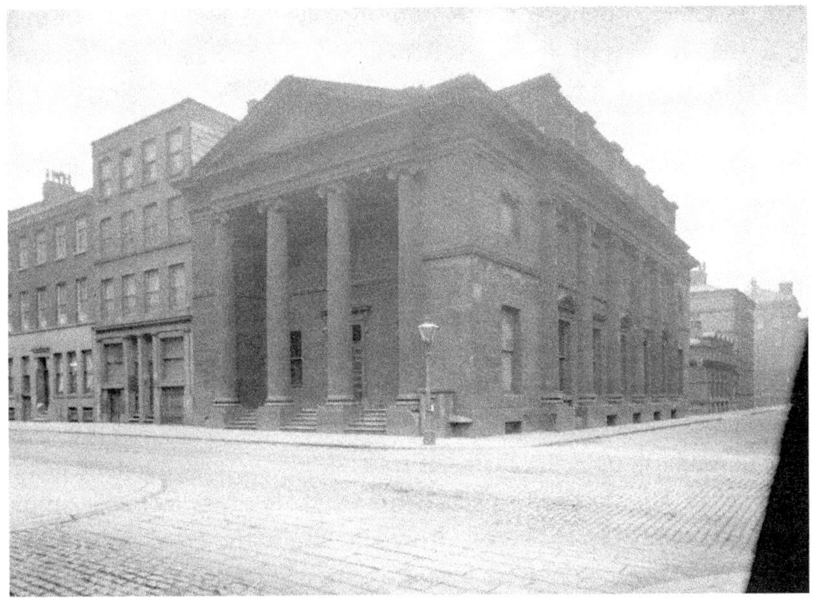

2 The Portico Library in Manchester

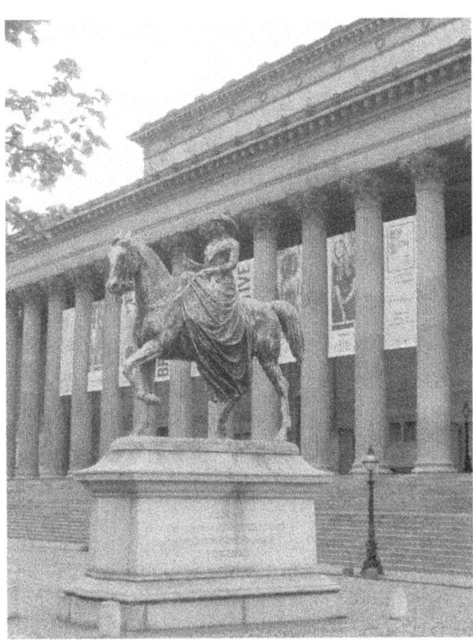

3 St George's Hall in Liverpool

the Greeks offered objective standards with universal application. For men like Hibbert, the architect of the Harris Art Gallery, the 'Hellenic race' had reached the highest standard in taste and public culture. Only by emulating their genius could taste be purified and advanced.[74]

The appeal of the objective standard was obvious in a period of rapid change and uncertainty. It is significant that it was the middle classes that were most closely associated with the neo-classical urban form. Few major neo-classical urban buildings were erected through aristocratic patronage. Almost all were products of middle-class cultural associations or individual middle-class entrepreneurs. Some, such as Manchester's original town hall and Preston's Harris art gallery, were publicly sponsored by the units of middle-class local government. The replication of ancient forms of architecture in the modern city was not merely an attempt to establish objective forms of taste, or even to articulate the forms of a particular class. It was a product of a desire to create a new form of community, reflecting the civic humanism and virtue inherent in the great cities of the past. Liverpool and Manchester were aware of the great economic transformation around them and their own unprecedented growth. The challenge was to turn this economic capital into a product of lasting value: to promote a notion of collective virtue and taste that would secure the stability of the political community and provide the basis for its future development.[75]

The city of the proto-industrial age was characterised by rapid expansion but also by economic and political insecurity. While historians have traditionally viewed the eighteenth century as one of growing political stability, in practice this 'stability' tended to be limited to the rather stagnant Hanoverian party system. In reality, the latter half of the 'long eighteenth century' was punctuated by what O'Gorman has viewed as a series of crises: the American revolution crisis of 1779–84, the French revolutionary crisis of 1787–1801, the constitutional crisis of 1816–20 and the reform crisis of 1828–32.[76] All these crises brought the fear of revolution, the toppling of the party system and the collapse of parliamentary rule. Even the 'religious question', supposedly settled after the repression of the 1745 rebellion, still caused political violence and instability, as the Catholic antique collector Charles Townley found when forced to flee from his London home at the time of the Gordon riots to escape the attention of a 'Church and King' mob.[77] Yet perhaps the most important political division was not between Protestants and Roman Catholics, but between the increasingly fragmented elements of the Protestant churches. The pre-1835 unreformed units of city government, the corporations, were often dominated by Anglican landowning interests associated with the Tory party. Many of the new urban middle class were Nonconformists allied to the Whig and Liberal parties. This politico-religious division was to cut across much of nineteenth-century urban political life and threatened the cultural fragmentation of the city's elite and perhaps even the destruction of urban forms of government. Following the 1835 Municipal Corporations Act, many Nonconformist Liberals, led by Cobden, urged urban populations to petition for new, more representative forms of city government. Sometimes, when these were granted, the Anglican Tories not only refused to co-operate but rejected the very legitimacy of these forms of administration.[78]

The economic fortunes of industrial cities were also prone to periodic shocks and instability. Britain had become a world trading power, and much of the country's expansion of trade was dependent on protecting its overseas commercial empire. The problems of the East India Company are well documented, but in Lancashire it was the American revolution that provided the greatest shock to the regional economy. Liverpool had emerged as a great international trading centre, but the abolition of the slave trade threatened to deprive it of an important component of its traditional business. The growth of French sea power threatened not only Britain's security, but all those ports tied into its growing maritime economy. Alongside these insecurities were the problems associated with the speculative nature of much of the early proto-industrial economy. The banking sector was relatively primitive and regionally fragmented. The collapse of one local bank could have profound repercussions for the whole of the city's economy. The most famous victim of a banking crisis was of course Liverpool's William Roscoe, whose own bank collapsed, resulting in the loss of almost all of his personal fortune. Roscoe was not the only 'man of culture' to suffer such an indignity. Henry McConnel, Manchester's pioneering collector of contemporary art, also suffered financial problems that forced the sale of much of his collection.[79] Even in the later nineteenth century, the unstable nature of mercantilist capitalist enterprise produced more victims. The plutocratic merchant Sam Mendel, famous for the ambitious development of a public art collection at Manley Hall, was a victim of the changing trade patterns brought about by the opening of the Suez Canal and ended his days in poverty.[80]

Given the instability in a rapidly expanding early industrial society, it is not surprising that much cultural debate focused on how to create stability and preserve progress. This debate was informed by an understanding of the rise and fall of past civilisations. The most famous contribution to this debate came, of course, with Gibbon's *History of the Decline and Fall of the Roman Empire*.[81] However, many eighteenth-century authors addressed the question of civil decline and often emphasised the relationship between stability and the flourishing of artistic and cultural endeavour. Shaftesbury, Winckelmann and Hume all made strong links between civil freedom, stability and artistic achievement. Thinkers from Thomas Paine to Adam Smith looked for the social causes that underpinned freedoms and provided the preconditions for the security of civil society.[82] A number of key Enlightenment thinkers helped to focus the debate about the failure of ancient civilisation and the contemporary progress of modern society.[83] Descartes's view that natural laws of God operated uniformly throughout all historical periods served to emphasise the importance of historical incidents and circumstances that created the discontinuities of history, such as the eclipse of Athens and the decline of the Roman Empire. Hume's account of human civilisation was one of very gradual progress, interrupted by breaks that over-turned the natural order. The difficulty was that few thinkers, if any, produced a theory of accident or incident that destroyed these patterns of progress or development.[84] It was only with Ferguson's *Essay on the History of Civil Society* that a broader comparative 'theory of stagnation' began to emerge and enter popular discourse. Decline, for Ferguson, was the product of:

> those revolutions of state that remove, or withhold, the objects of every ingenious study or liberal pursuit; that deprive the citizen of occasions to act as the member of a public; that crush his spirit; that debase his sentiments, and disqualify his mind for affairs.[85]

The revolutions were not natural or inevitable processes, but rather the product of apathy, neglect and corruption. Thus moral actions, principles and institutions could guard against decline. Ferguson's approach to civic republicanism, with its focus on enlightened citizenship, clearly owed much to Cicero and Tacitus. His concern for neglect and corruption reflected both contemporary constitutional debate surrounding the Hanoverian constitution and recent Roman historiography, notably Hooke's work on the Roman Republic and Gibbon's work on luxury and political decline. Since De Beaufort's 1737 *Treatise on Liberty in Civil Society* historians had generally followed Polybius and Tacitus in identifying personal ambition and corruption as the major destructive force in political commonwealths.[86] However, Ferguson is particularly notable because of the popularity of his writing and the influence of his central conceptual idea sur-rounding constitutionalism and human nature. By 1782 his popularity rivalled that of Gibbon, and his history of civil society was already in its fifth edition. His central idea, that decline could be defeated through the protection and advancement of civic virtue and liberal culture, became the dominant theme of civic humanist discourse. The idea was consistent with the emerging republic of taste and made the preservation and advancement of 'high culture' a moral necessity. The public nature of taste meant that it could not be too exclusive. A notion of taste that was defined too narrowly would fail to embrace the broad civic role that was essential if the civil state was to be protected.

The languages of civic humanism that emerged inevitably shaped the nature of art productions.[87] The traditional heroic school of epic paintings tended to be supplanted by one that emphasised softer, civic virtues related to cultured citizenship. This move is often associated with the lectures and writings of Sir Joshua Reynolds, but also reflects broader changes in literary taste away from the older notions of tragedy and epic.[88] These developments had a profound influence on practices of collecting and displaying art. As Pears observes, the possession of expensive objects had always been a way of achieving distinction, yet by the second half of the eighteenth century the notion of artistic connoisseurship had become increasingly important.[89] Knowledge and understanding of painting were central to the creation of a liberal public. From Richardson's guides to connoisseurship in the early part of the century, the discussion of taste was part of the public utility of art.[90] The creation of a liberal public required the creation of public spaces through which ideas and values could be disseminated. There existed printed media and the public meeting place, but the art institution could do more. Art institutions, like the RMI in the early nineteenth century or the Harris gallery fifty years later, could be monuments to specific concepts of taste or liberal virtue. They were physical and permanent manifestations of the ideas of their creators, shaping the assumptions and behaviour of the subsequent generations who passed through their gates.

Despite the increased scholarly interest in institutions as agents of social change, until recently art histories have been relatively silent on the general importance of institutional developments.[91] Other disciplines have increasingly begun to see institutions as important in shaping patterns of human behaviour rather than simply being reflections of that behaviour. In economics the 'institutionalist school' has a long history dating back to the late nineteenth century, when figures such as Veblen, Commons and Mitchell all but created a new orthodoxy as a reaction to modern neo-classical approaches.[92] Recently, the economic institutional school has enjoyed something of a revival, with an increasing awareness of the importance of institutions in shaping the assumed natural laws of human activity.[93] This 'new institutionalism' has also become influential in political science, especially with the current debates about the development of supra-national bodies and the growth of the European community.[94] Political and social scientists have often examined institutions for their capacity to deliver public goods and their ability to mediate social tensions and regulate external forces. Art institutions operate in similar capacities, conciliating competing groups and reflecting the notions of culture and taste with which those groups identify.[95] However, institutions are also agents of transformation, articulating and legitimising social activities and practices that in turn shape the politics and identities of those with whom they come into contact.

In order to understand the role of institutions as agents, it is essential to examine the formative principles, historical ambitions, internal culture and social self-identity of the institution's constituent elements. These shape the norms and values within an institution and provide both the framework and constraints of all future decision-making. Similarly, it is important to be aware of the organisation's understanding of its own history and its evaluation of previous policy decisions.[96] This is not, however, to suggest that one should take a historically deterministic or 'path dependency' approach to the study of art institutions, nor necessarily invoke neo-Weberian models of bureaucratisation. Indeed, many of the art institutions in this study are characterised by their ability to respond to the changes around them, and some were accused of being too willing to change policy on the basis of artistic fashion. It was rare for one individual or group of individuals to control any art institution for a long period of time. Even when many art galleries were brought under municipal control at the end of the nineteenth century, the nature of political recruitment and promotion meant that art committee chairs changed frequently. Only the largest galleries had anything like a specialist permanent staff, and the few special-ist curators that were in place were usually subject to close political control. Art committees were usually composed of shifting alliances of non-specialist public servants and a sprinkling of connoisseurs, which, as the studies illustrate, usually left the connoisseurs with a high degree of authority and autonomy. Art institutions tended to be characterised by informal systems of management and regulation, and were often dependent on the skill of a small number of interested enthusiasts.

The design, foundational principles and policy trajectory of an institution clearly provide an important framework for its ability to develop activities that will shape its members, participants and audience. Social and political scientists have spent much time engaged in studying the 'designs' of organisations and their relationship to their future productive capacities.[97] However, it is important to recognise how organisations are capable of undergoing metamorphosis while apparently retaining the same structure of governance. Thus structures that are theorised as representative or open may, in their operational sociological dynamic, turn out to be much less so.[98] Similarly, superficial similarities in the management and structure of organisations do not necessarily imply operational or policy convergence. Almost all the municipal art galleries in Lancashire were administered by the same structures, by the same legislation and often by similar ruling principles. Yet the diversity of policy pursued suggests that the rationalism of the public sphere fostered a considerable degree of pluralism. This, in turn, suggests that the notions of 'art public' created by the prevailing paradigms of culture and taste were far from identical. This study will suggest that the tension between the preservation of taste and the pressure of the expansion of the public sphere created a number of highly differentiated 'art publics'. The different notions of 'art publics' were, of course, partly reflective of local differences and prevailing political ideology. Differences were also due to the fragmentation of the civic humanist discourse that had informed so much late eighteenth-century political thought.

The controversies about exactly who constitutes a public for art are complicated by the complex nature of collective identities inherent in nineteenth-century urban life. The universalist principles embedded in the language of liberal popular politics were particularly important in shaping the discourse of the public. Joyce, Vernon and Lawrence, among others, have shown how the category of 'the people' became a powerful mobilising force, allowing disparate groups to come together in a politically virulent form of imagined collective identity.[99] While early forms of art institution, such as the RMI and LRI, often reflected the concerns of an intellectual elite and the desire to create institutions of 'high culture', by the mid-nineteenth century the intellectual climate had changed. Pioneering municipal museums, such as the Royal Museum and Library at Salford, were geared instead to a mass audience, responding to the demands for the provision of rational recreation, open space and mass public education. Yet, by the end of the century, the public debate about taste and culture had changed again. Influenced by the cultural pessimism and the *fin de siècle* atmosphere of the 1890s, there was an increasing preoccupation with the corrosion of culture by a mass audience and the failure of art institutions to have inculcated taste in their urban populations. The reactions, as this study shows, were many and various. Some attempted to assert a neo-liberal classicism, combining the universalistic language of modernism and the mass society with the objectivity inherent in Grecian standards of artistic excellence. Some sought a Ruskinian revolution in the nature and structure of museums, with the abandonment of the grand city museum and its replacement by communitarian forms of culture inspired by a largely imaginary pre-industrial past.[100] Others simply blamed the failure of modern British art and increasingly looked overseas to reinvigorate what was seen as a conservative and insular domestic art world.

These debates were not, of course, exclusive to Lancashire. One can see that museums in the United States also went through a complex phase of development as they attempted to wrestle with the problems inherent in their engagement with a growing mass society.[101] Art institutions in London faced comparable difficulties. The development of the first explicitly 'popular' metropolitan museum, the Victoria and Albert, has attracted particular interest from scholars. Goodwin has highlighted the difficulties of the museum in creating a coherent narrative and the tension between fine art and the more popular aspects of its activities.[102] Taylor shows how the dilemmas of mass society were also reflected in the access policy of the South Kensington Museum and, indeed, the types of behaviour to be permitted within its walls.[103] Debates about South Kensington were strategically important precisely because of the influence that the London authorities had over the development of regional museums.[104] However, in some respects, it was the traditional institutions of the nineteenth-century art world that were most disrupted by the disputed notion of 'art publics'. The narrowness and pernicious influence of the Royal Academy was so often a focus of criticism from outsiders. The long custom of using 'varnishing days' and private view days to provide commercial advantage to Academicians at the expense of outside painters was a long-running complaint and, for its critics, an example of how a supposedly noted public body used its power to secure private advantage for an established clique.[105] The difficulty was, of course, that the Royal Academy was not an exclusively public organisation; indeed it was really a private academy with state patronage. Yet it increasingly relied for cultural authority on its claim to be a national institution, rather than on its royal status. The academy had similar problems in its engagement with the commercial realities of late-nineteenth-century Britain. It was both a commercial organisation, dedicated to the sale of works of art, and an academy for the preservation of culture. In an earlier era when consumerism was limited to a relatively small class, the tension between consumerism and culture could be contained. When mass consumption became the norm, writers such as John Eagles were quick to identify its apparently corrosive impact, where art became commodified and culture debased.[106]

Various strategies were adopted to resolve this tension. Perhaps the most widespread was to try to combine the rhetoric and iconography of universal access and participation with an essentially paternalistic management style. Again, the appropriation of classical forms was apparent. First, the classical forms built on the pre-existing discourse and preoccupations of eighteenth-century civic humanism, while providing objective standards by which innovation and contemporary culture could be measured. Secondly, their representative and democratic rhetoric could provide popular legitimacy, while allowing, in practice, significant scope for a paternalistic form of cultural leadership. Prior's work on the National Gallery of Scotland demonstrated how museum architecture of classical temples supported the rhetoric of universal access and legitimised culture through links to ancient civilisation, yet concealed a somewhat authoritarian leadership style.[107] In this view classicism was not undermined by the growth of a bourgeois public; rather the rising middle class embraced classicism as a way of understanding and regulating both the patterns of civic virtue and the canons of taste. Marchand's work on Germany has also emphasised the continuing strength of museum classicism throughout the nineteenth century, highlighting the cultural unity that classical education offered.[108] Wiener has similarly been keen to demonstrate the importance of classical education to the British middle class as part of their broader identity as gentleman capitalists.[109] Although many aspects of Wiener's broader thesis have been disputed, there can be little doubt about the growth of importance of classical education in the nineteenth century and how this coincided with increasing middle-class access to university education.[110]

In some respects, the use of classical models to legitimise art institutions only created a second-order problem; it left the tension between the rhetoric of participation and the desire for paternalistic leadership unresolved. The increasing involvement of the state in art institutions was one way in which institutions could present themselves as an expression of the public good. Once municipalised, art institutions were part of the formal machinery of local government, administered by elected councillors and funded through taxes by the consent of the electorate. However, municipalisation did not necessary imply democratisation. Vernon's work on the British nineteenth-century constitution has illustrated how the creation of formally 'representative' institutions of government could lead to a reduction in certain forms of political participation and institutionalise the authority of existing political organisations. This could be done not only through formal patterns of exclusion, but also through the new cultural practices associated with 'representative' government.[111] The specialist nature of art knowledge ensured that most major decisions relating to art gallery management lay in the hands of a small group of councillors and officials with specialist understanding. Moreover, as several of these studies highlight, many councils continued to rely on unelected art advisors and private connoisseurs for the development of policy and for advice on hanging and purchases. In many cases the boundary between the activities of private organisations and the local state was blurred. Sometimes, as in the case of the RMI, the property of an art institution would be brought under public ownership, but that institution would still occupy the same premises and have a strong and formal influence over the city's art policy.[112] Similarly, art academies remained nominally independent, but were often dependent for their existence on either direct public grants or the use of municipal buildings for their operation. In the case of official corporation exhibitions, elected councillors rarely had a formal say in the selection and hanging of work, this task usually being left to a committee of private collectors or artists, sometimes joined by a sprinkling of elected representatives.

Few municipal art institutions or galleries were contemplated without some pecuniary assistance from private sources. Funding art institutions required a 'lumpy' pattern of finance. Large sums of initial capital were required, yet running costs were relatively low in comparison with other public facilities such as baths, libraries and schools. In most cases municipalities were prepared to pay operational costs from local taxation, but found it difficult to justify the capital investment inherent in the development of a new institution. The rapid growth in literacy, assisted by the 1872 Education Act, stimulated great public demand for circulating libraries, and throughout the 1870s corporations responded with large-scale investment in both central facilities and suburban branch libraries. This limited the funds available for art galleries, as those for art galleries and libraries came from the same budget, the limit of which was set by national legislation. The statutory restriction on spending could be circumvented only by an appeal to Parliament, but this was not always politically possible.[113] Large-scale investment in water and gas utilities between the 1850s and 1870s had led to significant increases in local government expenditure and taxation.[114] The regressive and inflexible nature of the local taxation system meant that the lower middle class and 'shopocracy', an aspirational group that might otherwise have been appreciative of public cultural resources, were particularly badly affected.[115] By the 1870s property owners had begun to organise themselves in an attempt to resist the apparently inexorable growth of the local state, some developing into significant federations such as the United Property Owners Association, which was particularly active in the north of England.[116] These developments inevitably had an impact on the willingness of established political parties to increase rates for non-essential activities, and especially for cultural activities where it was thought private patronage might be available.

This study examines in some depth the complex intersections between the private and public financing of art institutions. In some cases, municipalities solved the difficulty of capital funding by absorbing existing cultural institutions. Manchester Corporation took over the RMI and, in the twentieth century, the Manchester Athenaeum, to use for art gallery purposes. However, this strategy was not without its limitations. The RMI's members continued to demand influence over art policy and forced the corporation to enter into a covenant requiring it to spend £2,000 per annum of public money on works of art over the following twenty years. Alternatively, corporations could seek sponsors and patrons to cover the cost of the capital investment required. Both of the region's largest purpose-built art galleries were funded in this way. Liverpool's Walker gallery was built using finance provided by the town mayor, and Preston's Harris gallery was developed through the bequest of one of Preston's most well-known public figures. However, the 'gifting' process associated with such activity is not unproblematic. Anthropological and sociological research on gifting has revealed the complex meanings and power relationship in a 'gifting' economy and the difficult issues of reciprocity associated with the acceptance of supposed benevolence.[117] When applied to art institutions this type of analysis reveals the difficulty of simply regarding gifts as benevolent cultural acts. Gifts need to be located within the broader moral and political economy of the city. This study reveals how cultural gifts provided political as well as cultural status, especially in the case of Liverpool, where Walker's gift of an art gallery was closely followed by the acquisition of national political honours. The study of art institutions can also give an insight into the limitations of the gift economy and 'philanthropy' more generally. As Walker was to discover, gifting that was seen as too brash and self-serving could damage public reputations, however apparently 'generous' the donor.[118]

Gifting was, however, a key part of institutional development. Where it was not used to provide capital for art gallery development, it often played an essential role in the development of collections. Even galleries which were generously financed by their municipality, such as Salford, relied on large amounts of private curatorial assistance and private donations for the development of their collections. Most of the smaller town galleries were entirely dependent on donors for major collections. Oldham's impressive collection of nineteenth-century watercolours is almost entirely drawn from one major donation: that of Charles E. Lees in 1888. Even the collecting and exhibiting policies of larger galleries were heavily influenced by individual donations. Manchester's collection of watercolours was framed around the donated collection of Roger Ross, while most of Preston's important modern works came from the home of a local lawyer, Richard Newsham. While municipal collections were commonly seen as expressions of collective taste and civic virtue, they often owed much to political circumstances and the collecting practices of particular individuals. Sometimes donors made specific demands of their museum recipients, requiring their collections to be displayed in particular ways and to acknowledge the munificence of their donor. Even when such restrictions were not imposed, donations inevitably shaped the nature of future collecting. Once a gallery was known to specialise in a particular type of work, dealers would inevitably encourage it to develop these strengths. Gaps had to be filled to ensure that collections were 'representative', while hangings were influenced by the preoccupations inherent within the original donor's collecting practices. Donations not only memorialised the donor and his taste: they gave a personal taste a public visibility which could ultimately be viewed as a component of a broader civic identity.

Lancashire never faced a controversy of public and private taste equivalent to that surrounding the famous Chantrey bequest disputes of the late nineteenth and early twentieth centuries.[119] However, cultural debates were fought out through the region's art institutions, and it was clear by 1914 that the regional art world faced something of a crisis. Part of the crisis was associated with the growing centralisation of the art market and the increasing reluctance of municipal authorities to fund art projects. Successful artists from the region had long gravitated to London, but by the outbreak of the First World War, only one successful annual modern exhibition remained: that of Liverpool.[120] Manchester City Council had refused to fund the development of a new art gallery because of public hostility to rising taxation at a time of high unemployment. Debate about the corrosive nature of consumerism and popular culture had fragmented the art world into the neo-classicists on the one hand and the Ruskinian populists on the other. Large civic art museums were no longer seen as necessarily the most effective way of enhancing and diffusing culture and civic virtue. Critics argued that they were expensive and failed to meet their educational objectives. Some socialists saw the cultural forms of high art established by the middle class as offering little to working people and opposed public spending on new museums outright. Even middle-class urban cultural elites began to lose confidence in mainstream artistic canons of high art, including the work of leading figures in the world of British art. This was partly because British art had become an uncertain investment. The collapse of land values after 1901–2 sent shock waves through the luxuries market, and it soon became apparent that the 'bubble prices' paid for the works of many of the most popular Victorian artists could not be sustained. But the problem went deeper than this. Many Lancastrian patrons and opinion-formers had already begun to look overseas for cultural refreshment, often concluding that the British art scene was peculiarly insular. Lancashire was arguably more cosmopolitan and outward-looking than the London art world. Its international business connections, large European immigrant community and commercial networks encouraged a greater appreciation of overseas art than, perhaps, was possible in a metropolitan art world guarded by the canons of the Royal Academy. Liverpool was known for its interest in German art in the 1860s, Manchester developed a French proto-Impressionist school in the early 1870s, and by the Edwardian period both cities had thrown open their public galleries to modern overseas schools.[121] Municipal permanent collections, dominated by works of the modern British school, could appear less inspiring and, by 1914, somewhat out of date.

The economic decline of Lancashire from the late 1920s meant that the days of major public investment in visual art soon passed.[122] Yet an astounding institutional legacy remained. This volume will attempt to map the complexity of the cultural processes and preoccupations that created the public art institutions of Lancashire. Unlike some recent studies, it will not seek to locate the origins of public galleries in the ideas of one movement or set of ideas. Instead it will try to understand the complex urban processes that created the need and desire for public art institutions. Those processes not only changed significantly between 1780 and 1914, but could also differ between individual towns and often depended upon the preoccupations and values of individual promoter groups. While the desire to promote civic pride, disseminate high culture or educate a mass audience could be the stated goals of art gallery promoters, these could conceal the more fundamental motivations of local leaders. The creation of art institutions was also an opportunity for self-promotion or for consolidating collective cultural authority, or simply a platform for asserting a specific cultural argument. By examining and mapping these processes, the discussion that follows will facilitate a better understanding of Lancashire's cultural history and also of the social forces that shaped the leadership of the region's major industrial towns.

NOTES

1 H. Rees Leahy (ed.), *Art, City, Spectacle: The 1857 Manchester Art Treasures Exhibition Revisited* (Manchester, 2009); U. Finke, 'The Art Treasures Exhibition', in J. H. G. Archer (ed.), *Art and Architecture in Victorian Manchester* (Manchester, 1985), 102–26; G. Scharf, 'On the Manchester Art Treasures Exhibition, 1857', *Transactions of the Historic Society of Lancashire and Cheshire*, 10 (1857–58), 269–331. Also see *Catalogue of the Art Treasures of the United Kingdom Collected at Manchester* (London, 1857).

2 The classic statement of 1832's importance can be found in G. Trevelyan, *British History in the Nineteenth Century and After* (London, 1922). For recent critical assessments see J. Garrard, *Democratisation in Britain: Elites, Civil Society and Reform since 1800* (Basingstoke, 2002); E. Smith, *Reform or Revolution? A Diary of Reform in England, 1830–2* (Stroud, 1992): F. O'Gorman, 'Party Politics in the Early Nineteenth Century', *English Historical Review*, 102 (1987), 63–84; J. Phillips and C. Wetherell, 'The Great Reform Act of 1832 and the Political Modernization of England', *American Historical Review*, 100 (1995), 411–36.

3 For an introductory discussion of the industrialists' contribution to Victorian culture see A. Wohl, '"Gold and Mud": Capitalism and Culture in Victorian Britain', *Albion*, 23 (1991), 275–81.

4 For example, landmark contributions on private collecting include D. S. Macleod, *Art and the Victorian Middle Class: Money and the Making of Cultural Identity* (Cambridge, 1996); C. P. Darcy, *The Encouragement of the Fine Arts in Lancashire, 1760–1860* (Manchester, 1976); G. Chandler, *William Roscoe of Liverpool 1753–1831* (London, 1953); J. Seed, 'Commerce and the Liberal Arts: The Political Economy of Art in Manchester, 1775–1860', in J. Wolff and J. Seed (eds), *The Culture of Capital: Art, Power and the Nineteenth Century Middle Class* (Manchester, 1988), 45–81; M. Pointon, 'W. E. Gladstone as an Art Patron and Collector', *Victorian Studies*, 19 (1975), 73–98, M. Bennett, 'A Check List of Pre-Raphaelite Pictures Exhibited at Liverpool 1846–67, and Some of their Northern Collectors', *Burlington Magazine*, 105 (1963), 477–95.

5 C. Saumarez Smith, 'The Institutionalisation of Art in Early Victorian England', *Transactions of the Royal Historical Society*, 20 (2010), 113–25.

6 J. Treuherz, 'Ford Madox Brown and the Manchester Murals', in Archer (ed.), *Art and Architecture*, 162–207.

7 G. Waterfield, *The People's Galleries: Art Museums and Exhibitions in Britain, 1800–1914* (London, 2015).

8 K. Hill, *Culture and Class in English Public Museums, 1850–1914* (Aldershot, 2005). A. Woodson-Boulton, *Transformative Beauty: Art Museums in Industrial Britain* (Stanford, 2012).

9 Classic studies of British urbanisation include A. Briggs, *The Victorian City* (London, 1963, reprint 1990)'; H. J. Dyos and M. Wolff (eds), *The Victorian City: Images and Reality* (London, 1978); R. Morris and R. Rodger (eds), *The Victorian City, 1820–1914* (Harlow, 1993).

10 These complex fissures have been explored in a number of works, including E. P. Hennock, *Fit and Proper Persons: Ideal and Reality in Nineteenth Century Urban Government* (London, 1973); D. Cannadine (ed.), *Patricians, Power and Politics in Nineteenth Century Towns* (Leicester, 1982); J. Garrard, *Leadership and Power in Victorian Industrial Towns* (Manchester, 1983); J. Smith, 'Urban Elites c.1830–1930 and Urban History', *Urban History*, 27 (2000), 255–75; J. Moore and R. Rodger, 'Who Really Ran the Cities?', in R. Roth (ed.), *Who Ran the Cities: Elite and Urban Power Structures in Europe, 1700–2000* (Frankfurt, 2007), 33–70.

11 S. Gunn, *The Public Culture of the Victorian Middle Class: Ritual and Authority in the English Industrial City 1840–1914* (Manchester, 2000).

12 Agnews remained a family-owned firm until 2013.

13 J. Langton, 'The Industrial Revolution and the Regional Geography of England', *Transactions of the Institute of British Geographers*, 9:2 (1984), 145–67.

14 The first serious study of these developments can be found in Darcy, *Encouragement*.

15 C. Dellheim, 'Imagining England: Victorian Views of the North', *Northern History*, 22 (1986), 217; also see Macleod, *Art and the Victorian Middle Class*, 88–92.

16 C. Dickens, *Hard Times* (London, 1854).

17 For its origins see J. Stobart, *The First Industrial Region: North-West England, c.1700–60* (Manchester, 2004).

18 D. Chun, 'A History of the Leicester Family, Tabley House, and its Collection of Paintings', PhD thesis, University of Manchester, 2000; D. Chun, 'Patriotism on Display: Sir John Fleming Leicester's Patronage of British Art', *British Art Journal*, 4 (2003), 23–8.

19 H. Blundell, *An Account of the Statues, Busts, Bass-Relieves, Cinery Urns, and Other Ancient Marbles, and Paintings, at Ince, Collected by H.B.* (Liverpool, 1803); J. Fejfer and E. Southworth, *The Ince Blundell Collection of Classical Sculpture*, vol. 1, part 1 (London, 1991); J. Fejfer, *The Ince Blundell Collection of Classical Sculpture*, vol. 1, part 2 (Liverpool, 1997); E. Edwards, *Lives of the Founders of the British Museum* (London, 1870), 371–2; H. Ellis, *The Townley Gallery of Classical Sculpture in the British Museum* (London, 1846).

20 For background see J. Walton, *Lancashire: A Social History, 1558–1939* (Manchester, 1987), 103–25, 198–221; D. Farnie, *The English Cotton Industry and the World Market, 1815–1896* (Oxford, 1979).

21 A. Howe, *The Cotton Masters 1830–1860* (Oxford, 1984); H. W. Ogden, *The Geographical Basis of the Lancashire Cotton Industry* (Manchester, 1928).

22 A. Kidd, *Manchester* (Manchester, 1996), 115–18; D. Farnie, *The Manchester Ship Canal and the Rise of the Port of Manchester, 1894–1975* (Manchester, 1980); I. Harford, *Manchester and its Ship Canal Movement* (Keele, 1994); B. Leech, *History of the Manchester Ship Canal*, 2 vols (Manchester, 1907).

23 H. Roscoe, *The Life of William Roscoe*, 2 vols (London, 1833); J. Mayer, *Roscoe and the Influence of his Writings on the Fine Arts* (London, 1853); T. Baines, *The Liverpool Tribute to Roscoe* (London, 1853); G. W. Matthews, *William Roscoe: A Memoir* (London, 1931); Chandler, *Roscoe*.

24 R. Townley (ed.), *The Miscellaneous Works of Tim Bobbin* (London, 1806); H. Fishwick (ed.), *Works of John Collier (Tim Bobbin)* (Rochdale, 1904), 9.

25 See, for example the work of John Critchley Prince: R. A. D. Lithgow, *The Life of John Critchley Prince* (Manchester, 1880), 15–17.

26 G. Milner (ed.), *Poems and Songs of Edwin Waugh* (London, n.d.); B. Brierley, *Irkdale* (Manchester, 1868). For recent reflections on their work see T. Hakala, 'A Great Man in Clogs: Performing Authenticity in Victorian Lancashire', *Victorian Studies*, 52 (2010), 387–412.

27 M. Hewitt and R. Poole, 'Samuel Bamford and Northern Identity', in N. Kirk (ed.), *Northern Identities: Historical Interpretations of 'the North' and Northernness* (Aldershot, 2000), 111–32.

28 Townley (ed.), *Works of Tim Bobbin*, 5.

29 For simplicity, both are generally referred to as cities in this book, although Manchester did not officially become a city until 1853 and Liverpool did not achieve official city status until 1880.

30 P. Pickering, *The People's Bread: A History of the Anti-Corn Law League* (Leicester, 2000); N. McCord, *The Anti-Corn Law League 1838–1846* (London, 1958).

31 P. Clarke, *Lancashire and the New Liberalism* (Cambridge, 1971); J. Moore, 'Progressive Pioneers: Manchester Liberalism, the Independent Labour Party, and Local Politics in the 1890s', *Historical Journal*, 44 (2001), 989–1013.

32 J. Trepp, 'The Liverpool Movement for the Abolition of the English Slave Trade', *Journal of Negro History*, 13 (1928), 265–85; R. Anstey, *Liverpool, the African Slave Trade, and Abolition* (Liverpool, 1989); G. Cameron, *Liverpool: Capital of the Slave Trade* (Birkenhead, 1992).

33 F. Neal, *Sectarian Violence: The Liverpool Experience, 1819–1914* (Manchester, 1988). For background see S. Fielding, *Class and Ethnicity: Irish Catholics in England, 1880–1939* (Buckingham, 1993).

34 In some places this process had a long history. See, for example, J. Stobart, 'Building an Urban Identity: Cultural Space and Civic Boosterism in a 'New" Industrial Town. Burslem, 1761–1911', *Social History*, 29 (2004), 485–98.

35 J. Moore and R. Rodger, 'Municipal Knowledge and Policy Networks in British Local Government, 1832–1914', *Yearbook of European Administrative History*, 15 (2003), 29–58, esp. 35–6.

36 G. Timmins, *Made in Lancashire: A History of Regional Industrialisation* (Manchester, 1998). Recently the notion of 'industrial revolution' has been questioned. For the debate about growth rates see N. Crafts, *British Economic Growth during the Industrial Revolution* (Oxford, 1985); P. Mathias and J. Davis, *The First Industrial Revolutions* (Oxford, 1989); D. C. Coleman, Myth, *History and the Industrial Revolution* (London, 1992).

37 N. McKendrick, 'The Consumer Revolution of the Eighteenth-Century England', in N. McKendrick, J. Brewer and J. Plumb (eds), *The Birth of a Consumer Society* (London, 1982), 9–33.

38 C. Campbell, *The Romantic Ethic and the Spirit of Modern Consumerism* (Oxford, 1987).

39 B. Fine and E. Leopold, 'Consumerism and the Industrial Revolution', *Social History*, 15 (1990), 151–7.

40 T. Veblen, *The Theory of the Leisure Class: An Economic Study of Institutions* (New York, 1899).

41 P. Borsay, 'The English Urban Renaissance: The Development of Provincial Urban Culture c1680-c1760', *Social History*, 2 (1977), 581–603.

42 A. McInnes, 'The Emergence of a Leisure Town: Shrewsbury 1660–1760', *Past and Present*, 120 (1988), 53–87.

43 J. Beckett and C. Smith, 'Urban Renaissance and Consumer Culture in Nottingham, 1688–1750', *Urban History*, 27 (2000), 31–50.

44 P. Borsay, *The English Urban Renaissance* (Oxford, 1989), esp. 118–49, 129; J. Feather, *The Provincial Book Trade in Eighteenth-Century England* (Cambridge, 1985).

45 See, for example, H. Berry, 'Promoting Taste in the Provincial Press: National and Local Culture in Eighteenth-Century Newcastle upon Tyne', *British Journal for Eighteenth-Century Studies*, 25 (2002), 1–18.

46 T. Swindells, *Manchester Streets and Manchester Men*, 2nd series (Manchester, 1907), 99.

47 R. Sweet, *The English Town, 1680–1840* (Harlow, 1998), 231–2.

48 C. Chalkin, 'Capital Expenditure on Building for Cultural Purposes in Provincial England, 1730–1830', *Business History*, 22 (1980), 51–70.

49 P. Clark, *British Clubs and Societies, 1580–1800* (Oxford, 2000).

50 B. H. Grindley, *History and Work of the Liverpool Academy of Arts* (Liverpool, 1875, 2.

51 Sweet, *English Town*, 253.

52 For a broader outline of funding and organisation see R. J. Morris, 'Voluntary Societies and British Urban Elites, 1780–1850: An Analysis', *Historical Journal*, 26 (1983) 95–118.

53 For a useful short discussion of the meaning of culture see J. Gold and M. Gold, *Cities of Culture* (Aldershot, 2005), 8–10.

54 D. Solkin, *Painting for Money: The Visual Arts and the Public Sphere in Eighteenth Century England* (New Haven, 1992).

55 However, old masters continued to represent an important canon of high culture; see F. Haskell, *The Ephemeral Museum: Old Master Paintings and the Rise of the Art Exhibition* (New Haven, 2000).

56 J. Habermas, *The Structural Transformation of the Public Sphere* (Cambridge, 1989); W. Outhwaite, *Habermas: A Critical Introduction* (Cambridge, 1994); C. Chambers, *Reasonable Democracy: Jürgen Habermas and the Politics of Discourse* (London, 1996); M. Cooke, *Language and Reason: A Study of Habermas's Pragmatics* (London, 1994).

57 M. Arnold, *Culture and Anarchy* (London, 1869); F. Walcott, *The Origins of 'Culture and Anarchy': Matthew Arnold and Popular Education* (Toronto, 1970).

58 A. Bermingham, 'Introduction: The Consumption of Culture: Image, Object, Text', in A. Bermingham and J. Brewer (eds), *The Consumption of Culture 1600–1800* (London, 1995), 1–20.

59 For example, the case of Joseph Wright of Derby. See P. Diamond, 'Joseph Wright of Derby (1734–1797): The Importance of a Local Museum in the Formation of an Artist's Reputation', *British Art Journal*, 14 (2013), 18–23.

60 C. Duncan, *Civilizing Rituals: Inside Public Art Museums* (London, 1995), 48–71.

61 C. Trodd, 'The Authority of Art: Cultural Criticism and the Idea of the Royal Academy in Mid-Victorian Britain', *Art History*, 20 (1997), 3–22.

62 For an overview see W. J. Bate, *From Classic to Romantic: Premises of Taste in Eighteenth-Century England* (Cambridge, Mass., 1946).

63 I. Pears, *The Discovery of Painting: The Growth of Interest in the Arts in England, 1680–1768* (London, 1988), esp. 1–26.

64 Cited in Pears, *Discovery*, 11–12.

65 Pears, *Discovery*, 15–16.

66 For recent comparative perspectives on these issues see C. Paul (ed.), *The First Modern Museums of Art* (Los Angeles, 2012).

67 For ancient notions of urban life see J. Rykwert, *The Idea of a Town* (Princeton, 1976).

68 M. I. Finlay, 'The Ancient City: From Fustel de Coulanges to Max Weber and Beyond', *Comparative Studies in History and Society*, 19 (1977), 305–27, esp. 305–6.

69 A. Wilson, '"The Florence of the North"? The Civic Culture of Liverpool in the Early Nineteenth Century', in A. Kidd and D. Nicholls (eds), *Gender, Civic Culture, Consumerism* (Manchester, 1999), 34–46.

70 A. Brooks and B. Haworth, *Portico Library: A History* (Lancaster, 2000); T. Pratt, *The Portico Library: Its History and Associations* (Manchester, 1922).

71 W. Fairbairn, *Observations on Improvements of the Town of Manchester* (Manchester, 1836). For discussion of the scheme see J. Moore, 'Urban Space and Civic Identity in Manchester 1780–1914', *Transactions of the Historic Society of Lancashire and Cheshire*, 153 (2004), 87–123.

72 V. Skipp, *The Making of Victorian Birmingham* (Birmingham, 1983); G. Stamp, *Alexander 'Greek' Thompson* (Glasgow, 1999).

73 J. Stuart and N. Revett, *Antiquities of Athens*, 4 vols (London, 1762–1816); D. Watkin, *Athenian Stuart, Pioneer of the Greek Revival* (London, 1982); J. M. Crook, *The Greek*

Revival (London, 1972); D. Stillman, *English Neo-Classical Architecture*, 2 vols (London, 1988); D. Watkin, *The Life and Work of C. R. Cockerell* (London, 1974).

74 J. Moore, 'Periclean Preston, Public Art and the Classical Tradition in Late-Nineteenth-Century Lancashire', *Northern History*, 40 (2003), 299–323.

75 See discussion in J. Wolff and J. Seed (eds), *The Culture of Capital: Art, Power and the Nineteenth Century Middle Class* (Manchester, 1988).

76 F. O'Gorman, *The Long Eighteenth Century: British Political and Social History 1688–1832* (London, 1997); also F. O'Gorman, 'The Instability of Britain (1688–1832)', unpublished paper, British Society for Eighteenth Century Studies conference, Manchester, 2002.

77 B. F. Cook, 'Townley, Charles (1737–1805)', *Oxford Dictionary of National Biography* (Oxford, 2004), online edn, September 2014, www.oxforddnb.com/view/article/27601, accessed 7 August 2017).

78 D. Fraser, *Urban Politics in Victorian England* (Leicester, 1976), 119–20.

79 E. Conran, 'Art Collections', in Archer (ed.), *Art and Architecture*, 65–80, esp. 73.

80 *Art Journal*, April 1870, 106, *Art Journal*, June 1870, 209–11; T. Swindells, 'A Merchant Prince: The Romantic Career of Sam Mendel' (cutting) in 'Historical Manchester, Famous Manchester Men' (cuttings book), Manchester Central Library (hereafter MCL), 920.042 73 Sw1; M. Dobkin, 'Mendel of Manley Hall', *Jackson's Row Newsletter* (Manchester), 5:6 (1890), 8–9.

81 E. Gibbon, *History of the Decline and Fall of the Roman Empire* (London, 1766–88).

82 H. Weisinger, 'The English Origins of the Sociological Interpretation of the Renaissance', *Journal of the History of Ideas*, 11 (1950), 321–38.

83 J. Rendall, *The Origins of the Scottish Enlightenment 1707–1776* (London, 1978), B. Lenman, *Integration, Enlightenment and Industrialisation: Scotland 1745–1832* (London, 1981).

84 K. Bock, 'Theories of Progress, Development, Evolution', in T. Bottomore and R. Nisbet (eds), *A History of Sociological Analysis* (London, 1979), 55–7. See also J. B. Bury, *The Idea of Progress: An Inquiry into its Origin and Growth* (London, 1928); R. F. Jones, *Ancients and Moderns* (London, 1936).

85 A. Ferguson, *An Essay on the History of Civil Society*, 5th edn (London, 1782), 384; also cited in Bottomore and Nisbet (eds), *History*, 57.

86 W. Velema, 'Ancient and Modern Virtue Compared: De Beaufort and Van Effen on Republican Citizenship', *Eighteenth-Century Studies*, 30 (1997), 437–43.

87 For background see P. Monod, 'Painters and Party Politics in England, 1714–1760', *Eighteenth Century Studies*, 26 (1993), 367–98.

88 J. Barrell, *The Political Theory of Painting from Reynolds to Hazlitt* (London, 1986), 1–13. For discussion see K. Simonsuuri, *Homer's Original Genius: Eighteenth-Century Notions of the Early Greek Epic* (Cambridge, 1979).

89 Pears, *Discovery*, 181–206.

90 J. Richardson Snr and J. Richardson Jnr, *An Account of Some of the Statues, Bas-Reliefs, Drawings and Pictures in Italy, &c with Remarks* (London, 1722).

91 C. Smith, 'The Institutionalisation of Art in Early Victorian England', *Transactions of the Royal Historical Society*, 20 (2010), 113–25.

92 D. Seckler, *Thorstein Veblen and the Institutionalists* (London, 1979); M. Hodgson, *The Evolution of Institutional Economics* (London, 2004).

93 M. Rutherford, *Institutions in Economics: The Old and the New Institutionalism* (Cambridge, 1994).

94 P. Cammack, *New Institutionalist Approaches to Macro-Social Analysis* (Manchester, 1989); A. Jones, *The Modalities of European Union Governance: New Institutionalist Explanations* (Oxford, 2001).

95 R. S. Robins, *Political Institutionalisation and the Integration of Elites* (London, 1976), esp. 15–25.

96 For a summary of these issues see B. G. Peters, *Institutional Theory in Political Science* (London, 1999).

97 For a classic text see P. Khandwalla, *The Design of Organizations* (New York, 1977).

98 A problem long recognised. See, for example, the work of the pioneering political sociologist Ostrogorsky: M. Ostrogorsky, *Democracy and the Organization of Political Parties*, 2 vols (London, 1902).

99 P. Joyce, *Visions of the People: Industrial England and the Question of Class, 1848–1914* (Cambridge, 1991); J. Vernon, *Politics and the People: A Study in English Political Culture, c.1815–1867* (Cambridge, 1993); J. Lawrence, *Speaking for the People: Party, Language and Popular Politics in England, 1867–1914* (Cambridge, 2002).

100 M. Harrison, 'Art and Philanthropy: T. C. Horsfall and the Manchester Art Museum', in A. Kidd and K. Roberts (eds), *City, Class and Culture: Cultural Production and Social Policy in Victorian Manchester* (Manchester, 1985), 120–47; Woodson-Boulton, *Transformative Beauty*.

101 N. Harris, 'The Gilded Age Revisited: Boston and the Museum Movement', *American Quarterly*, 14 (1962), 545–66.

102 M. Goodwin, 'Objects, Belief and Power in Mid-Victorian England: The Origins of the Victoria and Albert Museum', in S. Pearce (ed.), *Objects of Knowledge* (London, 1990), 9–49.

103 B. Taylor, *Art for the Nation* (Manchester, 1999), esp. 74–81.

104 A. Burton, *Vision and Accident: The Story of the Victoria and Albert Museum* (London, 1999), esp. 104–15.

105 P. Gilbert, *The Victorian Painter's World* (Gloucester, 1990), 197–217.

106 C. Trodd, 'Representing the Victorian Royal Academy: The Properties of Culture and the Promotion of Art', in P. Barlow and C. Trodd (eds), *Governing Cultures: Art Institutions in Victorian London* (Aldershot, 2000), 56–68.

107 N. Prior, *Museums and Modernity: Art Galleries and the Making of Modern Culture* (Oxford, 2002), esp. 171–208.

108 S. Marchand, 'The Quarrel of the Ancients and Moderns in the German Museums', in S. Crane (ed.), *Museums and Memory* (Stanford, 2000), 170–85.

109 M. Wiener, *English Culture and the Decline of the Industrial Spirit, 1850–1980* (Cambridge, 1981).

110 M. L. Clarke, *Classical Education in Britain, 1500–1900* (Cambridge, 1959): R. M. Ogilvie, *Latin and Greek: A History of the Influence of the Classics on English Life from 1600 to 1918* (London, 1964), esp. 74–171; C. Stray (ed.), *Classics in 19th and 20th Century Cambridge* (Cambridge, 1999).

111 Vernon, *Politics and the People.*

112 R. F. Bud, 'The Royal Manchester Institution', in D. S. L. Cardwell (ed.), *Artisan to Graduate* (Manchester, 1974), 119–33, esp. 122–4.

113 For background see W. Lubenow, *The Politics of Government Growth* (Newton Abbot, 1971).

114 R. Millward, 'The Political Economy of Urban Utilities', in M. Daunton (ed.), *The Cambridge Urban History of Britain*, vol. 3: *1840–1950* (Cambridge, 2001), 315–49; P. J. Waller, *Town, City and Nation: England 1850–1914* (Oxford, 1983), esp. 298–316.

115 B. M. Doyle, 'The Changing Function of Urban Government: Councillors, Officials and Pressure Groups', in Daunton (ed.), *Cambridge Urban History*, vol. 3, 287–313, esp. 290–4.

116 A. Offer, *Property and Politics 1870–1914* (Cambridge, 1981), 297–301; D. Englander, *Landlord and Tenant in Urban Britain 1838–1914* (Oxford, 1983), 65–75.

117 For important contributions on this question see M. Mauss, *The Gift*, trans. W. Halls (London, 1990); P. Bourdieu and H. Haacke, *Free Exchange* (Cambridge, 1995).

118 See Chapter 6.

119 D. MacColl, *The Administration of the Chantrey Bequest: Articles Reprinted from 'The Saturday Review', with Additional Matter, Including the Text of Chantrey's Will and a List of Purchases* (London, 1904).

120 J. Partington, 'Manchester as an Art Centre', *Manchester Literary Club*, 3 (1876–77), 42–52, esp. 49.

121 Impressionism reached Manchester at an early date through the Corot-influenced Manchester school. See S. Thomson, *Manchester's Victorian Art Scene and its Unrecognised Artists* (Warrington, 2007), 71–86. For background of the movement in England see K. Flint, *Impressionism in England: The Critical Reception* (London, 1984).

122 For details of the region's economic decline see L. Sandberg, *Lancashire in Decline: A Study in Entrepreneurship, Technology, and International Trade* (Columbus, 1974); J. Singleton, *Lancashire on the Scrapheap: The Cotton Industry 1945–1970* (Oxford, 1991).

2

Lorenzo in Liverpool: William Roscoe, civic myths and the institutionalisation of urban culture

Cultural institutions reflected both personal interests and shared visions of the ideal civic life. Civic cultural leaders used languages of progress and civic humanism to mobilise support for their specific cultural agendas. Like the leaders of the ancient polis, cultural elites promoted histories and myths about the foundation of their own towns to promote new cultural formations and underpin their associated social bonds.[1] Liverpool's early nineteenth-century cultural dynamism was, in the popular mind, associated with one man and his artistic circle. In many respects, William Roscoe (1753–1831) created the cultural identity of nineteenth-century Liverpool. His legacy lay not only in his art collection, history writing and poetry, but also in the values and civic myths that he instilled in the city's cultural circles. His writings and authority were constantly appealed to on all manner of civic occasions, and his life was memorialised in a series of hagiographic biographies.[2] By the second half of the nineteenth century, he was Liverpool's Theseus, the founding father of the modern city who seemed to exist more in legends than history. Roscoe had associations with almost all the early cultural organisations in Liverpool and was directly responsible for the development of many of them. His artistic and humanistic civic values had been institutionalised in the cultural life of the city, ensuring that the direction of Liverpool's intellectual development would be heavily influenced by his ideas and writing. In some respects, the institutionalisation of Roscoe was a product of a planned and deliberative process by those within his circle. When Roscoe's bank got into financial trouble in 1816 his close friends rescued many of his cultural assets – including much of his library and art collection – to preserve them not only for Roscoe, but for future generations of Liverpool scholars.[3] On his death, his son Henry prepared a large-scale, two-volume heroic biography, recording the breadth of his father's achievements in the city.[4] However, the longevity of Roscoe's

36

influence can be explained more in terms of the relevance of his artistic and civic ideas for a developing commercial city. Roscoe's inspirational personality and views were often cited as a key cause of Liverpool's cultural achievements and the growth of a new public sentiment. Joseph Mayer famously remarked:

> Roscoe's honour lies not so much in deeds of his own – excellent and admirable though they were – as in those which he caused others to do. A leading man amongst people who regarded business as the one aim of life and title to respect, he boldly proclaimed another and a nobler idea ... He interested the public and thus, ensured a succession of disciples to labour in the cause after his own decease.[5]

This view of Roscoe and Liverpool culture requires close examination. What were the ideas and cultural conditions that allowed one man to apparently acquire so much influence over a city's development? Roscoe was, after all, something of a political outsider. He was a passionate and outspoken opponent of the slave trade in a city in which many merchants retained a large interest in the African traffic.[6] He expressed sympathy with the French revolution at a time when Britain was at war with France. Perhaps most controversially of all, his historical work on the Reformation appeared to betray pro-Catholic sympathies in a county where sectarian issues were still very sensitive.[7]

It is equally important to ask how Roscoe's values of civic humanism became institutionalised in the rationale of the new clubs, societies and organisations that appeared in the early years of the nineteenth century and what implications this process has for our understanding of the subsequent development of the Liverpool art world. Although Roscoe was often cited as a source of inspiration, the cultural and artistic priorities of the city's elites did undergo change. Even some of Roscoe's close friends, such as the head of the LRI, Dr T. S. Traill, tended to disagree with Roscoe on key artistic and aesthetic questions. While Roscoe famously focused on the art of the Renaissance as the key to understanding the vitality of an art republic, Traill focused on classical, and especially Grecian, models of artistic and cultural development. Traill's position as head of the LRI gave him the resources and organisational aptitude to put his classical vision into practical effect. His views on classical art and education were to shape the pattern of Liverpool's middle-class education system for much of the century. In contrast, Roscoe rarely remained at the head of any artistic or cultural society for any significant length of time. Yet, by the second half of the nineteenth century, Roscoe was institutionalised as a historical example of elevated citizenry, to be appropriated for almost any public purpose. While Traill stamped his authority and ideas on one particular powerful segment of the city's cultural life, Roscoe's influence was much more diffuse and was open for appropriation for any civic humanist purpose.

Liverpool in the second half of the eighteenth century was peculiarly suited to the early development of public cultural institutions.[8] The city was a key commercial gateway in an era of the rapid expansion of Britain's overseas trade.[9] The growth in the complexity of trade led to the development of new social networks, while the associated 'consumer revolution' created the demand for new structures of urban sociability.[10] Liverpool was not merely a gateway for international trade, but was also a key outlet for the bulk transport of sea-borne goods to Ireland and the south of England, ensuring that Liverpool merchants developed close connections with the key cultural centres of Dublin and London.[11] In many respects the economic structure of Liverpool was closer to those of the two capital cities than to that of late eighteenth-century Manchester; like London and Dublin, Liverpool was primarily a commercial city, not an industrial one. Liverpool's commercial elites tended to see their city as one of gentlemanly capitalism, rather than industrial production.[12] The city was also an important centre for the region's aristocracy and gentry. As the major port in the region, it catered for sea-borne passenger traffic, and for those seeking the adventure of overseas travel it offered an alternative to a long overland and uncomfortable trip to Bristol or the English Channel ports. Landed families also shipped many of their luxury goods through Liverpool. The antique sculpture collectors Charles Townley and Henry Blundell both shipped parts of their collections through the port, avoiding potentially dangerous overland routes. A number of landed families had estates close to Liverpool, such as the Knowsleys and the Seftons, for whom Liverpool was an important local centre.[13] Lancashire in the eighteenth century was a relatively remote palatine county and Liverpool was its commercial gateway, but the city had a cosmopolitan feel long before inland industrial centres, such as Birmingham or Manchester, did. While the port economy ensured that there was always a pool of unskilled dock labourers and seamen, the commercial shipping houses demanded a relatively large number of educated lower-middle-class scribes, clerks and managers.[14] Indeed, the fact that mid-eighteenth-century Liverpool was able to boast a significant commercial population that displayed high levels of literacy may give some indication as to why cultural institutions were so highly prized in the city and why Roscoe's message of civic humanism was so influential.

Much of the early associational life of Liverpool was the product of convivial rather than cultural pursuits. The curiously named Ugly Face Club of 1743 and Unanimous Club of 1753 attracted major gentlemen of Liverpool society but focused primarily on drinking and socialising.[15] However, 1758 saw the foundation of the Liverpool Library; this was the first subscription library in the country and was widely copied in other provincial centres. Roscoe's first appearance in the cultural life of the city came in the early 1770s. In 1769 the first society of artists was formed in the city, with Joseph Deare, uncle of the celebrated sculptor, renting modest premises for the society at 30 John Street. The society was the initiative of the local artists Richard Caddick, Thomas Chubbard and Ottiwell Worrall, but it did have a number of wealthy patrons, including the local watchmaker John Wyke.[16] It was the collapse of this society that prompted Roscoe to assist in the formation of a new group under William Caddick.[17] In August 1774 the society organised an open exhibition, which was claimed to be the first provincial art exhibition in Britain.[18] Although few details of this exhibition are known, the significance of the event was not lost on Roscoe, who composed an ode to celebrate the new society and its achievement.[19] Influenced by contemporary neo-classicism, the poem represents the Muses fleeing their old haunts and seeking refuge in Albion's grateful isle.[20] Although the ode is primarily a celebration of the receptiveness of Liverpool to artistic culture, it also hints at a broader political message. It was written in the wake of the brutal suppression of the 1770 uprising in Greece, the home of the Muses, and reflects contemporary dismay at the enslavement of Hellas, where the arts were born. In doing so it displays a preoccupation with the fragile and often short-lived nature of both political strength and cultural achievement. While this preoccupation was to inform much late eighteenth-century writing, most famously, of course, with the work of Edward Gibbon and William Mitford, the causes of the rise and decline of civilisation were to become a central concern of Roscoe in both his artistic and historical scholarship.[21] It was a concern that was to fuel his desire to organise and institutionalise Liverpool's cultural achievements and create the civic conditions for the perpetuation of liberal endeavour.

Some of the reasons for Roscoe's preoccupation can be seen in the nature of late eighteenth-century Liverpool society. The growth of Liverpool during Roscoe's lifetime was remarkable and unprecedented. When he was born the population of Liverpool was around 21,000; on his death it was 195,000, almost twice that of his beloved fifteenth-century Florence, which occupied so much of his time as a historian.[22] Much of Liverpool's commercial success had developed from the success of the American trade, a trade that was increasingly under threat because of the American revolution and, in particular, the naval power of the French. New markets would have to be found if Liverpool was to continue to experience the growth that it had enjoyed in the previous decades. The Liverpool of the 1770s was a city aware of the precarious nature of its commercial success.

Roscoe's concern about the permanence of the city's achievements was reflected in the difficulties inherent in establishing a permanent art society or institution in Liverpool. Despite the success of the 1774 exhibition, in little over a year the Liverpool society was dead and its property had been sold off. Liverpool had only a very small resident artist community, with many artists travelling between towns and aristocratic seats in search of commissions. The management of the society was in the hands of a small group of people, and, according to Roscoe, when one key member moved to Germany the society collapsed.[23] Roscoe and his circle, however, continued attempts to forge a permanent society in the city, and in 1781 they came together to create the Society for Promoting the Arts in Liverpool. Plans were brought forward for a painting and drawing academy and a new, regular exhibition based on the model of the Royal Academy.[24] While the management of the earlier societies had been primarily in the hands of artists, the new body sought to guarantee long-term institutional stability by placing the society in the hands of the permanent residents of the area. Roscoe's close friend Thomas Taylor wrote to the Manchester collector John Leigh Philips pointing out that Roscoe:

> has endeavoured, in forming the plan, to avoid the rock on which the former split, which was, that it was made to rest entirely on the artists, who being transient inhabitants, the matter dropt [sic] when they left town; but now the artists are secondary instruments only; the principal parts are in the hands of residents.[25]

Taylor's letter to Philips reveals that the new society sought to attract support from across Lancashire in an attempt to secure a strong foundation. Although Roscoe, as vice president, and Thomas Taylor, as secretary, were the main forces behind the society, they were able to attract some support from local landed gentry. Roscoe's close friend Henry Ince Blundell took the presidential chair. The society quickly moved to establish a series of lectures on anatomy and the theory of painting and encouraged the development of an academy formed by artist members of the society.[26] The society's most remarkable achievement was, however, the organisation of two major exhibitions. The first, in September

1784, attracted major works from Henry Fuseli, Paul and Thomas Sandby and Joseph Wright of Derby. Wright's contributions were particularly noteworthy and included the well-known history painting *Virgil's Tomb*.[27] The second took place three years later, and although the society struggled to find suitable accommodation for its exhibition, this did not discourage a large number of eminent contributors. Artists exhibiting included Sir Joshua Reynolds, Joseph Farrington, Thomas Gainsborough and George Stubbs, as well as Henry Fuseli, Paul Sandby and Joseph Wright of Derby, who had been represented at the previous exhibition.[28] Although it is not possible to say precisely why these artists were attracted to exhibit at a new provincial exhibition, it is clear that a number already had close connections with Roscoe's circle. John Leigh Philips was a major collector of Joseph Wright of Derby. Roscoe was a friend of both Henry Fuseli and George Stubbs, who, of course, grew up in Liverpool.[29] Henry Blundell had many metropolitan connections, especially through his close friend Charles Townley, who was a key figure in the London art scene of the 1780s. While the presence of the work of so many important artistic luminaries drew national attention to Liverpool as an art centre, it is interesting that the exhibition catalogues also reveal that a very significant number of professional artists were actually based in Liverpool. Some of these, such as William Jackson, Patrick McMorland and Joseph Parry, were to become well-known names in the city. They were supplemented by a number of artists from Manchester and Cheshire, including a female artist, Miss Gartside.[30] There is also evidence of a wider market for art in the city during this period, including a brisk trade in prints, and this may have helped attract exhibitors.[31]

The remarkable success of the two exhibitions might have seemed to have guaranteed the continuing success of the society and its related academy. Yet within two years the society had again ceased to exist. This may partly have been due to the decision of Roscoe and Blundell to withdraw from formal management of the society. There is no evidence of serious internal disagreement, and they may have withdrawn for business reasons or because of lack of support from the society's membership. Correspondence suggests that it was very difficult during this period to attract men of leisure to run artistic and literary societies in the city.[32] The situation was certainly not helped by the outbreak of the French Revolutionary Wars. In 1793 Roscoe joined with friends to form a small literary circle, which included some of the city's most prominent cultural leaders, including the Rev. W. Shepherd, the Rev. John Yates and William Rathbone. However, after Pitt's proclamations against seditious meetings, the circle's activities were apparently viewed with suspicion and it became necessary to suspend them.[33] It is not, of course, at all surprising that Roscoe was viewed with suspicion by the authorities. He was an abolitionist, was closely connected with liberal Unitarian thinkers and had important friends among Lancashire's Catholic gentry.[34] Yet it is clear that Roscoe's public work in the city and his energetic personality convinced Liverpool society of his generous and apparently disinterested intent. The following few years saw Roscoe at the height of his influence. In 1798 he assisted in the formation of the Liverpool Athenaeum and played a prominent role in the formation of its library. Four years later he was the motive force behind the formation of the Liverpool Botanic Gardens, which were opened with the assistance of the corporation.[35]

The success of these organisations encouraged many in Roscoe's circle to try to establish a more permanent institution dedicated to the promotion of art. The Athenaeum, in particular, revealed the large amount of latent interest in the liberal arts among the city's middle class.[36] The Athenaeum was widely emulated, even in the United States, where towns such as Boston copied the Liverpool example.[37] In 1810 Roscoe and Blundell supported the foundation of a Liverpool Academy based on the model of the Royal Academy. Blundell was elected patron while Roscoe served as treasurer.[38] Liverpool Corporation took an interest in the venture and encouraged a merger with a new literary and philosophy society to form what became the LRI in 1817. The idea for the creation of the institution did not come from Roscoe, but it was clearly influenced by the memory of the successful art exhibitions of the 1780s and mobilised many leading figures from Roscoe's cultural circle. John Theodore Coster had been studying the constitution of the Royal Institution in London with a view to copying it in Liverpool, and William Corrie had publicly advocated the formation of scientific and literary institute in the city. Roscoe's close friend T. S. Traill was a key organising force in the early years of the LRI and served as the institution's president for much of the 1820s. The public meeting which led to the formal creation of the LRI committee was chaired by Benjamin Arthur Heywood, the prominent Manchester banker, suggesting again that cultural societies in Liverpool were attracting interest and support from outside the city's boundaries. Perhaps inevitably, though, Roscoe was elected as chairman of the institution's general committee and drew up the formal plan for its creation. Unfortunately, the failure of Roscoe's bank forced his temporary retirement, following which Heywood and Traill took over effective leadership of the project.[39]

Roscoe, however, provided the intellectual mission for the institution. The opening of the LRI in 1817 saw Roscoe invited to provide a major speech, *On the Origin and Vicissitudes of Literature, Science and Art, and their Influence on the Present State of Society*.[40] The speech provided Roscoe with the opportunity to publicly expound his theories on the health of art and literary culture and its importance in civil society and revealed his attitude towards the relationship between art and the wider well-being of a civil community. As in his ode of 1774, Roscoe viewed art and civil culture as vulnerable and transient; the flight of the Muses from Greece to Albion demonstrated that civilisation in its highest form could collapse. It was the responsibility of the citizen to guard the conditions for art's survival through the institutionalisation of cultural practice.

Roscoe's own intellectual development reflected a preoccupation with the forms of civic humanism espoused by many thinkers of the eighteenth century. Much of this reflected the work of Shaftesbury a century before, which emphasised the moral purpose of painting and the associations between artistic progress and liberty.[41] Roscoe's early writings suggest that in the 1780s he had a relatively traditional attitude towards the moral qualities associated with painting, emphasising the importance of heroic subject matter as an elevating force. In a paper to the Manchester Literary and Philosophical Society he stated:

> From the contemplation of heroic actions, whether communicated by the pen or the pencil, feelings are excited, strongly connected with the first and leading object of our pursuit, and of great importance to the advancement of virtue and the improvement of human life.[42]

It was a period in which the rules for writing epic poetry and painting epic art were essentially the same.[43] Attention focused on the realistic depiction of heroic action and its ability to promote public virtue.[44] Two decades later, Roscoe adopted a more sophisticated position that viewed the social utility of art in much broader terms. This change reflected, in part, the developing intellectual climate and the influence of Sir Joshua Reynolds, who offered a more broadly based notion of civic humanism formed around a complex and softened sense of public virtue. Roscoe, however, took something of a post-Reynoldsian position by attempting to reconcile eighteenth-century notions of civic humanism with the commercial and industrial reality of modern Liverpool. The pattern of his friendships also gives some clues as to his scholarly development. Through Blundell he had access to the antiquarian scholarship of the Townley circle, including that of Richard Payne Knight. Knight had little sympathy for the traditional canons of heroic and history painting and developed a more natural-istic theory of art that was heavily influenced by the early Romantic schools.[45] Roscoe's friendship with Fuseli would also seem to suggest a growing interest in Romanticism and naturalism.[46] Roscoe was increasingly interested in naturalistic theories and, in particular, the relations between natural phenomena, social conditions and artistic production. This interest also reflected the naturalism inherent in new theories of the epic, from Thomas Blackwell's Homeric studies of 1735 to the influential work of Robert Wood forty years later.[47] Roscoe would have almost certainly been aware of this work through his friendship with T. S. Traill, an influential classical scholar in Liverpool, and the Cambridge historical school, most notably the modern historian William Smythe, with whom he corresponded.

Roscoe's writings give only very general clues as to his main conceptual authorities. His citations of David Hume suggest the influence of the Scottish Enlightenment. However, his own views on the epistemic root of civil art and culture differ very significantly from those of Hume. Roscoe spent much of his life trying to discover the fundamental causes for the development and collapse of art. While rejecting the old but still popular suggestion that the human race entered a period of cultural decline after the Trojan Wars, he was also determined to reject 'cyclical' theories of culture. While Hume saw the decay of the classical world as an inevitable process following an alteration of taste consequent on the achievement of perfection, Roscoe sought to find a find a fundamental pattern of causation to explain this decline.[48] For Roscoe, the apparently inevitable association between civil freedom and artistic achievement was also problematic. The apparent associations between freedom and creativity, identified by Shaftesbury and developed by Winckelmann and Hume, were, of course, very popular in the eighteenth century and appeared to explain the decline of the arts in the post-Augustan period. Indeed, Roscoe acknowledged that there was some truth in this association. Just as despotism in late imperial Rome destroyed the dignity and simplicity of the age of Cicero, the growth of authoritarian government in early sixteenth-century Italy destroyed a 'free and vigorous mode of composition' and artistic taste.[49]

Yet for the student of more recent European history, such as Roscoe, the success of the arts under despotic leaders such as Louis XIV suggested that the associations between artistic achievements and freedom were unclear. Roscoe sought, therefore, a more complex naturalistic model to understand the success of art: one where art productions echoed the events and circumstances of the times. Cultural products were 'only a reflexion or shadow or the transactions of real life'.[50] This view clearly echoed the opinions of some important classical and literary scholars of the period, who in seeking to explain genius saw the great artist as one who is able to replicate nature most effectively. For Robert Wood, Homer was 'the most original of all poets, and the most constant and faithful copier of nature'.[51] Societies with the most vivid and heroic social conditions would inevitably produce the conditions for the greatest art. Thus, although Roscoe did not reject the importance of freedom as a contributory factor to artistic advancement, it was dependent on more fundamental political conditions. For Roscoe, freedom was conditional 'on the degree of confidence which any government has in its own stability'.[52] Roscoe's opinions, clearly influenced by events in France, reflected the views of writers such as Lord George Lyttelton who sought to understand how liberty and creativity had historically been reconciled with civil peace. Lyttelton, in examining the reasons for the vitality of art in Pericles' Athens and Medici's Florence, saw strong benevolent leadership, which drew upon public spirit and affection, as essential if the arts were to reach maturity in a democratic state. Lyttelton's position was summed up in an imaginary composed conversation between the great leaders:

> PERICLES: In what I have heard of your character and your fortune, illustrious COSMO, I find a most remarkable resemblance with mine. We both lived in republicks where the sovereign power was in the people; and, by mere civil arts, but more especially by our eloquence, attained, without any force, to such a degree of authority, that we ruled those tumultuous and stormy democracies with an absolute sway; turned the tempests which agitated them upon their heads of our enemies, and after having long and prosperously conducted the greatest affairs, in war and peace, died revered and lamented by all our fellow citizens.
>
> COSMO: We have indeed an equal right to value ourselves on that *noblest of empires*, the empire we gained over *the minds* of our countrymen. – Force or caprice may give power, but nothing can give a lasting authority, except wisdom and virtue. By these we obtained, by these we preserved, in our respective countries, a dominion unstained by usurpation or blood, a dominion conferred on us by the publick esteem and the publick affection.[53]

This view was reflected in Roscoe's historical project. Art was an expression of the character of the times, but it required stability, freedom and benevolent direction for its fulfilment. In order to understand the conditions and process of this fulfilment, Roscoe advocated an empirically grounded social history of art that sought to understand the underlying values of society, the nature of cultural authority and the character of its leaders. This methodology was probably influenced his friend William Smythe of Peterhouse, Cambridge, who became Britain's leading historian of the French revolution. Smythe shared Roscoe's moderate liberalism and, like Roscoe, emphasised the importance of stability as a condition for political freedom. Like Roscoe, he was also highly sceptical of ahistorical doctrines of utilitarianism and human perfectibility, adopting instead a strongly empirical approach.[54] Roscoe's empiricism was also a reflection of the suspicion that many Liverpool merchants had of highly theoretical models of the human sciences, including those of Adam Smith.[55] To be successful, Roscoe's history had to engage with the material facts of commercial urban life in a way that would be persuasive to Liverpool's merchant community. This form of history writing was not merely an academic exercise; it was a history that sought to explain the elements essential to maintaining cultural life, and by implication the conditions for modern civic virtue.

Roscoe's own grand historical projects on the life of Lorenzo de' Medici and his son Pope Leo X reflect this. Roscoe also began a substantial work on the rise and decline of Greek art with a similar preoccupation, but this was never finished.[56] It is, therefore, in his six-volume *The Life and Pontificate of Leo X* that we have the most detailed exposition of his views on the social conditions necessary for the preservation of the liberal arts. This history is particularly concerned with locating the reasons for the development of a society's cultural attributes and the ways in which it may guard against the corruption of taste. In his introductory comments, Roscoe makes it clear that his aim is:

> to unfold the ever active effect of moral causes on the acquirements and the happiness of a people; and thereby raise a barrier, as far as such efforts can avail, against the torrent of a corrupt and vitiated taste, which if not continually opposed, may once more overwhelm the cultivated nations of Europe in barbarism and degradation.[57]

The relevance of this discussion for contemporary Liverpool is obvious when one considers Roscoe's views on the relationship between art and commerce. While industrial pursuits had a tendency 'to reduce the powers both of mind and body to a machine, in which the individual almost loses his identity', Roscoe regarded the mercantilist connections forged through trade as being inherently individualising and liberating.[58] The link between mercantile economies and artistic development could be shown in the trading economy of the ancient world, the Renaissance city states of Italy, the Hanse towns of Germany and, by implication, the modern city of Liverpool. This was not a new idea. The link between commercial economies and artistic development was noted in the work of some of the most literary figures of the eighteenth century including Thomas Paine, Adam Smith and Edward Gibbon, as well as historians of the Renaissance who were increasingly looking for sociological explanations for the rebirth of the arts.[59] What was unusual was that Roscoe was attempting to provide empirical validation of the theory, not merely for historical interest, but to inspire cultural leadership in a modern urban society, his home city of Liverpool.

Roscoe's determination to provide a forensic exploration of this association is reflected in the detail of research. He acknowledged in his foreword a considerable debt to the work of Angelo Fabrioni, principal of the University of Pisa, who had published a major work on Leo X in 1797. However, Roscoe's six-volume history does include a significant amount of original work. He made particular use of William Clarke, a resident of Everton, who was in Italy from 1789. Clarke helped Roscoe acquire rare Italian manuscripts and consulted a number of authorities in Italian libraries on his behalf.[60] Roscoe was also in contact with a number of British-based scholars, including, of course, William Smyth, and the Rev. William Parr Gresswell, author of the well-known *Memoirs of Italian Scholars who have Written Latin Poetry*.[61] Yet, in many respects, the work represents Roscoe's own priorities and eccentricities. Roscoe was determined to break from the circular arguments which saw the rise of culture as a result of the spirit of the age; indeed, he was extremely dismissive of the concept, stating that it was 'only another phrase for causes and circumstances which have not hitherto been sufficiently explained'.[62] Yet he had a tendency to explain the spirit of the age with an equally ambiguous concept, that of character and manners. For Roscoe, like Lyttelton, the character and manners of public figures were the principal agents in fostering and mobilising public spirit and virtue; he noted that of 'the predominating influence of a powerful, an accomplished, or a fortunate individual on the character and manners of the age, the history of mankind furnishes innumerable instances'.[63] Thus while celebrating the contribution of Leo X to the arts, he also felt compelled to devote almost a sixth of his entire work to rescuing the moral character of Lucretia Borgia.[64] His address to the LRI in 1817 identified the same theme; liberal arts were the product of a moral universe that secured rational liberty, tranquillity, prosperity and 'the wish to pay due honour to genius and talent'.[65]

Again, Roscoe emphasised the insecurity of art in the liberal state and the difficulties of protecting the moral conditions for the preservation of taste. Some aspects of his treatment of this issue were particularly controversial given the religious divisions in Liverpool. In particular, his criticism of the Reformation for destroying civil peace and undermining the conditions for artistic patronage brought a particularly hostile reaction from Protestant opponents. The *Edinburgh Review* accused him of outright prejudice against Luther, while the *Christian Observer* accused him of being 'uniformly hostile to Christianity'.[66] Yet there is little evidence that this issue caused Roscoe serious problems in Liverpool, perhaps because of his close friendships with many of Liverpool's religious leaders. Instead, Roscoe's works became a manifesto for Liverpool civic art and liberal studies. The parallels between the great commercial communities of the past and the Liverpool present were obvious, but so were the potential pitfalls if Liverpool was to fail to meet the moral challenge consequent on its privileged position. Even sixty years later, Roscoe's association of commercial Liverpool with Florence and Rome was still being advanced to mobilise the population in the name of civic humanism and art.[67] Yet the message was at its most powerful in the years immediately following the Napoleonic Wars, when Britain's naval supremacy was undisputed and its naval capital, Liverpool, stood at its commercial height. The example of Leo X appeared to show that however generous and liberal-minded one individual might be, leadership was essential to sustain a wider liberal public. Private support for art could not last beyond the death or departure of the patron. In Liverpool, private art associations had struggled and collapsed through the lack of a public spirit. In response, Roscoe sought to create a new moral public order that would institutionalise values of 'correct' taste and collective virtue.

The evidence of Roscoe's influence can be seen in the formation of the LRI art gallery in 1819. This was an important landmark in British art gallery history. While almost all of the other major public galleries of the period, such as the Dulwich gallery, the Fitzwilliam at Cambridge and Christ Church, Oxford, were essentially single bequests to established educational foundations, the Liverpool gallery was a carefully planned gallery and part of the LRI from its inception.[68] Its development was, in part, a product of Roscoe's own misfortune. The collapse of his bank and his failure to come to an agreement with his creditors forced Roscoe to put his entire art collection up for sale. An initial sale of September 1816 was unsuccessful, and in June 1818 he offered to sell the remaining part of the collection to the LRI for a sum of 1,200 guineas, substantially less than a contemporary valuation of 1,553 guineas. A committee of subscribers came together to bid for the pictures on behalf of the LRI, who ultimately paid £760 for the remainder of the collection, less six High Renaissance works that were sent to London instead. Most of the paintings that appeared on the walls of the LRI were, therefore, Italian primitives. The reason for the domination of the collection by Italian primitives is not entirely clear. There is evidence that Roscoe wanted to retain High Renaissance and Baroque pictures as part of the public display, but it is possible that the primitives stayed in Liverpool as they were simply the most difficult to sell.[69] However, in view of Roscoe's writing on the revival of the arts in the Italian republics and the moral value of art, it is likely that the LRI subscribers saw the primitives as having the greatest public utility. Roscoe's 1817 'vicissitudes' address to the LRI and his uncompleted history of art viewed the Italian primitives as representative of a key period of the rebirth of the arts in the fifteenth century, just as modern Liverpool was playing a key part in the rebirth of the arts in the nineteenth.[70] It is possible that, aware of these parallels, Roscoe's subscribers deliberately sought to retain those works which memorialised the period that Roscoe both celebrated through his work and represented through his collecting. The Italian primitives were an important piece of cultural capital that invited comparisons with the resurgence of the arts in mercantile Liverpool.

Roscoe's preoccupation with the forces that provided the foundation for the arts was reflected in the nature of the gallery's development. T. S. Traill, president of the LRI, shared Roscoe's art historical interests and believed that the scholarly focus of the gallery should be an examination of the emergence of artistic excellence. For Traill, however, the model was not that of the Italian primitives but that of the classical world and, specifically, fourth-century Athens. In many respects, his views merely reflected contemporary neo-classicism, being stimulated by the display of the Elgin marbles in London and the political philhellenism inspired by the Byronic revolution in Greece and the defeat of the Ottomans at Navarino.[71] Roscoe certainly had some interest in the classical period as well as contemporary philhellenism. He had begun to compose a treatise on the rise and fall of Greek art, and he wrote warmly of Leo X's resistance to the growth of Turkish power in the East.[72] However, Traill reoriented the gallery to more specifically classical models, rather neglecting the rare collection of primitives. In his annual address to the LRI in 1828, Traill asserted that 'the ancient Greek artists excelled all people that have ever existed' in the highest form of art, the depiction of the human form.[73] Studies of Greek sculpture were therefore to be central to the educational programme of the LRI. Drawing upon De Pauw's rather unscholarly *Recherches philosophiques sur les Grecs*, Traill argued that students should follow Greek methods, even to the point of drawing on life-sized tablets of boxwood, to ensure that the human figure was appreciated in its correct dimensions.[74]

Traill had yet greater ambitions for Liverpool. Just as Italian primitive art illustrated a key period in the revival of the arts in Renaissance Italy, so art of the early classical period illustrated the early stirrings of Greek genius. Bloomsbury had Phidias, but Liverpool could also have its cultural forefathers. In 1827 the Liverpool gallery obtained casts of what became known as the Aegina marbles, from the Temple of Jupiter on the island of Aegina.[75] These marbles were of a flatter and somewhat cruder type than the Elgin marbels and were widely interpreted as an early form of Greek art forming 'an important link in connecting the most finished productions of Grecian sculpture with the works of ruder ages'.[76] They were also important as they illustrated early arts of painting as applied to sculptured and raised surfaces. Using C. R. Cockerell's sketches, presumably those from the fourth volume of Stuart and Revett's *Antiquities of Athens*, the gallery committee assembled the casts in their original positions. Liverpool was the first British gallery to obtain these casts, the original works having been lost to rival bids from German museums. Not surprisingly, the Aegina marbles became a celebrated and central feature of the gallery, attracting artists and scholars from far afield.[77] The pride Liverpool showed in displaying the casts was of course not merely a reflection of their historical interest. They represented the seed of future perfection which had grown in a commercial state, some distance from the metropolis. Aegina, like Liverpool, was a commercial and maritime power. Like Liverpool, it was rendered subordinate to a mighty imperial city, yet retained its cultural strength and political vitality.

Traill's classicism and desire to rediscover the vital ingredients of cultural revival embraced all aspects of the LRI's activities. Debates about the vitality of public art, initiated by Roscoe, now infused the city's scholarly development. It was not enough merely to replicate Greek art; it was necessary to replicate Greek cultural practices. In 1828 Traill led initiatives to establish a gymnasium in connection with the institution. This was conceived as part of an extension of the art gallery in order to provide fine human specimens for study. Traill happily noted the benefits that Greek artists derived from 'the daily contemplation of fine forms afforded by their gymnastic exercises'.[78] Yet the gymnasium was intended for more than this; it was designed to shape the human body as a work of art.

You are all aware of the importance that the polished nations of antiquity attached to those exercises by which the symmetry and vigour of the human frame are improved. The Gymnasia of the Greeks and Romans were national concerns: the revival of Gymnastic exercises in modern times, and their introduction into some of our most flourishing public seminaries, and into many of our private schools, are circumstances which give importance to the subject in the eyes of all who have the superintendance [sic] of the education of youth.[79]

Here the link between art, human development and public welfare is made explicit. In some respects the statement echoes a Reynoldsian agenda for the public utility of art. Indeed, Reynolds was cited in the LRI annual report of 1828 for his emphasis on the importance of industry in the development of artistic genius.[80] However, Traill's agenda was a specific outgrowth of Roscoe's desire to provide the social conditions and leadership through which art and liberal pursuits can prosper. Human agency, expressed through public institutions, was to create a public art which replicated virtuous deeds through the emulative logic of its own operation.

This view, which placed classical learning at its core, was reflected in other aspects of the institution's operation. The LRI's success, of course, depended on its ability to marry Roscoe's civic humanism with the practical demands and aspirations of Liverpool's middle class. Traill was aware of this and saw the LRI as having an important educational function. It could be particularly useful in preparing students for university by organising advanced seminars and classes that could not be provided in the ordinary local schools.[81] For much of the nineteenth century, the LRI's educational programme focused on classics and philology. Although other subjects, such as mathematics, were available, classical studies dominated the curriculum. Of those LRI students who went on to university and get distinctions, the vast majority were classical scholars.[82] This pattern partly reflected the growing importance of Latin and Greek at the ancient universities during the mid-nineteenth century.[83] However, the complete domination of the curriculum by classical studies was unusual even in public schools; in a provincial bourgeois academy it was remarkable and was a testament to the views and influence of Traill. The success of the classical academy was even more remarkable when one considers that the LRI's general lecture programme was largely unsuccessful and had been abandoned by 1840.[84] The Liverpool Academy provided for a practical want by giving the sons of the middle class the opportunity to study for university entrance. The nature of the programme reflected the preoccupations of Roscoe by articulating enduring values of excellence that would create and replicate a culturally sophisticated public.

Unfortunately, Roscoe's legacy to the LRI was not entirely positive. The failure of his bank deprived the institution of around £5,000 of surplus capital that was intended for the LRI's development. Thus the early years of the institution saw little progress in plans for the formation of a permanent art gallery. It was not until 1840, when the public lecture programme was abolished, that £1,200 was made available for the construction of a permanent art gallery. The LRI made the grant conditional on a similar sum being subscribed by the general public. Although progress was initially rather slow, an entirely new gallery building was opened in Colquitt Street in 1843.[85] The main beneficiaries of the new gallery were local artists and art students, particularly those attached to the academy. On weekdays between 10 a.m. and 4 p.m. the galleries were thrown open to members and those nominated by members.[86] The gallery was not open freely to the general public but access arrangements were generally liberal. From the mid-1840s there were extensive attempts to transform the Colquitt Street building into a municipal museum and art gallery. In 1846 the president of the LRI, Samuel Turner, drew members' attention to the passing of the Museums Act and suggested that the institution should make an application to the council for a grant in return for a joint management arrangement. Unfortunately, there were a number of difficulties with the plan, not least of which was the need to apply for statutory permission to enact any new arrangements.[87] Formal negotiations did not begin until 1850 when Cllr James Picton, a formidable advocate of public libraries, persuaded the council to establish a joint committee to investigate the various proposals for municipalisation. By this time the Royal Museum and Library at Salford had already opened as the first municipal museum in the region, and the Liverpool authorities may have been influenced by the success of this initiative.[88] There a new facility had been developed solely by the initiative of the corporation and the local Liberal MPs. Unfortunately, municipalising an existing private institution proved much more difficult. Negotiations failed for two main reasons. First, some in the corporation resented being forced to guarantee an annual sum of £700 per annum for the upkeep of the LRI and its collection. Secondly, the LRI proprietors were reluctant to hand over their property without some guarantee from the corporation about the future extension of the museum and galleries. Feelings ran high, and public comments suggested that some LRI proprietors questioned the ability of town councillors to manage museum collections – one apparently expressing the fear that the council might use the geological specimens as material for road repairs.[89]

Reconciling the interests of Liverpool Corporation and the institution was never likely to be easy. Even in the 1880s the RMI and the Manchester Corporation found it difficult to arrive at a formula that would allow municipalisation while allowing institution members to retain some of their privileges. Ultimately, Manchester Corporation was forced to provide an annual picture purchase fund of £2,000 before the institution would allow the transfer of property to go ahead.[90] Thirty years earlier, in Liverpool, it was even more difficult to get agreement given the novel nature of the museums legislation and the weak political position of the city council. Liverpool Corporation was struggling to establish its political legitimacy following its reconstitution in the wake of the 1835 Municipal Corporations Act. Many ratepayers had opposed the constitution of new urban authorities, and it was not until the case of *Rutter* v. *Chapman* in the mid-1840s that the legal authority of the new local government units was finally undisputed.[91] The polarised nature of local politics in the corporation encouraged municipal leaders to be cautious. Salford, in contrast, was dominated by one party – the Liberals – which could experiment with new museum legislation without any effective opposition. In the first decades of the nineteenth century, Roscoe was able to overcome the polarised nature of local politics because the political class was still relatively small and, to a large extent, known to him personally. Those lobbying for cultural improvements tended to be either close friends of Roscoe or members of the Unitarian intellectual elite with whom he was associated. The expansion of the city and the institutionalisation of party politics made the building of civic consensus much more difficult. The techniques of cultural mobilisation that Roscoe had used were not so easy to apply by mid-century. Personal charm and charismatic civic idealism counted for less as urban governance was conducted more through the print media and less through personal contact. Moreover, the representative and bureaucratic nature of the new cultural institutions was perhaps less likely to lead to the emergence of strong, dynamic leadership. The new municipal government and 'subscriber democracy' had failed to produce a new Medici, much less a Pericles.

The failure of plans for the municipalisation and extension of the art gallery appeared to be symptomatic of the stagnation of the LRI's art policy. The institution did have its important collection of Italian primitives from the Roscoe collection and the extensive casts of classical sculpture obtained largely during Traill's time as president. There were also, of course, a number of miscellaneous donations and bequests, but there appear to have been few significant additions to the permanent collection between 1843 and Theodore Rathbone's revised catalogue of 1859.[92] It is interesting, therefore, that at this moment of apparent cultural stagnation and fragmented leadership, Liverpool's leading scholars and intellectuals should have attempted to rediscover Roscoe's artistic and historical thought as an exemplar for civic life.[93] In 1847 a small literary circle around Henry Sanbach founded a subscription society called the Roscoe Club 'for moral and intellectual improvement' in Liverpool.[94] The organisation was modelled on the 'Whittington Club' of London but took the name of Roscoe as its inspiration. Significantly, Roscoe's old friend T. S. Traill addressed one of its first meetings, while visiting Liverpool from his new home in Edinburgh.[95] Traill's precise involvement in the society is unclear, but there can be little doubt that his appearance in Liverpool and his address to the society did much to reinvigorate interest in Roscoe's life and scholarship. The Traill meeting received the endorsement of the mayor, and the society was able to attract a number of eminent patrons, including the Earls of Derby and Sefton, Lord Viscount Sandon and William Ewart MP.[96] In the autumn of 1847 it opened premises in Bold Street, and soon, on finding them inadequate for its growing membership, it moved to the Clayton Arms Hotel, where a library and newsroom were provided. Significantly, a gymnasium and baths were also available, reflecting Traill's belief in the relationship between art and physical culture.[97] The society continued to expand throughout the late 1840s and became an important agent in the propagation of the Roscoe myth. By 1849, it had developed a strategically important position at the heart of Liverpool's intellectual life and used its magazine, named after Roscoe, to report and comment on the proceedings of all Lancashire's and Cheshire's major scholarly and artistic societies.

The rediscovery of Roscoe as a Liverpool institution created a new demand for histories of his life and teaching. Mayer's *Roscoe and the Influence of his Writing on the Fine Arts*, read before the Historic Society of Lancashire and Cheshire, was perhaps the most important work of this genre.[98] Mayer emphasised Roscoe's pivotal role in the formation of the eighteenth-century art societies in Liverpool and highlighted his views on the public utility of art. Interestingly, his work also highlighted Roscoe's metropolitan connections and his associations with leading London artists, almost as if Roscoe had been solely responsible for their introduction into the region.[99] Another more folksy history was put together by Washington Irving, but it reflected similar themes. Irving stressed that Roscoe wrote about Lorenzo de' Medici because he regarded him as 'a pure model of antiquity' committed, like Roscoe, to a brand of civic patriotism that emphasised the centrality of art in the cultural health of a city.[100] Through his virtuous cultural actions Roscoe, like Medici, had established a memorial for himself; he had become institutionalised in the cultural consciousness of the city.

> the man of letters who speaks of Liverpool, speaks of it as the residence of Roscoe. – The intelligent traveller who visits it, inquires where Roscoe is to be seen. – He is the literary landmark of the place, indicating its existence to the distant scholar. – He is like Pompey's column at Alexandria, towering alone in classical dignity.[101]

Roscoe's centenary in 1853 thus saw a revival of the Roscoe myth. In some cases, the myth was reworked to provide an exemplar of generalised public generosity and benevolence, as in Baines's *The Liverpool Tribute to Roscoe*.[102] However, in general writers used Roscoe to remind the Liverpool citizenry of the importance of the liberal arts in the modern city state. While Mayer celebrated his contribution to the study of painting and sculpture, Aspinall and Tuckerman emphasised his literary and bibliographical pursuits.[103]

The revival of the Roscoe myth coincided with a growing sense of crisis in Liverpool's cultural elite. Attempts to form a municipal museum and art gallery through the municipalisation of the LRI had failed, and the Liverpool Academy was facing significant internal problems. At least one late nineteenth-century Liverpool historian saw the period as being one in which the city's leadership, secure in their social status, gradually withdrew from the field of public culture and continued to patronise art mainly for private consumption or aggrandise-ment.[104] Yet, interestingly, it was probably the decline of the private market for pictures in Liverpool that did most to undermine the position of the city's most publicly active art institution, the academy. The artistic and commercial success of the academy in the 1840s was illustrative of the emergence of the type of 'art public' that Roscoe had been so keen to foster. Its institutional growth appeared to indicate not merely a strong market for modern art, but the cultural health and virtue of the city more widely. Its contraction appeared to herald the city's decline.[105]

The academy's early development was closely associated with the LRI and it held its first exhibition on institution premises in 1822. Previous exhibitions had been held in less suitable accommodation in the Gothic rooms in Marble Street and in premises above the Union Newsroom.[106] After several years of disappointing exhibitions, the LRI provided financial assistance for the academy's exhibition of 1827. This decision appears to have revived the academy's fortunes. Picture sales reached a record £489 19s in 1827, and the following year the town council began to give grants to the academy.[107] The council's contributions allowed the academy to move to improved premises in Old Post Office Place. By the early 1830s, the Liverpool Academy Exhibition had been established as the leading exhibition in the region, especially after the collapse of the exhibiting society in Carlisle. Much of the academy's success clearly depended on the willingness of Traill's LRI to support it in its formative years. In contrast to the situation in Manchester, the Liverpool Academy also had a local corporation which, inspired by Roscoe's example, recognised the importance of public patronage of civic art. Moreover, a key factor in the success of the academy's exhibition appears to have been its ability to broaden the traditional system of art patronage through the introduction of an art union.

The Liverpool Art Union was established in 1834 and was the first of its kind south of the border. Edinburgh's art union had been established a year earlier and had, like Liverpool's, been conceived as a way of broadening financial support for the annual exhibition. In contrast, London's art union did not appear until 1837, and Manchester's did not begin operations until 1840.[108] The original idea for art unions came from Paris, and they were soon shown to be very effective ways of attracting support for exhibitions from those who were not necessary able or prepared to purchase works of art outright.[109] The unions operated essentially as open lotteries, with each winner either obtaining a specific picture or, as was the case in Liverpool, collecting a voucher from which an exhibition purchase could be made. By the late 1830s pictures bought through lottery winnings amounted to a very substantial proportion of the total value of pictures sold at the Liverpool annual exhibition. On some occasions art union sales counted for more than private sales; in 1839 the art union sales amounted to £1,623, while private sales were just £1,380. However, this was unusual. By the 1840s private sales grew considerably, and by 1844 exhibition sales were so successful that the academy was able to begin charging commission on sales.[110]

Sadly, the academy found it impossible to sustain this progress. Part of the difficulty was competition from the growing number of provincial exhibitions and the impact of the railways. The RMI exhibition at Manchester never produced as many sales as Liverpool's but in a good year could still draw a significant number of purchasers, who might otherwise have been drawn to Liverpool.[111] Yet it was probably the growth of the national rail network that had the greatest impact on the decline of the Liverpool and other provincial exhibitions, by revolutionising the relationship of provincial elites with the London market. Provincial dealers could now travel to London much more readily and buy directly from the Royal Academy on behalf of regional clients, and by the 1840s the Liverpool merchant could take an early breakfast in his home city and a late lunch in the capital. There had always been a suspicion that the metropolitan pictures that appeared in regional exhibitions were usually those that could not find buyers at the Royal Academy, or as the *Art Union* put it 'the refuse' of the marketplace.[112] Major pictures of the season almost always appeared in London first, and for serious collectors and connoisseurs a visit to the Royal Academy had become essential. The grip of the London market inevitably had a substantial impact on provincial artists too. When Liverpool's leading painter, Richard Ansdell, moved to London in 1850, he was reflecting a growing tradition of success-ful regional painters drawn by the centripetal tendency of the metropolitan marketplace.[113]

The forces of the marketplace were probably irresistible. However, the acad-emy's death knell came with the famous Pre-Raphaelite dispute of the mid-1850s. The decision of the academy to give its awards to Pre-Raphaelite artists sparked a total fragmentation of the society.[114] Almost immediately two of the society's leading non-resident members, Richard Ansdell and Henry Dawson, resigned in protest, sparking a decade of turbulence, which ultimately led to the town council withdrawing its annual grant and the emergence of two rival exhibiting societies. Despite attempts in 1863 at reconciliation between the academy and a new 'Society of Fine Arts', competition between the societies effectively led to their mutual destruction. The new society held its last exhibition in 1865, while the academy withdrew from organising exhibitions after the financial failure of its 1867 event.[115]

The revival of the spirit or myth of Roscoe was, therefore, closely associated with this growing sense of public crisis. The two Liverpool institutions that Roscoe had inspired, the LRI and the academy, had seemingly failed to satisfy the expectations of their supporters. This was at least partly because of the growth and fragmentation of Liverpool's cultural elites. The LRI was not brought under municipal control and expanded because of a fundamental dispute over the control and ownership of the city's most important civic resource. Many of those inspired by Roscoe and Traill were unwilling to hand control to a public authority which appeared to have no particular commitment to the cultural development of the city and was unwilling to commit substantial public funds to further the display of public art. The academy was a victim of the changing patterns of art patronage and the increasing tendency for members of Liverpool's business community to buy directly from the Royal Academy rather than from their own civic exhibition. Moreover, the academy was never really a public institution in the traditional sense. It was an unincorporated self-governing society that, despite receiving public patronage, essentially saw itself as a private organisation able to act upon its own initiative without reference to a broader public. This insularity was to prove fatal. Without the mechanisms or willingness to conciliate and resolve internal differences, the society was unable to sustain itself during a contentious period.

The apparent failure of the LRI and the academy would seem to suggest that whatever the power of Roscoe's ideas, they could not resolve the political struggles or prevent the social fragmentation of the city's cultural leadership that took place in mid-century. Liverpool grew rapidly, breaking up the remnants of Roscoe's circle, while the inland transport revolution relegated Liverpool to the fringe of a much larger metropolitan marketplace. Yet Roscoe's Liverpool was not entirely dead. The centenary of his birth saw a re-awakening of pride in Liverpool's cultural past. The foundation of the Liverpool public library and museum in 1852 marked the beginning of increasing municipal interest in civic culture.[116] The 1860s were to see a period of strong public agitation for the formation of an art gallery in the city, and when in 1873 a local brewer, A. B. Walker, offered to fund the construction of a municipal gallery, the spirit of Roscoe was once again invoked. Roscoe had ceased to be a philanthropist, or even an institution; he had become an idea. Art was the means through which a commercial community could express its identity, purify its taste and preserve its greatness. This did not mean that the Roscoe idea would necessarily lead to a consensus about the ultimate direction of a civic art policy. With the death of Roscoe, Liverpool lacked a Pericles or a Medici with the political and cultural authority to provide just this leadership. Traill helped to revive the ideological corpse of Roscoe, but the growth of Liverpool as a complex urban society with competing claims of authority meant that the political purchase of Roscoe's ideas about virtuous civic leadership was considerably weakened. Disputes about the formation of the Walker Art Gallery would reveal the difficulties of realising Roscoe's civic vision in the institutionalised partisan space of municipal government.

NOTES

1 For background and discussion see J. Rykwert, *The Idea of a Town* (Princeton, 1976).

2 T. S. Traill, 'Memoir of William Roscoe', *Edinburgh New Philosophical Journal*, 26 (c.1832), 193–221; H. J. Tuckerman, *Characteristics of Literature: The Philanthropist William Roscoe* (London, 1849); Joseph Mayer, *Roscoe and the Influence of his Writings on the Fine Arts* (London, 1853); T. Baines, *The Liverpool Tribute to Roscoe* (London, 1853); G. W. Matthews, *William Roscoe: A Memoir* (London, 1931); G. Chandler, *William Roscoe of Liverpool 1753–1831* (London, 1953).

3 F. Espinasse, *Lancashire Worthies*, 2nd series (London, 1877), 274–85.

4 H. Roscoe, *The Life of William Roscoe*, 2 vols (London, 1833).

5 Cited in Matthews, *William Roscoe*, 46.

6 J. Trepp, 'The Liverpool Movement for the Abolition of the English Slave Trade', *Journal of Negro History*, 13 (1928), 265–85; R. Anstey, *Liverpool, the African Slave Trade, and Abolition* (Liverpool, 1989). For background see F. E. Hyde, B. B. Parkinson and S. Marriner, *The Nature and Profitability of the Liverpool Slave Trade* (London, 1953), and G. Cameron, *Liverpool: Capital of the Slave Trade* (Birkenhead, 1992).

7 R. B. Rose, 'The Jacobins of Liverpool', *Liverpool Bulletin*, 9 (1960–61), 35–49.

8 For an overview and description see G. Chandler, *Liverpool* (London, 1957), 439–71; R. Brooke, *Liverpool as it Was during the Last Quarter of the Eighteenth Century, 1775 to 1800* (Liverpool, 1853).

9 V. Burton (ed.), *Liverpool Shipping, Trade and Industry: Essays on the Maritime History of Merseyside 1780–1860* (Liverpool, 1989); F. Hyde, *Liverpool and the Mersey: An Economic History of a Port 1700–1970* (Newton Abbot, 1971); J. R. Harris, *Liverpool and Merseyside: Essays in the Economic and Social History of the Port and its Hinterland* (London, 1969).

10 P. Borsay, *The English Urban Renaissance* (Oxford, 1989); P. Clark, *British Clubs and Societies, 1580–1800* (Oxford, 2000), 142–6, 415–16.

11 C. Walford, *The Commercial Greatness of Liverpool* (London, 1883).

12 A. Wilson, '"The Florence of the North"? The Civic Culture of Liverpool in the Early Nineteenth Century', in A. Kidd and D. Nicholls (eds), *Gender, Civic Culture, Consumerism* (Manchester, 1999), 34–46, esp. 34. For the broader debate about the nature of 'gentlemanly capitalism' see P. Cain and A. Hopkins, 'Gentlemanly Capitalism and British Expansion Overseas, I: The Old Colonial System, 1688–1850', *Economic History Review*, 39 (1986), 501–25; W. D. Rubinstein, *Elites and the Wealthy in Modern British History* (London, 1988); M. Daunton, '"Gentlemanly Capitalism" and British Industry 1820–1914', *Past and Present*, 122 (1989), 119–58; W. D. Rubinstein, '"Gentlemanly Capitalism" and British Industry 1820–1914', *Past and Present*, 132 (1991), 150–70.

13 D. Ross, *Sketch of the History of the House of Stanley, and the House of Sefton* (London, 1848); W. Pollard, *The Stanleys of Knowsley: A History* (London, 1869).

14 R. Muir, *The History of Liverpool* (Liverpool, 1907), 308.

15 A. Wilson, 'Cultural Identity of Liverpool, 1790–1850: The Early Learned Societies', *Transactions of the Historic Society of Lancashire and Cheshire*, 147 (1997), 55–80, esp. 57.

16 H. C. Marillier, *The Liverpool School of Painters* (London, 1904), 1–4.

17 Marillier, *Liverpool School*, 3–4.

18 B. H. Grindley, *History and Work of the Liverpool Academy of Arts* (Liverpool, 1875), 2.

19 W. Roscoe, *An Ode on the Institution of a Society in Liverpool for the Encouragement of Designing, Drawing, Painting* ... (Liverpool, 1774).

20 The ode became well known and was referred to in Axon's popular histories; see W. E. A. Axon, *Lancashire Gleanings* (Manchester, n.d. [1882?]), 252.

21 E. Gibbon, *History of the Decline and Fall of the Roman Empire* (London, 1766–88); W. Mitford, *The History of Greece* (London, 1784–1810). There was also a broader cultural preoccupation about the transitory nature of civilisation. For a brief overview see C. Woodward, *In Ruins* (London, 2002).

22 Chandler, *Roscoe*, xx.

23 Grindley, *History*, 2.

24 C. Morris, 'History of the Liverpool Regional College of Art 1825–70', MPhil thesis, Liverpool Polytechnic, 1985, 10.

25 Thomas Taylor, letter to J. L. Philips, 28 October 1783; J. Mayer, *Roscoe and the Influence of his Writings on the Fine Arts* (Liverpool, 1853), 5.

26 Mayer, *Roscoe*, 9–10.

27 *The Exhibition of the Society for Promoting Painting and Design, in Liverpool, September 1784* (Liverpool, 1784) (copy), 14–23.

28 *The Exhibition of the Society for Promoting Painting and Design, in Liverpool, September 1787* (Liverpool, 1787) (copy), 26–34.

29 For details of Roscoe's associations with Fuseli see H. Macandrew, 'Henry Fuseli and William Roscoe', *Liverpool Bulletin*, 8 (1959–60), 5–52.

30 *The Exhibition of the Society for Promoting Painting and Design, in Liverpool, September 1784*, 14–23.

31 M. Hopkinson, 'The Print Market in Liverpool in the Late Eighteenth Century', *Print Quarterly*, 24 (2007), 107–15.

32 Daniel Daulby, letter to Holt, 4 June 1794, cited in Grindley, *History*, 3.

33 Matthews, *William Roscoe*, 24–5.

34 For background see I. Sellers, 'William Roscoe, the Roscoe Circle and Radical Politics in Liverpool 1787–1807', *Transactions of the Historic Society and Lancashire and Cheshire*, 120 (1968), 45–62.

35 Matthews, *William Roscoe*, 28–30.

36 For a contemporary description see *The Stranger in Liverpool; or An Historical and Descriptive View of the Town of Liverpool and its Environs* (Liverpool, 1823), 99–100.

37 Wilson, '"The Florence of the North"?', esp. 38.

38 Grindley, *History*, 3.

39 H. A. Ormerod, *The Liverpool Royal Institution: A Record and a Retrospect* (Liverpool, 1953), 10–13.

40 W. Roscoe, *On the Origin and Vicissitudes of Literature, Science and Art, and their Influence on the Present State of Society* (Liverpool, 1817).

41 J. Barrell, *The Political Theory of Painting from Reynolds to Hazlitt* (London, 1986), 1–13.

42 W. Roscoe, 'On the Comparative Excellence of the Science and Arts, by Mr William Roscoe Communicated', *Memoirs of the Society at Manchester*, 3 (1787), 244–59, esp. 258.

43 H. T. Swedenberg, *The Theory of the Epic in England, 1650–1800* (New York, 1972); R. Lee, 'Ut Pictura Poesis: The Humanistic Theory of Painting', *Art Bulletin*, 22 (1940), 197–269.

44 Barrell, *Political Theory*, 19–20.

45 J. Brewer, *The Pleasures of the Imagination: English Culture in the Eighteenth Century* (Chicago, 1997), 273–6; A. Ballantyne, *Architecture, Landscape and Liberty: Richard Payne Knight and the Picturesque* (Cambridge, 1997).

46 For details of Fuseli and the early Romantic school see N. L. Pressly, *The Fuseli Circle in Rome: Early Romantic Art of the 1770s* (New Haven, 1979).

47 T. Blackwell, *An Enquiry into the Life and Writings of Homer* (London, 1735); R. Wood, *An Essay on the Original Genius and Writings of Homer* (London, 1775).

48 Roscoe, *Origin*, 24–6.

49 Roscoe, *Origin*, 27.

50 Roscoe, *Origin*, 36.

51 See K. Simonsuuri, *Homer's Original Genius: Eighteenth-Century Notions of the Early Greek Epic* (Cambridge, 1979), esp. 133–4.

52 Roscoe, *Origin*, 33.

53 G. Lyttelton, *Dialogues of the Dead* (Worcester, Mass., 1790), 182–3, cited in H. Weisinger, 'The English Origins of the Sociological Interpretation of the Renaissance', *Journal of the History of Ideas*, 11 (1950), 326; and C. Tite, 'Sensation, Danger and New Protagonists of Taste in Mid-Eighteenth Century Britain', *Anglia – Zeitschrift für englische Philologie*, 123 (2005), 26–44.

54 K. Balfour, 'A. "Petty" Professor of Modern History: William Smythe (1765–1849)', *Cambridge Historical Journal*, 9 (1948), 217–38; H. Ben Israel, 'William Smythe, Historian of the French Revolution', *Journal of the History of Ideas*, 21 (1960), 571–85.

55 S. G. Checkland, 'Economic Attitudes in Liverpool, 1793–1807', *Economic History Review*, 5 (1952), 58–75, esp. 59–61.

56 Several chapters of this book were, however, completed. See H. Roscoe, *Life of William Roscoe* (London, 1833), vol. 1, 461–2.

57 W. Roscoe, *The Life and Pontificate of Leo X*, 2nd edn, vol. 1 (Liverpool, 1806), xlvi–ii.

58 Roscoe, *Origin*, 44, 47.

59 Weisinger, 'Sociological Interpretation', 321–38.

60 Roscoe, *Life of William Roscoe*, vol. 1, 148–9.

61 Roscoe, *Leo X*, vol. 1, xxxvi–ii.

62 Roscoe, *Leo X*, vol. 1, xxxviii.

63 Roscoe, *Leo X*, vol. 1, 506–7.

64 Roscoe, *Leo X*, vol. 5.

65 Roscoe, *Origin*, 73.

66 Roscoe, *Life of William Roscoe*, vol. 1, 332–4.

67 *Daily Post*, 30 September 1873; *Liverpool Leader*, 4 October 1873.

68 E. Morris, 'The Formation of the Gallery of Art in the Liverpool Royal Institution, 1816–1819', *Transactions of the Historic Society of Lancashire and Cheshire*, 142 (1992), 87–98, esp. 88–9.

69 For a detailed discussion of events surrounding the sales see Morris, 'Formation', 92–5.

70 Roscoe, *Origin*, 47, 59, 63, 66.

71 For background see W. St Clair, *That Greece Might Still Be Free: The Philhellenes in the War of Independence* (Oxford, 1972); D. Dakin, *British and American Philhellenes* (Thessaloniki, 1955).

72 Roscoe, *Leo X*, vol. 4, 462–3.

73 T. S. Traill, *Address Delivered February, 1828 at the General Meeting of Proprietors of the Liverpool Royal Institution* (Liverpool, 1828), 14.

74 Traill, *Address Delivered February, 1828*, 15–16.

75 In fact the temple from which they were taken was the Temple of Aphia, Aegina. However, early nineteenth-century archaeologists were misled by somewhat confusing designations in Pausanias.

76 Traill, *Address Delivered February, 1828*, 27.

77 Traill, *Address Delivered February, 1828*, 24.

78 Traill, *Address Delivered February, 1828*, 12.

79 T. S. Traill, *Address Delivered February, 1829 at the General Meeting of Proprietors of the Liverpool Royal Institution* (Liverpool, 1829), 13–14.

80 Appendix to Report of the Academy of Art, in Liverpool Royal Institution Report 1828 (Liverpool, 1828), 34, Liverpool Record Office (hereafter LRO), H q027 2 ROY.

81 T. S. Traill, *Address Delivered February, 1827 at the General Meeting of Proprietors of the Liverpool Royal Institution* (Liverpool, 1827), 7.

82 'Distinctions Attained at the University [sic] by Pupils of the Royal Institution School [1846–73]', in H. A. Bright, *Address Delivered to the Annual Meeting of the Proprietors of the Liverpool Royal Institution* (Liverpool, 1873), 12–14.

83 R. Jenkyns, *The Victorians and Ancient Greece* (Oxford, 1980); H. Lloyd-Jones, *Blood for the Ghosts: Classical Influences in the Nineteenth and Twentieth Centuries* (London, 1982); R. M. Ogilvie, *Latin and Greek: A History of the Influence of the Classics on English Life* (London, 1964); F. M. Turner, *The Greek Heritage in Victorian Britain* (London, 1981).

84 Ormerod, *Liverpool Royal Institution*, 33.

85 Ormerod, *Liverpool Royal Institution*, 33–4.

86 'Regulations Respecting the Gallery of Art', in T. Duguid, *Address Delivered at the Annual Meeting of the Proprietors of the Liverpool Royal Institution* (Liverpool, 1861), 34.

87 Ormerod, *Liverpool Royal Institution*, 42–3.

88 See Corporation of Salford Museum and Library Committee, Minutes, 5 July 1849, SRML.

89 Details of the negotiations can be found in Ormerod, *Liverpool Royal Institution*, 42–53.

90 Royal Manchester Institution, Council General Meeting, Minutes, 8 March 1882, MCL, M6/1.

91 J. Moore and R. Rodger, 'Municipal Knowledge and Policy Networks in British Local Government, 1832–1914', *Yearbook of European Administrative History*, 15 (2003), 29–58, esp. 35–6.

92 T. Winstanley, *Catalogue of the Pictures, Casts from the Antique, &c in the Liverpool Royal Institution, June 1836* (Liverpool, 1836); T. Rathbone, *Descriptive and Historical Catalogue of the Pictures, Drawings, and Casts in the Gallery of Art of the Royal Institution* (Liverpool, 1859).

93 Muir was perhaps first to note this 'rediscovery'. See Muir, *History*, 292–318.

94 *The Laws and By Laws of the Roscoe Club* (Liverpool, 1847).

95 *Roscoe Magazine*, March 1849, 21–3.

96 *Laws and By Laws of the Roscoe Club*.

97 *Roscoe Magazine*, March 1849, 22–3.

98 Mayer, *Roscoe*, esp. 5–9.

99 Mayer, *Roscoe*, 23–5.

100 W. Irving, *A Sketch of William Roscoe* (Liverpool, 1853), 9.

101 Irving, *Sketch*, 14.

102 Baines, *The Liverpool Tribute to Roscoe*.

103 J. Aspinall, *Roscoe's Library* (London and Liverpool, 1853); Tuckerman, *Characteristics of Literature*.

104 B. G. Orchard, *Liverpool's Legion of Honour* (Birkenhead, 1893), 213, 689, cited in Wilson, '"The Florence of the North"?', 46.

105 E. Morris, 'The Liverpool Academy and Other Art Exhibitions in Liverpool 1774–1867', introduction to E. Morris and E. Roberts (eds), *The Liverpool Academy and Other Exhibitions of Contemporary Art in Liverpool 1774–1867* (Liverpool, 1998), 3–4.

106 Marillier, *Liverpool School*, 11–12.

107 Morris, 'Liverpool Academy', 4.

108 Morris, 'Liverpool Academy', 5–6.

109 V. Whitfield, 'A Lottery for Art: The Manchester Art Union 1840–1850', BA thesis, University of Manchester, 1997, vi–vii, 8–9. They were also developed in the United States. See R. Klein, 'Art and Authority in Antebellum New York City: The Rise and Fall of the American Art-Union', *Journal of American History*, 81 (1995), 1534–61.

110 Morris, 'Liverpool Academy', 6.

111 Total picture sales in 1851 were £1,339. See RMI, Council Proceedings, General Meeting, 31 March 1852, MCL.

112 *Art Union*, 1 January 1843, 17, cited in C. Darcy, *The Encouragement of the Fine Arts in Lancashire, 1760–1860* (Manchester, 1976), 87.

113 Morris, 'Liverpool Academy', 9.

114 For details of these works see M. Bennett, 'A Check List of Pre-Raphaelite Pictures Exhibited at Liverpool 1846–67, and some of their Northern Collectors', *Burlington Magazine*, 105 (1963), 477–95.

115 Marillier, *Liverpool School*, 21–5.

116 Muir, *History*, 318.

3

An 'ornament to the town'? The Royal Manchester Institution and early public art patronage in Manchester

Manchester's iconic status as the world's 'first industrial city' has inevitably attracted the attention of historians of cultural production. Alongside the new factories and industrial landscape came a middle class with surplus capital to devote to art and luxury consumption. Although Manchester's cultural life was not mobilised by the work and myth of a single 'heroic' individual such as Roscoe in Liverpool, its institutions were shaped by its status as a rising industrial city and an awareness of its sudden economic predominance and latent political power. The city was to become an enigma: it was both the 'shock city' of industrialisation and a major centre of modern art patronage and philanthropy. Yet Manchester, like other northern industrial cities, was often perceived as a place of cultural philistinism.[1] This reputation reflected popular prejudices against the city's ruling class, its industrial character and regional rivalries. Manchester was a place that represented the emerging economic and political power of a new industrial middle class – advocates of the new politics of free trade, commercial enterprise and religious free thought. Consequently, the city's elite were frequently the butt of Tory caricatures which depicted them as 'bluff, plain-speaking, uncultured, Nonconformist, Liberal, self-made men wholly concerned with making money'.[2] Manchester also suffered from metropolitan and southern prejudices that became interwoven with this political conflict. While southerners were stereotyped as 'genteel, graceful, romantic, idealistic, and benevolent', northerners were regarded as 'independent, practical, rough, calculating and enterprising'.[3] Although these characterisations of the north and Manchester were not entirely negative, they emphasised the commercial and materialistic aspects of the new industrialists and neglected their contributions to the arts and sciences. Even within the north, Manchester suffered denigration from its rivals and especially from its chief eighteenth-century rival Liverpool. The

65

phrase 'Liverpool gentleman and Manchester man' continues to be in common parlance as a jibe at the alleged relative unsophistication of Mancunians. Modern historians of Manchester have thus been very keen to emphasise the differences between the real nineteenth-century Manchester industrialist and the Dickensian caricature of Josiah Bounderby of Coketown:

> He was a rich man: banker, merchant, manufacturer, and what not. A big loud man, with a stare and a metallic laugh. A man made out of coarse material, which seemed to have been stretched to make so much of him … A man with a pervading appearance on him of being inflated like a balloon and ready to start. A man who could never sufficiently vaunt himself a self-made man. A man who was always proclaiming his old ignorance and old poverty. A man who was the bully of humility.[4]

These caricatures hardly did Manchester justice. By 1840 the city had a buoyant local art market, a nationally significant exhibition, a school of art and, most significantly of all, a prestigious art institution that attracted royal patronage. Indeed, as Darcy has noted, it is somewhat surprising that Manchester failed to develop a public art institution before the 1820s, especially given the presence of important local collectors and the success of the nearby Liverpool exhibition.[5] Manchester had a strong cultural life even in the late eighteenth century, and the Manchester Literary and Philosophical Society, formed in 1781, was one of the earliest English scientific associations outside the capital.[6] However, the early cultural institutions that developed in industrial towns were primarily the product of the private interests of a small number of men. It is doubtful whether late eighteenth-century art in Liverpool would have developed so rapidly had it not been for the pioneering enthusiasm of William Roscoe. Similarly, in Manchester, early public cultural activities were primarily the outgrowth of the private interests of a few art enthusiasts.[7] Although no single individual established predominance over Manchester's cultural life as Roscoe did in Liverpool, some early Manchester institutions benefited from the presence of entrepreneurs seeking fame as cultural pioneers. The classic case of such an institution is that of the Ashton Lever Museum, located at Alkerington, now Piccadilly.

Ashton Lever, educated at Manchester Grammar School and Oxford, was responsible for developing the city's first museum. He began by establishing an aviary, then moved on to collecting stuffed birds and eventually accumulated a large miscellaneous collection covering natural history, ethnography and art. By 1773 it was being described as 'one of the grandest collections of the most perfect specimens of Natural History that perhaps are to be seen in any private gentleman's possession in Europe'.[8] In all Lever had accumulated 60 species of quadruped, 160 species of bird, over 200 shells, 100 fish, 100 amphibians, 1,100 types of fossil, 200 specimens of marble, 1,000 types of medal and almost 200 weapons – 'diabolical instrument of destruction, invented, no doubt, by the Devil himself'.[9] Although the promotion of fine art was not a core aim of Lever's museum, his curious collections attracted artists and sketchers, and he may have actually commissioned artists to reproduce images of items in his collection. Lever was reported to have amassed a total of 200 drawings 'highly finished after natural subjects in this Museum, and done by gentleman eminent in the art', many of which were on public display.[10] Unfortunately for Manchester, in 1774 Lever decided to move the museum's contents to London, where he took a large house in Leicester Square belonging to the Sidneys, Earls of Leicester, and opened a new museum entitled 'The Holophusicon'. For the next eleven years it was a major cultural attraction in the metropolis, with travellers such as Sir William Hamilton and Baron Dimsdale regarding it as the best in Europe.[11] Despite the critical success, Lever's enthusiasm for collecting placed him in a troubled financial position and he decided to dispose of the collection, eventually through a public lottery, after the British Museum declined to purchase it. Although the main collection went to London, Lever retired to his house in Alkerington, where he lived until 1788, and it seems that at least some of his exhibits remained in Manchester.[12]

Limited sources make it difficult to say very much about the influence that the Ashton Lever museum had on local taste for art and scientific knowledge in Manchester, but it clearly attracted visitors and artists to the city. Early directories show only a small number of artists and art dealers in Manchester at this time. The first directory of 1772 lists just a single print seller, William Newton, who combined print selling with a position as a bookseller and stationer, and a single professional artist, Joseph Legard Jnr, who was also listed as a 'Musick-maker'.[13] Of course, it is important to view directories of this early period with caution as they may only partially reflect the business activity being undertaken, particularly in the art world, where many dealers and artists would have been semi-itinerant. It seems likely that few artists in Manchester during this period would have operated exclusively as artists. William Green, who later gained fame as a Lakeland artist, is a case in point. Green was the son of a schoolmaster and writing master who spent his early years primarily surveying and map-making. In 1783 he opened an afternoon school for drawing and painting, which by 1786 had moved to his home in Brazenose Street, and he then spent a period of eight years working on a new map of Manchester. Unfortunately, this proved unremunerative. By the early 1790s he began concentrating on landscape painting, especially in Wales and the Lake District, but he continued to run a drawing school with his half-brother Hartley, until he left Manchester for London and then the Lake District during 1796.[14] Others also came to specialise as the market expanded. Joshua Shaw spent his early career as a chair painter in the 1790s before establishing himself as a professional artist who could command up to sixty guineas for his landscapes.[15] By the 1790s a number of artists were able to make a significant living from local patrons, with Joseph Parry and William Tate of Liverpool both obtaining considerable local work.[16]

By the end of the eighteenth century, several artists were offering tuition in drawing and painting in Manchester. In December 1802, William Craig launched an initiative to begin an 'Academy on a plan something like that of the Royal Academy, for the gratuitous instruction of one hundred young men, in the different departments of Drawing and Designing'.[17] In fact the plan drawn up by Craig was somewhat different from that of the Royal Academy. The prospectus made it clear that, although the drawing arts represented 'elegant amusement', there were also commercial advantages to be obtained from 'improvements in mechanics and manufactures'.[18] Craig offered 100 or more drawings to aid the development of the academy, and membership was to be limited to 100 subscribers, with an annual subscription of one guinea allowing each subscriber to nominate a pupil for three months. The format of membership was designed to appeal to manufacturers and those in artistic trades, who could use the academy as a training ground for workers. The academy was to be limited to men only, and there were ambitious plans for an annual exhibition and the purchase of a collection of antique casts for study. Quite why the initiative failed is difficult to see. The academy attracted aristocratic support in the shape of the Earl of Wilton, who became president, while the subscribers included representatives of the leading industrial families such as the Hardmans and the Heywoods. Although the academy was operating in 1805 it closed shortly afterwards.[19]

War with France naturally diverted some public attention from public art and associational life, but the early years of the nineteenth century were not without some advances in civic culture. 1806 saw the opening of an important subscription library, the Portico, in one of the city's most fashionable streets: Mosley Street.[20] Ashton's guide of 1804 recorded that Mosley Street contained 'many capital houses, and if it had fortunately been a few yards wider it would have been one of the best streets in the north of England'.[21] The new Portico Library was by no means the first library in Manchester – Chetham's library could claim a fourteenth-century foundation – but it represented an important cultural meeting place for the city's leading industrialists and professionals.[22] During the first quarter of the nineteenth century, there built up in Manchester a small but important cadre of supporters of the fine arts. Of these perhaps the two most important in Manchester social circles were William Hardman and John Leigh Philips. Hardman occupied a large house on what was then the edge of Manchester, in Quay Street, which became an important centre for social entertaining and onto which he built a music hall for recitals and gentlemen's concerts.[23] His fortune came through his success in business as a drysalter and his marriage to an heiress.[24] However, it is as an art patron that he is most celebrated. By the time of his death, his art collection was said to be worth around £30,000 and to include works by Titian, Canaletto and Rembrandt, as well as modern artists such as Wright of Derby.[25] Although the authenticity of the old masters may be questioned, Hardman was undoubtedly a collector of major significance. He had been making important purchases in the region since the 1790s and was closely connected with William Roscoe's circle at Liverpool.[26] After Hardman's death in 1813 his son Thomas inherited some of his cultural interests and kept up the city centre property and its art collection until 1828, when the death of Hardman's widow brought a move to Higher Broughton.[27] Even following this move, the Hardman family still maintained part of the collection, lending works to old master exhibitions at the RMI into the 1830s.[28]

John Leigh Philips was a contemporary of William Hardman who compiled a similarly important collection. Although Philips's interests were somewhat broader than Hardman's – like many cultured men he had a particular interest in natural history and antiquarianism – his art collecting habits were similar. Like Hardman, he collected some old masters, including two works attributed to Rubens and two to Rembrandt, but he also collected modern British painting, including works by Sandby, Walmsley and Girtin. He was particularly noted for his patronage of Joseph Wright of Derby. On his death he owned twenty-nine works by Wright, including notable items such as *A View of the Bay of Naples, from Pausilipo* and *An Eruption of Vesuvius, Destroying the Vineyards*. He also possessed two finely finished drawings by Wright of caverns on an Italian shore, which were studies from which two pictures in William Hardman's collection were painted. Philips did not collect Wright's Italian scenery exclusively; he also possessed works such as *The Bridge and Waterfall, at Rydall in Westmoreland*. A major part of his collecting activity was devoted to prints and etchings, which comprised the majority of the items in his disposal sale.[29] Philips was also a bibliophile, and his interest in landscapes and travel featured prominently in his book collection. Important works that he owned included Joseph Farrington's *Views of the Lakes*, Samuel Prout's *Instructions for Drawing Landscapes* and a number of Italian travel books.[30] His interest in classical travel and antiquarianism was reflected in his ownership of Lord Elgin's *Pursuits in Greece*, Hasselquist's *Voyage to the Levant* and Goldsmith's *Grecian History*.[31]

An interest in antiquarianism was a common feature of a number of Manchester art collectors. Some, such as William Yates, verged on the eccentric. Yates, a manufacturer of upholsterers' trimmings, developed a reputation for collecting almost any and every antiquarian and art object with little discrimination. When two old houses in Market Street were being demolished to make way for road improvements, Yates stepped in, dismantled the properties and re-erected them on a specially purchased plot of land at Stony Knowls, Roman Road, near the newly developing suburb on Bury New Road. He soon filled the building with 'a large assortment of curiosities, some valuable and many the reverse'.[32] Although the house was never formally opened as a public museum, the property became a landmark, and Yates took great delight in showing visitors his acquisitions.[33] Yates was a major customer of William Ford, one of the city's best-known booksellers and picture dealers, but his eccentricity and lack of judgement in purchases meant that he won little respect from more 'serious' art collectors and dealers. Ford remarked that Yates 'has so strange a natural affection for worm-eaten speculation that it is apparent he has a worm in his skull'.[34] Yates's Folly, as Yates's house became known, lasted just seven years until 1829, when the land and library were sold by auction.[35] However, the house represents an interesting example of an early semi-public museum of art and antiquarianism.

The fashion for antiquarianism provided important opportunities for Manchester's art community. Artists and illustrators were required to examine, record and represent all manner of historical remains, from stone circles to drawings and sketches in books and manuscripts. Thomas Barritt, from Withy Grove, Manchester, was typical of the late eighteenth-century and early nineteenth-century antiquarians for whom detailed artistic illustration was vital to record the progress of history. One of his major projects was the recording of the history of the various branches of the Barritt, or Barret, family. His subsequent manuscript included half-length portraits in oils of family members, sketches of heraldic devices and watercolour drawings of supposed incidents in the family's history. Although one may scoff about the rather fanciful nature of the research, this type of antiquarianism was popular and used visual art as a key medium for its expression. Antiquarians were often local celebrities. The legend of Yates's Folly was enthusiastically recalled almost a century later, while a portrait of Barritt was drawn and engraved by Charles Pye of London and published for circulation in 1820.[36]

By the early nineteenth century, Manchester's cultural elite of art patrons, antiquarians, natural historians and bibliophiles had access to a number of local commercial dealers who attempted to cater for the needs of this emerging community. Typically, dealers were non-specialists who operated a number of related cultural trades from one business address. Specialisation tended not to emerge until well into the nineteenth century. William Ford was a publisher and bookseller as well as an art dealer. Vittore Zanetti's shop sold pictures but also scientific instruments, barometers, artists' materials and furniture. The firm continued to do so well into the 1840s, after the well-known Thomas Agnew had taken over the business.[37] The miscellaneous nature of many art dealers' businesses should not be taken to imply that the fine art sold through these outlets was of second-rate quality. Certainly there were unscrupulous picture dealers in the city, and a number of prominent local men had fallen victim to what were termed 'picture jockeys' – dealers who sold faked paintings, usually old masters, as original works. Even Manchester collectors such as R. D. Ashworth and William Townend were not immune from 'the *rascally* part of the profession'.[38] The difficulty for the collector – and indeed the historian – was in attempting to discriminate between originals and forgeries. It seems, for example, unlikely that all the works attributed to Rembrandt, Da Vinci, Rubens and Canaletto in Zanetti's commercial Manchester exhibition of 1811 were genuine originals, but at the same time the exhibition did contain significant modern works such as Joseph Wright's *An Eruption of Vesuvius*, J. Parry's *A View from the Pier Head, Liverpool* and a landscape by Thomas Gainsborough.[39] By the 1820s the Manchester art market was sufficiently buoyant that dealers were bringing major modern works from the capital for sale in the city. These works were often collected from major London sales. In 1821, John Ford, son of William, sold works formerly in Sir Joshua Reynolds's collection in this manner.[40] It is, however, important to recognise that the sale of oils, watercolours, drawings and sketches was only one part of the emerging regional market for fine art.

Even those who could afford to collect original works, such as William Hardman and John Leigh Philips, also collected large numbers of prints. Although the individual value of such items was considerably less, the volume in which they were sold illustrates how they played an important role in spreading a taste for fine art in the region. An auction of the stock of William Ford in 1816 reveals the huge variety of prints available from a relatively small provincial dealer. In all there were 581 lots up for sale, many of which contained multiple items. Portraits of the famous, particularly the royal family, represented the core of the sale, but there were also a number of topographical prints illustrating all parts of the country, from Oxford and Cambridge colleges to aristocratic seats, and from panoramas of the Lake District to prints of St Helens.[41]

By the early 1820s, Manchester was home to a significant number of major patrons, and the city could support a buoyant and diverse local art market. Art also penetrated popular culture, with novelty touring exhibitions of large-scale canvasses providing dioramas of foreign countries and exotic landscapes. These would often be presented in theatrical style with dramatic lighting effects to bring them to life.[42] However, the city had no artistic institutions, academies or fellowships, and the only formal exhibitions were the periodic shows assembled by commercial dealers. The initiative behind the formation of the RMI came not from patrons or groups such as the Manchester Literary and Philosophical Society or the Portico Library, but from Manchester's growing community of artists. Following the visit of three Manchester-based painters to an exhibition of the Northern Establishment of Artists held in Leeds, thoughts turned to trying to establish a similar society of artists in Manchester. A preliminary meeting was held on 6 August 1823, and some of the city's leading artistic names attended, including Arthur Perigal, Charles Calvert and the Parry brothers. It was immediately decided to establish a new society and that outside patrons should be sought. 'Noblemen' and 'gentlemen' were to be elected by the artistic membership to conduct the management of the society (see Figure 4).[43]

The proposal for a society of artists clearly provoked much discussion in Manchester art circles. Opinions differed as to how the society should be managed and what its precise functions should be. The issue of establishing an academy attached to the society proved to be particularly contentious. Many artists derived a significant part of their annual income from teaching painting and drawing, and there were naturally fears that an academy would deprive them of this important private business. At the third meeting of the society, Charles Calvert

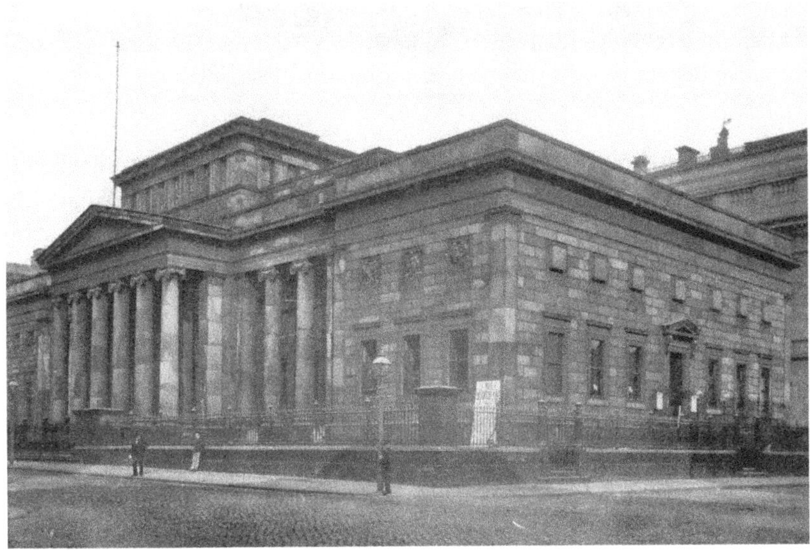

4 Royal Manchester Institution, showing an advertisement for the Manchester School of Art

made clear his strong opposition to the formation of an academy on the grounds that it would 'eventually prove highly detrimental to the Professional Tutors in Art'.[44] Others saw benefits in a more systematised form of art teaching in Manchester, but the idea of an academy was rejected following a show of hands. The issue of management proved to be even more controversial. A number of artists felt strongly that the society should be self-governing: that artists rather than patrons should be responsible for managing the affairs of the organisation. Otherwise, it was feared, the society's proposed exhibitions might just become a form of commercial speculation, with wealthy men becoming involved and diverting profits from art to their own private interests. However, there was also a broader objection. Many saw the society as a sort of trade association and felt that the only way in which their interests could be looked after was by professional artists managing their collective affairs. For some the dangers of ceding control to patrons were already evident in other societies:

If the Leeds the Bath and some other similar institutions be consulted as regarding the general management it does appear from their rules that the artists possess not an iota of power or influence on the proceedings of the

73

donors or proprietors. They are excluded from all meetings they have no voice either in Election [gap] directions or in any point of their transactions and no resultive benefit beyond that of being tributary [?] exhibitions.[45]

Others saw the formation of the society as a key opportunity to attract wealthy patrons in the creation of a broader art institution. Perigal argued that although it might appear preferable for the society to be self-governing it would be unlikely to be successful without the support of wealthy supporters of the arts, and he felt there was little danger that Manchester patrons would appropriate exhibition profits for themselves or act from primarily commercial motives.[46] During September, negotiations were opened with leading patrons and a committee was formed that included Robert Christie, Thomas Hardman, Robert Hindley and William Townend.[47] Little is known about the details of these meetings, but it is clear that with Perigal as one of the society's two-man delegation, his view of how the society should develop became most influential. Proposals put to a public meeting on 1 October went far beyond those put forward by the society of artists. Plans emerged for a general educational institute not only for 'opening a channel through which the works of meritorious Artists may be brought before the Public' but also for the 'encouragement of literary and Scientific pursuits'.[48] Membership of the organisation was to be through a hierarchy of governorships. Forty guineas would purchase a hereditary governorship that could be passed on to descendants, and twenty-five guineas a life governorship, while two guineas per year would provide an annual governorship. The society would be run by a council elected by governors from within the membership. Interestingly, the institute was never conceived as simply a place where only men would socialise, despite the prevailing homosociality of many artistic activities.[49] Governorships were confined to men, but all governors were permitted to bring their wives and other members of their immediate families to lectures, exhibitions and other educational activities.[50] Artists, however, took little part in the governance and organisation of the institute. Although they were not explicitly excluded from membership, the high subscription costs were not designed to facilitate their involvement.

The proposals captured the attention of many in Manchester's commercial community, with the committee claiming that 'an Institution in this Town has long been contemplated by many Gentlemen'.[51] By February 1824 over £16,000 had been raised from the sale of hereditary and life governorships.[52] Much of this support came from merchants expressing not only their local civic loyalties, but also their loyalties to a broader idea: that of a particular notion of urbanity and civilisation. By patronising art, the process of commercial activity was given a new social dignity. As in Liverpool, parallels were drawn between the nobility and liberality of ancient merchants and those of the modern day:

> the Arts have uniformly pursued the footsteps of Commerce. The Merchants of the Italian Republics were the patrons of genius; and the effects of commercial munificence in fostering the growth of Art are still conspicuous in the cities of Holland and Flanders.[53]

The institute was designed to express individual generosity and collective taste.[54] The building was to be 'an honourable proof of the liberality and good taste of the Governors, and accord with the wealth and importance of the town of Manchester'.[55] The merchant George Wood noted that an artistic body of this kind would be 'an ornament to the town, and a monument of its prosperity'.[56] The desire to ornament Manchester in order to commemorate its commercial success continued to be a powerful idea for at least a decade and found its strongest expression in William Fairbairn's unsuccessful visionary plan for the city of 1836.[57] The RMI would ornament the city and commemorate the contribution of the citizens who subscribed. This desire to memorialise commercial success seemed to be combined with awareness of the precarious nature of that commercial success and how important it was to pass something of lasting value on to future generations. Governorships were hereditary so that they could be left as family heirlooms, echoing the aristocratic practices of the Royal Institution in London.[58] While Manchester's middle class could not bequeath physical property on the scale of aristocratic estates, they could leave cultural and intellectual capital in the form of hereditary governorships. The references to past times can be read as a plea by the new middle class for the type of social status that was afforded to ancient merchants who acquired vast wealth through trade. By turning economic wealth into cultural capital, members of the new class would be remembered beyond their deaths. Even if commercial success could not be sustained, art could still memorialise a golden age of commerce. Benjamin Heywood, on making a contribution of £500 to the institution, stated that the aim was to 'obtain for the town a character as enduring as that which, surviving the loss of wealth and commerce, still rendered illustrious those communities where the refinements of art were once united to the enterprises of trade'.[59]

This desire for prestige and memorialisation strongly influenced the type of institution that was to develop. Initially, the retail premises of an artist and dealer located in King Street were purchased for £5,750.[60] However, it soon became clear that these facilities would be inadequate for the more ambitious objectives now in mind. By March 1824, the institute had attracted support from almost all the leading figures in the city's public and political elite, Liberal and Tory, including Samuel Jones Lloyd MP, George Philips MP, H. H. Birley, Louis Schwabe and J. E. Taylor. The list of governors also included a number of minor noblemen and gentry including Sir Oswald Mosley, who still had extensive manorial rights in Manchester, the Earl of Wilton and the Marquis of Stafford.[61] Royal patronage was obtained in April, and it was soon decided to obtain a more prestigious site for the institute.[62] Unfortunately, this did not prove to be easy. The committee tried to obtain land in Market Street and Brown Street from Mosley, but he declined to sell.[63] After considering several sites the council decided to purchase land in Mosley Street, close to other cultural institutions such as the Portico Library and the Assembly Hall. This plan was, however, rejected at a general meeting of governors and the council was required to investigate other sites.[64] While Mosley Street was a fashionable location, the road itself was narrow and enclosed and, it was feared, would do little to set off a prestigious building.[65] Forced to rethink its plans, the RMI decided to advertise for land 'in a central part of Manchester, with good approaches'.[66] Some governors felt that the institute should be set apart from commercial and residential buildings in its own square. The only suitable central location that fell into this category was Piccadilly. Land could be obtained here relatively cheaply because it was slightly further away from the most fashionable district and because of the presence of the city infirmary close by. Unfortunately, it was the very proximity of the hospital that undermined the case for the Piccadilly site. Hospitals were not regarded as adding to the prestige of a location. Speakers denounced 'the incongruity of a building apportioned to the purposes of Science adjoining a public Hospital, as [a] matter of taste'.[67] Others were more blunt, declaring that the institute 'ought not to be confronted by the gable end of a Lunatic Hospital'.[68]

With few viable sites available, the RMI council continued to support the Mosley Street option. As a number of governors lived in the Mosley Street area, several had vested interests in a development that could only add to the prestige of the neighbourhood and stimulate property values. In June 1824, it was finally decided to opt for the Mosley Street site and obtain neighbouring property to allow the institute to stand freely in its own grounds, detached from other buildings.[69] There is little evidence that those who had initiated plans for an artistic body – the society of artists – played any role in developing the final scheme, or were consulted about their own needs. Indeed, attempts to persuade the RMI to organise an art exhibition in temporary buildings while more extensive plans were developed did not prove successful.[70] This may have been partly because the council of the RMI was becoming increasingly concerned about its ability to raise the very large sums required to erect the type of building it had promised Manchester. In December, it issued an appeal for further funds together with a statement warning that 'a Building of more limited extent or humbler character would not prove satisfactory to the Public, or be adequate to the objects contemplated'.[71]

The council attempted to broaden the basis of its patronage network by making a direct appeal to known aristocratic supporters of art. Of course, by the beginning of the nineteenth century there were no resident aristocratic gentry in Manchester as such, except for the De Trafford family of Trafford Park. The RMI's leadership hoped that the institute would develop into a nationally significant body and would merit the support of art patrons from across the country. When John Fleming Leicester of Tabley House, Cheshire, drew up a shortlist of likely aristocratic supporters of the institution, he included most of Britain's major titled families known to have an interest in art.[72] Leicester was an important, pioneering collector of modern British art, and one might have expected his influence to be very significant.[73] Unfortunately, the letters requesting support drew a largely unfavourable response, with few showing any inclination to support an institution in a far-off industrial centre. The Duke of Bedford declined on the grounds of 'having no connection with Manchester, or that part of the Kingdom connected with it'.[74] Similarly, Lord Lansdowne elected to support art institutions in those towns in which he had a personal interest, namely Bath and Dublin. Sir Edmund Antrobus responded somewhat tersely that he 'already subscribes to several Institutions in London for the same Objects'.[75] MacDonald has interpreted these rejections as evidence of the reluctance of the aristocracy to support educational institutions in industrial centres that might stir class unrest.[76] However, with other provincial centres developing similar artistic institutions, it was perhaps only natural that landed patrons would become more selective in those they chose to support. It is more surprising that leading public men with commercial links to the county were sometimes reluctant to provide financial support. The chairman of the

RMI, James Davenport Hulme, was particularly dismayed at the failure of Sir Robert Peel to support the institution, especially given Peel's professed support for public art museums and his family's commercial roots in Lancashire.[77] The RMI did attract a small number of patrons from outside the region, although at least one withdrew from membership after realising that a financial contribution was required.[78]

Failure to attract major aristocratic patrons, together with a deterioration in the Lancashire economy in the mid-1820s, brought about significant delays to the construction of the new RMI building. The majority of architects who were consulted on the plans felt that the sum set aside for construction of £15,000 was far too limited and that around £20,000 would be necessary. This cost reflected the RMI's desire for a design for an imposing building from the pen of Charles Barry, one of the leading neo-classical architects of the period. It was eventually decided to investigate the possibility of constructing the building in stages, thus deferring the construction of the proposed natural history wing. This met with little enthusiasm from architects, and it was instead decided to try to budget for a building costing between around £18,000 and £20,000. This, it was felt, would obviate the need for construction in stages, which would undermine the prestige of the project. A new appeal for funds was launched to ensure 'that in point of architectural design, it should rank as a conspicuous ornament to the town'.[79] Once again, the ornamental and monumental functions of the building were regarded as being of primary importance. However, attempts to raise extra funds during an economic recession were largely unsuccessful, and for a period of around nine months the council met irregularly and made no further progress.[80]

The RMI had become a victim of its own grandiose vision, and for a time it seemed that the plans might collapse. Yet there continued to be a strong underlying interest in art in Manchester during this period, and commercial dealers continued to prosper. In the winter of 1824, Arthur Perigal delivered a series of formal lectures on the art of painting in the rooms of the Manchester Literary and Philosophical Society and provided a display of 'the grandest composition of the most celebrated masters'.[81] Manchester also continued to attract commercial touring exhibitions of metropolitan works.[82] Improvements to Market Street forced Zanetti and Agnew from their old shop there but, after battling for compensation, the firm moved to a much more prestigious location in Exchange Street, from where its business developed into one of the most successful dealerships in the country.[83] Moreover, the establishment of bodies such as the mechanics' institute helped foster further interest in art education and high culture.[84]

Despite the problems in completing plans for a permanent building, it was decided to go ahead with the organisation of an exhibition of modern painting. This decision may have been reached because of pressure from local artists, but it seems more likely that the RMI council simply felt that an exhibition would be the most effective way to publicise its plans among a wider audience. The RMI sought advice on the organisation of the exhibition from the Northern Society for the Encouragement of Fine Art at Leeds, London artists were contacted for contributions, and advertisements were placed in the Manchester and London press.[85] The exhibition regulations seem to have been largely inspired by those of Leeds. Carriage expenses were to be met by the RMI for all unsold pictures, but those sold in the gallery had their carriage expenses deducted from the sale price. No pictures without frames or pictures copied from originals were allowed, and contributors were responsible for their own insurance arrangements. Although the RMI wanted to attract London artists, its art advisor W. Linton was careful to warn it against becoming too closely dependent any one body of artists; the regulations allowed individual artists to submit just one picture that had been previously exhibited for sale elsewhere.[86] The principal difficulty was in finding a suitably prestigious location for such an exhibition. The only purpose-built rooms were, of course, those of commercial dealers, and therefore the RMI had little choice but to hire an exhibition room in Jackson's gallery in Market Street.[87] It took on the appearance of a large-scale private commercial exhibition, with the dealer and auctioneer Thomas Winstanley acting as honorary secretary of the exhibition.[88]

The exhibition opened on 7 May to governors and one week later to the public at large. Governors naturally had free admission, while members of the public were charged one shilling for a single admission and five shillings for a season ticket. A printed catalogue was also available for a further shilling.[89] In most respects, the exhibition was a success. It attracted works from five Royal Academicians, namely A. W. Callcott, A. Cooper, James Northcote, W. A. Pickersgill and James Ward, together with painters from most of the major northern industrial towns including Bolton, Lancaster and Newcastle, with Leeds and Liverpool being particularly strongly represented. Local Manchester artists were also very prominent, with works by Charles and Michael Calvert, Henry Liverseedge, Arthur Perigal, James Parry, John Ralston and a number of lesser-known artists. The exhibition was interpreted by the RMI as 'more numerous and replete with talent than could have been expected' and as demonstrating 'a sufficient pledge of the readiness of London, as well as Provincial Artists, to aid them more effectually on future occasions'.[90]

The exhibition was important not only in promoting Manchester as an emerging art centre but also in stimulating the RMI leadership to finalise its building plans. Benjamin Heywood, who had been actively involved in the successful formation of the mechanics' institute, exhorted RMI governors to forge ahead with a building that would 'do honour to the Town and Nation'.[91] The public address published in the exhibition catalogue issued a rallying call, emphasising the importance of the fine arts in 'adding lustre to the national character' and the development of a 'high degree of civilisation' and 'in rendering the manufactures of Great Britain so superior in most instances to those of other nations'.[92] By May 1827, a revised construction budget had been agreed, Charles Barry's designs had been accepted, and the contract for the erection of the shell of the new RMI building had been authorised.[93] Unfortunately, although construction work was officially completed in the autumn of 1829, in time for an exhibition of living British artists, some difficulties remained.[94] Manchester's artists were hardly consulted at all in the development of the plans and consequently their primary needs were largely overlooked. The RMI council was forced to admit somewhat shamefacedly that it had made no specific provision in the building for facilities for professional artists to work and study, even though this had been a key intention of the initial proposals. Artists were, of course, allowed access to exhibition rooms for the purpose of copying, but overall the facilities fell well short of their expectations. Led by Arthur Perigal, Charles Calvert, James Parry and George Evans, several local artists formed a new society with the aim of trying to establish better facilities and then somewhat cheekily asked the RMI council to assist.[95] Lighting in the exhibition gallery was also problematic, and Charles Barry was commissioned to make improvements to the roof. Unfortunately, however, a somewhat ambitious plan for improvements fell victim to cost-cutting, and additional lights were removed from the scheme.[96] Despite the desire to build a grandiose monument to memorialise middle-class achievement, the RMI council was not above rather niggardly cost-cutting, even when this was at the expense of important local artists or the quality of exhibition facilities.

> The state of the funds of the RMI made it difficult for it to improve facilities. Despite attempts to attract more subscribers by organising more varied events, such as an exhibition of old masters in 1831, the numbers enrolling as annual governors remained small.[97] This may have been because these annual governors

effectively counted as 'third-rate' members, carrying little social prestige. In 1832 it was felt that by raising annual subscriptions to three guineas and increasing the privileges of annual members, more support might be attracted.[98] The initiative did little to secure more income for the institution: annual income was little more than £400 per year while fixed costs, chief rents and salaries amounted to £300. Only 'a very trifling sum' was left over for lectures and educational programmes.[99] It was even decreed that parts of the building currently not in use should not be fully decorated unless there was a firm prospect of them being let to outside bodies.[100]

Manchester artists often organised their own small-scale events, sometimes in co-operation with local dealers who provided additional works. One such example was the regular series of *conversaziones* for 'Artists and Amateurs'.[101] Unfortunately, this particular series was handicapped by lack of suitable rooms in the RMI. The 'conversaziones' were relegated to rooms usually occupied by the choral society, and ceased in spring 1838.[102] Attempts to form societies of local artists tended to be short-lived, and, in the absence of an academy, the teaching of art was conducted on an informal basis through private tuition. The eventual formation of a school of art came through a combination of central government action and the initiative of a small group of manufacturers, led by George Jackson.[103] Following the creation of the first government-supported school of design in June 1837, it was almost inevitable that Manchester manufacturers should take an interest in similar schemes. Jackson, a local decorator and manufacturer of ornaments, led a campaign, through a series of lectures at the mechanics' institute, for a similar school in Manchester. The plans initially focused on mass education, with further plans for a free exhibition gallery of technology, natural history and art.[104] The exhibition was to be one whose 'door should always swing easily on its hinge; no law but decorum should guard admission to its treasures'.[105] This was envisaged as a first step towards a democratic school of design where workmen could learn the fundamental principles of art, not simply for the purposes of fine art, but for application to items of everyday use and manufacture.[106] In reality, the development of the school of design was somewhat different. Instead of emerging spontaneously from the members of the mechanics' institute, the school developed from a meeting held in the exclusive premises of the RMI. Far from being organised by and for workers, it was headed by the merchant James Heywood, the engineers William Fairbairn and Joseph Whitworth, the architect Richard Lane and the manufacturer George Jackson.[107] Despite Jackson's radical emancipatory rhetoric addressed to workers at the mechanics' institute, when he was faced with an audience at the RMI or the middle-class Athenaeum Club his language was a little different. Rather than discussing the personal benefits to be obtained by art education, he stressed instead the dangers to British commerce brought about by the lack of a skilled workforce.[108]

Just as the school of art struggled to obtain local patronage, the RMI itself found it difficult to obtain the level of support necessary to achieve its lofty ambitions. At the end of the 1830s the RMI's key event, the annual exhibition of modern paintings, was struggling to fight off competition from other towns for leading works from London. In order to obtain pictures the RMI found it was required to employ an agent in London to collect and organise the packing of works. This increased the RMI's costs as by this time it was clear that artists were unwilling to send works unless exhibition organisers offered these facilities. A significant number of pictures continued to be sold – in 1836, sixty-three pictures were sold for a total value of over £1,400 – but it was acknowledged that the exhibitions barely covered their costs.[109] The quality of the exhibitions was variable, and the press was not slow in pointing out the RMI's failings. The 1837 exhibition was described as 'meagre and common-place' with 'nothing that repays the trouble of the survey'.[110] A year later no catalogues were available for the private view – normally the time when most of the major purchases were made.[111] Critics rounded on the RMI as simply providing 'an annual exhibition of the unsold pictures from the London Galleries' and noted that, for all the showiness of the RMI's royal title, little of educational value had been achieved.[112] Although Manchester was gradually developing a reputation for its support of modern artists, interest in old masters continued to be strong. An exhibition of old masters held at the RMI in 1838 seemed to attract at least as much local attention as the annual exhibition of modern art, despite the fact that one of the centrepieces of the exhibition, a *Salutation* attributed to Rubens, owned by the Rev. John Clowes, was regarded as a probable fake.[113]

By 1839 it was widely recognised that action was required to revive the exhibition. Quite apart from the need to improve the artistic quality of the exhibition, financially the RMI was not in a strong position to subsidise exhibition losses and, with a number of tenancies set to expire, future levels of income were uncertain.[114] In order to improve the popularity of the annual exhibition, it was decided to establish a local art union – effectively a public art lottery – which would guarantee sales. The Manchester art union followed the lines of the successful Edinburgh plan, where annual subscriptions had risen from £728 to £6,118 in just six years.[115] A promotional circular was drafted which frankly acknowledged the decline of the annual exhibition, noting the reduced sales and that the quality of exhibitions had 'greatly fallen off'.[116] The initial rules placed the prize fund in the hands of a committee of private patrons, who were empowered to purchase works from the exhibition which would become the lottery prizes.[117] Subscribers were not permitted to choose their own prizes, but instead prizes were chosen for them by an appointed body of experts who regarded themselves as having superior artistic knowledge. The committee existed not simply to administer the lottery fairly but also to fulfil a crucial educational role in the development of public taste:

> ... a Committee composed of persons known to have devoted both time and attention to the fine arts, it is reasonably certain that their standard of taste is above the average standard of taste among the subscribers or the public; and this of itself must tend to raise the standard of art.[118]

It was clear that the success of many art unions was dependent not just on providing a picture lottery, but also on the provision of complimentary quality engravings to subscribers. Some art unions spent more on providing engravings than on fine art prizes. In 1844, the Birmingham art union spent just £620 on picture purchases although its subscription list stood at well over £1,500.[119] The Manchester committee provided a Lucas engraving of Constable's *The Vale of Dedham* to every subscriber.[120] The new art union also required a very active marketing offensive. Advertisements were taken out in all the major provincial papers, including titles in Newcastle, Edinburgh, Glasgow, Dublin, Leeds, Bristol, Birmingham and Chester.[121] The committee made widespread efforts to recruit agents, or secretaries as they were termed, in towns across Britain, but especially in northern England. By 1841 the union had secretaries in twenty-seven towns.[122] The experiment was initially a success. Almost 800 subscriptions, or shares, were taken up at a cost of a guinea each. This allowed for thirty-two paintings and ten proof engravings to be purchased as prizes, providing a significant boost to exhibition sales.[123] Private galleries noted the success of the art union principle. Grundy's Repository of Arts copied the RMI scheme almost immediately, issuing 1,200 shares for the disposal of a collection of watercolours.[124]

Following these promising beginnings, the art union committee, led by its honorary secretary, the art dealer Thomas Winstanley, hoped that its subscription list would enjoy the same growth as that in Edinburgh. However, following the 1841 draw the committee decided to abandon hopes of competing directly with London and Edinburgh and to concentrate on developing the market in the north and north-west.[125] This did not, unfortunately, prevent a fall in the number of subscriptions for the 1842 draw, in which just 687 shares were taken in comparison to 830 in 1841 and 780 in 1840. Some clearly objected to prizes being selected by a committee, and consequently it was decided to take the pragmatic step of allowing lottery winners to choose their own prizes, despite the earlier reluctance to do so.[126] Although this was probably more popular with the general public, critics did not altogether welcome the step, particularly when the year's prizewinners overwhelmingly plumped for rather conservative landscapes.[127] Some felt the union was, in any case, doing little to encourage art in Manchester, and accused it again of simply attracting unsold 'refuse' from London exhibitions.[128] The art union organisers faced other problems too. In 1843 the keeper of the exhibition rooms defrauded the committee, leaving the exhibition organisers in the embarrassing position of working out how to make up the deficit.[129] There was also a suspicion that the draw for pictures was not entirely fair in its conduct. Despite the fact there were some 700 subscribers, some names made multiple appearances in the winners' lists. Uriah Cook won two major prizes in three years.[130] Elias Chadwick won two within four years.[131] Even those closely involved in the organisation of the exhibition, such as the honorary secretary T. W. Winstanley, took part and won prizes.[132] Although it is not possible to say whether any dishonesty was involved, some potential subscribers may have interpreted these patterns as being the product of something more than good fortune.

In 1847, the Manchester union reconstituted itself with the aim of trying to broaden its appeal and reverse its apparently flagging fortunes. Subscription rates were cut to just half a guinea, the distribution of engravings was abandoned, and, no doubt under pressure from local artists, it was agreed that prizes could be chosen from works exhibited either at the RMI or at the recently formed Manchester Academy of Arts.[133] Unfortunately, these rule changes only served to place the union in even more difficulties. The reduction in the level of subscriptions did not generate a significant increase in the number of subscribers but it did dramatically reduce the prize income available. It was also clear that the abandonment of complimentary engravings was unpopular.[134] The decision of the union to loosen its ties with the RMI by allowing prizes to be selected from another exhibition irritated some in the RMI, who demanded that the union pay rent for use of RMI property. In response the union threatened to suspend its operations.[135] Although the union eventually relented, the breakdown in relations with the RMI did nothing to help the union's revival and, as the leading figures gradually lost interest, the union was quietly wound up in 1858.[136]

It is difficult to assess precisely what impact the art union had on the fortunes of the RMI's annual exhibition, but it is clear that during the early 1840s it did, at least, guarantee a minimum number of sales at a time when the national economy was in recession. The 1841 and 1842 exhibitions were particularly disappointing in terms of the aggregate number of private sales, and the contribution of the art union was acknowledged as very important in ensuring that the total number of sales remained at a respectable level.[137] However, the main reason for the revival of the exhibition in the mid-1840s was probably the decision to reschedule it earlier in the year. Previously the exhibition had opened at the close of the Royal Academy and London exhibition season, in the hope that pictures from these exhibitions would then be attracted to Manchester. This meant that the season most favourable for the display of pictures was lost. It was a worthwhile sacrifice when important pictures were attracted from the south, but recent experience showed that most of the best pictures of the season were bought in London and never found their way north. The decision to open the Manchester exhibition in June proved to be an unqualified success – 'the most successful in every point which has been held for several years'.[138] Press comments were favourable, and far from discouraging leading artists from exhibiting, the re-timed exhibition seemed to have actually attracted more, particularly those specialising in British landscape.[139] Some of the Royal Academicians' works on display in Manchester admittedly included what were regarded as second-rate efforts, such as *Rockford Mill, Devon* by F. R. Lee RA. Others, however, received genuine critical acclaim. *A Mountain Lake* by T. Creswick ARA was described as 'one of the finest landscapes it has ever been our lot to contemplate' and 'and honour to the British school'.[140] The 1844 exhibition was also marked by renewed attempts to popularise and attract working-class visitors. For the last month of the exhibition doors were open between 7 p.m. and 9 p.m. for an average charge of 6d. An average of sixty-five visitors per hour took up the offer.[141]

In 1845, the exhibition expanded further and was the largest and most profitable held to date, generating a net income of over £216.[142] Exhibition space was increased to make way for a record number of works. Again, far from deterring London artists from exhibiting, the date change seemed to attract more metropolitan names. The long list of Royal Academicians included C. Stanfield, W. Etty, David Roberts, F. R. Lee, W. F. Worthington, E. F. Chalon, J.

J. Chalon, W. Collins and Sir W. J. Newton. Celebrated works included Newton's *The Homage*, which represented the Duke of Sussex at the Queen's coronation.[143] The success of the exhibition saw even more contributions being sent the following year, with works of Collins, Etty, Eastlake and Hart being among the 850 works sent for display.[144] In some respects, the exhibition had become too popular. The sixpenny evenings had become particularly successful, so much so that the RMI council noted that 'the reduced price of admission had been taken advantage of by many parties for whom the indulgence was neither necessary nor intended'.[145] Although the RMI officials were clearly dismayed at members of the middle class taking advantage of cheap admission, this did not discourage them from further steps to popularise the exhibition. In 1846, it was decided that during the last two weeks of the exhibition, evening admission rates should be cut to just 2d. The RMI was rewarded with 11,000 people paying for admission over twelve nights.[146] Although this produced some overcrowding in the galleries, a more serious problem was the increasingly overcrowded wall space. By 1850, the council had a more selective hanging policy in an attempt to prevent overcrowding and eliminate poorer-quality works.[147]

After a few years of success, however, the exhibition again went into decline, with fewer prominent names appearing as contributors. It was thus decided to change policy again and move back the opening of the exhibition to September. It was also agreed to offer a prize of 100 guineas for the best painting at the exhibition and to organise a deputation from Manchester to visit the president of the Royal Academy and London artists in order to obtain pledges of support. The initiative was successful, with pictures sold to a total value of £1,339, more than double that generated in previous years.[148] The episode, however, reveals just how difficult it was to maintain a successful exhibition in Manchester. If it was held during the summer, London artists had to be persuaded that their works stood a good chance of being sold in Manchester, and this could be done only if year on year the Manchester exhibition generated good sales. If it was held in the autumn, Manchester was left to fight over unsold works with other provincial exhibitions. With relatively limited sales at the Manchester exhibition, only very energetic promotional efforts could attract leading works.

The exhibition of modern paintings was the annual highlight of Manchester's cultural life, but the efforts required to maintain its position were probably one of the reasons for the failure to develop a successful public gallery of art. The RMI had collected miscellaneous works from the outset, but the lack of a purchase fund meant that it was largely dependent on the generosity of its own members in order to develop its own gallery.[149] It did receive some important donations, most notably when William Grant donated Etty's *The Sirens and Ulysses* in 1839.[150] However, there was no systematic collecting policy, and the RMI's private gallery developed piecemeal. In the early 1840s, the RMI developed a library in which a number of pieces from its permanent collection were hung. Unfortunately, it was little used and closed after an experimental period of six months.[151] Following the failure of this initiative, the RMI exhibited little interest in developing its permanent collection or a permanent gallery. The rearrangement of the building for the annual exhibition, however, afforded more space, and in 1849 a small annual exhibition of the modern collection commenced in the spring.[152] There is no evidence that this encouraged local art collectors to donate works, but a few local artists clearly saw commercial advantages in having their works in the RMI's permanent collection, especially after the RMI agreed to offer artists associate membership of the institution in return for donations.[153] Despite the stated aim of the RMI to become 'the home and centre of the Art and Science of Manchester', it did little to realise Jackson's dream of a public gallery for the city.[154]

The RMI was a complex body. Although initiated by an association of artists, it was taken over almost immediately by Manchester's economic and cultural elite. A society that was designed to promote the economic interests of artists was transformed into an institution designed to promote and memorialise the cultural arrival of Manchester's rising middle class. For the RMI's leadership, appearance was all. Only the most prestigious building in the most prestigious location would be acceptable. Therefore, almost from the outset, the artistic activities of the RMI were handicapped by ambition. Although the shell was completed quickly, the completion of the building's interior took almost a decade, and limited funds were left over to subsidise artistic or cultural activities. The RMI constantly struggled to obtain the level of patronage it had anticipated, and although it did obtain a royal title this did little to help it attract the type of nationally significant status or aristocratic patronage that it sought. Although the market for art in Manchester was strong, local collectors were not particularly enthusiastic patrons of Manchester exhibitions. By mid-century the city's annual exhibition had achieved a limited amount of success, but its position was precarious and was maintained only through the great efforts of the organising committee. The city's art school was all but bankrupt and struggling to find suitable premises, while plans to form a permanent exhibition gallery in Manchester had all but been abandoned.

Much attention has been given to middle-class patronage of cultural institutions in emerging industrial cities, but it is important to recognise that the position of many of these institutions was precarious and that many initiatives failed. Any explanation must go beyond the allegedly parsimonious nature of 'Manchester man'. There were many successful aspects to the RMI's activities: it provided Manchester with a major annual art exhibition, and its lecture programme was undoubtedly effective in stimulating interest in the arts and sciences.[155] However, it never achieved quite the national status its founders sought, and it failed to provoke large-scale public benefaction in public art. Visionaries such as William Fairbairn, who sought to transform Piccadilly into a Grande Place surrounded by classical buildings in the 1830s, faced the same difficulties as the RMI did in the 1820s. Rapidly increasing land values made the development of prestigious sites expensive. Despite the wealth generated in the Manchester region during the period of industrialisation and the growth of large private art collections, relatively few private citizens dedicated a significant proportion of their wealth to public purposes. The process of suburbanisation began early in Manchester, with leading merchants abandoning their homes around the central Mosley Street area for fashionable private suburbs.[156] Exclusive estates such as Victoria Park were already in existence by the mid-1820s.[157] Palaces of commerce were soon to overshadow the Mosley Street portico. The fluctuating fortunes of the textile-based economy meant that the capital available for art patronage could quickly dry up. Economic problems at the end of the 1820s nearly killed off the RMI project altogether. The annual modern exhibition almost collapsed during the 'hungry forties'. Later plans for a city art gallery, paid for by public subscriptions, were fatally undermined by the cotton famine of the early 1860s. Although Manchester was a wealthy city, periodic slumps caused great hardship. With local government powerless to formally support local art institutions, private patronage was the only form of support available. When central government did patronise art institutions, it largely patronised those in London, as members of the Manchester School of Art were quick to point out. In this respect it was London, not Manchester, which was the 'modern Athens': a city that raided its provincial empire through taxes to provide monuments to its own cultural and economic imperialism.

NOTES

1 D. S. Macleod, *Art and the Victorian Middle Class: Money and the Making of Cultural Identity* (Cambridge, 1996), 91–2.

2 J. Seed, '"Commerce and the Liberal Arts": The Political Economy of Art in Manchester, 1775–1860', in J. Wolff and J. Seed (eds), *The Culture of Capital: Art, Power and the Nineteenth Century Middle Class* (Manchester, 1988), 45–81.

3 C. Dellheim, 'Imagining England: Victorian Views of the North', *Northern History*, 22 (1986), 217, cited in Macleod, *Art and the Victorian Middle Class*, 88.

4 C. Dickens, *Hard Times* (London, 1854; Penguin edn 1985), 85, cited in A. Kidd, *Manchester* (Keele, 1993), 73. For an alternative view of 'Manchester man' see Kidd, *Manchester*, 72–9.

5 C. P. Darcy, *The Encouragement of the Fine Arts in Lancashire, 1760–1860* (Manchester, 1976).

6 Kidd, *Manchester*, 75.

7 The Unitarian community – particularly members of Cross Street Chapel – seem to have been influential in the leadership of many of the city's cultural institutions. See H. M. Wach, 'A "Still, Small Voice" from the Pulpit: Religion and the Creation of Social Morality in Manchester, 1820–1850', *Journal of Modern History*, 63 (1991), 425–56, esp. 426–30; R. F. Bud, 'The Royal Manchester Institution', in D. S. L. Cardwell (ed.), *Artisan to Graduate* (Manchester, 1974), 119–33, esp. 122–4.

8 *Gentleman's Magazine*, May 1773, 219.

9 *Gentleman's Magazine*, May 1773, 220.

10 *Gentleman's Magazine*, May 1773, 220.

11 C. Hayes (ed.), *Stories and Tales of Old Manchester* (Manchester, 1991), 20–1; originally published in F. Hird, *Lancashire Stories* (London, 1911).

12 Hayes (ed.), *Stories*, 23–4.

13 Seed, 'Commerce', 47–8.

14 C. Roeder, 'William Green, the Lake Artist', *Transactions of the Lancashire and Cheshire Antiquarian Society*, 14 (1896), 100–30.

15 Seed, 'Commerce', 49.

16 Seed, 'Commerce', 48–9.

17 W. M. Craig 'of Market-street-lane', circular letter, 1 December 1802, MCL, H910.

18 Craig, circular letter.

19 *Laws and Regulations of the Manchester Academy for Drawing and Designing* (Manchester, 1805), MCL, H910.

20 A. Brooks and B. Haworth, *Boomtown Manchester 1800–1850: The Portico Connection* (Manchester, 1993).

21 T. Swindells, *Manchester Streets and Manchester Men*, 1st series (Manchester, 1906), 4.

22 Kidd, *Manchester*, 78.

23 Swindells, *Manchester Streets*, 1st series, 9.

24 L. H. Grindon, *Manchester Banks and Bankers* (Manchester, 1878), 49.

25 Kidd, *Manchester*, 76.

26 Hardman is mentioned as making purchases in a 20 November 1793 reference in the Farington diary. See Manchester Cuttings Collection, MCL, F942.7 M10, vol. 12, 31–2.

27 Grindon, *Manchester Banks*, 50–1.

28 E. Conran, 'Art Collections', in J. H. G. Archer (ed.), *Art and Architecture in Victorian Manchester* (Manchester, 1985), 65–80, esp. 68.

29 *Catalogue of the Valuable Collection of Paintings and Drawings, Prints and Etchings, Cabinets of Insects etc* (Manchester, 1814), MCL, 708 2733 Cal. There were 52 lots of drawings, 34 lots of sketches and 1,096 lots of prints and etchings.

30 *Manchester: A Catalogue of Books etc* (Manchester, n.d.) (property of John Leigh Philips), MCL, M84/3/8/1.

31 J. L. Philips, Library Catalogue, 1805, MCL, M84/3/7.

32 T. Swindells, *Manchester Streets and Manchester Men*, 2nd series (Manchester, 1907), 254.

33 W. Ford, 'Characters of the Different Picture Collectors, in, and about Manchester' c.1827, MCL, MS 827.79, fol. 43.

34 T. Swindells, *Manchester Streets and Manchester Men*, 4th series (Manchester, 1908), 185–6.

35 Swindells, *Manchester Streets*, 2nd series, 254.

36 For details on Barritt see 'Collectanea Relating to Manchester and its Neighbourhood', *Chetham Society*, 68 (1866), 240–58.

37 Seed, 'Commerce', 52–3.

38 Ford, 'Characters', 8, 28.

39 *A Catalogue of the Manchester Exhibition of Paintings by Various masters of the Italian, Flemish, Dutch, German and English Schools* (Manchester, 1811), MCL, S&A 378.

40 Seed, 'Commerce', 54.

41 *A Catalogue of the Valuable Amateur Topographical and Illustrative Prints, English and Foreign Portraits being a Part of the Stock in Trade of Mr Wm. Ford Smith, Bookseller* (Manchester, 1816), MCL, 769 9 F1.

42 See the description of a touring diorama of European and Asian scenery in *Manchester Mercury*, 24 February 1824, 9 March 1824.

43 RMI, Council Minute Book (hereafter CM), Society of Artists Meetings , 6 August 1823, MCL, M6/1/1/1.

44 RMI, CM, Society of Artists Meetings, 12 August 1823. Calvert operated a drawing school, known as the Academy, at 17 Lloyd Street. See S. MacDonald, 'The Royal Manchester Institution', in Archer (ed.), *Art and Architecture*, 28–45, esp. 28.

45 Comments of Thomas Dodd, RMI, CM, Society of Artists Meetings, 12 August 1823.

46 RMI, CM, Society of Artists Meetings, 26 August 1823.

47 RMI, CM, Society of Artists Meetings, 5 September 1823.

48 RMI, CM, 1 October 1823.

49 For example, see D. MacLeod, 'Homosociality and Middle-Class Identity in Early Victorian Patronage of the Arts', in A. Kidd and D. Nicholls (eds), *Gender, Civic Culture and Consumerism* (Manchester, 1999), 65–80.

50 RMI, CM, 1 October 1823. Rule 15 stated that the family of a governor was entitled to free admission to such activities, the term 'family' to 'include the Wife and Daughters, and other female relatives, permanently resident in his [the governor's] house; and Sons and Brothers, being unmarried, and under 24 years of age, and permanently resident in his [the governor's] house'.

51 RMI, CM, 5 November 1823.

52 *Manchester Mercury*, 3 February 1824.

53 RMI, CM, 5 November 1823.

54 For background to its formation see S. D. Cleveland, *The Royal Manchester Institution* (Manchester, 1931).

55 See the wording of a resolution passed at public meeting, *Manchester Mercury*, 3 February 1824.

56 *Manchester Mercury*, 3 February 1824.

57 W. Fairbairn, *Observations on Improvements of the Town of Manchester* (Manchester, 1836).

58 Bud, 'Royal Manchester Institution', 121. The Royal Institution in London had hereditary governorships until 1810.

59 Comments of B. A. Heywood, *Manchester Mercury*, 3 February 1824.

60 RMI, CM, 9 September 1823.

61 *Manchester Mercury*, 2 March 1824.

62 RMI, CM, 5 April 1824.

63 RMI, CM, 27 February 1824.

64 *Manchester Mercury*, 6 April 1824.

65 See comment in *Manchester Mercury*, 18 May 1824.

66 *Manchester Mercury*, 13 April 1824.

67 *Manchester Mercury*, 4 May 1824.

68 Mancuniensis, letter, *Manchester Mercury*, 18 May 1824.

69 RMI, CM, 21 June 1824; *Manchester Mercury*, 22 June 1824.

70 *Manchester Mercury*, 20 July 1824.

71 RMI, CM, 23 December 1824.

72 RMI, CM, 6 January 1825. For background on the artistic interests of Leicester see D. Chun, 'A History of the Leicester Family, Tabley House, and its Collection of Paintings', PhD thesis, University of Manchester, 2000.

73 See H. Hoock, '"Struggling against a Vulgar Prejudice": Patriotism and the Collecting of British Art at the Turn of the Nineteenth Century', *Journal of British Studies*, 49 (2010), 566–91, esp. 577–80.

74 RMI, CM, 31 January 1825.

75 RMI, CM, 31 January 1825.

76 MacDonald, 'Royal Manchester Institution', 33.

77 Macleod, *Art and the Victorian Middle Class*, 96–7.

78 W. Fawkes of Baker Street, London: see RMI, CM, 14 February 1825.

79 *Manchester Mercury*, 4 January 1825.

80 RMI, CM, 15 September 1825, 26 July 1826.

81 *Manchester Mercury*, 5 October 1824.

82 See advertising notice for the exhibition in the Emporium Room, Exchange Street, *Manchester Mercury*, 1 November 1825.

83 *Manchester Mercury*, 26 April 1825.

84 RMI, CM, 9 August 1826.

85 RMI, CM, 25 September 1825.

86 However, the council reserved the right to lift this restriction at its discretion. RMI, CM, 1 January 1827.

87 RMI, CM, 26 September 1826.

88 *Catalogue of the Exhibition of Pictures by Living British Artists in the Gallery, No 83 Market-Street – the First* (Manchester, 1827), MCL, S&A 378.

89 RMI, CM, 1 May 1827.

90 *Catalogue of the Exhibition of Pictures.*

91 RMI, CM, 15 January 1827.

92 RMI, CM, 2 May 1827.

93 RMI, CM, 17 May 1827.

94 RMI, CM, 14 March 1831.

95 RMI, CM, 1 March 1831.

96 RMI, CM, 20 February 1833, 2 March 1833.

97 RMI, CM, 14 March 1831.

98 RMI, CM, 18 July 1832.

99 RMI, CM, 29 March 1833.

100 RMI, CM, 23 June 1833.

101 *Manchester and Salford Advertiser*, 1 April 1837.

102 *Manchester and Salford Advertiser*, 28 April 1838.

103 For more details see Chapter 5.

104 D. Jeremiah, *A Hundred Years and More* (Manchester, 1980), 2.

105 G. Jackson, *Two Essays on a School of Design for the Useful Arts, Delivered at the Mechanics Institute'* (Manchester, 1838), 9, in *Tracts on the Arts etc*, MCL, 751 243 Ku1.

106 Jackson, *Two Essays*, 39–40.

107 'Laws and Regulations of the School of Design, Manchester' (Manchester, 1839), 6, in Manchester School of Design etc, MCL, 707.0942 M2; Jeremiah, *Hundred Years*, 2–3.

108 G. Jackson, 'On the Means of Improving Public Taste' (Manchester, 1844), 5–6, in Manchester School of Design etc.

109 RMI, Council Proceedings, General Meeting (hereafter GM), 22 March 1837, MCL.

110 *Manchester and Salford Advertiser*, 16 September 1837.

111 *Manchester and Salford Advertiser*, 8 September 1838.

112 H. Heartwell, 'Characteristics of Manchester V', *North of England Magazine*, 1 (1842), 564, cited in Seed, 'Commerce', 76.

113 RMI, Council Proceedings, GM, 27 March 1839; *Manchester and Salford Advertiser*, 5 May 1838.

114 RMI, Council Proceedings, GM, 27 March 1839.

115 RMI, Association for the Patronage of the Fine Arts (hereafter APFA), Minutes, 13 May 1840, 17 June 1840, MCL, M6/1/6.

116 RMI, APFA, 17 June 1840.

117 Whitfield, 'A Lottery', 12.

118 See circular, RMI, APFA, 17 June 1840.

119 Whitfield, 'A Lottery', 18.

120 RMI, APFA, 23 October 1840.

121 RMI, APFA, 8 July 1840.

122 However, it is not clear how successful these agents were in attracting subscriptions. It appears that as many as half may have not raised any subscriptions in 1841. See the list in RMI, APFA, 26 April 1841.

123 RMI, Council Proceedings, GM, 24 March 1841.

124 *Manchester Guardian*, 2 September 1840, cited in Darcy, *Encouragement*, 89.

125 RMI, APFA, 4 October 1841.

126 RMI, APFA, 3 May 1843.

127 'We do not think much taste or judgement has been displayed in the selection.' *Art Union*, November 1844, 341, cited in Whitfield, 'A Lottery', 21–2.

128 *Art Union*, 1 January 1843, 17, cited in Darcy, *Encouragement*, 87.

129 RMI, APFA, 17 November 1843.

130 RMI, APFA, 28 November 1842.

131 RMI, APFA, 1 November 1843.

132 RMI, APFA, 28 November 1843. Few subscribers held multiple shares, so it seems unlikely that this could account for the 'good fortune' of certain shareholders. See RMI, APFA, 3 May 1843.

133 RMI, APFA, 21 May 1847.

134 RMI, APFA, 22 June 1848, 30 April 1849.

135 RMI, APFA, 20 September 1848.

136 Whitfield, 'A Lottery', 32–4.

137 RMI, Council Proceedings, GM, 23 March 1842, 7 March 1843.

138 RMI, Council Proceedings, GM, 27 March 1844.

139 *Manchester Guardian*, 12 June 1844.

140 *Manchester Guardian*, 26 June 1844.

141 RMI, Council Proceedings, GM, 10 March 1845.

142 RMI, Council Proceedings, GM, 30 March 1846.

143 *Manchester Guardian*, 25 June 1845.

144 *Manchester Guardian*, 18 July 1845.

145 RMI, Council Proceedings, GM, 29 March 1847, MCL, M6/1/2.

146 RMI, Council Proceedings, GM, 27 March 1847.

147 *Manchester Guardian*, 3 July 1850.

148 RMI, Council Proceedings, GM, 31 March 1852.

149 This was also true of its developing natural history and ethnographic collection, whose varied exhibits included aboriginal weapons, a mammoth's tooth and a Peruvian mummy. MacDonald, 'Royal Manchester Institution', esp. 40.

150 RMI, Council Proceedings, GM, 27 March 1837.
151 RMI, Council Proceedings, GM, 23 March 1842.
152 RMI, Council Proceedings, GM, 26 March 1846.
153 Astbury Hammersley was the first thus elected following his donation of his *Mountains and Clouds – a Scene from the Top of Loughrigg, Westmoreland*. RMI, Council Proceedings, GM, 6 November 1850.
154 See the aim in the plans for co-ordinating cultural and intellectual bodies in Manchester: RMI, Council Proceedings, GM, 26 March 1856.
155 H. M. Wach, 'Culture and the Middle Classes: Popular Knowledge in Industrial Manchester', *Journal of British Studies*, 27 (1988), 375–404.
156 S. Gunn, 'The Middle Class, Modernity and the Provincial City: Manchester c.1840–80', in A. Kidd and D. Nicholls (eds), *Gender, Civic Culture and Consumerism* (Manchester, 1999), 112–27, esp. 114–15.
157 M. Speirs, *Victoria Park, Manchester* (Manchester, 1976).

4

From private to civic: the diverse origins of the municipal art gallery movement

Lancashire and Cheshire have a strong claim to be the birthplace of the municipal art gallery. The Salford MP Joseph Brotherton promoted the legislation that allowed local authorities to finance public art galleries, and it was in the towns of Salford and Warrington that the first municipal galleries appeared. Like the campaigns for public art schools, the municipal art gallery movement was stimulated initially by concerns about the deficiency of public taste and, more specifically, the poor quality of British calico and textile design. It began as part of a broader movement for design education reform in the 1830s. Yet, paradoxically, the leaders of the calico and textile industries played little part in the development of the municipal art galleries and their educational agenda. The major textile towns were relatively slow to adopt the legislation, and most of the early municipal galleries developed from cultural initiatives largely unrelated to the problems of design education.

The Salford gallery was mainly the work of the Brotherton family and benefited from both local civic rivalries and the success of the 1840s mass campaign for public parks. In nearby Warrington, the new museum was the product of a merger between existing, largely middle-class, educational and cultural bodies. Stockport's art museum was the result of the private donations of the local MP, consisting of a collection of wares brought back from the grand tour. Yet, despite the mixed origins of these galleries, all attracted significant numbers of visitors and did much to shape the emerging cultural identity of their respective towns. For their supporters, the museums were a vital step in the creation of a more sophisticated visually literate public and an audience for art. They were also to play a fundamental role in strategies of cultural embourgeoisement and urban governance. In doing so, they highlighted the paradoxes inherent in nineteenth-century civic cultural policy. Municipal museums existed to promote

95

artistic knowledge among an urban public, yet their success often depended on their incorporation into a broader public spectacle of pleasure gardens and promenading. They sought to be educators of high culture, yet constraints on finance and acquisitions often forced them to become agents of commercial art. Galleries sought to reflect and shape the taste of a community, yet in reality they frequently reinforced the power of the private donor. Through municipal museums, the private collector's taste was rendered public, ensuring that the tastes of contemporary urban capitalists often became the canons of civic art.

In order to understand the cultural trajectories of the municipal art gallery movement, it is necessary to examine the emergence of the first galleries to appear in the region, namely those of Salford, Warrington and Stockport. The early history of the municipal art gallery is closely connected with the history of the civic art school. In 1844, at a meeting of the formative committee of the Manchester School of Design, the Salford MP Joseph Brotherton argued that schools of design, while desirable, needed to be supplemented by the development of provincial art museums (see Figure 5).[1] These would not only provide objects for study, but support the wider, popular diffusion of artistic knowledge. With assistance from George Jackson, later the head of the Manchester school, Brotherton drafted a parliamentary bill enabling local corporations to establish schools of design and museums. He then asked William Ewart, the chairman of the 1836 parliamentary committee that had recommended the formation of schools of design, to introduce the bill into Parliament.[2] Under the subsequent Museums Act of 1845, the council of any municipal borough with a population of over 10,000 was empowered to levy a rate of up to a halfpenny in the pound 'to promote the Establishment and Extension of Museums of Art and Science in large Towns, for the Instruction and Amusement of the Inhabitants thereof'.[3] However, the 1845 Act placed important limitations on the nature of rate support: municipal corporations could finance only buildings, fixtures and fittings, and support staff. They were not empowered to purchase specimens or works of art. These restrictions were to fundamentally influence the shape of the very early municipal museums, which were, therefore, almost entirely dependent on private benefactors for their contents and exhibitions.

Corporations were generally slow to adopt the 1845 Act, partly because of general resistance to additional rates and partly because, unlike other educational institutions, museums did not attract parliamentary grants-in-aid to act as incentives for local initiative. In some cities, the museum rate was ridiculed as 'the Beetle rate' – a sarcastic reference to the amateur natural history

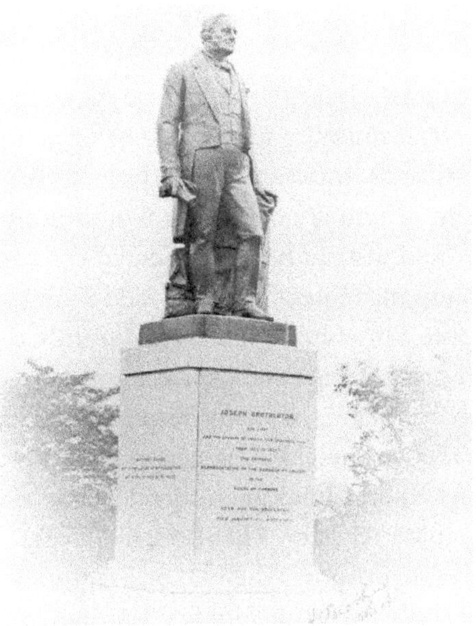

5 Statue of Joseph Brotherton

collections which were often the mainstay of early museums.[4] While art schools were to receive substantial state subsidy and become part of a national network of art education, there was no provision for central support of regional museums, however large and successful they were. For a time the Salford museum claimed more visitors than South Kensington and the British Museum, yet unlike these metropolitan institutions, it had to rely entirely on local sources of support.[5] For smaller towns, a halfpenny rate generated insufficient funds to cover annual costs, let alone the necessary capital expenditure. Even in Warrington, a relatively wealthy town with established middle-class learned societies, a halfpenny rate raised just £50 per annum. This represented less than half of the annual running costs of the museum, the rest being met by private sources.[6] The Public Libraries Act of 1850 allowed for a penny rate to be levied in support of both museums and libraries, increasing the flexibility of the funding formula. Yet, in practice, demand for library facilities absorbed much of this extra funding. By the 1880s, a few towns, such as Oldham, had promoted private Acts to allow them to levy a higher museum rate. This was, of course, politically contentious, and, in practice, most local authorities were heavily dependent on sources of private support to supplement the museum rate. This dependence ensured that the first municipal museums were shaped as much by the taste of private patrons and local political preoccupations as by national educational agendas and cultural goals.

Salford was the first provincial city to embrace the spirit of the new legislation and to attempt to create a museum that would be of national, as well as merely local, importance. Salford's ambition was driven by Brotherton's vision of a visually literate public, where art education would not be limited to scholars at art schools, but would instead be disseminated through popular instructive museums. The museum movement also provided Salford's city fathers with the opportunity to promote a new cultural identity for the city and its leadership, an identity that would attract British and overseas royalty to celebrate its cultural and institutional achievements. In many respects, Salford was England's lost city. Living in the shadow of neighbouring Manchester, it has long struggled to express its individuality and retain its political independence. Economically, it was indistinguishable from Manchester. The *Guide to Manchester and Salford* of 1877 noted that 'for mercantile purposes the two boroughs may be reckoned as one' and, tellingly, devoted only five of its fifty-five pages to Salford.[7] Geographically, only a small river, which for much of the nineteenth century was little more than an open sewer, divided the twin towns. Often modern urban developments ignored the boundary completely. The largest railway station in Salford was named Manchester Exchange, and its main entrance was orientated to deliver passengers to the Manchester side of the river. Politically, the city of Salford was forced to fight off a series of attempts from Manchester to incorporate it into a greater Manchester corporation. Indeed many of Salford's suburban residents who worked in Manchester city centre welcomed such a move, identifying more with Manchester than with their home city.[8] Other administrative borders overlapped: Manchester was in the hundred of Salford, but Salford was in the parish of Manchester. As the essayist Thomas De Quincey observed in 1856, Salford held 'the same relation to Manchester as Argos did to Mycenae'.[9]

By the mid-nineteenth century, Manchester had emerged as the economically dominant of the twin cities, even though for centuries Salford had been the more administratively significant. Manchester was almost certainly created from the royal estate of Salford, and Salford retained these royal connections into the modern era. After incorporation Salford became a royal borough, and royal patronage was regularly granted to many of its social institutions. It used this royal patronage and assumed prestige to good effect in the development of its new cultural facilities. For a time, its Royal Museum and Library was one of the most influential in the country, attracting visitors as diverse as Queen Victoria,

Gladstone, Dom Pedro and the Duke of Wellington. Joseph Brotherton was an important cultural link not only between Lancashire and the metropolis, but also between new industrial wealth and the rural gentry – a man capable of mobilising town and country. Brotherton was one of the most successful industrialists in the region, yet he dressed in the manner of a country squire and held on to his stout Lancashire accent and dialect.[10] Following the 1832 Reform Act, he became the first MP for the new borough of Salford and made a key contribution to his constituency's cultural achievement.

In order to mobilise support for a Salford art gallery, Brotherton exploited both national cultural unease about design education and the growing civic rivalry between the new corporations of Manchester and Salford. Salford Corporation's annoyance at Manchester's growing political dominance of the region was first apparent in the campaign to establish urban public parks. In September 1844, a huge appeal for public subscriptions was launched at the Manchester Free Trade Hall with a view to establishing public parks around the rapidly expanding Manchester and Salford conurbation. By Christmas 1845, over £32,000 had been subscribed, with contributions coming from over 5,000 firms and individuals.[11] The new parks committee identified four sites for the development of public parks, including one in the borough of Salford on the Lark Hill estate. However, in what was taken as a direct snub by Salford's political leadership, the committee planned to gift the park not to Salford corporation, but instead to Manchester. Salford, as a newly incorporated borough which had struggled to assert its independence from Manchester, was outraged.[12] The mayor, John Kay, described the proposal as an insult, and the council refused to take part in any opening proceedings or support the acquisition of further land for the park's extension.[13] The parks committee soon realised that it was in an untenable position and reversed its decision. However, even during the opening ceremony, the Salford Corporation was made to feel a junior partner. The mayor of Manchester was asked to open the formal proceedings, while the mayor of Salford took only a supporting role.[14]

Despite Salford's somewhat subservient political position, its political elite were determined to use the opportunity provided by the new park to provide cultural facilities and attractions to rival those of Manchester. There was a long tradition of Mancunians crossing the river to Salford for public entertainments, including the regular race meetings and theatre productions.[15] The new public park, library and art gallery were from the start conceived as offering 'rational recreation' for the masses, while providing cultural facilities that would enhance

Salford's reputation. Speakers at the park's opening ceremony argued that the facility would be responsible for 'harmless enjoyment' for the whole family while 'winning men from those low and dangerous sports, or from those debasing occupations'.[16] The corporation was fortunate in that within the park was a large and elegant mansion house dating from 1790. Although not ideally suited for museum purposes, it was a building that could be modified at little cost.[17]

Brotherton played an important role in popularising the idea of a museum for Salford, but it was the enthusiasm of the local authority which enabled plans to develop so rapidly. Crucial to the success of the venture was the 1848 mayor of Salford, Edward Ryley Langworthy. Langworthy owned mills in Greengate and eventually became one of the most prominent members of Manchester's banking community.[18] He even represented Salford in Parliament for a few months, following the death of Brotherton in 1857. Langworthy's main contribution to Salford's political life was, however, as the guiding force being the formation of the city's art gallery. He was chairman of the city's library and museum committee for much of its first decade and during his lifetime contributed around £6,000 for the development of the gallery.[19] Contemporaries took the view that it was his financial support of the institution that persuaded the council to adopt the plan.[20] Attempts to form museums also, of course, required the practical and pecuniary support of local patrons. Bizarrely, Salford did not adopt the Public Libraries Act, even though it levied a library rate.[21] The museum was essentially viewed as a project funded by private subscriptions and simply vested under the supervision of the corporation. A private association, the Salford Borough Museum and Library Association, was, in effect, the management body of the museum and library. In the first few years of the museum's existence, the gallery was largely administered by the executive committee of this association, until it was finally disbanded in 1857.[22] By then its functions had passed to a committee of the corporation, although not before the association had contributed £6,677 3s 3d to support the museum's development.[23]

The management committee envisaged the development of a museum funded largely by public subscription, with books, objects and works of art donated by those living not just in Salford but for many miles around. Their aim was to develop a nationally important museum, and the committee's annual reports noted proudly how support had been obtained from those with no previous connection with the borough.[24] They also recorded exchanges of gifts with museums and libraries overseas, including the Smithsonian Institution in Washington and the New York State Library.[25] The members of the management committee were keen to stress the wider significance of their work, emphasising that the failure of Britain to establish institution 'for the amelioration of the intellectual condition of the working classes' was 'a reproach upon our national character'.[26] They also sought, and obtained, royal patronage for the venture.[27]

In September 1849, the committee appointed a curator, John Plant, to assemble a suitable collection for exhibition.[28] Following an appeal to the public over 5,000 volumes, maps and specimens were obtained.[29] The collection was of a very miscellaneous character. The natural history section was the largest; it was a collection that encompassed some 1,000 specimens of British and foreign birds, together with separate cabinets of insects, shells and plant life.[30] Brotherton, whose primary interests were connected with art education, stressed the importance of developing a significant art collection and encouraged the executive committee to appeal to the Board of Trade for grants of casts from antique sculpture from the British Museum.[31] The request was granted, but the Salford authorities soon discovered they had no suitable room for displaying sculpture and larger works of art.[32] Initially, large works and the casts of antiquities from the British Museum were crowded into rooms set aside for the natural history collections.[33] The matter became more pressing during the mayoralty in 1851 of the art dealer Thomas Agnew, who encouraged the development of a picture gallery through the donation of a series of engravings of modern works.[34] During 1852, plans were drawn up for a museum extension, which were to include a purpose-built picture gallery measuring seventy-five feet by thirty feet.[35] The estimated cost of the extension was £1,902, but the final cost was more than £5,300, a figure that even Langworthy had to admit was 'considerably beyond the estimates'.[36] The episode again highlighted the dependence of the corporation museum on voluntary assistance. The council offered just £1,000 for the scheme, with £3,000 coming from voluntary subscribers and the rest of the shortfall from members of the executive committee themselves.[37]

The building of the new gallery brought a restructuring of the management of the museum. Previously members of the executive committee – a group of subscribers headed by G. Leeming – had supervised the collections. However, in 1852 Leeming stepped down, prompting the committee to give Plant, the professional curator, full day-to-day charge of the museum.[38] The new gallery, opening on 1 October 1853, was a popular addition (Figure 6). During the first ten months of 1854 it was estimated that some 330,000 people attended the museum and library, and it continued to attract major dignitaries, including, in June of that year, the King of Portugal.[39] The opening of the gallery also encouraged

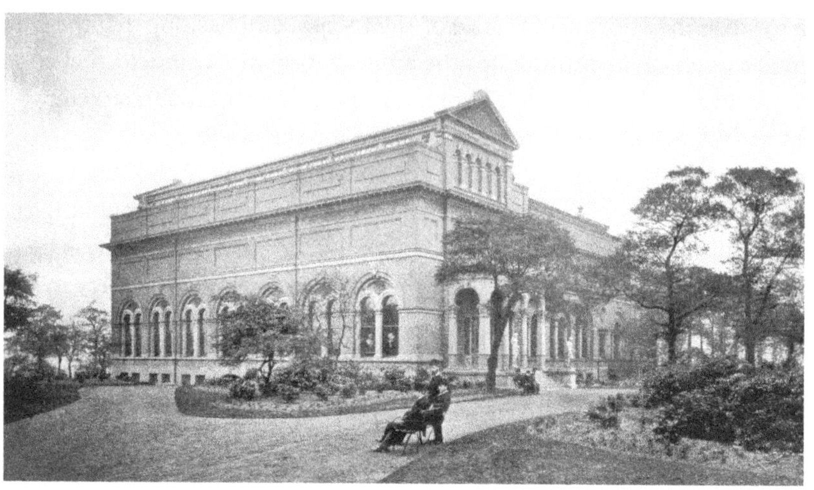

6 Peel Park Museum and Art Gallery

further donations by local art collectors, including an obscure portrait in oil of Handel. In general, the quality of donated works was poor. The engravings were a particular cause for curatorial concern. Eighty were regarded as such poor quality as not to be worth the cost of framing.[40] Relying on donations had not yielded the quality of contributions anticipated. Brotherton felt that the best hope for Salford was to persuade the British Museum to lend some of its duplicate works to the developing provincial museums. He held talks in Westminster aiming to promote an Act of Parliament to allow British Museum trustees to sanction loans, but made only limited progress. Even if legislation could be passed, it was clear that British Museum trustees would be reluctant to lend original works.[41] The Salford committee thereafter made renewed attempts to solicit donations. These met with more success, but rendered the gallery increasingly dependent on local commercial interests. The local art dealers Thomas Agnew and Sons and J. Clowes Grundy donated important works, partly as a form of advertisement for their own businesses. Agnews provided a life-sized statue of John Dalton and a bust of Humphrey Cheetham. Grundy contributed a series of higher-quality engravings of local portraiture and landscape.[42] The gallery also attracted the predicable donations of 'subscriber portraits', including one of William Lockett, the first mayor of Salford, together with modest copies of old masters.[43]

The rather mixed quality of the collection did not deter visitors. Spectacle mattered as much as content. Located in an attractive setting and within walking distance for several hundred thousand people, the museum and park became a popular place of resort. Unlike the RMI, which organised exhibitions primarily for a middle-class audience, the Salford museum was intended 'to afford gratuitous instruction and amusement to all classes of society'.[44] By 1855, the museum had begun to attract day trippers, with cheap transport provided from the surrounding districts, and the museum committee claimed that visitor numbers had increased to 450,000 per year.[45] During the public holidays, the museum was so busy that at peak times it was estimated that over 100 people were entering per minute, causing real danger to young children, who, it was feared, could be trampled underfoot.[46] Yet the museum and library had become part of a much wider public attraction. The sheer popularity of the park made it difficult for the committee to regulate public behaviour. When the committee decided to ban Sunday music in the park, the local brass bands simply ignored it.[47] A key part of the attraction of the park and museum was, of course, that admission to them was free, in an era when many recreation grounds and art exhibitions made a charge for admission or deliberately tried to deter working-class visitors. By 1859, excursions were being organised from Cheshire, Yorkshire and Derbyshire, and the museum was one of the leading holiday attractions in the north of England.[48] Although the committee was reluctant to antagonise Sabbatarians by allowing music on Sundays, it was proud of the park's ability to attract visitors from outside the area and did all it could to provide the park with popular appeal. In addition to the erecting a statue of Peel, the committee contacted the War Office and obtained two guns reputedly captured at Sebastapol for display in the park, believing that such acquisitions would be 'highly interesting and gratifying to the numerous frequenters of the Park and Museum, most of whom are working people'.[49] Such was the success of Peel Park and its museum that other corporations began to send deputations to study the achievement. The authorities at Stockport based their museum and park directly on the Salford model, while there can be little doubt that the development of the Whitworth Institute, more than half a century later, was also influenced by Salford.

The committee recognised that the Whitsuntide holiday was a time when many chose to take advantage of the park's facilities, and it naturally made sense to organise the major exhibition of the season to coincide with this holiday. Although the museum's collection was a little sparse, Agnew enthusiastically offered to provide exhibits to fill the gaps; the museum offered him an excellent opportunity to display sale works to a large audience at no cost to himself.[50]

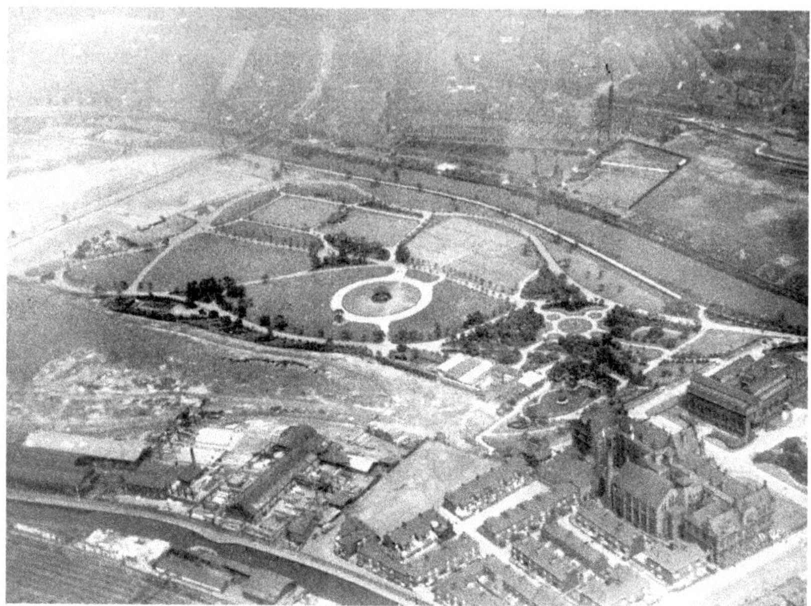

7 Aerial view of Peel Park and the Peel Park Museum and Art Gallery

Agnew organised the rearrangement of the work and then helped persuade the council to use profits from the sale of gas to fund the development of a further extension.[51] The new south wing extension was opened in 1857 by the Prince Consort during the Manchester Art Treasures Exhibition (Figure 7).[52]

The death of Brotherton in January 1857 deprived the museum of its foremost supporter, but the gallery continued to innovate. Faced with competition from the RMI there was little opportunity to establish a major annual sales exhibition, so instead the museum authorities became increasingly interested in promoting the work of prominent artists in the Manchester region. In March 1853, Charles Mitchell, the honorary secretary of the Manchester Academy, held talks with committee members, suggesting that the corporation organise an exhibition of members' works.[53] Three years later their plans came to fruition, with the emergent academy organising a local exhibition 'to foster and develope [sic] a taste for art', stressing the wider educational advantages rather than their own commercial interests.[54] The exhibition, held during the 1857 Manchester Art Treasures Exhibition, was a great success and included 670 works, hung by a committee of artists. The collection was inspected by the Prince Consort, and over a period of six months around half a million people passed through the gallery.[55] The exhibition helped establish the Manchester Academy as a leading association of regional artists and convince the Salford authorities that loan exhibitions need not be excessively costly.

Despite the opening of the new wing, the Museum and Library Association was increasingly frustrated at its inability to attract high-quality donations for the gallery, and therefore began to encourage more loan exhibitions. The chairman of the committee, James Renshaw, noted that the passing of the museums legislation of 1855, enabling corporations to levy a rate for the purchase of permanent collections of art, had actually made it even more difficult to attract contributions. Renshaw felt that rate support deterred voluntary donations, lamenting that despite numerous appeals 'very few persons have responded to the call'.[56] Little less than a year earlier, the committee had assured the council that funds would not be required to acquire further items for exhibition because 'ample means to accomplish this part of the undertaking will be afforded by voluntary contributions'.[57] In practice, the voluntary committee that had supported the museum since its inception was so frustrated at its inability to raise voluntary subscriptions that it folded in an air of disillusionment in 1857. This was, somewhat ironically, at the same time as the Manchester district was being hailed as an emerging force in the art world owing to the success of the Manchester Art Treasures Exhibition.[58]

Rather than try to assemble a large permanent collection, the committee looked instead to organising a series of loan exhibitions, drawing on the collections of well-known local patrons. In this venture it enjoyed much more success. The first exhibition of 1858 was primarily a local affair, attracting loans from the Bishop of Manchester, the local dealers Agnew and Grundy and a number of local art collectors and city councillors.[59] Encouraged by the success of this exhibition, the following year the committee drew up more ambitious plans to attract a much wider range of modern works. A deputation waited on the authorities at Buckingham Palace, who agreed to contribute a number of items from the royal collection. The committee also attracted aristocratic patronage, with a long-standing supporter of the RMI, Lord Egerton, contributing several items and the Earl of Derby lending works by Gainsborough and Thomas Lawrence. W. J. Legh MP provided items from his Cheshire seat, Lyme Hall, while many of the area's leading merchants also contributed, including R. N. Philips, J. Moss and J. Barratt. Significantly too, the Salford authorities continued to encourage local artists, many of who felt excluded from the RMI. The most prominent of these was probably H. H. Hadfield, who supplied a number of landscape views of local beauty spots.[60]

In 1860, an even larger exhibition was held, supported by contributions from over eighty of the region's leading art collectors, headed by the Earl of Ellesmere, who provided a number of important drawings and sketches from Italian old masters. Again, however, the exhibition focused primarily on the work of leading artists from the modern British school. Both Agnew and Armitage contributed works by Richard Ansdell. Two important works by Etty, *The Idle Lake* and *The Toilette*, were also in evidence, together with E. M. Ward's *The Greenwich Pensioner's Story*. There was also the celebrated documentary painting *Garibaldi at the Siege of Rome* by G. Barket, together with works of historical genre, including F. Newenham's *The Princes in the Tower*. The South Kensington authorities sent a number of watercolour drawings by E. W. Cooke, and the work of local artists was again in evidence. With three important exhibitions held in as many years Salford was by now becoming one of the most visited museums in the country. In the years 1857–59, it again claimed to have attracted more visitors than the National Gallery, the British Museum and the South Kensington Museum.[61] Although it would not be wise to take these claims too literally – Salford still had no entrance turnstile and no way of accurately measuring visitor figures – it was clear that the museum was attracting very large numbers. Its exhibitions commanded the support and interest of all social classes, including almost all of the major artists and collectors in the Manchester region. Although it is always difficult to measure the influence of the exhibitions among the city's working classes, the establishment in 1860 of drawing classes at Salford Working Men's College suggests that the success of the museum may have led to a rising demand for elementary drawing instruction.[62]

The success of the gallery encouraged the Salford authorities to view their museum as a nationally important facility, deserving national recognition. In the spring of 1860 the mayor, town clerk and borough treasurer organised a series of interviews in London with the authorities of the royal estates, the South Kensington Museum, the Chief Commissioner of Works, East India House and others who, it was thought, might be prepared to assist in the organisation of future Salford exhibitions. The responses were somewhat mixed. The Salford authorities were clearly upset when Sir Charles Phipps informed them that no future contributions from the royal residences would be forthcoming, on the grounds that there had been a policy change by which contributions would not be provided to 'local' exhibitions. South Kensington agreed to provide loan works, but only for a fee. As Salford did not charge an admission fee, it was very difficult for the committee to enter into any agreement which involved significant financial commitments. Henry Cole of the South Kensington Museum seemed impressed with the 'extraordinary number of visitors' to the museum and declared there to be 'no insuperable difficulties' in obtaining items from the national collections in future.[63] He was not, however, prepared to lend his authority to the application.[64] The museum did have some success in gaining recognition from South Kensington. In 1860 it obtained the loan of an important national collection, including items by the Royal Academicians E. W. Cooke, C. W. Cope and R. Redgrave and, a year later, a travelling exhibition of vases and 'choice examples of Ancient and Antique objects'.[65] Despite its royal patronage, however, the Salford gallery was still perceived as a 'local' facility. Even local dealers, such as Agnews, sometimes treated the committee in a high-handed way, withdrawing pictures from exhibition at short notice because of customer demands.[66] Over the next two decades, Salford's position as the leading free museum in the north of England was to be eclipsed.

The status of the Salford museum depended primarily on its ability to attract large number of visitors to its exhibitions. It was designed as a facility created for the advancement of taste and rational recreation among, primarily, the working classes. However, its reliance on scale and spectacle to attract visitors undermined its educational rationale. Furthermore, the onset of the cotton famine and the resultant economic distress presented the museum with a fundamental problem. Despite the economic uncertainties of 1863, there was a strong desire on the part of the committee to organise an exhibition, with the committee's new chairman, J. W. Weston, arguing that it was 'the more urgent when the straitened means and distressed circumstances of the working classes of this district was considered'.[67] Pictures to the value of £300,000 were attracted on loan, and John Plant canvassed exhibitors at the international exhibition in London for further contributions. These efforts could not, however, do much to rescue the Salford exhibition. There was a significant fall in visitor numbers during Whit week, as few from outside the immediate district had money available for rail excursions. Those who did come from far afield were mainly those from Yorkshire and Staffordshire and 'distant places far removed from the influence of the distress now prevailing in the Cotton districts'.[68] Visitors during the summer months fell to around 250,000, around half of the total in the previous year.[69]

E. R. Langworthy's withdrawal from the chairmanship of the museum and library committee in 1862 was unfortunate as it came shortly before the museum faced its most significant challenge. Langworthy had been the inspiration for the major exhibitions of 1858–61, and his successor, J. W. Weston, struggled to maintain the progress that had been made. The summer loan exhibition of 1864 was the last that could be said to have attracted a large number of celebrated artists from outside the area. The success of this exhibition was largely due the patronage of one man, John Chapman MP, who provided a number of pictures by Wilkie, Turner, Landseer, Linnell and Webster.[70] In 1866 it was decided to abandon the annual loan exhibition completely because of the drop in support, although, Weston declared defensively, 'the number of visitors to the Institution has not been much less than in former years'.[71] The cotton famine cannot be directly blamed for the loss of the exhibition, but it disrupted patterns of business, made patrons more cautious about investing and prevented many from attending what had become a popular cultural ritual. After 1863 the museum never quite regained either its visitor numbers or its national reputation as a popular museum.

The reasons for the decline in visitor numbers were complex, but it can partly be accounted for by increasing competition from other parks, museums and commercial entertainment facilities. By the end of the 1860s, there were two other similar museums in the Manchester area, albeit on a smaller scale. The museum at Queen's Park (Figure 8) catered for those in the centre and east of Manchester, while the museum in Vernon Park, Stockport, was accessible for those living in the southern suburbs. The Manchester Natural History Museum on Peter Street was located centrally and more easily accessible for Manchester city centre's population. Commercial entertainment parks, such as those at Belle Vue and the botanical gardens at Old Trafford, made a charge but provided a wider range of activities and a more socially exclusive experience for the visitor.[72] The Salford authorities were aware of the challenge they faced, recording in their annual report of 1873 that Peel Park 'no longer offers the same undivided attractions to visitors as it did in its earlier years; other places for public recreation and resort having sprung up in the district'.[73] The museum committee could do little to compete with these alternative visitor attractions in Manchester, still less with the rise of the cheap day trip and the seaside holiday. In 1884 the committee recorded banefully that 'experience in former years had shown that when the weather is bright and fine, the holiday people prefer to go into the country and to the seaside, for doing which there are abundant and cheap facilities'.[74] The economic problems of the late 1870s may have contributed to a further drop in visitor numbers, with the official figures falling to just 381,000 in 1879.[75]

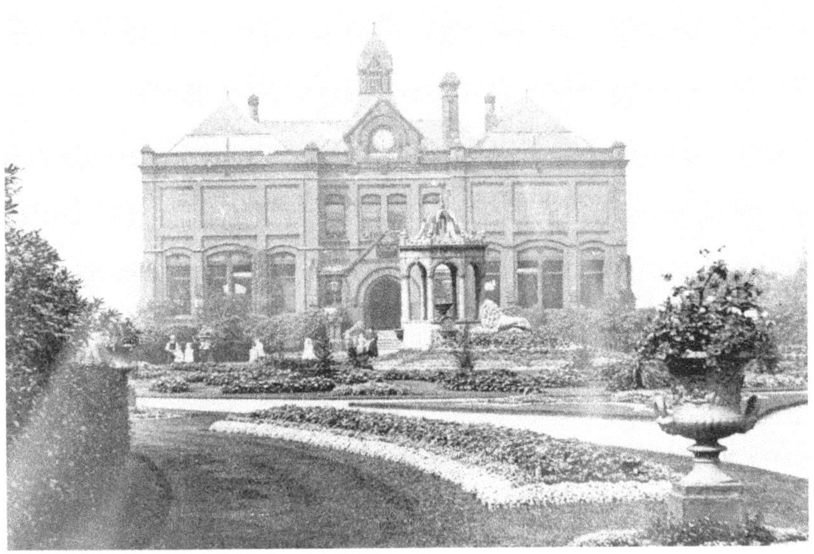

8 Queen's Park Museum and Art Gallery in Harpurhey

This reduction in admissions may also be explained by the change in tone of the museum and art gallery. When it opened in the 1850s the Salford authorities attempted to appeal to wide cross-section of tastes, collecting a wide variety of objects designed to instruct and amuse. From the 1860s, there was a discernible shift of emphasis to the collecting of high-value works of fine art that would appeal to more 'refined' tastes. This move was partly a response to Manchester City Council's own initiative in forming a permanent art collection. The collapse of Fairbairn's attempts to establish a public fine art gallery for Manchester encouraged Manchester City Council to offer a home for fine art bequests in the small museum in Queen's Park. Alderman J. M. Bennett, the mayor of Manchester, noted 'a very large number of gentleman who were collectors of pictures and curiosities, [who] would be glad to deposit their work of art within that building… and so prevent their being distributed on their decease'.[76] In 1866 the Salford committee persuaded the council to establish a fund dedicated to art acquisition.[77] Its first purchases were somewhat modest affairs, mainly British landscape and seascape pieces.[78] The initiative, however, encouraged Agnew to donate a series of thirty-six paintings to supplement the permanent collection. These included well-known works such as Sir Joshua Reynolds's *Portrait of a Cabinet Minister* in addition to a number of items of local interest.[79] Agnew may have hoped that this generosity would strengthen the position of his firm in future dealings with the committee, particularly if it was to devote a large annual sum for the purchase of works of art. In May 1869 Agnews offered the committee a work by J. R. Herbert, *The Assertion of Liberty of Conscience in the Westminster Assembly of Divines, 1644*, for the sum of £400. The Agnew family offered to make a contribution of £100 and hoped the rest could be made up by the committee and private subscribers. The committee, however, was very reluctant to spend up to 200 guineas on one work and, in any case, did not believe the rest could be found by private subscription.[80] Eventually a compromise was found and the picture acquired, but the incident highlighted the limitations of the corporation's budget.[81]

The corporation retained a small acquisitions fund and throughout the early 1870s collected significant works of the British landscape and seascape schools. These included S. R. Percy's *The Highland and Ben Nevis* and Montague's *Wreck near the North Foreland*.[82] Yet the development of the permanent collection was not only inhibited by lack of funds, but also by lack of space. The museum building had undergone some changes, including the addition of a handsome classical portico, but no additional gallery space had been provided.[83] The inability of the museum to charge for admission to specialist exhibitions made it impossible to raise significant funds from its own resources and, therefore, it inevitably had to wait for a large benefaction before any developments were possible. This came in 1874, following the death of E. R. Langworthy. Langworthy, once the gallery's most important patron, played little part in the administration of the museum following his retirement to south Manchester, but his bequest of £10,000 provided the resources for a significant expansion of gallery space.[84] The new Langworthy wing, built at a cost of £5,760, featured a reading room on the ground floor and a new picture gallery on the upper tier.[85]

The extension stimulated something of a revival in the fortunes of the gallery and encouraged more ambitious exhibitions. Throughout the previous decade, the Salford authorities had organised few sales exhibitions. Yet in 1867 they controversially, and somewhat opportunistically, hosted the exhibition of the Manchester Art Society. The Manchester Art Society was a society of artists who, angry at what they regarded as the RMI's neglect of local artists, established their own independent exhibition. Salford not only provided a suitable location, but assisted in the hanging and organised a mayoral reception for those participating.[86] The corporation regarded it as an opportunity to both publicise the work of younger artists and re-establish the Salford gallery as a venue for important exhibitions.[87] However, attempts to persuade Manchester artists to view Salford as the primary exhibition venue for their works were soon thwarted. By the end of the 1860s, the RMI had become more sympathetic to the interests of local artists and agreed to host the Manchester Academy's nascent annual exhibition.

By the 1870s, William Agnew and his brother Thomas were the main force behind the organisation of exhibitions at Salford. In 1876, the corporation gave over most of its gallery to an exhibition of works lent by William.[88] Two years later, on the inauguration of the Langworthy gallery, he offered his entire personal collection on loan. This provided the core of the exhibition in the new wing, although it was supplemented by important works from other local collectors, such as Benjamin Armitage of Halton Bank, William Cottrill of Didsbury, Charles Galloway of Old Trafford and Charles Rickards of Seymour Grove.[89] The Salford authorities also continued the tradition of supporting local artists and organised for them a sales exhibition, encompassing over 300 works. This was not a great success, with 'the bad state of trade generally which has prevailed throughout the year deterring many admirers from purchasing luxuries as paintings until better times'.[90] Special exhibitions were held again in 1880 and 1881, following a similar pattern, but were again discontinued until 1890, when the corporation organised an exhibition which focused on loaned works from other corporations. Liverpool, Nottingham, Southampton and Bolton all sent contributions, and the exhibition claimed to have attracted 200,000 in 100 days.[91] The committee organised a further exhibition four years later to mark the jubilee of the museum, limiting exhibits, as far as possible, to works produced in the previous fifty years.[92]

The special free exhibitions held at Salford fulfilled several functions. They gave local artists a space to display their works, they provided collectors with a chance to display their taste, and they gave dealers, particularly Agnew, opportunity for commercial promotion. After 1863, however, they were primarily local affairs aimed at a local audience. The building of the new Langworthy wing and the Langworthy financial bequest allowed the Salford committee to begin to build a worthwhile permanent collection. Almost all of the gallery's earlier acquisitions had been by donation and bequest, leaving the committee with a miscellaneous collection of works of mixed quality. Even the normally supportive *Salford Weekly News* remarked in 1880 that some pictures were 'undeniably good, but others of them are indifferently regarded as works of high art'.[93] The Langworthy fund at least allowed the committee to adopt a slightly more adventurous acquisitions policy. In 1878 it purchased ten paintings using this fund, including two important historical works by E. M. Ward, *The Last Sleep of Argyll* and *The Execution of the Duke of Montrose*. Salford Corporation, like many others in the north-west, also exhibited much interest in the Welsh landscape school, buying two works by Joseph Knight, *The Welsh Grandmother* and *Conway Marsh – Evening*. Sculpture was not forgotten either, with the acquisition of Heinrich M. Imhof's *Hagar and Ishmael* and S. H. Wolff's *The Wounded Fawn*.[94] This spending spree rather limited the works that could be acquired in subsequent years.[95] By the mid-1880s, the committee was suffering from financial pressures associated with the expansion of public libraries and the 'penny in the pound' statutory restriction on expenditure.[96] Consequently, few significant works were obtained during this period, although the museum did expand its sculpture collection with donations from the collections of Benjamin Armitage of Sorrel Bank, Samuel Pope QC and the recently deceased Henry Tootal.[97]

During the latter years of the century the Salford authorities increasingly chose to devote what little funds they had to works of instruction – such as Turner's *Liber Studiorum* – somewhat ironically returning the museum to its unfulfilled mid-nineteenth-century ideal as a popular educator.[98] Visitors were encouraged to bring children into the museum, and lectures with lantern slides were organised to illustrate and explain the nature of the various collections.[99] Part of the reason for this change in emphasis was the decision of Salford Corporation to promote the construction of a new technical college and locate it on a plot of land immediately adjacent to the museum. Opened with much pomp and circumstance by the Duke and Duchess of York in March 1896, the new facility helped breathe life into the museum.[100] In 1899, the new chairman of committee, Alderman J. G. De Mandley, visited the Victoria and Albert Museum, obtaining casts and bronzes for use in the Salford galleries by art students.[101] The development of the technical school may have prompted a reorganisation of the collections. Following the appointment of a new curator, B. H. Mullen, there was a rearrangement and reclassification of the entire permanent collection. The original marbles, including those by Gatle, Ball, Swinnerton and Schwanthaler, were rearranged in a prominent position, as was the pottery and porcelain collection. The curatorial practice aimed to stress the intellectual indivisibility of the collections. Reflecting the curriculum of art schools, natural history collections were essential for inspiration in art. In particular, it was urged that 'the decorative artist should not forget that in natural history collections he will find birds in brilliant plumage, well suited for panel work or for reproduction into renaissance designs'.[102]

The Salford gallery was important not merely because it was a pioneer, or because of its popularity, but because it created a model for other corporations to emulate. Yet in trying to emulate the Salford model, other art institutions were prone to the same financial limitations and logistical problems that confronted Salford. Just as the role and function of Salford's museum depending on changing patrons, management and commercial interests, so did those who followed Salford's example. Stockport's Vernon Park Museum was one of the first to pursue the model established by Salford, yet it tried to do so with considerably fewer private supporters and little backing from the corporation. One of Stockport's MPs, John Benjamin Smith, visited the Salford museum in 1856 and was 'very much struck by the value of such institutions'.[103] Together with his fellow MP James Kershaw and the local Reform Association, he drew up plans for a similar 'people's park and museum' in Stockport. Earlier attempts to create a public park for Stockport had met with little success, and a possible central site near Chestergate had been built upon. Finally, in 1858, a public park was opened on the outskirts of the town, following a donation of land by Lord Vernon. As in nearby Salford, the opening of the public park proved extremely popular, with thousands turning out to an official opening celebrated with triumphal arches and a hog roast.[104] Kershaw and Smith, enthused by the success of nearby Salford, were keen to see the development of a museum on the site. The corporation was more cautious, suggesting that if a museum were to be built a more central location should be found. However, with Kershaw and Smith offering to pay for the capital cost of the museum, it was their view which was to prevail. In April 1859 plans were approved for a building in a 'domestic' style, with two galleries measuring 45 feet by 25 feet. The original plan was to use the lower room for the museum and the upper storey for an art gallery, although in practice it seems that both were used as a common museum space, with pictures hung on available wall space.[105]

Although Smith had ambitious plans to match the success of the Salford gallery, its educational objectives were undermined by a lack of financial support. He had hoped that his generosity would be matched by other townspeople, but in practice neither the corporation nor private citizens provided much encouragement. Over the winter of 1841–42, Smith had stayed with the Marquis of Brancadori at his palace in Rome. During his time there he was offered almost the entire contents of the Brancadori gallery, which were then shipped back to England.[106] These were thought by Smith to be old masters and were loaned to the Stockport museum to inspire further donations and to act as the basis of its emerging art gallery.[107] However, by this time the collecting of old masters had declined in popularity, and it is significant that much of the popularity of the Salford gallery was based on the display of modern loan works. In any case, the veracity of the 'old masters' supplied by Smith were soon brought into question and they proved to be of little interest to the local art community. The corporation, although forced to accept the patronage of the local MPs, showed little interest in the project and initially declined to finance its maintenance. For several months the building remained closed, with the windows whitewashed and doors locked. Contributors to local newspapers complained about the dull and unsightly nature of the building, demanding that it 'look more like a public building and less like a public house'.[108]

The political motivation for the construction of museums was wholly transparent. Brotherton's enthusiasm for museums was based on their educational capacity and their ability to diffuse artistic knowledge to a broader public. Kershaw and Smith shared this view, noting that the museum was 'of the greatest importance in the education of people at large and ... in regulating the taste of the young'.[109] It was also an opportunity for them to demonstrate their public patronage and promote a particularly liberal notion of political citizenship. Public generosity in the provision of cultural tropes was to be repaid, not by obedience, but by mutual respect and the mutual protection of property. Opening the museum, Kershaw reportedly commented:

> Treat the working classes liberally, and they would not disappoint them. That they had appreciated the advantages of the Vernon park was amply shown by the way in which they had protected and preserved the property. He honoured them for it.[110]

Yet, in practice, those who made use of the museum and park often fell short of the ideal standard of citizenry expected. Before the museum opened a statue of Napoleon I, donated by a local councillor, was attacked while on display in the park, raising concern that potential donors would shy away from making contributions to the museum.[111] The worst fears of the museum committee were realised in March 1863, when the museum's coin collection was stolen in a burglary.[112] Despite moves to improve museum security, a fear of disorder remained. Stockport's open spaces were regarded as an 'arena of gambling transactions', with complaints of 'low blackguards, principally Irish' appearing to play pitch and toss to the annoyance of local inhabitants.[113] The theft of dahlias and geraniums seemed to prove a particular point of concern.[114] An illiterate girl caught picking flowers in Vernon Park was forced to make a humiliating public apology to the parks committee, with public notices of her contrition displayed around the town:

> I, the undersigned, having been GUILTY of PLUCKING FLOWERS in the VERNON PARK, on 16th July, do hereby express my deep Contrition for the Offence, and humbly thank the Park Committee for not Prosecuting me. I further agree to pay all the Expenses incurred in making Public this Apology. Mary [her X Mark] Kelly, 24 Howard-street, Stockport – [dated 27 July 1864].[115]

The park and museum may have been seen as a monument to the civility of the town and the benevolence of local liberalism, but in practice it often drew attention to the somewhat authoritarian nature of local municipal governance.

Once the museum was established, the Stockport Corporation parks committee showed little interest in developing its collection in any specific direction. It was pleased to receive donations, but failed to allocate a budget to acquire works or encourage loan exhibitions. The local artist Robert Cheetham was employed to hang gallery pictures and there were some interesting donations, including a portrait of George Washington bought from America.[116] However, the museum was the model of disorganisation, with no significant permanent picture collection and a small, cluttered gallery space. The local art community took little interest in the project. Worse still, the museum was unsuccessful in attracting large numbers of the wider community. Unlike Peel Park in Salford, Vernon Park was a considerable distance from its town centre, with only smaller suburban districts in its immediate vicinity. The park was celebrated for its natural beauty and for being isolated from the most polluted industrial districts. Yet it was this isolation that undermined its popular appeal. An additional wing was added to the museum in 1866 for use mainly as a public library. The location proved unpopular, and in 1874 the library was moved to a town centre location, with the newly vacant wing being converted to refreshment rooms to raise additional income.[117] Subsequently, the museum was largely neglected, although in the latter years of the century the Stockport authorities did take advantage of loans of exhibits from South Kensington. The main difficulty was that the museum was primarily the project of the town's local MPs. The corporation had misgivings about the wisdom of the museum's location and its value, but had little choice but to accept the 'generous' gift of the local parliamentary representatives. There was very little other voluntary support for the museum, and there were no major donations of art. Therefore, unlike Salford, Stockport was required to draw almost exclusively on the municipal exchequer. Stockport authority's tax base was relatively small and, in the 1870s, a penny rate generated only around £590. Faced with demands to expand the town's library provision, the authority was forced to allocate around £300 for the provision of books and related expenses.[118] Of the £584 raised by the penny rate of 1876, more than £523 was spent on library services.[119] Even if Stockport Corporation had been more enthusiastic about museum development, it had very limited resources for expansion. Without a network of private patronage little could be achieved.

The difficulties of Stockport contrasted with the relative success of Warrington. Warrington, like Stockport, was a town on the edge of the Manchester conurbation, although slightly more distant from the cultural attractions of Manchester and Salford city centres. By the early nineteenth century, Warrington had become a rapidly expanding industrial town with a diverse and independent industrial base. Unlike those of Stockport and many other towns in the Manchester region, its local economy was not dominated by the cotton industry, and it instead became a town of many industries, including soap, wire and glass making, brewing, tool-making and tanning.[120] Yet the most remarkable feature of the town's growth was the emergence of a network of cultural and educational organisations that were to be crucial in the development of the town's museum. As early as 1757, a non-denominational centre of higher education was established in the town. The Warrington Academy lasted until 1786, establishing a national reputation and giving Warrington the honourable nickname of the 'Athens of the North'. Around twenty-five of its alumni found their way into the *Dictionary of National Biography*, including the pioneer of modern demography, Thomas Malthus, the chemist Joseph Priestley, the naturalist John Forster and the classicist Gilbert Wakefield.[121] The success of the academy fostered a broader cultural life in the town. The Warrington Town Library was established in 1760 and in the first half of the nineteenth century other learned organisations followed, including the botanical society in 1807, the Warrington Institution in 1811, a musical society in 1834 and a Warrington Natural History Society in 1838.[122]

Although Warrington had a strong and dynamic cultural life, the Warrington museum movement was also driven by strong political motivations. William Beaumont, the town's first mayor, was a key figure in the promotion of the museum. Beaumont had led the campaign for the incorporation of the town under the 1835 Municipal Corporations Act, and the town's charter was finally granted in April 1847.[123] The museum project offered the opportunity to commemorate and memorialise the town's newly acquired municipal identity and its acquisition of a representative form of local government. It was conceived explicitly as a way of expressing a new civic vision, creating 'an Institution which might be expected at no distant period to be worthy of the Town'.[124] As mayor, Beaumont placed the museum project before the community and subscribed in all £450 towards the museum and the later art gallery building.[125] On his death in 1889 he provided a further legacy of £500 and a number of pictures from his private collection.[126] As with Salford and Stockport, the initiative and direction for the project were provided by a charismatic local politician with specific social objectives. However, in the case of Warrington, the objective was primarily to secure the town's reputation as a culturally sophisticated community with a distinctive and independent identity.

The town's reputation as a cultural centre had been in gradual decline since its eighteenth-century heyday and the closure of the Warrington Academy. The old town library attracted little support, with its 'wholly useless' reading room in a 'cold and comfortless apartment'. The library committee feared that unless the corporation took over its operation it would face closure. Meanwhile the private museum of the natural history society was suffering badly for want of accommodation. Both organisations were all too willing to hand over their property to the corporation, if public funding could be used to help guarantee their existence.[127] Unlike other towns, Warrington had existing collections, so the town was less reliant on new, individual donations. However, in practice, the museum authorities were also very successful in attracting new funds from private sources. John Marsh, the town clerk, recognised that the 'the prosperity of the Museum and Library will in a great measure depend upon the extent of annual subscriptions' and opened up a successful subscription book.[128] In the early years of the museum, the income from subscriptions made up at least half of its income, the rest being brought in from the rate. As the tax base of Warrington increased, the dependence on annual subscriptions declined, although annual subscriptions remained a useful supplement to library and museum income right up to the end of the century. In 1856, income from subscriptions was little over £71; it increased to £200 in 1876 before gradually falling back to £121 by 1890.[129]

Unlike the Stockport museum, the Warrington institution was not associated with any one politician or political party. The museum represented a common cultural endeavour attracting support from across partisan divides. Its leading patrons included John Wilson-Patten, Conservative MP for North Lancashire; Peter Rylands, the Liberal MP for Burnley; Gilbert Greenall, a prominent Liberal soap manufacturer and Warrington's own MP; and William Beaumont, a Conservative. Peter Rylands remarked, on opening the museum extension in 1877, 'while at times they [the Liberals] might be found in hostile camps, it was a source of the deepest satisfaction ... that there were now and again occasions when they could be found upon the same platform'.[130] Strenuous efforts were even made to attract the patronage of the local gentry, and the Warrington museum committee was able to gain the nominal support of the Earl of Derby, Lord Stanley, Lord Linsey, Lord Lilford, and the Bishop of Chester.[131] Significantly, however, none made any financial contribution with the exception of the Earl of Ellesmere, famous for his Bridgewater House gallery in London, who made a modest contribution of £5 to the museum extension fund. Instead, it was local professionals, merchants and manufacturers who provided the finance for the project. William Beaumont, mayor and local solicitor, provided an initial £200, while the railway contractor William Allcard, the businessman Benjamin Pierpoint and the industrialists Joseph Crosfield and Joseph Stubbs each provided £100.

After the opening of the museum in temporary premises in 1848, it soon became clear that more commodious accommodation was required. The construction of a permanent museum was facilitated, again, by a donation, this time of land. The local politician John Wilson-Patten provided a plot of land in Bold Street, near to the town centre. Private funds were the main source of finance for the project: more than two-thirds of the total £2,867 cost was provided by private subscriptions. However, despite the relatively large amount of support for the museum project, the initial plans for construction were abandoned on grounds of cost, and the eventual building, opened in 1857, was a plain brick affair. Yet this modest building proved to be a catalyst for the cultural renaissance of Warrington. Until 1884, the museum also provided a convenient home for the Warrington School of Art. The rationale for the school was, as for other provincial schools, to provide training in design to the industrial population in order to help British-designed products compete more effectively in the international marketplace; like many other schools, it required the fees from fine art classes to be financially viable. Under the distinguished mastership of Jonathan Christman Thompson, Warrington produced an array of distinguished artists who gained national and international fame. The most prominent of these were Samuel Luke Fildes,[132] his brother-in-law Henry Woods and the sculptor John Warrington Wood.[133] The Warrington museum extension of 1877, designed to provide a purpose-built art gallery, was prompted by the need to find a home for Warrington Wood's celebrated marble sculpture *St Michael and Satan*, a work commissioned by his old townsfolk.[134]

The success of the art school helped to maintain a network of support for the museum's activities. In Salford the museum went into a period of decline after its founders passed away and visitor numbers fell. Warrington, in contrast, benefited from the continuing presence of a network of committed patrons and concentrated on the specialist task of appealing to a largely middle-class fine art audience. The opening of the new gallery in 1877 was met with an ambitious loan exhibition of art from neighbourhood collections. The exhibition included 274 oil paintings, 139 watercolours and a range of other works of fine art, as well as loan items from South Kensington collections. The loan exhibition was supplemented by a commercial exhibition, attracting the region's most prominent dealers, including Grundy and Smith and Thomas Agnew and Sons. In common with many provincial exhibitions of the period, a number of these items had been formerly at the Royal Academy, and some prominent Royal Academicians were represented, the exhibition containing including several works by Frith.[135]

Although the formation of the museum had been driven mainly by a political desire to memorialise the municipalisation of the borough and to revive its cultural reputation, it always had a strong and specific educational function. However, while the Salford and Stockport museums focused on appealing to a mass public, Warrington focused on the training of fine artists. By 1870 the alumni of the school were already well known and the art school was an important regional centre for fine art training. This was enhanced in 1877 when the paintings of the former Warringtonian Thomas Robson were donated to the public collection. Robson had begun his career studying the Derby collection at Knowsley before attending the Royal Academy schools and becoming Sir Thomas Lawrence's assistant. He exhibited at the Royal Academy from 1824 but later specialised in the copying of old masters. Many of these copies were donated to the Warrington museum by Thomas's brother William, who regarded them as having a key educational function for young artists unable to consult the originals.[136] This donation was to set the tone for future collecting practices. When Beaumont left a £450 legacy to the museum in 1890, the art gallery committee decided to purchase 'Reproductions of acknowledged masterpieces' to 'assist directly in the acquisition of a taste for art by persons as yet uninstructed'.[137] Education in matters of fine art had emerged as the central function of the museum, even though the museum had begun with broader and more diffuse cultural objectives. The numbers attracted to the Warrington museum were relatively modest, but by retaining a more specifically fine art profile it continued to command a substantial amount of middle-class patronage well into the final decades of the nineteenth century.

The municipal art gallery movement may have sprung from concerns about the paucity of design skills in the industrial population but, in practice, early museums showed limited interest in serving the specific needs of industrial design. There was sometimes little direct connection between art schools and municipal museums. Even in cases such as Warrington where the two institutions shared the same premises, the art school did not necessarily encourage the museum to adopt practices to assist industrial designers. The Warrington school's influence was mainly in encouraging specialist fine art in the museum through the success of its famous alumni, such as Warrington Wood. Similarly, in Salford, the museum's role in the development of industrial design skills was a very limited one. Its greatest achievement lay in its ability to attract middle-class fine art patronage, winning the support of both collectors and dealers through the organisation of successful loan exhibitions. It was then in a position to serve the needs of the local artist community and played a crucial role in the Manchester Academy of Fine Art. Stockport had few pretensions to serve the needs of technical education and existed mainly as a local curiosity.

Early municipal museums need to be understood in broader context of mid-century campaigns for popular education, rational recreation and mutual improvement. Although the creation of a visually literate public was an important consideration, there was little specific debate about how this should be achieved and no evidence of systematic plans to create a specific category of artistic culture. Stuffed animals and obscure mineral samples were packed into crowded rooms alongside copies of old masters. Little guidance was offered to the visitor, and the municipal museums themselves were little more than enlarged domestic houses. Museums focused on providing a rich visual experience of the unusual. They were places in which visitors were free to form their own narratives and interpretations with a relative absence of direction and regulation. It was only when artists gradually gained more influence over hanging that curatorial direction became evident. Even then, this direction was limited, given that curators at Salford, Stockport and Warrington were required to be authorities on ornithology and mineralogy as much as fine art. It was in the 1870s that specialist fine art curators began to appear in municipal museums, and then only in larger galleries such as the Walker in Liverpool.

This is not to say that museums lacked a specific purpose, but merely that the purpose was often concealed in a broader cultural and educational agenda. The first three municipal museums were all expressions of the local civic culture of the newly formed municipal corporations. Through a nationally significant popular museum, Salford could express its cultural independence from Manchester, attracting royalty and dignitaries from across the world. Similarly, Warrington, a town in apparent cultural decline since its fame in the eighteenth century, could consolidate its standing and memorialise its inheritance through the municipal museum movement. Even Stockport, a town that had shown little interest in museums, could create a haven of culture and refinement in its midst, celebrating the rise of a local liberal public and distracting attention from its crime and social disorder. Yet although all these initiatives were designed as corporate activities, they were heavily dependent both on individual private initiative for their directions and on private patronage for their financial viability. Even after the 1850 Public Libraries Act liberalised the municipal funding regime, most municipal museum collections were dependent on private patronage to supply their exhibits. Therefore early municipal museums were more the reflection of the interests and tastes of benevolent collectors than of a broader consensus about art. Indeed, museums were an important means by which collectors ensured that their own tastes became exemplars of a broader public taste. The donation of a specific type of painting, such as old master copies in Warrington, helped the local resurgence of this particular canon and shaped the future of later municipal collecting. Dealers such as Agnews could add value to their wares by placing them in a public gallery, a place of communal celebration, thereby legitimising their cultural status. There were, however, important limitations to this strategy. The process of legitimisation and canonisation inevitably depended on the existence of an engaged, if somewhat compliant, municipality and a network of patrons prepared to indulge the civic ritualism of this practice. In a town such as Stockport, where museum activities were driven mainly by the force of the local MPs, the lack of a network of public patrons to support the initiative soon became a significant handicap. Municipal museums could build civic identity only if they were successful in engaging with pre-existing patron networks and their cultural preoccupations.

NOTES

1 See Chapter 5.

2 J. S. Cowan, 'Joseph Brotherton and the Public Library Movement', *Library Association Record*, 59 (1957), 156–9.

3 *An Act for Encouraging the Establishment of Museums in Large Towns*, 21 July 1845, 8 and 9 Vic. c. 43.

4 George Dawson, evidence, in *Minutes of Evidence Taken before the Select Committee on Public Libraries*, vol. 1 (London, 1849), 1297–8.

5 These claims need to be treated with caution as they were dependent on rather haphazard calculations made by junior museum attendants.

6 Edward Edwards, evidence, in *Minutes of Evidence Taken before the Select Committee on Public Libraries*, vol. 1, 348–52.

7 *The Guide to Manchester and Salford* (Edinburgh, 1877).

8 T. Bergin, D. Pearce and S. Shaw, *Salford: A City and its Past* (Salford, 1974), 92.

9 Quoted in F. A. Bruton, *A Short History of Manchester and Salford* (Manchester, 1927), 2.

10 E. O'Brien, *Eminent Salfordians*, vol. 1 (Salford, 1982), 31–2.

11 *Manchester Courier*, 26 August 1846.

12 Salford was incorporated in 1844; for details see Bergin, Pearce and Shaw, *Salford*, 90.

13 *Manchester Courier*, 19 August 1846.

14 *Manchester Courier*, 26 August 1846.

15 Bruton, *History*, 143–4.

16 *Manchester Courier*, 26 August 1846.

17 Report from the General Purposes Committee to the Council, 13 June 1849, in Salford Royal Museum and Library (hereafter SRML) Annual Report 1849, Salford Library Local Studies Centre.

18 *Salford Weekly News*, 11 April 1874, in Manchester Cuttings Book, MCL, F942.7389 Sc4.

19 G. Simpson, 'Historical Notes on South Manchester' (cutting from *South Manchester Gazette*, 1885–86), MCL, F942.7395 M128.

20 Manchester Cuttings Book, MCL, F920.04273 o1.

21 Indeed, as Mullen points out, when the Public Libraries Act of 1850 was enacted on 14 August, the Salford public library had already been open for seven months. The corporation levied a library rate with questionable legality until 1893, when a local improvement Act finally enabled the provisions of the 1855 public libraries legislation. B. Mullen, *The Royal Museum and Libraries, Salford* (Salford, 1899), 15.

22 Cowan, 'Brotherton', 156–9.

23 However, much of this sum had been contributed by Langworthy. O'Brien, *Eminent Salfordians*, vol. 1, 10.

24 SRML Committee, Report, 4 July 1849, in SRML Annual Report 1849, 63.

25 SRML Executive Committee, 9 November 1853, Salford Library Local Studies Centre.

26 SRML Executive Committee, 21 August 1849.

27 SRML Executive Committee, 21 August 1849.

28 Report, 1 October 1849, in SRML Committee Annual Report 1849.

29 SRML Executive Committee, 12 February 1850.

30 William Jenkinson, report, 1 November 1850, in SRML Annual Report 1850.

31 SRML Executive Committee, 23 July 1850.

32 SRML Executive Committee, 18 February 1851.

33 SRML, Third Report of the Executive Committee, 1851, 82.

34 SRML Executive Committee, 18 March 1851; Third Report of the Executive Committee, 1851, 82.

35 SRML Committee, 31 May 1852.

36 SRML Committee, 17 June 1852; E. R. Langworthy, report, 9 November 1852, in SRML Annual Report 1852.

37 E. R. Langworthy, report, 9 November 1852, in SRML Annual Report 1852.

38 SRML Committee, 22 June 1852, 182–3.

39 E. R. Langworthy, 7 November 1854, in SRML Annual Report 1854.

40 SRML Committee, 1 March 1853. The implication is that the quality of reproduction was very poor; many were probably 'shilling engravings'.

41 Brotherton, letter to Langworthy (copy), SRML Committee, 1 March 1853.

42 SRML Committee Annual Report 1855, 11–16; Annual Report 1857, 14–18.

43 SRML Committee Annual Report 1855, 11–16; Annual Report 1857, 3.

44 SRML, Third Report of the Executive Committee, 1851, 83.

45 E. R. Langworthy, report, in SRML Committee Annual Report 1855, 8.

46 SRML Committee, 21 June 1859, 285.

47 Salford Corporation, Proceedings of Council, Seventh Report of the Executive Committee, 1855–56, 159–63, Salford Library Local Studies Centre.

48 SRML Committee, 25 October 1859, 339.

49 Salford Corporation, Proceedings of Council, 1856–57, 105–6, 8 July 1857.

50 SRML Committee, 22 May 1855.

51 SRML Committee, 10 June 1856, 151–3.

52 Mullen, *Royal Museum*, 29.

53 SRML Committee, 24 March 1853, 252; 7 June 1853; 15 November 1853.

54 E. R. Langworthy, report, in SRML Committee, Annual Report 1857, 10.

55 E. R. Langworthy, report, in SRML Committee, Annual Report 1857, 10.

56 James Renshaw, Executive Committee Report, SRML Committee, 24 July 1857, 12.

57 SRML Committee, 10 June 1856, 153.

58 Some members of the former voluntary committee did, however, continue to work for the museum and were admitted to the corporation's own management committee. These included James Renshaw, Charles Bradbury, William Foyster, Thomas Davies, Robert Lomas and William Watkinson Platt. SRML Committee, 11 August 1857, 397.

59 E. R. Langworthy, SRML Committee, Annual Report 1858, 3–4.

60 E. R. Langworthy, SRML Committee, Annual Report 1859, 3–12.

61 E. R. Langworthy, SRML Committee, Annual Report 1860, 3–21. The committee claimed to have attracted 2,110,831 visitors in the period, compared with 1,658,484 at the British Museum, 1,98,4017 at the National Gallery and 1,216,506 at the South Kensington Museum.

62 *Salford Weekly News*, 20 October 1860.

63 SRML Committee, 27 March 1860, 410–12.

64 SRML Committee, 27 March 1860, 410–12.

65 E. R. Langworthy, SRML Committee Annual Report 1861, 3.

66 SRML Committee, 19 June 1860, 445.

67 J. W. Weston, SRML Committee Annual Report 1863, 3–4.

68 Salford Corporation Minutes, 2 June 1863, vol. 4, 442–3.

69 J. W. Weston, SRML Committee Annual Report 1863, 6–7.

70 J. W. Weston, SRML Committee Annual Report1864, 3–4.

71 J. W. Weston, SRML Committee Annual Report, 1866, 5.

72 *Manchester Guardian*, 23 May 1863.

73 Thomas Davies, SRML Committee Annual Report 1873, 5.

74 Thomas Davies, SRML Committee Annual Report 1884, 4.

75 Thomas Davies, SRML Committee Annual Report 1879, 8.

76 *Manchester Guardian*, 14 May 1864.

77 SRML Committee, 10 July 1866, 81.

78 J. W. Weston, SRML Committee Annual Report 1867, 5; Annual Report 1868, 4–5.

79 Such Sir M. A. Shee's portrait of William Roscoe and S. W. Reynolds's portrait of P. Thompson, the first MP for Manchester. Peter Gendell, SRML Committee Annual Report 1869, 13–14.

80 SRML Committee, 25 May 1869, 490; 8 June 1869, 497.

81 Peter Gendell, SRML Committee Annual Report 1869, 6.

82 Peter Grendell, SRML Committee Annual Report 1870, 14; Annual Report 1871, 6.

83 *Manchester Guardian*, 3 June 1865.

84 Thomas Davies, SRML Committee Annual Report 1874, 6.

85 Thomas Davies, SRML Committee Annual Report 1876, 3.

86 *Manchester Guardian*, 21 May 1867.

87 J. W. Watson, SRML Committee Annual Report 1867, 34.

88 Thomas Davies, SRML Committee Annual Report 1876, 3–4.

89 Thomas Davies, SRML Committee Annual Report 1878, 6.

90 Thomas Davies, SRML Committee Annual Report 1878, 7–8.

91 I. Bowes, SRML Committee Annual Report 1890, 4.

92 Advertisement for *Catalogue of the Loan Collection of Pictures, Jubilee Exhibition 1894*, MCL, L 708.273 SALa.

93 *Salford Weekly News*, 15 May 1880.

94 Thomas Davies, SRML Committee Annual Report 1878, 8.

95 Thomas Davies, SRML Committee Annual Report 1879, 8–9.

96 I. Bowes, SRML Committee Annual Report 1885, 4.

97 I. Bowes, SRML Committee Annual Report 1889, 4–5.

98 Thomas Davies, SRML Committee Annual Report 1879, 8–9.

99 *Salford Weekly News*, 15 February 1896.

100 *Salford Weekly News*, 28 March 1896.

101 J. G. De Mandley, SRML Committee Annual Report 1899, 5.

102 *Salford Weekly News*, 15 February 1896.

103 J. B. Smith, letter to William Gosling, 11 September 1856, cited in 'The Opening of Vernon Park' (cutting), Stockport Reference Library Miscellaneous Cuttings Collection, S C 71.

104 *Stockport Advertiser*, 17 April 1858.

105 H. Fancy, *A History of Stockport Museum* (Stockport, 1971).

106 E. Hewitt, 'Stockport Museum: Its History and Aims', Conference of the Museums Association, 25 April 1912.

107 J. B. Smith, letter, Stockport Borough Parks Committee Proceedings, 26 September 1861, Stockport Reference Library.

108 Fancy, *History*, 1–2.

109 *Stockport Advertiser*, 26 October 1860.

110 *Stockport Advertiser*, 26 October 1860.

111 'When Napoleon was Attacked in the Park …', *Stockport Heritage Magazine*, 3:6 (Summer 1995).

112 Fancy, *History*, 4–5.

113 *Stockport Advertiser*, 22 March 1861.

114 Stockport Borough Parks Committee Minutes, 2 June 1862, Stockport Reference Library.

115 Public Notice, Stockport Reference Library Miscellaneous Cuttings Collection, S C71.

116 Stockport Borough Parks Committee, 2 December 1861; Stockport Borough Manorial Tolls Committee Minute Book, 14–28 May 1862, Stockport Reference Library.

117 Fancy, *History*, 4–5.

118 *Stockport Chronicle*, 24 September 1874; *Stockport Libraries: A Century of Service* (Stockport, 1975).

119 Extract from *Report of the Libraries and Museums Committee* (Stockport, 1876), 12–13.

120 I. Sellers, *Early Modern Warrington 1520–1847* (Lampeter, 1998).

121 P. O'Brien, *Warrington Academy 1757–86* (Wigan, 1989).

122 W. B. Stephens, *Adult Education and Society in an Industrial Town: Warrington 1800–1900* (Exeter, 1980), 26–36.

123 G. Carter, 'William Beaumont (1797–1889) and the Town of Warrington in the 19th Century', diploma thesis, University of Liverpool, 1983.

124 Warrington Council Minutes, vol. 4, 3, Warrington Public Library Local Studies.

125 Broadside Collection, Warrington Public Library Local Studies, W352.921.

126 Warrington Council Minutes, vol. 23, 631.

127 Warrington Council Minutes, vol. 6, 3.

128 Warrington Council Minutes, vol. 6, 3.

129 Warrington Museum Committee Annual Report 1890, Warrington Public Library Local Studies.
130 *Warrington Guardian*, 6 October 1877.
131 Warrington Museum Committee Annual Report 1848, 2.
132 Fildes was knighted in 1906 for his services to art.
133 Warrington Wood was one of the most celebrated nineteenth-century British sculptors. After a local education he spent most of his career in Rome.
134 *Warrington Guardian*, 3 October 1877.
135 *Catalogue of the Exhibition Held at the Opening of the Art Gallery* (Warrington, n.d.), Warrington Public Library Local Studies, P.S. 20.
136 *Warrington Guardian*, 6 October 1877.
137 Warrington Council Minutes, vol. 50, 32–3.

5

A 'solid foundation'? Art schools and art education

Schools of art and design became part of the urban infrastructure of the Lancashire region many years before the creation of major municipal art galleries. By the mid-1840s, both Liverpool and Manchester had established schools of art or design, and thirty years later almost every major town in the north-west had an art school of some sort.[1] This remarkable growth in public art education was partly the product of local initiatives and partly the work of government policy at a time when the promotion of art design education was seen as essential for the development of Britain's design- and craft-related industries. It is important to stress, however, that demands for artistic education came from a number of sources, many of which were unconnected with industry or government.[2] For many in the upper middle classes, art education formed a central part of liberal education. It was also regarded as an important polite art, especially for ladies, to be pursued as part of a sophisticated leisured lifestyle. Thus some of the earliest art schools were developed not in industrial towns, but in older county towns such as Norwich and York, which were home to a large middle-class population.[3] A system of art education was also essential to those who sought careers as professional fine artists, and while Lancashire could support only a limited number of these, their ranks were bolstered by those who worked in the decorative arts and related craft trades. Thus a widespread demand for art education existed in the region well before the formation of formal art schools. In the eighteenth century, most artistic training was conducted in the home or in the studio of a local drawing master – usually a professional artist who took on young men for what amounted to apprenticeships. Drawing masters would also visit the houses of the urban elites, giving instruction in the polite arts to the wives and children of the middle class. As early as the 1770s, regional artists recognised the important role that societies and academies could play in the development of young artists and the dissemination of new ideas and techniques. However, as with other forms of eighteenth-century associational life, small and transitory memberships often made it difficult for artists' societies to be sustained for more than a few seasons of activity.[4]

The first society of artists in the region was formed in Liverpool by three local drawing masters, Richard Caddick, Thomas Chubbard and Ottiwell Worrall. The society held its first meetings in 1769, with Joseph Deare, uncle of the celebrated sculptor, renting modest premises for the society at 30 John Street. Although an apparently autonomous professional organisation, it seems to have had significant support from wealthy patrons, most notably the local watchmaker and philanthropist John Wyke.[5] Little is known about the early activities of the society, but classes of study from cast models seem to have featured prominently. A number of plaster casts were obtained from Flaxman, and the society attracted at least twenty-two members, with the notable engraver P. P. Burdett acting as president.[6] The original society lasted only a year but was revived in 1773 with William Caddick, one of its former members, as president. Details of its activities are unclear, although William Roscoe clearly assisted in its reformation.[7] This new group had a significantly larger membership – fifty-nine are recorded on its rolls – and had a much more specific educational function. A lecture series was the key feature of its published programme, with addresses on architecture, anatomy, the theory of forms, perspective and the art of design. Drawing classes also featured; new casts were purchased, and payments were made to living models. In August 1774 the society organised a public exhibition, open to all artists, which came to be regarded as the first provincial art exhibition in Britain.[8] Despite these early successes, the society struggled, and on 2 November 1775 it was dissolved and all its property sold. The tendency of artists to lead a somewhat nomadic lifestyle, moving from town to town in search of commissions, made it extremely difficult for an academy to be sustained adequately. It also seems that the actual management of the academy was in the hands of a very small group of people. Roscoe is known to have observed that the society's failure was primarily due to the departure of one key member to Germany.[9]

In 1783 a new artistic circle was formed, the Society for Promoting the Arts in Liverpool. This group revived plans for a painting and drawing academy and put in place an ambitious scheme for a new exhibition in the city.[10] In contrast to previous societies, the management of this new body was largely in the hands of art patrons. Roscoe served as a vice president, with his friend and fellow collector Henry Ince Blundell as president and Thomas Taylor as secretary. Although little is known about the educational work of the society, its exhibitions again drew the attention of nationally recognised artists. Its 1783 exhibition attracted two works by Sir Joshua Reynolds – a portrait of Colonel Tarleton and a view of the Thames – while a second exhibition of 1787 attracted the work of not only Reynolds, but also Gainsborough, Wright of Derby, Beechey, Farrington and Fuseli. Seven years later, the society was again practically extinct. Blundell and Roscoe had both stepped down as officers of the society, and it was, it seems, extremely difficult to find 'men of leisure' in Liverpool to run such an organisation.[11]

There appear to have been few attempts to establish drawing academies in Manchester before 1802. This is a little surprising, as there were clearly a number of professional artists and drawing masters active in the city in the late eighteenth century. In 1783 William Green opened an afternoon school for drawing and painting, which three years later operated from his home in Brazenose Street.[12] However, this seems to have been a largely private initiative. It was not until 1802 that William Craig drew up the first plans for a formal public academy, based on those of the Royal Academy, for drawing and designing.[13] Craig offered over 100 drawings to aid the development of the institution, and it is clear from the prospectus that it was intended to be broad in scope, appealing to those who sought an artistic education as a polite accomplishment and to the growing number of industrial designers in the city. The initiative attracted influential support, from representatives of the local gentry such as the Earl of Wilton, art collectors like William Hardman and influential industrialists such as the Heywood family. It was another short-lived venture. Although still operating in 1805, it closed shortly afterwards.[14]

Liverpool was the first city in the region to develop a sustainable society and academy of art, despite the failure of previous attempts. On 11 April 1810 a group of artists met to form a new society, with the object of organising regular exhibitions and establishing a constitution based on the Royal Academy model. Again, Blundell and Roscoe were important figures in the success of this initiative. Blundell was elected patron while Roscoe served as treasurer.[15] The society's first exhibition was held in the August of the following year, and included work by a number of prominent artists outside the academy, including Benjamin West. The academy, perhaps aware of how difficult it was to sustain private artistic societies, began discussions on possible co-operation between itself and other learned societies in the city. It was soon evident that there was strong support for a merger with the literary and philosophy institution, with the Corporation of Liverpool offering to provide £1,000 in support of a new institution in the city. A sum of £1,600 was also invested from the estate of the late Henry Blundell in support of the plans, although it seems doubtful whether this latter sum was ever paid. The new institution, established in 1817, brought the academy under its aegis as the Academy of the Liverpool Royal Institution. However, it is clear that the academy always maintained a degree of independence, and in 1830 it moved out of the LRI buildings altogether to a new location in Post Office Place, provided rent-free by the corporation.[16] It was the support given by the corporation that enabled the academy to continue to have an independent existence: for many years it provided it with an annual grant of £200.[17] The academy provided the first systematic form of art education in the region. From the mid-1820s, both antique and life classes were held regularly, with senior members of the academy giving instruction to students in rota. No fee was charged to the students, and access to the school was on the basis of merit alone. However, as the academy aimed to provide principally higher artistic education to its members, applicants for admission had to demonstrate a significant level of artistic accomplishment. Prospective members were required to submit a drawing or model of an antique statue and a testimonial from the academy or someone known to the academy.[18] In practice, therefore, only students who had already undergone a course of instruction under the supervision of a local drawing master could obtain entrance to the academy.

From the outset, many in the LRI recognised that there was a need to provide a more elementary system of education for artists, draughtsmen and designers that would eventually allow them admission to the higher schools, both in Liverpool and further afield. The LRI took a lead by establishing a school for boys in 1819 and then, five years later, began discussions on the formation of an apprentices' library to serve a wider spectrum of students engaged in the trades of the district. In March 1825 a committee of the LRI met to consider more ambitious plans for the formation of a mechanics' institution. The first classes of the new institute began in an old chapel, and from the outset drawing was a central feature of the curriculum. Curiously, local drawing masters seem to have played little part in the early teaching work of the institution. William Yelverton, a slate merchant from Everton, led the first formal drawing classes in the new school.[19] Teaching tended to focus on elementary and applied skills, with training in perspective, the drawing of plans and architectural design.[20] Some classes unmistakably reflected the priorities of local industrialists. A specialist programme on the art of ship draughting was led by Andrew Morrison, a shipwright of Birkenhead. Yet, surprisingly, this practical training was less successful than some of the general courses and was abandoned in 1826 because of lack of support.[21] Few large local industries had specific requirements for draughtsmen and designers. The potteries, the original craft industry of Liverpool, had closed by 1815, and few other local enterprises had specific demands for drawing skills. This may explain why the teaching institutions of Liverpool tended to place greater emphasis on the fine arts, rather than on the applied arts with specific industrial application.[22]

Yet, despite Liverpool's position as a commercial rather than manufacturing centre, the promoters of the mechanics' institution were keen to emphasise the practical applications of the courses studied at the institute. Dr T. S. Traill noted that although Liverpool could not compete with Manchester for the scope and magnitude of its industrial enterprises, there were many for whom practical artistic training was important, from high-grade occupations such as architecture to the skilled trades of joinery and carpentry. Traill took the view that the institute should not look to the wealth of outsiders to sustain its activities and that those most likely to benefit from it – the lower middle class and working class – should share the costs of its upkeep.[23] In order to attract the fees and support of this group, the institute had to demonstrate how the skills taught would be of direct benefit to their individual trades. However, the school was also to have a broader educational function, namely to allow the labouring classes 'to obtain instruction in the Sciences most immediately connected with their daily occupations'.[24] Traill's comments were designed to demonstrate that the institution was of general cultural value to the city and not merely to individual manufacturers. This way he could mobilise the financial support of local commercial and political elites. The initial subscribers included many of Liverpool's most prominent public men including William Huskisson, John Gladstone MP, Alderman Thomas Case, B. A. Heywood and William Rathbone. Subscriptions from wealthy donors were always an important component of the institute's income.

Patron support was important because the institution's finances were rarely in the black. The autumn of 1830 brought a crisis for the school, and the keeper's salary had to be cut from £80 to just £50 per annum.[25] Subsequent years saw increasing efforts to increase the popularity of the institute and broaden its financial base. Circulars for a series of lectures on plaster casting and modelling in 1832 offered all sculptors, modellers, carvers, stucco workers and ornamental designers access to the lectures, whether they were members of the institute or not. The rather high entrance fee of 2s probably deterred all but the most enthusiastic. Of course, offering non-members cheaper admission would have inevitably discouraged others from becoming members, and thus the institute's directors were caught in a difficult position.[26] Annual membership of the institute cost 21s, so heavy charges had to be made to non-members in order to prevent annual members from allowing their subscriptions to lapse and simply buying into the classes that were most relevant to themselves or their children. One way of encouraging wider support for the institution was to provide members with broader privileges; thus members who did not have sons in attendance at any of the classes were allowed to send one of their apprentices at the reduced rate of 8s per annum. These initiatives seem to have helped stabilise the fortunes of the school, and by 1832 a wide range of art classes was available, including mechanical drawing and practical engineering, perspective landscape and figure drawing and ornamental design, human figure and modelling.[27] However, the attendance figures for these early classes again suggest that fine art classes were much more popular in Liverpool than those dedicated to mechanical or applied art. In 1834 those attending landscape and perspective drawing classes numbered 100, while those in the ornamental, human figure and modelling classes totalled 53. The most poorly attended classes were those in mechanical drawing; just 23 students were enrolled in these programmes, and the average nightly attendance was around a dozen.[28]

The early 1830s saw closer associations between the schools of the Liverpool Academy and the Liverpool Mechanics' Institution, which had opened in 1825 as the Liverpool Mechanics' School of Arts. Although no formal connection existed, a number of the younger members of the academy assisted in teaching at the schools. Until 1832, Edwin Lyon, a pupil at the academy, taught regularly in the institution.[29] In 1834 W. J. Bishop, an associate of the Liverpool Academy, established a new class in ornamental drawing. The classes were established at the behest of painters themselves and were based on small group tuition. They represented a move towards a more specialist form of tuition, offering students a bridge between the elementary art education offered at the institution and the higher-grade work demanded of academy students.[30] By 1835 the institute's school was enjoying increasing numbers of students and looking to expand to new premises. In 1837 the school moved to premises in Mount Street, although this did not entirely solve the overcrowding problems. Only the figure drawing and modelling students had rooms reserved exclusively for their own use. The other art classes were forced to share with the existing day classes.[31] However, art teaching was recognised as a key part of the elementary curriculum of the school. Students were required to undertake at least two classes a week in art instruction and undertake a varied programme of drawing, including landscapes, perspective, figures and flowers. While drawing was obligatory for all elementary students, classics – traditionally the foundation of a liberal education – could be omitted.[32]

Mechanics' institutes were, of course, common across urban Britain by the 1840s. Few, however, gave such prominence to art education. The Liverpool institution's art classes were some of the most successful in the provinces and were to lead to the development of the Liverpool School of Art in subsequent decades. Few cities followed Liverpool's example, and it was the failure of private enterprise to provide a system of art education in its industrial centres that prompted parliamentary action. Fears about foreign competition in craft trades, especially from France and the Low Countries, led to the formation of the parliamentary Select Committee on Arts and Manufactures in 1835. The report of this commission led to the foundation of the Government School of Design at Somerset House and plans for the promotion of provincial schools throughout industrial Britain.[33] From the beginning, there was a fundamental disagreement as to what the precise role of the new schools should be. William Dyce and members of the Royal Academy wanted to see new institutions based on the German model – the *Gewerbeschulen* – which were allied to the specific requirements of industry. Others, most notably Benjamin Haydon, saw them primarily as providing foundational training in the arts, focusing on broad principles rather than simply teaching applied skills.

The debate between these two approaches continued for many years. Both Manchester and Liverpool rejected attempts to direct local art teaching towards the needs of specific industries. Haydon's influence was particularly strong in Manchester, where he was invited to give a series of twelve lectures on painting to the Manchester Mechanics' Institute during the autumn and winter of 1837–38. Haydon found Manchester 'in a dreadful condition as to art' and did much to promote the formation of a new school of art.[34] During January 1838 he dined with some of the city's most influential citizens including Edmund Potter, members of the Heywood banking family and the city's leading engineer

Thomas Fairbairn. Within a month, the new Manchester School of Design had been formally established. Its first academic season began in October the same year, with thirty-six students taking classes in basement rooms of the RMI in Mosley Street.[35] From the outset, it was clear that the school was to be conducted on the lines laid down by Haydon. In an initial address to supporters Edmund Potter set out the aims of the school:

> The School of Design at Manchester is based on the same views of public utility as the School of Lyons, teaching the principles of design as applicable to all industrial art, and laying a solid foundation of instruction for all those who may decide upon the pursuit of higher Arts hereafter.[36]

Although there appeared to be unanimity in Manchester as to the direction of art teaching, the practical problems of financing the operation of the school ultimately ensured that compromises had to be made at the behest of the London authorities. The school's first art master, John Zephaniah Bell, was a prominent artist and a committed follower of Haydon with strong views on teaching method. Bell had studied at the Royal Academy in London and with Baron Gros in France. He had travelled extensively on the continent, including Italy and Portugal, and had painted the royal portrait of Queen Maria II.[37] Following Haydon's method, he emphasised the importance of the study of the human form, although a scandal soon threatened the life class. The local artist Robert Crozier recorded that 'a private model of Mr. Bell was seized with a fit in the corridor and a lady and gentleman hearing her moans made a bother'.[38] It is impossible to know how serious this incident was or if Bell was guilty of any misconduct. It was enough to ensure that life classes with female models ceased. Bell then found himself in more difficulty when the directors of the school decided to surrender their independent status and seek financial support from the authorities at Somerset House. The precise reasons for this move are unclear, although it seems that the influence of James Thompson, an important calico printer from Clitheroe, was decisive. Thompson, the school's original patron, had close associations with the Government School of Design in London and negotiated an interim grant of £150 in March 1842, followed the following year by a sum of £250 to be paid annually for three years. The grants were provided on the basis that the Manchester authorities would provide matching funds.[39] It is unclear whether the directors of the Manchester school were aware of how much they would be forced to compromise their own teaching methods in order to receive this grant. The London authorities made it clear that the teaching methods of Bell were inconsistent with the policy of the federal school:

> You will perceive from this that the Council desire you to look upon the drawing of the human figure as a special acquisition, to be learned after the pupil has undergone a preliminary course of ornamental drawing; and which is not to be entered upon at all unless the future purposes of the student should render it desirable …[40]

Initially, it seems that Bell was confident of the support of the Manchester directors and made little effort to comply with the regulations. Eventually his position became untenable, because the Manchester authorities were dependent on the central government grant. Bell resigned in 1843 and the directors clearly felt relieved, hoping that the internal disputes over the management of the school would be over.[41] Unfortunately, Bell's departure continued to be something of an embarrassment. Several of his students instituted a private society for life drawing known as 'The Roman Bricks', which for twenty-two years flourished in an attic room in King Street.[42] Bell himself set up a private continental-style academy in Upper Charlotte Street, Fitzroy Square.[43]

Perhaps the greatest problem for the school was that it was increasingly dependent on government financial support. Mark Philips, a leading patron of the school, was, like many other Manchester Liberals, embarrassed that the school should have to look to London for finance. He saw central subsidy as a degrading affront to local pride and pointedly reminded the committee that 'so long as you receive support from Government you are not left to a free and independent action, as you would be if the support came from yourselves'.[44] Philips's comments were partly a reflection of the ongoing debates about fundamental teaching methods, but there was also a concern that the central authorities were trying to impose a uniform system of industrial training, without appreciating the different industrial characteristics, and thus educational demands, of different cities. Much of the work done in London would be irrelevant to the manufacturers of Manchester.[45] This was to be a concern that was to be repeated frequently in Manchester and elsewhere over the next forty years.

The school's new headmaster, George Wallis, proved to be as controversial as his predecessor. Wallis was a strict disciplinarian whose teaching was, in the words of the school's official reports, 'more directly applicable to the study of the Decorative and Industrial Arts'.[46] His methods were not popular with many of the established students, and there were resignations in almost every quarter of his first two years of office.[47] It is also clear that the directors were aware that the policy of following the regulations of Somerset House threatened to drive away the lucrative support of middle-class students who were more interested in fine art. Consequently, in March 1844, private classes in fine art were established. Although these were not dramatically successful in terms of the numbers enrolled, they proved to be highly lucrative. The directors continued to fight hard to make the school more financially independent, but could do so only by offering fine art courses to wealthier students – precisely the sort of practice the Government School of Design was trying to discourage.[48]

Ironically, although Wallis was viewed as a headmaster who would follow the methods of Somerset House more closely, he too eventually fell foul of the government school's policy. Wallis was very disappointed with the level of support from local industrialists and made it known that he wanted to improve relations between the school and the local textile producers.[49] In this aim he appeared to have the sympathy of the school's directors, who expressed their own concern that their recent industrial exhibition did 'not seem to have been sufficiently understood or appreciated by the manufacturers of this district'.[50] So, in order to attract the interest of manufacturers and apprentices, Wallis attempted to gear teaching to the creative aspects of the local calico trade. One of his first actions as headmaster was to establish a creative drawing class, which, while very successful with students, was not in accordance with central policy. Somerset House directed the Manchester authorities to discontinue the class. Initially, the Manchester committee showed its support for Wallis by ignoring the directive. However, within a week the headmaster received a further letter 'reminding him that he was subject to orders from London, independent from any other party'.[51] Wallis's students and supporters in the school rallied to his cause but the plain facts were that, as James Heywood observed, if central government provided funds for his salary, it had the right to direct teaching policy.[52] Without the government grant it was unlikely that the school could have continued at all.[53] Wallis's resignation was inevitable.

The financial weakness of the Manchester school made it impossible for the directors to defend the professional integrity of their teaching staff against the diktat of Somerset House. Although the central authorities had stressed the importance of local fundraising to support provincial schools, it was in many respects in the interests of Somerset House to make such schools more dependent on the centre by offering generous salaries to teaching staff that could never be met out of local resources. Shortly after the resignation of Wallis as headmaster, the annual grant rose to £350. The Manchester authorities were clearly concerned about their dependence on the centre, but could do little to revive the financial fortunes of the school. An Exposition of Arts and Manufactures, intended as a fundraising as well as educational enterprise, resulted in a loss to the school of £110. The directors recruited the Earl of Ellesmere to head an appeal in a somewhat desperate attempt to eliminate debts, but very few new subscribers were forthcoming.[54] Among the directors and leading subscribers there seems to have been genuine bewilderment about the failure of local manufacturers to support the school. Again, however, discussions revealed a fundamental disagreement as to why the school was failing. The board of directors condemned the lack of interest that the textile trade had shown in the school, arguing that a city which spent £20,000 annually on French patterns and designs should be able to support a school of art. The implication was clear. The school should ally itself even more closely to local trades in order that those trades would render it self-supporting and independent. This was, however, by no means the unanimous view of all subscribers. A leading donor, Salis Schwabe, argued that most of the problems arose from the popular perception that the school was valuable only to those who made pattern designs as part of their trade. For Schwabe and others, the school could be successful only if it made a more general appeal.[55] There were also complaints about the level of education on offer. Joseph Lockett, an engraver to a local calico printer, complained that apprentices were required to spend too much time on severe elementary studies and were required to return to this work with each change of master.[56] George Jackson, a decorator and ornamental manufacturer, took a similar view. Jackson had lectured at the mechanics' institute before the formation of the school of design and had a good knowledge of student demands. For him, the error of the Manchester authorities was in merely creating a drawing school and ignoring the more advanced creative aspects of design.[57] Government policy had provided a steady income for the school but at the cost of stifling educational development and alienating many in Manchester's manufacturing community.

Following the resignation of Wallis, the Manchester School of Design almost collapsed. According to Jackson's evidence to the 1849 Select Committee on the School of Design, student numbers fell from 220 to fewer than 100.[58] Within days, Wallis opened an independent school of art in a house on the site of the Prince's Theatre. The new school was not particularly successful and appears to have been short-lived, but it did attract a number of students from the government school.[59] After Wallis's departure, three headmasters came and went in short succession. The first, Henry Johnson, a historical painter, was chronically unsuccessful, quarrelling with the authorities even more than Wallis had done, and resigned shortly after his appointment.[60] A temporary replacement was made in the shape of a Mr Cooper, but he was dismissed within a year.[61] By this time the Manchester school was on the verge of closure. In the autumn of 1848 it was so desperate to reduce costs that it removed from the RMI to cheaper premises in nearby Brown Street.[62] A private appeal raised £314 to pay off the worst of the debt, although it was only through the generosity of the local MP Alex Henry, who contributed £100, that the deficit could be reduced to a manageable level. By now, far from being embarrassed and reluctant to accept government grants, the Manchester authorities recorded that 'without the Government aid none of the Schools could have been carried on'.[63] This view seems to have been borne out by national comparisons. By 1850, the only government schools of art and design that were not in debt were those in Coventry, Cork and Paisley – and the latter two institutions had been in operation for only a short period.

Was it, then, impossible for schools of art to be self-funding? Or was it the straitjacket of government policy that suppressed local initiative and made it impossible for local schools to break even? The case of Liverpool suggests that art schools could be self-funding, but only if they were allowed to seek out students who were prepared to pay a premium for their studies and to offer the type of art education that would attract this wealthier class of students. Although the key force behind the 1836 parliamentary select committee, William Ewart, had strong Liverpool connections, there is little evidence that the Liverpool authorities copied the findings of his committee in any detail.[64] In particular, there was little in the way of a concerted effort to seek government recognition of the school, despite the fact that the school was suffering renewed local competition. By 1842 the Church of England Collegiate Institute was offering its own programme of art and general education in nearby Shaw Street, with the result that the mechanics' institution lost almost 400 annual subscribers.[65] Worst still, the drawing instruction at the collegiate institute was led by William Bishop, the former head of drawing at the original school of art.[66] Yet Liverpool, instead of modifying its teaching programme and constitution to attract an annual grant from London, took a different approach. The Liverpool school had always had a strong bias towards attracting students in the fine arts and so concentrated on this market. In 1843 it had 160 students in its landscape classes, while mechanical drawing attracted only 38 and naval architecture just 7. Significantly too, the

Liverpool authorities were prepared to encourage smaller classes in higher and more specialised forms of art, such as oil painting.[67]

For a while, in the early 1840s, the Liverpool directors appear to have tried to move the school's teaching practice closer to that of the government schools, perhaps with a view to firm affiliation. The art master Richard Norbury was certainly a strong devotee of the South Kensington approach, having been trained at Somerset House. However, he came into conflict with other masters at the school, most notably John Oakes, who was determined to maintain more flexible teaching methods. Oakes, it seems, largely ignored Norbury's instructions and encouraged students to adopt a more *plein air* approach.[68] Moreover, the Liverpool school had long retained close connections with the Liverpool Academy, which provided teaching staff for the school. Without the co-operation of figures such as John Oakes, William G. Herdman, Charles Seddon, William Bishop and Ephraim Pugh, the school would have found it almost impossible to provide teaching cover for the broad art curriculum it offered.[69] By the mid-1840s, the fine art section of the school appeared to be operating almost as a junior branch of the Liverpool Academy.

The school had long been aware of the problems of providing adequate facilities for those wanting to pursue higher studies.[70] The response of the Liverpool authorities was typically bold. By 1843, a new sculpture gallery had been assembled in the school, with casts from the Elgin marbles and other famous collections, principally those of Henry Ince Blundell, an early pioneer of art education in Liverpool, and his friend and fellow Lancashire collector Charles Townley.[71] Over the next fifteen years the sculpture gallery was extended with further purchases and soon became a key attraction for new students. An 1861 school circular boasted proudly that the gallery 'contains the most numerous public collection of specimens of Ancient and Modern Art to be found anywhere in this country, except in the Galleries of London and Edinburgh'.[72] The presence of such an important resource within the school ensured that figure drawing and drawing from the cast would always play an important role in its educational programme. To have such a collection and not to offer fine art classes would have been foolish, especially as there was a large body of Liverpool Academicians prepared to offer their teaching services.

The independent nature of the Liverpool school was not, however, simply the product of the presence of the Liverpool Academy in its midst. It is doubtful whether Liverpool's local industrial elite had any direct interest in promoting the South Kensington system. Without any significant local industries that required technical forms of drawing education, there was little incentive to adopt the central curriculum. When the school moved briefly to a more South Kensington-style system in 1843–44, student enrolment fell significantly.[73] Even if the Liverpool authorities had wanted to try to attract a central grant, it is doubtful if they would have been able to do so under the pre-1849 conditions of award. It was well known that the government authorities were reluctant to fund schools attached to mechanics' institutes, partly because of fears that they were 'political' bodies. In any case, the Liverpool school was not an isolated institution, or an outgrowth of another institution like the school at Manchester. Instead, it was part of a broader educational facility offering a programme of liberal education to the sons of its members. As part of a federal college, it enjoyed some financial protection from its governing body, guaranteed tenure and could generate sufficient income from within its own resources by offering a broad curriculum.

It is significant that shortly before Henry Cole reformed the system of central government funding for provincial art schools in 1854, the Manchester authorities had themselves begun to move to a broader and more creative curriculum of art education, similar to that in Liverpool. One might have expected the Manchester school's new headmaster, J. A. Hammersley, appointed in 1849, to have been even more committed to London practices than his predecessors. Hammersley, a pottery designer by trade, had worked in Somerset House as an art master and then spent three years as head of the Government School of Design in Nottingham.[74] Yet the Manchester school was in such a parlous state that the key priority was to attract students and generate revenue. Hammersley achieved this objective in a similar way to Liverpool, namely by emphasising the non-vocational aspects of art training and providing more advanced classes for those interested in pursuing fine art. His decision to put his own landscape works on public exhibition as a form of self-promotion may have antagonised South Kensington purists and the dogmatic *Journal of Design*, but the gamble appears to have paid off.[75] By 1850, Hammersley had boosted the numbers of adult students with the promotion of a life class. The strategy made strong commercial sense. While artisan trainees who tended to be concentrated in the technical classes paid just two shillings per month in fees, the wealthier students who largely sought fine art teaching paid two guineas per quarter.[76] Only by promoting fine art and higher-grade teaching could the school be viable.

When Hammersley took over the headship of the school, it is clear that many directors felt the institution was practically insolvent and would have to close.

Fortunately, a majority 'entertained the opinion that its languishing condition was more attributable to injudicious interference on the part of the Central Government than to local indifference …'.[77] Yet the Manchester authorities found it difficult to resist this interference, dependent as they now were on London for a £600 per annum annual grant covering Hammersley's higher salary and related teaching costs. Worse still, from Manchester's point of view, was that there was increasing political concern about the rising cost to the Exchequer of the government art schools. Many argued that the huge sums offered to subsidise the schools were simply being wasted. Instead of producing artisan designers for the needs of industry, public money was being used to subsidise fine art study and the recreational interests of the middle class.[78] Professional artists and independent drawing masters tended to share this concern, worrying that their students were being lost to a publicly subsidised form of fine art study. The Manchester drawing masters were particularly vocal in their hostility to Hammersley's new fine art classes and issued a petition to Parliament in 1850 condemning 'the perversion of the School into an ordinary drawing academy'.[79] For the drawing masters, the subsidy of an institutional system of fine art education was an attack on the free trade principles of Manchester Liberalism, and they called for complete withdrawal of the grant 'allowing art education in Manchester to proceed on a system of free and unrestricted competition – in short, on free trade principles'.[80] The concern at the alleged unfair competition and waste alarmed the local Liberal establishment, and it is significant that it was a Manchester MP, Thomas Milner Gibson, who moved the motion for the 1849 Select Committee on the Government School of Design.[81]

The 1849 select committee brought about, in effect, the nationalisation of art education. The committee's proceedings revealed considerable scepticism among the business community about the value of teaching fine art in any form to commercial designers. Manchester's Joseph Lockett 'went so far as to say that if Raphael himself could be recalled in all his glory, he would find a man for 20s. a week who would be more useful to him as a designer'.[82] The committee's report acknowledged that there were many differences of opinion about the value of art schools but felt that public subsidy could be justified if the schools concentrated on providing mass education for artisans and focused attention on more practical matters of vocational education.[83] The government's response to the report was to establish the Department of Practical Art, under Henry Cole, and what amounted to a national curriculum, with a national course of instruction, a national competition and a national system of examinations. For the provincial schools of design, this move had a number of important financial implications. The first important change was the abolition of fixed salary payments to masters. In future, salary payments would have to be paid directly from fee income, with central government merely guaranteeing a minimum figure of £70. In January 1853 the Board of Trade laid down tighter rules requiring each school to pay a portion of its fees to its staff. Little over a year later, in March 1854, the Board of Trade abolished annual salary subsidies in favour of a series of graduated payments based on the number of teaching certificates that individual art masters held. This, of course, immediately placed the jobs of non-certified teachers and drawing masters in jeopardy, as art schools would receive no direct grants in support of their teaching work. The move was intended partly to raise standards, partly to reduce costs and partly to drive out fine artists not educated at the government schools. A year later, a further change was introduced, aiming primarily to encourage art schools to focus on the teaching of children in 'schools for the poor' – the public elementary schools. After 1856, payments made to art schools were dependent on the examination results that local schoolchildren obtained. Art masters were required to recruit actively from the public elementary schools; if they failed, not only would the school receive no payments on results, but it would also lose the state contribution to the masters' salaries.[84]

Although the rationalisation of the payments system was driven by Benthamite logic and principles of Liberal meritocracy, there were immediate practical problems. First, how would art schools who had very highly-paid headmasters funded from the centre, like Manchester, be able to meet the funding gap consequent on the new regulations? Secondly, how would schools in poorer industrial areas with very ill-educated populations be able to attract sufficient quality students to pass enough exams in order to pay for teaching programmes? Even if schools were successful in examinations, their level of funding would not necessarily increase in absolute terms. It was clear that Cole did not intend to allow provincial art schools, however successful they were in examinations, to force an increase in overall aggregate spending. The overall level of expenditure would be capped by raising the standards required to pass examinations.[85]

The changes to the system of government funding caused further problems for the Manchester school. The early 1850s were a difficult time for the Manchester authorities. Their school had been severely criticised, somewhat unfairly, by the 1849 select committee report, and the local directors found it difficult to persuade the Manchester public to provide sufficient support to the school through private subscriptions. This was partly because of the internal disputes over teaching methods, but also partly because the 1850s saw a number of major public subscription projects in the city that competed for philanthropic attention – from the Royal Infirmary and the Peel Monument to the free public library and the development of Owens College.[86] In fact the Manchester public were more generous than most. The 1864 Select Committee on Schools of Art reported that the Manchester school attracted a larger amount of private subscription income than any other school that returned figures.[87] However, this 'success' concealed significant problems. Manchester was forced to engage on a major subscription drive to protect its voluntary income, although this income still fell after the new funding code was introduced.

Initially, the school did benefit from South Kensington's decision to give local art schools more discretion over the details of teaching policy. With the new headmaster taking more interest in fine art, the well-known art dealer Thomas Agnew began to assist in the revival of the school, and the school of design was reopened in 1853–54 as the Manchester School of Art.[88] Following visits to art schools in Munich and Nuremburg, Hammersley proposed that the school should promote and develop a formal academy of art in Manchester for the benefit of professional artists.[89] 1854 also saw the school move back to better premises in the RMI. Yet much of the progress that the school had made was undermined by the changes to the system of government funding. The Manchester committee was among those who protested the loudest at the changes that were introduced. At first it simply sought assurances that there was no intention on the part of South Kensington to reduce overall levels of funding. However, these assurances were not forthcoming, and Thomas Bazley responded by launching a fierce attack on Cole's new funding schedules. While money was lavished on the London establishment, the provincial schools were left to starve:

Art Education cannot be conducted without large and expensive class-rooms, galleries, and collections of sculpture, engravings, specimens of natural history, &c; and salaries adequate to obtain the services of able Masters. This principle, it has to be said, is fully avowed by Government as regards the metropolis, but exactly the reverse is the rule assumed for the provincial Schools and 'the Department of Science and Art' so far disavows for them what it builds upon in the metropolis, as to rule that 'no portion of the funds afforded by Government shall be applied to the maintenance of *establishment,* or to any purpose but direct instruction – that is to say partial payment of the salary of Masters, and part purchase of examples – save only in London, where everything is to be done at the public expense.[90]

The imposition of the new funding code left Manchester with a huge hole in its finances. The first year of the new code saw the government grant drop to just £394 11s 6d, compared with £600 in previous years. This change came at a particularly difficult time when the school had recently incurred additional expenses consequent on its return to the RMI.[91] An individual donation of £95 helped meet some of the deficit, but there was serious doubt about whether the school would be sustainable unless other revenue sources could be tapped.[92] Subscription income, which had reached a high of £295 in 1855, fell to £255 in 1858 and then to less than £230 by 1861.[93] The school attempted to meet this shortfall by expanding its teaching activities in order to boost overall fee income. In the short term, this was successful: its fee income rose from £313 in 1855 to £513 three years later.[94] However, the fee income seems to have been somewhat volatile, and by 1861 the total sum brought in by student fees had again dropped below £400. Around a third of the overall fee income came from Hammersley's private classes, conducted mainly for the benefit of middle-class students who were undergoing instruction more for amusement than for professional development.[95] It is likely that demand among this group was most sensitive to the fluctuations in disposable income consequent on the general economic conditions of the early 1860s. In order to try to make the school viable, Hammersley had made particular efforts to tap this source of income, yet it was a source that would quickly diminish in the years of economic depression.

Ironically, it was Hammersley, who had done so much to rescue the school, who almost unwittingly brought about its collapse. In 1862 he left his Manchester post, and with him went his protected salary grant of £300.[96] Cole was, of course, keen to eliminate such grants but was unable to cancel existing contracts. However, when a master moved on, a grant could then be paid on the basis of the new regulations. Instead of a block grant of £300 with additional payments for extra teaching, future payments to Manchester were to be purely on the basis on the number of certificates the new art master held.[97] Bazley again complained about the school being left to starve and lobbied his parliamentary colleagues for a change in the law.[98] Eventually, there was some liberalisation of the financial codes after the appointment of a new parliamentary select committee on art schools in 1863. The changes were already too late for many schools. Between 1854 and 1863 eleven schools of art or design closed, including those in Llanelli,

Merthyr Tydfil, Westminster, Camden Town, Swansea, Dunfermline, Plymouth, Belfast, Burslem, Tavistock, Hereford and Sunderland.[99] Without the political support of Thomas Bazley and the financial support of his friend R. N. Philips, the Manchester school might have joined this list.[100]

The school's declining subscription list may also have indicated increasing frustrations with the way in which South Kensington treated provincial art schools. Bazley and his Liberal colleagues were among the most outspoken opponents of the national curriculum of art instruction, believing that it would inevitably mean a diminution in their national position. The Manchester School of Design was one of the first to be established and had been created largely by local effort and local subscriptions; it was a source of local pride as much as the new free library and Royal Infirmary. Consequently, the Manchester committee made it clear that it was 'not prepared to be reduced to the rank of an infants' school, or a nursery for the metropolitan establishment at Marlborough House'.[101] The authorities at Marlborough House do appear to have been more than a little concerned about the Manchester protests and, partly to stem opposition to the new system, they sent Sir Charles Eastlake to distribute prizes in Manchester the following year.[102] However, nothing could disguise the fact that the school had become merely a branch school teaching a national curriculum that many in Manchester were uncomfortable with – and if they were uncomfortable with the teaching methods they could hardly be expected to underwrite a higher proportion of the teaching costs.

While Manchester got into financial difficulties as a result of the new code, the authorities in Liverpool seem to have sought recognition, partly because of Cole's reforms. Affiliation to South Kensington not only provided for additional income but would also finance an expansion of the school's outreach activities into the local elementary schools – a key policy objective for the Liverpool Institute. During the 1840s, the school had gone into steady decline following the death of its pioneers and more lukewarm support from the increasingly conservative corporation. By 1851, the school was in financial difficulty following the downturn in the economy, and drastic action was required.[103] The committee's decision to seek official recognition, however, may have come more from fears about local competition than from the immediate financial concerns. William Bishop's rival art classes in the Church of England Collegiate Institute continued to be successful, and if the collegiate institute had obtained funding while the mechanics' institution remained independent, it would have been very difficult for the latter to compete successfully with subsidised classes nearby. In the event, the mechanics' institution obtained recognition but was not provided with a monopoly. Both the mechanics' institution, now called the Liverpool Institute, and the collegiate institute were recognised and funded by South Kensington. The initial plans envisaged the establishment of an entirely new central school and two branches – the Liverpool Institute becoming the south district branch and the collegiate institute the north one.[104] Plans for the new central school never materialised, partly because of competition between the two branches. However, it seems that it was not until Bishop's retirement that the Liverpool Institute came to be regarded as the central school. By 1863 it seems that the collegiate institute's classes were actually generating a significantly higher income from student fees, although the Liverpool Institute's classes were more successful in terms of attracting prizes and government aid.[105]

A major reason for the Liverpool Institute's success, at least in comparison to Manchester, was the Liverpool committee's support of the headmaster and the adoption of a consistent teaching policy. While Manchester underwent many changes of personnel and teaching method, Liverpool was much more stable. After the school's affiliation to South Kensington in 1855, Marlborough House appointed the Scotsman John Finnie to take over the headship, a position that he held until his retirement in 1896. One might have expected this to have been something of a problematic appointment for an independent-minded school like Liverpool with a strong bias towards the fine arts. Finnie had begun his career as an apprentice in the decorating trades before training at the government school at Newcastle and teaching in the Central School of Design in London. However, it seems that his interests in the fine arts grew in Liverpool, and he gradually developed a reputation as a noted landscape painter. He acted as a consulting artist in the early Liverpool autumn exhibitions and was later a leading figure in the Royal Cambrian Academy.[106] During his first few years of headship at Liverpool, he oversaw a significant expansion of the school's activities in both the applied and fine arts. He was particularly interested in increasing provision for women painters. A new day class for ladies was opened on Mondays and Thursdays, and a few years later, in 1860, he formed an additional landscape class. By this time, over 1,713 young people were being taught art under the auspices of the school, including 274 based in the central institute.[107] Despite the fact the Liverpool was now an affiliated school, many classes operated outside the national curriculum. Classes for ladies, naval architects and builders made little reference to the national curriculum and were financed largely from student fees.[108]

Liverpool benefited from the presence of a dynamic master, a consistent policy and an independent-minded committee prepared to support its master in offering a broad curriculum relevant to local needs. While Manchester was constrained by the view that the city, as an industrial centre, should teach applied design, Liverpool, it seems, was allowed to follow a more independent course. This was, no doubt, in part because it was part of a larger, autonomous educational institution that gave it some degree of protection from central encroachment. Manchester depended on the generosity of annual subscribers who received little in return. Liverpool had a membership scheme that provided direct benefits to subscribers in the form of reduced fees and access to club benefits. Most significant of all, perhaps, was that Manchester was required to find £200 per annum from its own resources in the form of rent while Liverpool lived de facto rent-free, as part of a larger federal institution. Without this latter perk there can be little doubt that Liverpool would also have struggled. By 1863 it was widely recognised that the new funding scheme had resulted in the impoverishment of most schools and the closure of several. The Select Committee on Schools of Art of 1864 was an attempt to fend off a crisis.

The crisis was provoked by what became the infamous Science and Art Minute 441 of the Council on Education. This took away art masters' certificate payments, the last remaining element of their guaranteed income, and replaced it with a revised schedule of payment by results. Not only did this upset regional art schools, but it also antagonised the art teachers, who promptly established what amounted to a new trade union, the Association of Art Masters, to fight the plan.[109] The select committee may have been an attempt to defuse the conflict, but in practice it served to highlight just how intractable the problem of art education had become. In Lancashire, Liverpool and Manchester provided the largest schools and those most focused on the fine arts. However, by 1864, most of the major towns in the region had attempted to establish art classes of some kind, and almost all were facing difficulty. The Birkenhead school of art used premises above a piano warehouse, provided by the local MP John Laird, and like most schools depended on the success of the middle-class day school to subsidise artisan evening classes. Bolton had no dedicated building and despite having few facilities had become £800 overdrawn at the bank. Preston's school used rooms in the Institution for the Diffusion of Useful Knowledge but was also £500 in debt. Very few schools had any museums, libraries or dedicated study space for students. Where libraries were being formed, as in the case of Chester, their development was usually dependent on the generosity of the subscribers and donors. The Macclesfield school used money raised from the awarding of national medallions to develop a small museum, but this was never sufficient to meet the needs of students. Other towns were a little more fortunate. Warrington Corporation had pioneered the development of municipal museum and library facilities and the art school was located in the same building, providing students with convenient access to a range of specimens.[110] Yet Warrington was a rare example of a municipality developing art school and art museum facilities in parallel. Other pioneering municipal museums, notably Salford and Stockport, appear to have taken little interest in the art school movement. However, it is important not to exaggerate the importance of museums in the success of schools. Warrington also struggled to recruit enough students to be successful under the system of payment by results. Like Manchester and Liverpool, it had to look to middle-class students in the fine arts to cover funding deficits. Although the new code was an attempt to focus teaching attention on technical subjects, it actually forced schools to provide more special classes in the fine arts in order to compensate for cuts in government funding.[111]

The 1864 select committee did little to resolve the funding problems. Both Cole and the government were reluctant to return to direct subsidy of masters' salaries. The previous decade had seen a rapid expansion in the number of art schools, and it was clearly felt that it would not be financially viable to maintain this expansion if block subsidies were reintroduced. Any return to the old system would have meant a net reallocation of funds from the central schools to the provinces, something which neither Cole nor the government was prepared to countenance. In fact, the average annual cost of supporting provincial schools of art was remarkably low. It was estimated that the average subsidy of a provincial school was just £154 per annum, while the annual subsidy for South Kensington was a colossal £56,542 8s 7d.[112] The select committee did, however, come out strongly in criticism of the existing system of payment by results. It was therefore replaced by a more straightforward capitation payment, whereby schools received a fixed payment for each artisan student who received forty lessons within a year. The new system continued in its basic form until the end of the century.[113]

It is very doubtful whether the new capitation payment had much practical effect on the overall financial fortunes of the schools. It did mean that schools' finances were less volatile and less dependent on the unpredictable nature of examination results. Other aspects of the funding regime were also rationalised, making the system more flexible and recognising the difficulties schools faced in meeting non-teaching costs. A grant of 2s 6d per square foot up to a maximum of 4,000 square feet was made available for the construction of new buildings or buildings adopted for art school purposes. South Kensington would provide half the cost of 'art examples' or specimens used in art schools, provided that they were approved by the central authorities, and there were various small grants and prizes for those successful in the national competition.[114] Manchester welcomed the fact that the new regulations were not so stringent and that masters could direct their attention 'to the specialities of the various localities'.[115] Overall, however, the Manchester authorities were unimpressed by the new regime and were gravely disappointed that the special grants awarded on the basis of examination results amounted to just £60. Manchester's new headmaster, W. J. Muckley, was, broadly speaking, much more sympathetic to the South Kensington system than his predecessor, but even he accused the department of trying 'to bring about as speedily as possible its entire severance with every School of Art in the kingdom'.[116] Although Muckley was committed to a much more applied form of art education, he, like Hammersley, had to expand the day schools in fine art to meet the funding shortfall. By 1867, 'public' classes were bringing in just over £225 in fees, while private classes generated almost £470.[117] Eight years later the difference became even more marked, with private classes accounting for over £835 in fee income and public classes just £330.[118]

Liverpool adopted a similar course to Manchester, promoting day schools and fine art classes very strongly. Satirical commentators had long enjoyed ribbing the institute about the middle-class nature of its 'mechanics', and this tendency seems to have been exacerbated as the century passed.[119] Central government funding for artisan training had been cut so much that there was little incentive to reverse this trend. In 1869, the Liverpool directors hoped that a new, supposedly more liberal funding regime would result in an increase in the number of artisan students. The problem was that the Liverpool school had always enjoyed a large number of students undertaking elementary studies as part of a broader programme of educational instruction, but it was difficult to attract much additional income from their examination results; in 1866 the additional income totalled just £10.[120] It is not surprising to learn, then, that by 1871 the numbers enrolled in elementary classes had been reduced, while those in the advanced classes was allowed to expand. Indeed these classes had expanded to such a degree that new rooms had to be provided above the old museum. By 1874, the lucrative ladies' class enrolled ninety students per annum.[121]

The success of art schools in the late 1860s and early 1870s occurred partly because they became more consumer-oriented, offering the fine art courses that students were prepared to pay for, and partly because the number of potential consumers increased rapidly as the major cities expanded. The development of cheap mass rail travel meant that poorer students were prepared to travel longer distances for higher-class education. The geographical consumer catchment areas of the major schools of Liverpool and Manchester expanded as they began to attract students from across the region. By 1899, the Manchester School of Art had students from as far afield as Chester, Matlock, Mansfield and Halifax, and of the 574 who were enrolled for that year only 230 came from the city of Manchester itself.[122] The major cities were able to obtain this position of influence only by offering higher-quality facilities and training than those in the smaller towns. Yet Liverpool, Manchester and the larger towns were slow to develop purpose-built facilities to house their schools. The first purpose-built schools of art generally appeared in older cities and county towns rather than the new industrial metropolises. Wolverhampton built its school in 1854, Norwich in 1857, Bristol in 1858, Lambeth, Coventry and Nottingham in 1863 and Lincoln and Exeter in 1865. Interestingly, MacDonald argues that schools of art first appeared in towns with a large middle-class population that saw a school of art as a fine art academy and a contribution to the high culture of their own locale.[123] It is, however, important to emphasise the importance of specifically local factors in the development of some schools. The construction of a new building for the Oldham school of art – the Oldham Lyceum – was the work of one local family. In the early 1860s the Lyceum had suffered badly as a result of the mass unemployment in the town brought about by the cotton famine. Elementary class numbers fell off badly, and the art teacher Charles Potter worked without pay in order to help keep the classes going.[124] Partly in order to revive the institution, the local mill owner John Platt provided around £2,000 for the construction of a magnificent Gothic building to house the school, and between 1868 and 1873 the number of students doubled.[125] Self-interested philanthropy could often be a feature of cultural developments in towns where prominent men like Platt constructed 'a monument of his munificence'.[126]

The scale of large industrial metropolises and the nature of cultural politics of larger urban centres made it difficult for one individual to monopolise phil-anthropic effort and become a symbol of the town's progress in the way Platt did with Oldham. Moreover, in practical terms the larger cities needed larger and more expensive facilities to meet the cultural demands of their populations, with most major projects for libraries, museums and schools running into at least five figures. In any case, many clearly felt, by the 1870s, that such public buildings should be paid for out of local taxation and that the newly expanded urban electorate should not, as matter of pride, look to the patronage of the wealthy to satisfy their cultural needs. In theory the Public Libraries Act 1855 gave local authorities power to make grants for the construction of art schools and subsidise their operation. However, the legislation was so badly worded that it seemed to imply that councils could fund museums and libraries or schools of art, but not both.[127] This point of law was not tested until the 1880s, and as most cities already had free libraries or museums, they seem to have been reluctant to fund art schools for fear of having the expenditure struck down by auditors. Had municipalities been keen to fund art schools they could have done so through the promotion of private local improvement Acts. Many towns used these Acts to circumvent rating limits and increase expenditure on municipal museums and libraries. In the case of art schools this was rarely, if ever, attempted.[128]

The result was that even large and successful schools found it difficult to obtain suitable premises. Liverpool Corporation's generosity towards the fine arts is well known. It was one of the first councils to set up a fine art committee and provided generous sponsorship for an annual autumn exhibition. Its leading figures Edward Samuelson, Philip Rathbone and J. A. Picton became high-profile local celebrities, and the exhibition soon became one of the most successful in the provinces, especially after its move to the newly constructed Walker Art Gallery in 1877.[129] Yet the corporation never tested the legislation on the funding of art schools, and it was left to the private initiative of school's directors to raise finance for the new building by fundraising and borrowing. By the time Liverpool's new school opened in 1883, the nearby middle-class suburb of Birkenhead had had a purpose-built art school for some years.[130] The total cost of the Liverpool project was around £12,000, and despite all the efforts to raise funds from other sources, most of the costs were met by a single member of the board of directors.[131]

In Manchester the problem of providing accommodation for the art school proved to be much more acute. In 1875 the school was given notice to quit its rooms in the RMI as the RMI required the facilities as exhibition space.[132] The city council leaders made it clear that the corporation could not be expected to provide funds. The whole of the budget from the penny rate was expended on public libraries and, as branch libraries were soon to be expanded, there was little prospect of the art school receiving money from this source.[133] Unlike

Birmingham, Manchester was not prepared to promote private legislation to circumvent the restriction of the penny rate and increase local taxation to fund the school. While Birmingham opened the country's first municipal school of art in 1885, Manchester was forced to rely on private enterprise to fund its new building.[134] Land was purchased in Cavendish Street for £10,500 following a public subscription supported by the Earl of Derby, the Earl of Wilton, Lord Egerton of Tatton and many of the city's leading industrialists and traders, including Edmund Potter, James Worthington, Richard Peacock and Thomas Ashton.[135] This, however, left a large sum still required for the building. Some monies were promised from the commissioners of the exhibition of 1851, but the trade depression of the late 1870s made it very difficult for the directors to raise the remaining additional capital from local sources. A fundraising art exhibition held in the summer of 1878 had actually lost money, and it was soon decided to construct a building that was 'architecturally less ambitious'.[136] Unfortunately, by the time this decision was made the directors had already entered into contracts for the construction of the school, and it was not easy to identify any major economies.[137] F. W. Grafton, the treasurer of the school, was so appalled that the stone façade was to be removed from the plans that he offered to meet the cost himself, but even this generous offer did little to reduce the overall shortfall. A further fundraising exhibition was held to mark the opening of the school, and a 'Grand Art Union' helped to provide additional income, but a deficit of over £2,000 remained.[138] Servicing a debt of this size threatened to strangle the school's operations. Capitation payments were being received for only about 60 per cent of the students in the school, and the government grant was less than £250 per annum.[139] Aware of these difficulties, Grafton first agreed to pay off the bank interest from his own resources and eventually, with little prospect of the capital sum ever being repaid from school resources, agreed to meet the rest of the debt too.[140] There can be little doubt that without Grafton's contribution the early years of the new school would have been extremely difficult.

It had become clear, by the late 1880s, that even the most successful art schools found it impossible to make an operational profit. The new Manchester school appears to have been remarkably successful in the first decade of its existence, more than doubling its capitation payments and being recognised by South Kensington as one of the most high-ranking institutions in the country. However, the directors frankly admitted that it was impossible for a school made up mainly of artisans to be self-supporting. Even with government grants of £500 per year, the school made a loss of over £250.[141] By now, national government recognised the problem. The 1881 Royal Commission on Technical Instruction recommended a significant increase in the amounts spent on technical education and stated that this should be found from local resources. Although some ambiguity existed as to whether funds should be found from the voluntary or state sector, thanks to the campaigning work of the Manchester MP Sir Henry Roscoe and the National Association for the Promotion of Technical Education, there was increasing recognition that more public money would have to be found. The Technical Instruction Act of 1889 enabled local authorities to raise a penny rate in support of technical instruction. Local funds for technical education were also supplemented by what became known as the 'whiskey money'. The 1890 Local Taxation (Customs and Excise) Act allowed certain revenue from customs and excise duties to be allocated to local authorities either to relieve the rate burden or to support technical education. By 1898, £740,000 of this £807,000 'whiskey money' was allocated to art and technical teaching.[142]

The response of art schools to this change was mixed. Most immediately sought to be municipalised in order to receive rate support. Even though the Manchester committee had, by 1890, attracted the financial support of the legatees of Sir Joseph Whitworth, it immediately looked to the city council for rate aid.[143] Money had been made available through the Whitworth fund and the Jubilee Exhibition profits for an extension, but it was soon found to be insufficient.[144] Thus, in 1893, negotiations were completed to transfer the building to the corporation. The following years saw a rapid expansion of the school's activities and facilities. An impressive plant conservatory was added to the building in 1893 for the study of nature, and a jubilee extension was begun in August 1896. The new extension included a large hall and two galleries, with provision for a textile room and tapestry displays.[145] Municipalisation also brought about changes in the teaching programme of the school. Walter Crane was appointed as a visiting director of design and worked with the permanent staff to arrange applied art study.[146] Although he occupied his position only until the summer of 1896, the quality of teaching at the school continued to attract the praise of the South Kensington authorities, with R. Glazier, T. C. Horsfall and William Burton assisting with higher-grade teaching and lecturing (see Figures 9, 10 and 11).[147]

Not all schools, however, were keen to be municipalised. Despite the adoption of a penny rate for technical instruction, some were disappointed about how much money actually found its way to art and technical schools. In the academic year 1892–93 the Liverpool Technical Instruction Committee was provided with

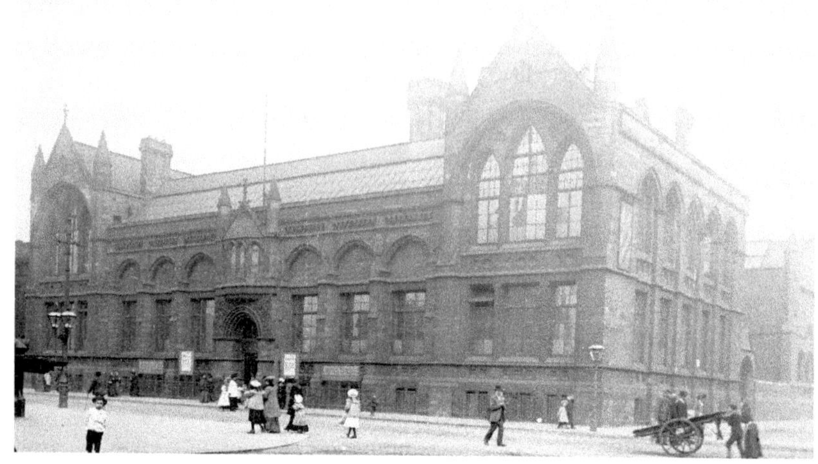

9 Manchester School of Art

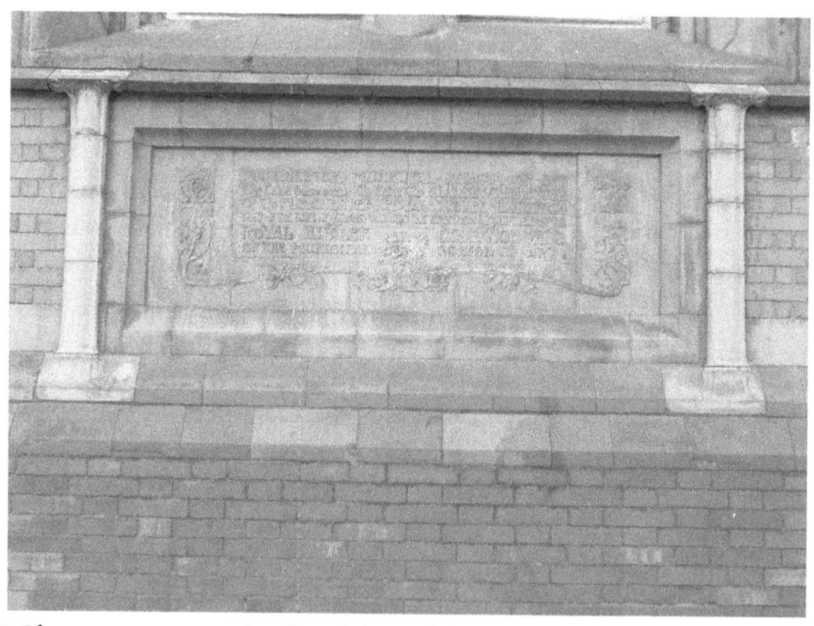

10 Plaque commemorating the Jubilee Exhibition gift to the Manchester School of Art

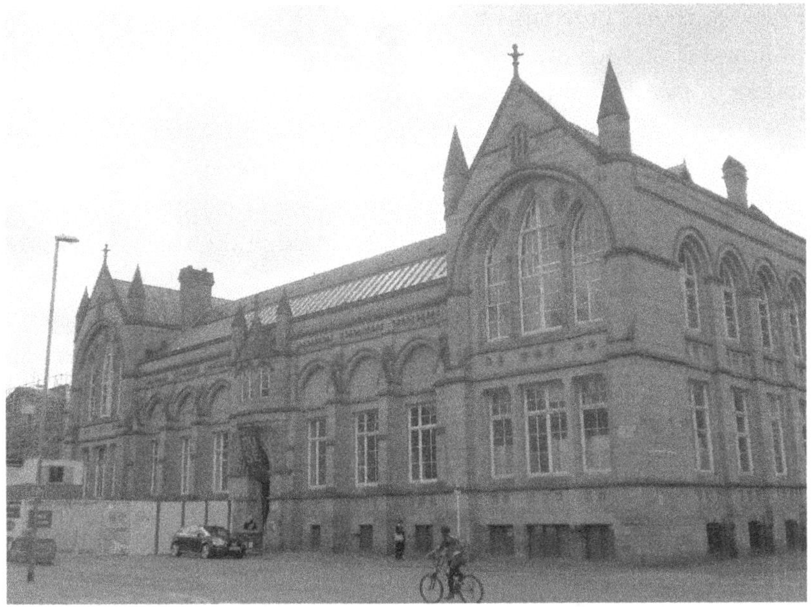

11 The Manchester Municipal School of Art today, now part of Manchester Metropolitan University

a budget of £18,495 for the support of technical education. Yet, in practice, this sum was divided between a whole range of cultural organisations providing further and secondary education classes in the city. The largest portion, £4,275, was given to the museums and libraries sub-committee of the city council, and the University College obtained £1,940, while the school of art received just £250.[148] The Manchester School of Art fared little better. Of the £4,000 raised from the penny rate in 1890, only £500 found its way into the coffers of the school.[149] Faced with such figures, it is not surprising that the more independent-minded institutions such as Liverpool School of Art were cautious about the benefits that municipalisation might bring. In Liverpool co-operation between the school and the municipality was difficult from the start. In December 1890 the school asked the council for a grant of £770 to stabilise its financial position, but received a grant of just £140 for equipment costs. Negotiations with the city council about the possibility of amalgamation continued for some time, but the school was unhappy with the corporation's plans for the school to have a new constitutional relationship with University College. This may have been related to the decision of the University College to change its Roscoe Chair of

Fine Art, which had previously been occupied by senior figures such as Martin Conway and R. A. M. Stevenson, into a chair of architecture.[150] The change to the nature of the chair and the decision of the school to break off negotiations occurred at roughly the same time in 1894.

Following the break-off of negotiations, the University College's applied art department underwent a programme of rapid expansion. Most of this expansion was funded by the city council, although the college also provided some funds from accumulations from the Roscoe chair.[151] New buildings – the famous 'art sheds' – were begun in 1894–95, and the school attracted some of the most prominent artists and art teachers in the north-west, notably R. Anning Bell, C. J. Allen, J. H. MacNair, R. B. Rathbone and Augustus John. Between them they represented some of the most important artistic currents of the period – from the Arts and Crafts influence of Bell and the art nouveau of MacNair to the 'New Sculpture' of C. J. Allen and the English Impressionism of Augustus John.[152] The success of the art sheds and the expansion of the University College's department of fine art clearly had a significant effect on the school of art. The rather conservative landscape work of the school's master, John Finnie, was very staid compared to the work being produced by the younger teachers in the art sheds. Within two years of the opening of the art sheds, Finnie announced his decision to retire.[153] By the time he officially left the school in February 1897, the school was seriously struggling to compete with a University College department in receipt of a large municipal grant and managed to survive only by severely cutting back its teaching staff.[154] Although the school struggled on independently for a few years under the leadership of a new head, Frederick F. Burridge, formerly of the Royal College of Art, the 1902 Education Act practically obliged the corporation to bring forward plans to incorporate it within a co-ordinated municipal plan for further education. However, the city council's plan to fuse the department of applied art and the School of Art met with opposition from all sides and was not executed until 1905. Even then some teachers continued to resist the plan, with J. H. MacNair and Gerard Chowne breaking away to establish an independent school in Sandon Terrace.[155] Interestingly, it was former directors of the Liverpool school who were most marginalised by the new management plans for art education. While the University continued to have guaranteed representation on the governing body of the art school, the council's sub-committee, the school's governors were given no place beyond that necessary to make transitional arrangements.[156] The city council, responsible for implementing a plan for further education in the city, seemed reluctant to engage the co-operation of outside bodies. While the 1902 Act had largely released schools from the tyranny of the South Kensington, the response of the Liverpool artists to the municipal plan suggested a continuing antipathy to state intervention in the direction of art education.

The reality was, however, that art schools had always operated on broadly commercial lines, while the importance of their business made government intervention in their management inevitable. They attempted to attract students from local communities and provide a service to local business engaged in artistic trades, yet the government required them to fulfil a broader national function in artisan education. However, artisan education was inherently unremunerative. Schools were prohibited from providing artistic training in specific trades on the German model, and therefore industrialists were generally reluctant to support them directly or to provide scholarships. Those who required the education offered did not have the resources to meet the full cost of that education and, therefore, some cross-subsidy was necessary. Even schools that attracted a very large amount of private subscription income, such as Manchester, were unable to make an operating profit and had to look elsewhere to keep deficits under control. As Manchester, Liverpool and Warrington soon discovered, the easiest way to do this was to provide more fine art classes for wealthier groups and use these to cross-subsidise artisan classes. Yet when Cole and others discovered the extent of this practice they were outraged, fearing that grants for artisans were being diverted to subsidise those who could pay. In a sense, this was true. Block grants to headmasters who taught artisan and middle -lass students did represent some diversion of funds. However, the cutting of block grants only encouraged the development of more middle-class fine art teaching in art schools and, in some cases, a reduction in the resources applied to elementary education.

Perhaps the most damaging effect of the funding formula was the impact it had on the status of art masters. Senior art masters could obtain a comfortable income, but only by engaging in private work to supplement their core employment.[157] It is notable that in Liverpool and Manchester, prominent artists such as Augustus John and Walter Crane became closely involved in the operation of art schools only after they were municipalised and the position of tutors was guaranteed. Although the schools in Liverpool and Manchester were high-profile, training several hundred fine and applied artists every year, few artists of national prominence chose to teach and work in them until the schools were given improved status and more independence by becoming municipal schools. Many of the early problems of art schools arose precisely because

South Kensington-trained masters and art committees sometimes had different priorities. In Manchester it was found that even those who had trained under the South Kensington system often resented central interference in their teaching methods. It is not surprising, then, that Liverpool gave up its independence only with reluctance and then ignored, whenever it could, strictures from London. Only after the gradual liberalisation of teaching policy in the 1870s did the conflicts die down. However, the basic issue of the system of funding remained. The directors of the Manchester school of art were making the same complaint in 1897 that they had been making for almost forty years: the funding system was bureaucratic, the capitation and examination grants were inadequate, and the volatility of the grant income awarded made long-term budgeting almost impossible.[158]

Municipalisation helped to solve some of the financial problems of the art schools but, as the case of Manchester shows, it did not always end tensions between the major cities and the central bureaucracy. In some respects, municipalisation created new problems for art schools. With new public funds available, it was unlikely that figures like F. W. Grafton would be prepared to underwrite the costs of new art schools. However, in many cases the public sums set aside for technical education never reached the art and technical schools. Instead they were used to provide a general subsidy for further education, or to subsidise existing cultural assets, such as libraries and museums. In some ways, municipalisation took the management of art schools further away from those who had most interest in them – local artists and patrons. In Liverpool, the old art school authorities were excluded from the management of their school, while the new university authorities were cheerfully included in council committees. Many artists clearly disagreed with the city's plans and left to found a private institution. In Manchester, the presence of the philanthropist Charles Rowley on the art gallery committee suggests a more inclusive tone to management there. Yet interestingly, Rowley's account of the development of the school ignores the contribution of Grafton and the many other large donors who paid for the building in Cavendish Street, and instead emphasises his own work and that of the municipality.[159] While there can be little doubt that municipalisation was important in allowing for an expansion of art education, it also cut links with those who had previously supported art schools and rode roughshod over the wishes of artists and consumers. Municipalisation did not necessarily lead to a more inclusive form of art education.

There can be little doubt that art schools made a powerful contribution to the artistic culture of the region. By 1909, there were over sixty publicly-funded schools teaching drawing or art in Lancashire and Cheshire.[160] Although the major schools of art were in almost perpetual financial crisis and subject to ongoing disputes with the South Kensington authorities, they provided elementary art education to thousands of artisan students and were responsible for developing the careers of some of the region's most important artists. William Huggins was one of the first products of the Liverpool Mechanics' Institution to find fame. A noted animal painter, he later diversified into other forms of fine art and made a significant contribution to the artists' colony at Betws-y-Coed. Robert Tonge, regarded as 'the greatest master of landscape painting the Liverpool School of painters produced', was also a product of the mechanics' institution and became a prominent figure in Liverpool before his tragically early death at thirty-three.[161] The close relationship between the school and the Liverpool Academy continued for many years. James Pelham Jnr, the eldest son of the secretary of the academy, attended classes at both the school and the academy. He later established a flourishing practice as an art teacher in Liverpool and, in 1874, helped to reorganise and re-establish the Liverpool Academy following the famous Pre-Raphaelite crisis.[162] Of course, not all of the school's most successful students were entirely impressed by its teaching methods. James Hamilton Hay, who later found fame as an important English Post-Impressionist, was particularly critical of the South Kensington system, which he endured in the art schools of Birkenhead and Liverpool, but he was quick to acknowledge the help of Augustus John, who was then working at the department of applied art in the city.[163]

Although the Manchester school of art tended to place greater emphasis on applied art than Liverpool, it too made a significant contribution to the development of several generations of fine artists. H. C. Whaite, later the long-serving president of the Manchester Academy, was among some of the first prizewinners of the school in 1847, when he took a first-class prize for painting from casts.[164] His academy colleague Robert Crozier was also a student at the school, and he too went on to lead the Manchester Academy. Indeed most of the painters belonging to the famous 1870s 'Manchester School' of artists studied at the local school of art, including George Hayes, Warwick Brookes, E. M. Bancroft, J Houghton Hague, J. Anderson Hague, William Meredith and J. H. E. Partington. The school was responsible for the early training of some of the city's leading architects, such as Thomas Worthington and Edward Salomans, while in later years it also helped develop the careers of the prominent women artists Gertrude Thompson and S. J. Dacre.[165] One would expect the larger regional art schools to produce prominent fine artists, but even smaller schools could boast nationally significant artists among their alumni. Warrington was particularly successful in this respect. Henry Woods began his studies at the Warrington School of Art at the age of nine before becoming a prominent illustrator, a well-known Italian genre painter and a full member of the Royal Academy in 1893. John Warrington Wood studied at the school in the early 1860s before establishing himself in Rome as a sculptor of international fame. However, perhaps the most famous son of the Warrington school was Luke Fildes, who began his studies at Liverpool in 1859 at the age of sixteen. He was soon a student teacher before winning a £50 scholarship to South Kensington school of art in 1863. After entering the Royal Academy, Fildes went on to become a pioneer of social realism painting and, later, a prominent portrait painter, with royal commissions for state portraits of Edward VII and George V.[166] The parliamentarians and government officials who had encouraged the development of schools of art and design had not envisaged them as a training ground for fine artists. The policy of Henry Cole was aimed at discouraging fine art teaching in art schools and ending public subsidies for fine art training. Despite this constraint, the art schools of Manchester, Liverpool and Warrington not only provided a foundational art education for thousands of students seeking work in applied design, they also furthered the careers of a nationally prominent cohort of fine artists.

NOTES

1 For the history of elementary art teaching see G. Sutton, *Artisan or Artist? A History of the Teaching of Arts and Crafts in English Schools* (London, 1967).

2 The general history of teaching provision is outlined in R. Carline, *Draw They Must: A History of the Teaching and Examining of Art* (London, 1968).

3 M. Allthorpe-Guyton and J. Stevens, *A Happy Eye: A School of Art for Norwich 1845–1982* (Norwich, 1982); Q. Bell, *The Schools of Design* (London, 1963), 124–5.

4 For a discussion of the instability of urban associational life see P. Clark, *British Clubs and Societies, 1580–1800* (Oxford, 2000).

5 H. C. Marillier, *The Liverpool School of Painters* (London, 1904), 1–4.

6 B. H. Grindley, *History and Work of the Liverpool Academy of Arts* (Liverpool, 1875), 1–2.

7 Marillier, *Liverpool School*, 3–4.

8 Grindley, *History*, 2.

9 Grindley, *History*, 2.

10 C. Morris, 'History of the Liverpool Regional College of Art 1825–70', MPhil thesis, Liverpool Polytechnic, 1985. 10.

11 Daniel Daulby, letter to Holt, 4 June 1794, cited in Grindley, *History*, 3.

12 See Chapter 2.

13 W. M. Craig 'of Market-street-lane', circular letter, 1 December 1802, MCL, H910.

14 *Laws and Regulations of the Manchester Academy for Drawing and Designing* (Manchester, 1805), MCL, H910.

15 Grindley, *History*, 3.

16 Marillier, *Liverpool School*, 10–12.

17 J. Willett, *Art in a City* (London, 1967), 29.

18 Grindley, *History*, 6.

19 Morris, 'History', 19.

20 H. J Tiffin, *A History of the Liverpool Institute Schools* (Liverpool, 1935), 23.

21 Morris, 'History', 18.

22 E. Roberts, 'The Liverpool Academy as a Teaching Institution', in E. Morris and E. Roberts (eds), *The Liverpool Academy and Other Exhibitions of Contemporary Art in Liverpool, 1774–1867* (Liverpool, 1998), 21–2.

23 Liverpool Mechanics' Institution School of Arts, Addresses, in Lancashire Pamphlet Collections, British Library (hereafter BL), 1866 e7,vii.

24 Liverpool Mechanics' Institution School of Arts, *Address Delivered by Thomas Stewart Traill* (Liverpool, 1825), iii, in Lancashire Pamphlet Collections, vol. 14: Liverpool, BL, 1866 e7.

25 Morris, 'History's, 19.

26 Lectures on Plaster and Wax Casting, Modelling etc, 1 June 1831, in Lancashire Pamphlet Collections, vol. 13, BL, 1866 e7.

27 Liverpool Mechanics' Institution circular (n.d. [1 June 1832]), in Lancashire Pamphlet Collections, vol. 14.

28 Report of the Directors of the Liverpool Mechanics' Institution, 19 March 1834, in Lancashire Pamphlet Collections, vol. 14.

29 Morris, 'History', 21–5.

30 Report of the Directors of the Liverpool Mechanics' Institution, 4 March 1835, LRO.

31 Tiffin, *History*, 112.

32 *Prospectus of the Course of Instruction, Terms and Regulations of the School Attached to the Liverpool Mechanics' Institution* (Liverpool, 1837), 12–14.

33 The standard history of this development is Bell, *Schools*.

34 S. Heydari, 'Manchester School of Art', BA thesis, Manchester Metropolitan University, n.d., 2–3.

35 Heydari, 'Manchester School of Art', 3–4.

36 Cited in Bell, *Schools*, 111.

37 C. Stewart, *Regional College of Art, Manchester – a Short History* (Manchester, n.d.), 2–3.

38 D. Jeremiah, *A Hundred Years and More* (Manchester, 1980), 4.

39 Jeremiah, *Hundred Years*, 5–6.

40 Dyce, quoted in Bell, *Schools*, 112–13.

41 *Manchester School of Design: A Report*, 15 January 1844 (Manchester, 1844), MCL.

42 Stewart, *Regional College*, 3–4.

43 Bell, *Schools*, 114.

44 *Manchester School of Design: A Report*, 15 January 1844, 7–8.

45 *Manchester School of Design: A Report*, 15 January 1844, 9.

46 *Manchester School of Design: A Report*, 13 January 1845 (Manchester, 1845), 5, MCL.

47 However, the total number of students increased. Bell, *Schools*, 117.

48 *Manchester School of Design: A Report*, 13 January 1845, 8.

49 Jeremiah, *Hundred Years*, 6–8.

50 *Manchester School of Design*, 24 February 1846 (Manchester, 1846), MCL.

51 *Report from the Select Committee on the School of Design*, 14 May 1849, in Reports from Committees, 12 of 14 vos, Select Committee vol. 18 (London, 1849), 218–19, paras 2411–20.

52 Bell, *Schools*, 119–20.

53 *Report from the Select Committee on the School of Design*, 219, para. 2421.

54 Manchester School of Design, Annual Report 1847, 6–7, MCL.

55 Manchester School of Design, Annual Report 1847, 11–23.

56 *Report from the Select Committee on the School of Design*, 211, paras 2316–26.

57 *Report from the Select Committee on the School of Design*, 218–19, paras 2411–40.

58 *Report from the Select Committee on the School of Design*, 220, paras 2428–9.

59 Stewart, *Regional College*, 3–4.

60 Bell, *Schools*, 120.

61 Manchester School of Design, Annual Report 1848, 6; Bell, *Schools*, 120.

62 Manchester School of Design, Annual Report 1849, 6.

63 Manchester School of Design, Annual Report 1849, 7.

64 Morris, 'History', 30.

65 *Report of the Directors of the Liverpool Mechanics' Institution*, 8 March 1843 (Liverpool, 1843), 19–20.

66 Morris, 'History', 31.

67 *Report of the Directors of the Liverpool Mechanics' Institution*, 8 March 1843, 20–5.

68 Morris, 'History', 39–42.

69 See details in Roberts, 'Liverpool Academy', 28.

70 The ornamental and figure drawing classes suffered from the lack of casts and models and of suitable premises for study. Report of the Directors of the Liverpool Mechanics' Institution, 14 March 1838, in Lancashire Pamphlet Collections, vol. 14.

71 *Report of the Directors of the Liverpool Mechanics' Institution*, 8 March 1843.

72 *Liverpool Institute Mount Street, Established 1825* (Liverpool, 1861), LRO.

73 Morris, 'History', 40–1.

74 *Report from the Select Committee on the School of Design*, 225–6, paras 2497–508.

75 Bell, *Schools*, 120–1.

76 Manchester School of Design, Annual Report, 7 May 1850, 3–7.

77 Manchester School of Design, Annual Report, 6 June 1851, 8.

78 C. Ashwin (ed.), *Art Education Documents and Policies 1768–1975* (London, 1975), 26–7.

79 Stewart, *Regional College*, 7.

80 Stewart, *Regional College*, 8; Bell, *Schools*, 121–2.

81 Ashwin, *Art Education*, 26–7.

82 *Report from the Select Committee on the School of Design*, 215, para. 2378.

83 Ashwin, *Art Education*, 26–31.

84 For more details on the changing patterns of funding see S. Macdonald, *The History and Philosophy of Art Education* (London, 1970), 208–11.

85 This principle was revealed in the proceedings of the 1864 Select Committee on Schools of Art. See Macdonald, *History and Philosophy*, 211.

86 Manchester School of Design, Annual Report, 6 June 1851, 10–15.

87 *Report of the Select Committee on Schools of Art* (London, 1863), Appendix 14: 'Table of Local Subscriptions, Fees, Government Aid, Donations and Local Expenses', 346–8.

88 Manchester School of Art, Annual Report, 28 February 1853, 3–5, MCL.

89 Manchester School of Art, Annual Report, 28 February 1853, 17.

90 Thomas Bazley, in Manchester School of Art, First Annual Report, 31 July 1854, 11–12.

91 Manchester School of Art, First Annual Report, 31 July 1854, 7.

92 *Manchester Examiner*, 10 March 1857.

93 Manchester School of Art, Annual Report, 22 February 1859, 5; Annual Report, 11 April 1861, 8.

94 Manchester School of Art, Annual Report, 22 February 1859, 5.

95 Manchester School of Art, Annual Report, 11 April 1861, 8.

96 Manchester School of Art, Annual Report, 27 March 1862, 5–6.

97 Jeremiah, *Hundred Years*, 16.

98 Manchester School of Art, Annual Report, 10 April 1863, 13.

99 *Report of the Select Committee on Schools of Art*, Appendix 13, 'Schools of Art Established, Changed or Closed since 1852', 335.

100 R. N. Philips seems to have made good the school's deficits on several occasions, including in 1863 when he underwrote the cost of a loss-making exhibition. Manchester School of Art, Annual Report, 20 April 1864.

101 Manchester School of Art, First Annual Report, 31 July 1854, 13.

102 *Manchester Examiner*, 10 March 1857.

103 Willett, *Art*, 36.

104 Morris, 'History', 49–50.

105 In 1863 the North District attracted £472 13s 3d in student fees and £114 2s 3d in government aid; the South District attracted £413 11s 8d in student fees and £154 1s 3d in government aid. *Report of the Select Committee on Schools of Art*, Appendix 14, 346–8.

106 arillier, *Liverpool School*, 119–21.

107 Liverpool Institute, 35th Annual Report of the Directors, 18 January 1860, 6, 23, LRO.

108 Morris, 'History', 56.

109 Macdonald, *History*, 216.

110 *Report of the Select Committee on Schools of Art*, Appendix 16, 375–446.

111 G. Regan, 'Art Education in an Industrial Town: Warrington School of Art 1853–93', BA thesis, Manchester Metropolitan University, 1982, 56.

112 *Manchester Guardian*, 9 April 1863; also cited in Macdonald, *History*, 216.

113 Macdonald, *History*, 220–2.

114 For details of the new schedule see Manchester School of Art, Annual Report, 1865, 10.

115 Manchester School of Art, Annual Report, 12 September 1866, 6.

116 Manchester School of Art, Annual Report, 12 September 1866, 7.

117 Manchester School of Art, Annual Report, 19 December 1867, 22.

118 Manchester School of Art, Annual Report, 15 March 1876, 23–4.

119 *The Porcupine* (Liverpool), 28 (13 April 1861), 13.

120 Liverpool School of Art, *44th Annual Report of the Directors*, 20 January 1869 (Liverpool, 1869), 8, LRO.

121 Tiffin, *History*, 114.

122 Technical Instruction Committee of the Manchester City Council, Annual Report, year ending October 1899 (Manchester, 1899), 40.

123 MacDonald, *History*, 182–3.

124 Oldham Lyceum, 23rd Report of the Directors of the Oldham Lyceum, 1863, BL.

125 B. Law, *Oldham, Brave Oldham* (Oldham, 1999), 182–3.

126 Oldham Lyceum, 25th Annual Report of the Directors of the Oldham Lyceum, 1865, BL.

127 MacDonald, *History*, 182.

128 Birmingham famously used this route to finance city centre improvements in the 1870s and 1880s.

129 Willett, *Art*, 41.

130 Morris, 'History', 67–8.

131 Tiffen, *History*, 115.

132 Heydari, 'Manchester School of Art', 6.

133 See comments of Alderman Heywood in Manchester School of Art, Annual Report, 21 December 1877.

134 J. Swift, *Changing Fortunes: The Birmingham School of Art Building 1880–1995* (Birmingham, 1996), esp. 6–15.

135 See Manchester School of Art, Annual Report, 21 December 1877.

136 Heydari, 'Manchester School of Art', 10–12, 16.

137 Manchester School of Art, Annual Report, 19 December 1879, 12.

138 *What to See & Where to See it or the Visitor's Guide to the Opening Exhibition, Manchester School of Art* (Manchester, 1881); *Preliminary Prospectus – Grand Art Union* (Manchester, 1881).

139 J. Murgatroyd, *Remarks Concerning the Manchester School of Art and Schools of Art Generally* (Manchester, 1881), 4.

140 Heydari, 'Manchester School of Art', 28.

141 Manchester School of Art, Annual Report, 30 January 1888, 5–7.

142 For details see G. W. Roderick and M. D. Stephens, *Education and Industry in the Nineteenth Century: The English Disease?* (London, 1978), 72–4.

143 Manchester School of Art, Annual Report, 22 January 1890, 10.

144 Manchester School of Art, Annual Report, 14 January 1892, 8.

145 Heydari, 'Manchester School of Art', 33–9.

146 Technical Instruction Committee of the City Council of Manchester, Annual Report, 19 October 1893, 15.

147 Technical Instruction Committee of the City Council of Manchester, Annual Report, year ending October 1897, 26.

148 Roderick and Stephens, *Education and Industry*, 75.

149 Manchester School of Art, Annual Report, 15 January 1891, 7.

150 For background see M. Bennett, *The Art Sheds 1894–1905* (Liverpool, 1991).

151 £1,000 came from the city council and around £300 from the Roscoe funds. Morris, 'History', 85.

152 Bennett, *Art Sheds*.

153 *Memorial Exhibition of the Art of John Finnie, RE, RCA* (Liverpool, 1907), 11–12.

154 C. Crouch, *Design Culture in Liverpool* (Liverpool, 2002), 82–3.

155 Willett, *Art*, 55–7.

156 City of Liverpool Education Committee, Proceedings and Appendix to Proceedings of the Education Committee, 1903–4, LRO, H370 EDU.

157 Finnie of Liverpool earned over £600 per annum by the end of his career. Morris, 'History', 75.

158 Technical Instruction Committee of the City Council of Manchester, Annual Report, year ending October 1897, 16–17.

159 C. Rowley, *Fifty Years of Work without Wages* (London, n.d. [1913]), 71–9.

160 *Handbook to the Technical and Art School and Colleges of the United Kingdom* (London, 1909), 21–95.

161 Marillier, *Liverpool School*, 143–53, 213–21.

162 Marillier, *Liverpool School*, 191–2.

163 T. Stevens (ed.), *James Hamilton Hay* (Liverpool, 1973), 4–5.

164 Manchester School of Design, Annual Report, 1847, 18.

165 Murgatroyd, *Remarks*, 5.

166 Regan, 'Art Education', 62–5.

6

The art of philanthropy? The formation and development of the Walker Art Gallery

The period 1870–1914 saw the rapid spread of municipal art galleries across the region. Although these galleries were under municipal control, they often depended upon the successful intersection of private and public forces. The galleries of Liverpool, Manchester and Preston became the largest and best-known in the region, yet in none of these towns did the municipalities initiate the schemes or fund the construction costs. The formation and early development of these galleries owed much to the activities of private philanthropists and sponsors. Perhaps the most notable and controversial instance of private philanthropy in gallery formation is the case of Liverpool, where a local brewer, Andrew Barclay Walker, not only provided the full funds for the gallery's construction, but also supported its later extension and development. Other galleries in Lancashire also received significant amounts of private support, but this was usually in the form of bequests. Harris's funding of the Preston gallery took this form, as did the funding for the Whitworth gallery. Walker was relatively unusual in sponsoring the construction of a gallery during his own lifetime, creating a living memorial for himself in his own city of residence and business (see Figure 12). However, Walker's philanthropy provoked controversy, and the disputes surrounding the Walker gallery highlight how public gifts could be used to obtain social and political status. Walker's business interests in the brewing trade made him a controversial political figure in a city riven by sectarian and religious differences. Many saw his philanthropy as a crude attempt to establish his own cultural status in the city and to curry favour with metropolitan artistic elites. Others accused him of attempting to buy a knighthood through showy displays of philanthropy. Nonconformist churchmen even criticised the gallery itself and regarded it as the fruits of drunkenness, crime and immorality.

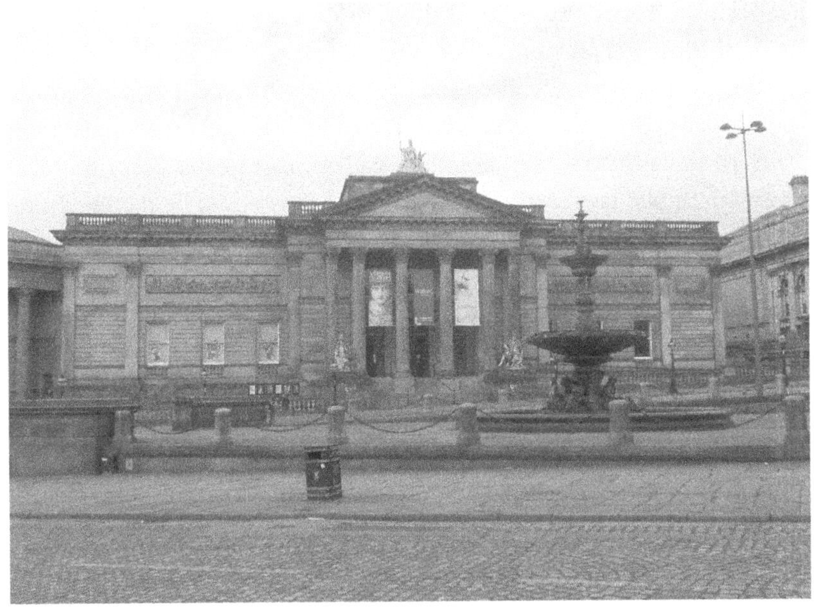

12 The Walker Art Gallery

The early history of the Walker provides an opportunity to examine the very notion of philanthropy in the context of the cultural development of the mid-Victorian city. Philanthropy was neither a value-neutral benevolent activity nor a straightforward act in the exercise of power. It was a negotiated activity that not only operated in the context of complex expectations of the donor and receiver but also acted against the background of costs and expectations shared by wider civil society.[1] In Liverpool, as in many urban centres, philanthropy was a competitive business, with leading politicians from the major parties attempting to outbid each other's generosity. Supposed public-spirited activity created complex patterns of expectations and obligations.

Early historians of philanthropy tended to emphasise the selfless, other-regarding aspects of the activity. For Kirkman Gray, voluntarism was the key element of philanthropy: it was an activity carried out through benevolence without any sense of compulsion, duty or right and without any reciprocal expectation of service.[2] This is, however, a somewhat naïve approach. Classically educated Victorians were aware of the power of philanthropy in conferring status but also of its potential pitfalls. Those familiar with Isocrates, Xenophon, Plutarch and Polybius would have been aware of the term in its Greek form and its position in ancient political thought and historiography.[3] Philanthropy was part of Aristotelian notions of political prudence and had an important role in the promotion of enlightened self-interest.[4] But it had its limitations as a political weapon. Cicero was careful to advise his son Marcus about the problems of philanthropy, warning that while philanthropic contributions were a tool to win public favour, too much philanthropy could be damaging in both financial and political terms.[5] Philanthropy was not always associated with fulfilling a pressing public need, or even the needs of a specific group. It was sometimes an act of existential display focused on the promotion of specific values or simply the reputation of the individual associated with it. The fact that so much philanthropy does not appear to respond to specific normative demands has stimulated a significant re-evaluation of the historiography of public giving.[6]

Until recent times there has been a tendency to assume that the decline of philanthropy was closely and inexorably associated with the rise of the state. Philanthropists and voluntary organisations identified social needs, but it was the failure of 'voluntarism' to adequately meet the needs that led to the gradual growth of statutory collective provision.[7] However, as Gorsky has noted, recent literature has attempted to 'deteleologise' this approach and question the role of philanthropic activity in processes of social and cultural modernisation.[8] These revisionist accounts also, of course, have significant implications for the development of the local state and, for our purposes, the development of art institutions. It is important not to read the rise of the municipal art gallery as simply the product of the 'failure' of private provision. In the case of the Walker Art Gallery, a private subscriber provided that which the local state had failed to supply. However, without the long-term support of the local state, the private subscriber might have declined all involvement. Philanthropy needs, therefore, to be understood in the context of a network of multiple agencies attempting to meet the needs, or the perceived expectations, of a given community.

The classic works of E. P. Thompson and Harold Perkin have reminded us how class and status are often important in understanding the operation of philanthropic effort.[9] Mauss's work on gifting and the gift economy has illustrated how gifts can be expressions of power and superiority, rendering the receiver indebted and subordinate. Much of the power inherent in gifting lies in the receiver's inability to refuse the gift without being placed in a morally or politically embarrassing position.[10] Mauss also emphasises how important this process is in the formation of human bonds and social alliances.[11] This theme has been taken up by a number of modern urban historians. Morris, for example, sees the creation of voluntary societies, often with a philanthropic purpose, as crucial in processes of class formation and emerging group identities in the early industrial city.[12] There has been an increasing tendency to emphasise the capacity of philanthropic effort as a unifying, conciliatory force, embracing those from different cultural backgrounds in the exercise of shared values and identity. Harrison's work on charity emphasises how the values of the workers and the elite could be remarkably similar, reflecting a process of mutual recognition and negotiation.[13] More recently, Vernon and Joyce have identified the importance of the displays of public virtue and philanthropy in the broader governance of the modern city.[14] Such activities are viewed a not only important at the individual level but, as both Aristotle and Cicero may have observed, essential in understanding the generation of new patterns of civic political legitimacy.[15]

This is not to say that selfless and altruistic motives were always absent from the gifting process. McCord's work on the relief of poverty in the early nineteenth century argues that straightforward liberality could sometimes provide an adequate explanation for philanthropic effort.[16] Many sociologists are now keen to rescue 'genuine' altruism from reductionist cynics, who have long claimed that it must inevitably collapse into self-referential feelings of personal satisfaction.[17] Empirical research on late twentieth-century patterns of philanthropic giving has identified a complex pattern of motivations, including, in many cases, a strong sense of altruistic obligation partly derived from the possession of surplus capital.[18] The notion that material wealth brought social obligations was important in Victorian industrial society, and, however hypocritical it could sometimes be, the idea became enmeshed in the conscious and unconscious modes of urban governance as financial capital was converted into symbolic social capital.[19] As A. B. Walker was to discover, successful philanthropy had to be perceived as a disinterested act aimed at the public good. If suspicions arose that an act of philanthropy was undertaken for private or partisan advantage, it lost its political and cultural purchase. The power of philanthropy lay in its ability to create for the donor a universally accepted narrative that presented him as a benevolent, selfless servant of the polis, dedicated to the good of all men. The narrative was one that would be transmitted not only in the announcement of the benefaction and the public ceremonies associated with its realisation, but in the permanent monument that it created – such as the Walker gallery.[20] Inevitably, charges of partisanship and selfishness challenged this narrative, threatening its rearticulation and encouraging the circulation of contradictory interpretations. It was Walker's failure to be aware of this threat that ultimately challenged his public image.

In many towns and cities public corporations funded art galleries because of the perceived failure of private philanthropy to provide these important cultural assets. In Liverpool, however, almost the reverse was true. Liverpool Corporation had, for many years before Walker announced his project, assembled plans for the construction of a publicly-funded art gallery, but had consistently failed to take them beyond the planning stage. The famous Pre-Raphaelite disputes of the 1850s and early 1860s effectively destroyed the Liverpool Academy, ended its annual exhibition and fundamentally threatened Liverpool's position as a major regional art centre.[21] In 1860, at the height of the dispute, the corporation took the first steps towards the development of its own gallery, but financial constraints and the economic problems associated with the American civil war saw the plans quietly shelved. It was not until five years later that a serious proposal emerged for the erection of a specific building for an art gallery. Sadly, the committee lost a portion of its anticipated rate support, which rendered the plans unsustainable. Sir William Brown's provision of a civic museum for the city in 1867 only served to postpone the development of an art gallery further. Brown's museum provided a suitable home for the art treasures of Joseph Mayer, which had recently been donated to the city, but the running costs of the museum fell on the city rate, ensuring that fewer resources were available for the development of a separate art gallery.[22]

The development of Brown's museum did, however, provide a suitable location for the revival of Liverpool's annual modern exhibition. By this time the academy's exhibition had effectively collapsed. Small exhibitions were held in 1864 and 1867 at Griffith's private gallery and in 1865 at Old Post Office Place, but these failed to attract major metropolitan artists and were subsequently discontinued for financial reasons.[23] The corporation was persuaded to promote a new exhibition, at Brown's museum, by Philip Henry Rathbone and Edward Samuelson. Both were municipal leaders and prominent figures in Liverpool's business and social circles. Rathbone was the son of the Liverpool merchant and banker William Rathbone, and had risen to the presidency of the Liverpool Chamber of Commerce.[24] Samuelson was a leading tobacco broker and the son of Henry Samuelson, a shipping merchant of Liverpool and Hull. Significantly, the two men represented rival factions of Liverpool's deeply divided political community: Rathbone was a Liberal, Samuelson a Conservative.[25] The revived exhibition at Brown's was a considerable success, and, by excluding artists from the management of the exhibition, the corporation was able to avoid the worst of the controversy that had afflicted its predecessor.

The success of the new exhibition only served to highlight the need for a purpose-built gallery that could do justice to the work of the country's leading artists. In the summer of 1873 Picton brought forward new proposals for a publicly funded gallery. Although the cost of the gallery was relatively modest – an estimated £18,000 exclusive of fixtures and fittings – the proposals provoked considerable opposition from the city's small shopkeepers and the lower middle class. The proposed costs, although not great compared with those of similar projects in other cities, seemed considerable at a time when the corporation was reluctant to fund even pressing commercial projects, such as the city's fish market.[26] Moreover, there was increasing recognition of the injustices inherent in the system of local taxation, which appeared to fall disproportionately on the lower middle class. Merchant princes, and indeed many councillors, lived outside the boundaries of the city, escaping the city's high domestic rates and paying only business rates to Liverpool Corporation.[27] Critics argued that the building would be 'almost exclusively used by the upper classes',[28] and that it should therefore be provided by the wealthy men who would frequent it.[29] Picton also experienced significant opposition from within the council. Alderman Weightman of the finance committee criticised the vagueness of the plans, the failure to provide working drawings for the scheme and the apparent reliance on uncertain exhibition profits to provide revenue funding for the day-to-day operation of the proposed gallery. Worse still, it was argued that the construction of an art gallery would only serve to cripple the development of the lending libraries, which had been shown to be especially popular in working-class districts.[30] Ultimately, it was probably Picton's attempt to take £300 from the lending library budget for the development of an art gallery that persuaded his fellow councillors to reject the plans.[31]

Protestors against the plans for a municipally funded gallery accused Picton of attempting to use public funds to satisfy the recreational needs of a civic cultural elite. The *Liberal Review* noted that it would be well if Picton and his followers 'would ride their hobby only at the expense of their funds'.[32] Similarly, the *Liverpool Leader* called upon Picton and Samuelson to organise an effort to secure a gallery by private gift, if they really regarded it as important for the cultural well-being of the city.[33] Statements like this in the press clearly put Picton and his followers under some pressure and demonstrated the societal expectations that came with civic leadership. Willingness to offer philanthropic gifts was an important factor in marking out a civic leader's selflessness and commitment to public duty, particularly when that civic leader was calling upon his electorate to make continuing sacrifices in the shape of ever rising rates. This became abundantly clear during a protest meeting against rising civic expenditure in late August 1873. Picton, under pressure from Conservatives attempting to exploit his associations with high public expenditure, withdrew his plans for a municipal art gallery. He then offered, in a clear move to outflank his opponents, to fund an art gallery for the city, providing that his main Conservative opponent, Councillor Richard Minton, would provide a lending library.[34]

Picton's offer to finance the construction of a gallery seems to have been a rather rash one, prompted by the emotion of the moment and the desire to defuse personal criticism. Minton's Conservatives, however, were determined to see Picton's hand and engaged in what can only be described as an exercise in competitive philanthropy. The following day, Minton announced, through his agent, that he would provide a new lending library for the city, so long as Picton made good his pledge to construct an art gallery.[35] Picton was clearly somewhat taken aback by events and, unwilling to meet the entire cost of a new gallery, sought to relieve himself of the commitment:

> I never offered to build an art gallery at my own expense, but I did say whatever Mr Minton might be prepared to give in aid of his pet project of an additional lending library, I would give double the sum towards the erection of an art gallery. However, let that pass. I do not wish to make the progress of art dependent on Mr. Minton's generosity connected with the extension of lending libraries.[36]

Picton's offer to provide finance for an art gallery was clearly not the product of disinterested commitment to the public good. His very public dispute with Minton turned the affair into a somewhat sordid political and philanthropic competition. Any gift given in these circumstances would be tarnished by its partisan associations. As the press observed, it was at best an 'undignified controversy', at worst a 'broad farce'.[37] Picton, clearly desperate to salvage both his own reputation and the art gallery scheme, offered to put down £1,000 to fund the gallery if another nineteen benefactors would follow suit.[38] Unfortunately the response was disappointing. The only patrons prepared to match Picton's offer were the manufacturing chemist George Kurtz, the brewer John Parrinton, the merchant James Houghton and the collector Thomas Harding.[39]

The collapse of the scheme is somewhat puzzling given the success of the revived Liverpool autumn exhibition. The exhibitions of 1871 and 1872 had both generated considerable surpluses for the organisers which were in turn utilised to develop the municipal collection. In 1871 £495 was spent on three pictures for the corporation's collection, and a year later £600 was spent on major acquisitions, including F. W. Topham's celebrated *The Fall of Rienzi*.[40] Yet this level of support was not manifest in the plans for a public gallery. This may have been partly because some resented Picton's associations with the project and his apparent withdrawal of the offer to finance the gallery himself. It was clear that many were also sceptical about the long-term viability of the gallery, even if £20,000 could be found to finance the initial construction. In the absence of a major patron, there was a danger that it would simply fall to the local ratepayers to fit out and complete it. Commentators took the view that a gallery to reflect Liverpool's importance would cost over £100,000 and it would be impossible to achieve anything of significance with the sums projected by Picton. The *Liberal Review* proffered that a gallery 'filled with daubs, the refuse from rich merchants' dining rooms, would be a far greater disgrace that having none at all'.[41] The *Review*, for its part, offered an old hat last worn in 1861, two Chinese tea boxes, a copy of *Punch* and a half-pint china cup labelled 'A Present from Staffordshire'.[42] For Picton, the failure of the scheme presented little occasion for amusement. In a last desperate attempt to rescue the project Samuelson, in his capacity as mayor, called a town's meeting to rally support. Despite attempts to gain support for the scheme by reviving the spirit of Roscoe and reminding citizens of the supposed cultural connections between the mercantile city of Liverpool and Renaissance Florence and Rome, just twenty-five attended the meeting. A public subscription list was opened, but to little practical effect.[43]

The failure of Picton and Samuelson to assemble an effective philanthropic plan for the construction of an art gallery provided a significant opportunity for the politically and socially ambitious Andrew Barclay Walker. By 1870, Walker had established himself as head of the city's most extensive chain of public houses. His business reputation was, however, somewhat chequered, and he had been accused of conspiring with Conservative interests on the council to grant a free trade in alcohol licences. He had then used his market power to drive out independent competition and buy up licences from free houses at nominal cost. When free trade in licences was abandoned several years later he retained his licences, further consolidating his grip on the city's drink traffic.[44] In 1867 he entered the town council, and in 1872 he was elected by the ruling

Conservative group as an alderman, despite apparently showing little interest in municipal work and having a reputation for missing committee meetings.[45] Remarkably, just a year later, he was elected mayor. Many commentators clearly saw a close association between the Conservatives' decision to elect him as mayor and his offer to construct a £20,000 art gallery for the city. His offer to support the art gallery scheme was closely associated with the political manoeuvring inherent in mayoral elections.[46] The Liberals were in a difficult position. Many, having argued that the gallery should not be paid for by the rates, could hardly oppose Walker's apparently generous offer, especially as their own leader, J. A. Picton, had withdrawn his apparent offer to fund a gallery himself.[47] Philip Rathbone made an explicit reference to Conservatives buying the office of mayor, though, significantly, not through the agency of public philanthropy but through subscriptions to the Conservative association.[48] Press commentators also suspected malpractice but were circumspect in their criticism. The *Daily Post*, while noting that 'there has hitherto been no precedent for nominating a Mayor who has made no mark whatever in municipal matters', also stated that Walker would always be remembered with honour as the man who provided the city with an art gallery.[49]

Perhaps aware of the controversy surrounding his mayoralty, Walker rarely spoke publicly about his gift to the city. In an attempt to unify public opinion on the question, it was Walker's rival, Picton, who moved the resolution in council naming the new gallery the Walker Art Gallery (Figure 13).[50] The council also planned major public events to celebrate the various stages in the gallery's construction. Even metropolitan newspapers, such as the *Illustrated London News*, provided detailed coverage of the plans for the gallery and the laying of the foundation stone by the Duke of Edinburgh.[51] Cornelius Sherlock's plans for a grand neo-classical building with over 1,000 lineal feet of hanging space on the upper floors and sculpture galleries below gave the public a taste of what to expect.[52] However, Walker was never allowed to forget the political nature of the gift and its associations with his mayoral ambition. Those in the radical wing of the Liberal party objected to the donation of public land with a rental value of £1,200 per annum in support of Walker's supposed philanthropy and the continuing commitment of the rates to support the building. As the economy began to slump into the 'Great Depression' of the mid-1870s their criticism became increasingly powerful. As the *Liberal Review* noted, 'A magnificent home for pictures, and none but miserable hovels for poor frail human

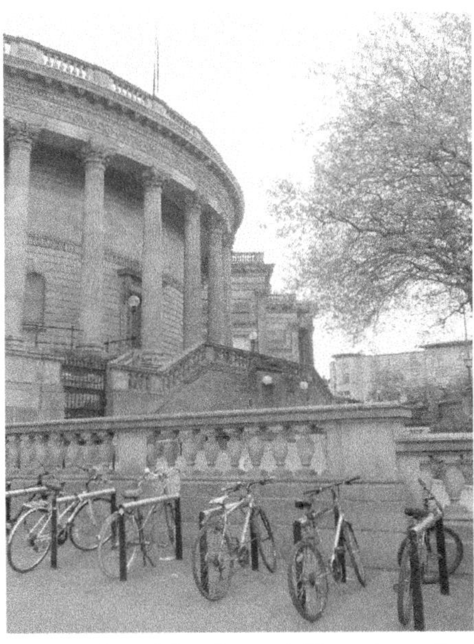

13 The landscape of competitive philanthropy? Picton's reading room and public hall (left) and Walker's art gallery (right)

beings, is, indeed, a deep satire upon our boasted civilisation of the nineteenth century.'[53]

The most effective way to respond to this criticism was, in the view of the corporation, to organise exhibitions and activities that would justify its decisions in the eyes of the wider art community. Above all it needed to avoid the accusation that the gallery would be home to only the refuse of mercantile living rooms. The corporation was fortunate in that it had received a number of donated pictures in the period when the possibility of a municipal art gallery was first mooted. Between 1852 and 1870 it had obtained sixteen significant works, including Richard Ansdell's *The Hunted Slaves*, donated by G. Winter Moss, and Benjamin West's *Death of Nelson*, provided by Bristown H. Hughes. Following the announcement of the commencement of the Walker gallery, several more pictures were added through donation, perhaps most notably E. J. Poynter's *Faithful unto Death*, given by Charles Langton in 1874. The success of the autumn exhibition was also generating large surpluses that could be invested in new works. In 1874 £1,200 was set aside for the purchase of new works, including £350 for David Roberts's *London – the Lord Mayor's Show*.[54] It was always recognised that the success of the new gallery would be dependent on contributions from outside. These would not only improve the quality of the exhibition and fill wall space but also help to legitimise the Walker as a gallery for all Liverpool's people – and not merely an exercise in political sophistry or 'The Mayor's White Elephant'.[55] A large representative committee was formed of Liberal and Conservatives, municipal leaders, businessmen, collectors and MPs to oversee an appeal for paintings.[56]

The highpoint of the opening day of the gallery would be a grand procession through the city. The procession would not only include the city's officials, the corporation and the police, but also encompass trade unions, voluntary societies and religious groups, in a show of civic unity. The demonstrations would be a celebration of the culture of the Liverpool and the generosity of its leading philanthropist. Yet, in practice, the political divisions of the city stirred beneath the surface. Working-class organisations and trade societies were initially excluded from the formal procession for fears that 'political organisations' would attempt to use the day's events to publicise their particular causes. Ultimately, the trade societies were allowed to take part, but on the strict understanding that no party badges or emblems of any kind would be displayed.[57] The organisers were even careful to provide directions on the types of national flag that could be carried. Royal standards and union flags with orange borders were strictly prohibited, as were any other emblems associated with the Orange order.[58]

The main problem that Walker and the civic authorities faced was not, however, from sectarianism but from temperance opinion that objected to Walker's role in the Liverpool drinks trade and the extravagant attempts of self-promotion inherent within his philanthropy. Almost as soon as the corporation had announced plans for the art gallery's opening ceremony, the temperance campaigners announced their own plans for a counter-demonstration.[59] The temperance activists were particularly annoyed at plans for a working-class fund for a testimonial to mark Walker's generosity. The local press reported allegations that large employers had been putting pressure on workers to give to the fund, despite the objections of many to Walker's business activities.[60] On the day of the opening ceremony temperance activists presented their own testimonial casket to Walker: handbills and posters representing the gallery as the reward of iniquity. The new gallery was depicted as a building built upon the foundation of Walker's alehouses. On its walls were chalked the statistics of drink-related crime – '472 brothels known to police', '23,556 drunkards', '2,318 licensed drunkeries' – with the

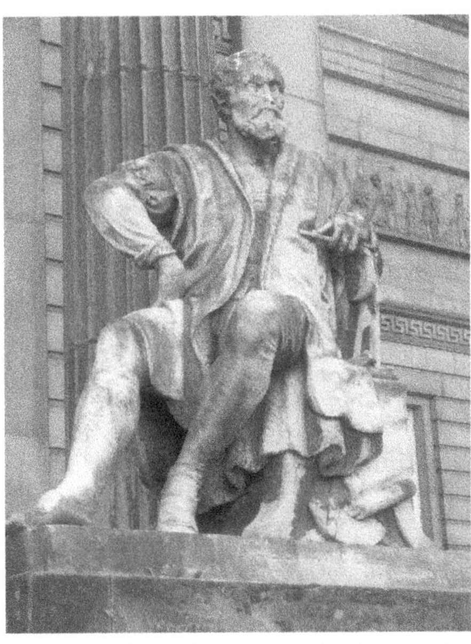

14 Statue of Michelangelo outside the Walker Art Gallery

legend 'All these will I give for a baronetcy?'[61] The elegant statues of Michelangelo and Raphael by Warrington Wood at the gallery's entrance (Figure 14) were replaced by a common prostitute and a drunkard in rags, with the 'Spirit of Liverpool' statue above the gallery's cornice replaced by the figure of the devil.[62]

Walker's attempts to establish a cultural and philanthropic reputation were shattered by 'respectable' criticism of his business activities. Rather than diverting attention from his drink trade activities, his high-profile patronage of the arts simply brought his associations with brewing industry into sharp focus. Liverpool's 'respectable opinion' became even more dubious about Walker's motivations when, shortly after the opening of the gallery, it was announced that he was indeed to receive a knighthood.[63] By the 1890s, even those who sought to defend Walker's reputation from scurrilous attacks accepted that the baronetcy was 'deliberately bought', merely denying that there was anything improper in this practice.[64] It is interesting that even during the opening of the gallery, many in Liverpool's elite appear to have been suspicious of Walker's motives. Although Liverpool Corporation and the city's 'official society' paraded in support of the opening ceremony, many of the city's leading merchant families were absent from the festivities. Not surprisingly this absence was noted by the Liberal press, which observed:

> People from the first have viewed his present with suspicion ... They appreciate generosity, of course, but they well question the motives of a gift which is proclaimed from the housetops with the blare of trumpets and the beat of drums.[65]

Modesty and a degree of circumspection were essential in the delivery of philanthropic gifts. Both Walker's friends and enemies ensured that his generosity was put on public display. It was inevitable, then, that the gallery was born into a public controversy.

Significantly, Walker seems to have played only a limited role in the operation of the gallery that was donated by him and named in his honour. Although he, as mayor, was involved in the organising committee for the opening ceremony there is little evidence that he proffered strong views about its future development. Some questioned whether he had any real interest in the cultural life of Liverpool at all. His early business associations were with Warrington, and it seems that he initially planned to fund the cost of a large art gallery there. This was at a time when Warrington was home to a number of prominent artists such as Luke Fildes, George Sheffield and the man whose sculptures were to eventually decorate the Walker, Warrington Wood. It emerged that Walker turned his attention to Liverpool only after a somewhat petty planning dispute with Warrington Town Council persuaded him to withdraw his philanthropy from that town.[66] Walker rarely intervened in policy matters concerning the Walker gallery, leaving operational matters to the connoisseurs Rathbone and Samuelson.

Both Rathbone and Samuelson appear to have been aware of the criticism of the gallery and immediately tried to stimulate the widest possible interest in its activities. Although the annual autumn exhibition inevitably focused on attracting the cream of London artists for reasons of both financial viability and prestige, there was strong support for local and regional artists. In order to avoid the conflicts of the past, local artists were officially excluded from the hanging committee of the exhibition, but there were representatives from the Liverpool Academy, the art school and the LRI.[67] One of the first pictures bought following the revival of the exhibition in 1871 was a landscape of Snowdon produced by John Finnie, headmaster of the Liverpool School of Art.[68] Over the next few years local artists would continue to receive the patronage of the corporation. In 1877 the art committee spent 130 guineas on an important landscape by the leading Manchester artist H. C. Whaite.[69] Whaite went on to be an influential president of the Manchester Academy of Fine Art and a founder of the Royal Cambrian Academy. The support that the Walker gave to local artists in its formative years suggests a strong desire to foster links with the local artistic community, and by supporting the efforts of local landscape painters the Walker was providing accessible art which even those regarded as visually illiterate could enjoy.

While many feared that the Walker would become a storehouse of merchants' refuse, in practice the gallery obtained a number of important paintings through voluntary donation in its first two decades of existence. Although some in Liverpool's merchant community were reluctant to support the gallery, once it was open the building undeniably became central to the cultural life of the city. With Walker himself taking little part in its operation, prominent citizens could support the gallery's activities without necessarily being directly associated with Walker's attempts at self-publicity. Indeed, by offering donations themselves, other groups in Liverpool society could draw attention to their own disinterested benevolence in contrast to the partisan benevolence of Walker. It is notable that shortly after the Walker's opening, Picton provided a donation of £1,000 for the fitting-up of the city's reading room.[70] One of his supporters in the original art gallery scheme, A. G. Kurtz, followed with the donation of the valuable *Lady Macbeth* by T. F. Dicksee.[71] Less than two months later, there were a number of donations from the Arkle family, the most notable of which was probably *Ruins of a Temple and Amphitheatre* by David Roberts. It was also during this period that the Walker began to receive its first major bequests, including a number of items by Thomas Creswick, Birket Foster and T. S. Cooper from the collection of Robert Ellison Harvey.[72]

Once the gallery opened its operational costs fell upon the corporation and, ultimately, local taxation. From the start, civic leaders were keen to depict the institution as one designed for the enjoyment and education of all classes. The Walker was the largest gallery in the region and thus one of the most costly to maintain. Only by emphasising the relevance of the gallery to all classes could the corporation avoid complaints about the high level of public subsidies. B. H. Grindley of the art gallery committee attacked those who saw art as merely the hobby of the rich, arguing that culture and refinement were required at all levels of society. For Grindley, many adults in the population had become 'so sensual in their nature, and so low and debased in their pleasures' that what they needed was 'not so much education, as cultivation'.[73] Rathbone expressed similar sentiments in a lecture at the free library in 1875. In his view, the great strength of art was its ability to inspire and represent the common people. This, for Rathbone, was the great genius inherent in classical Greek art. By placing art on public display in the Greek marketplace, the artist and the people were brought into dialogue. Public taste was educated and purified, and the artistic products which emerged came to reflect the values and interests of the whole nation. Such was the collective power of this process that it could still awaken and inspire the consciousness of a people generations later. Rathbone, echoing the sentiments of T. S. Traill a generation before, argued that it was 'not Homer, Euripides, Plato, or Aristotle, that delivered Greece from the Turks, but Phidias and the Parthenon'.[74] Clearly, Rathbone recognised that some saw the Liverpool art gallery as a product of one man's self-serving vanity. However, by demonstrating the capacity of art to purify the taste and express the consciousness of a people, he was able to rescue the future of the gallery from the political partisanship associated with its birth. Equally he was responding to the insecurities that many Liverpudlians felt about the future of their city. Art provided an enduring image to immortalise their wealth and importance. Those who failed to leave behind evidence of their artistic taste would soon be forgotten, and with it their civilisation. Liverpool was faced with a choice. Would it build a memorial to its civility 'or be content to rot away as Carthage, Antioch, and Tyre have rotted away, leaving not a trace to show where a population of more than half a million souls once lived, loved, felt, and thought'?[75]

In trying to establish an artistic reputation for the city, Rathbone faced the same key difficulty as that faced by Roscoe almost three-quarters of a century before. Liverpool had few associations with artistic and craft industries and had failed to foster a distinctive school of painting or sculpture. In the early nineteenth century Liverpool had successful pottery and earthenware enterprises, but these were short-lived. The Herculaneum pottery works, situated near the docks, was particularly well known, but even the import of skilled Staffordshire craftsmen failed to prevent its demise and with it that of the pottery industry in Liverpool.[76] The break-up of the Liverpool Academy had done little to help encourage the development of a distinctive Liverpool school, however much the academy had helped foster the work of metropolitan Pre-Raphaelites. Worse still, Liverpool artists faced the danger of losing their identity altogether as the Manchester school of Corot-inspired Impressionists became more prominent across the region. Rathbone seems to have been aware of this threat and was unusually critical of the Mancunians' technique. Although he had some sympathies with the Impressionist movement, he had little time for the Manchester school, even going as far as to offer public condemnation of its 'slip-shod cant and pretentiousness' in a Liverpool exhibition review of 1883.[77] The unfortunate truth was, however, that Liverpool artists of the 1870s had offered little in response to the radicalism of their colleagues in Manchester. If Liverpool was to express its cultural identity through art, it was hard to see how it could do so through the agency of its own art and artists.

Liverpool's great strength lay in its history of organising successful autumn exhibitions of modern art. Although these had folded for a time, the corporation's decision to organise its own exhibition from 1871 demonstrated that there was still a significant market for pictures in Liverpool and that profitable modern exhibitions could still be organised. The opening of the Walker gave the annual exhibition a renewed impetus, not only by providing a purpose-built gallery in order to display the 'works of the season' to best effect, but also by providing significantly more wall space than had ever been available at previous venues. At the first autumn exhibition at the Walker in 1877, over 200 more exhibits were placed on display than in the previous year.[78] In some respects, the relocation of the exhibition was poorly timed, occurring when the effects of the 'Great Depression' were all too evident. The total picture sales fell from £10,989 6s in 1877 to just £7,340 7s a year later.[79] Yet, remarkably, Liverpool's exhibition soon revived, and by 1881 the aggregate value of sales topped £12,000.[80]

Part of this success was undoubtedly due to the work of Rathbone. He was not only a prominent business leader, but was also closely involved in the London art world.[81] His artistic contacts were considerable, and it was his influence that brought figures such as Alphonse Legros and Hubert von Herkomer to Liverpool for public lectures.[82] Rathbone bought works by Legros and donated his *The Pilgrimage* to Liverpool's permanent collection. While Manchester struggled to attract major metropolitan artists to its annual exhibition, Liverpool continued to attract leading Royal Academicians. Even in the relatively unsuccessful exhibition of 1878, E. W. Cooke, E. Ermitage, Ford Madox Brown, P. H. Calderon, C. G. Lawson and Alma Tadema all sent works. In turn the financial success of the exhibitions generated significant surpluses that could be used to finance the development of the permanent collection. In a good year the commission on sales alone could generate over £500, and even in a poor one at least £250. This allowed Liverpool Corporation to bid for the great works of the season and build up a permanent collection that, if not actually representing the consciousness of the people of the city, provided an impressive cultural resource.

During the 1880s, it was Rathbone who led the development of the gallery, and there is little evidence that Walker ever took a leading role in gallery policy. Walker did finance a major extension of the gallery in 1882 but seems to have exercised little influence over the expansion of the permanent collection. Rathbone encouraged the corporation to collect all manner of British art, and there was never a formal collecting policy. However, Liverpool's permanent collection did develop some important characteristics. In general, the art committee collected high art and subject pictures, often with a strong historical theme and those that reflected the city's association with the Pre-Raphaelites. This trend is typified by perhaps the most celebrated picture in the Walker collection, D. G. Rossetti's *Dante's Dream*. For many this was Rossetti's most ambitious imaginative work, and its appearance at the Walker in November 1881 was occasioned by a formal civic reception.[83] Formal historical pictures were also prominent, notably E. J. Poynter's *Faithful unto Death*, depicting a Roman guard at Herculaneum, and F. W. Topham's *The Fall of Rienzi*, illustrating the attempted escape of a tribune from an angry shouting people. According to Liverpool's art advisor, E. R. Dibdin, many of the pictures chosen for purchase were selected with an eye to gaining public favour and stimulating interest in the new gallery. Pictures including children and animals were regarded as particularly popular among the 'uncultivated', and it is interesting that many of the most celebrated works of high art in the gallery include these subjects. Frederick Goodall's *New Light in the Harem* had a baby as its central subject, and many other paintings, including Topham's *Fall of Rienzi*, also featured infants in their midst. There were also a number of more obviously sentimental pieces, such as J. R. Reid's *Rival Grandfathers*, Thomas Faed's *When the Children are Asleep* and Arthur Stocks's *Motherless*. The Walker authorities, although determined to collect high art, continually had one eye on public opinion. If Rathbone wanted Liverpool's art collection to represent the consciousness of the people, rather than the vanity of one man, it had to be made attractive to a wider audience. As Dibdin noted, 'Children and animals, beloved of all but the utterly debased, are the surest baits for wide popular appreciation.'[84]

The other major bait for public attention was, of course, the landscape. Many municipal galleries focused on the collection of landscape painting, often buying works of questionable quality. Liverpool, under Rathbone's guidance, largely avoided this pitfall. The corporation did buy some rather hackneyed

Welsh landscape scenes, such as J. D. Watson's watercolours of scenery near Betws-y-Coed, but in general the works acquired were of a superior quality.[85] E. A. Waterlow's *A Summer Shower* was one of the collection's earliest acquisitions and one of the most popular. There were also important works by G. A. Fripp, Joseph Knight, J. Aumonier, Peter Ghent and many leading British landscapists of the second half of the nineteenth century.[86] Nor was this populist approach at the expense of foreign works, with Rathbone pioneering interest in leading continental schools.[87] It was in the area of portraiture that the Liverpool collection was, perhaps, the slowest to develop. This aspect was gradually strengthened, and the gallery could eventually claim representative samples of Sir Joshua Reynolds, Sir Godfrey Kneller and Sir Thomas Lawrence. By the end of the century, the Roscoe collection of Italian primitives had also found its way into the corporation art gallery. Although it was still owned by the LRI, the financial difficulties of the institution meant that the collection had, in effect, been placed on permanent loan.[88]

Rathbone's approach to collecting was driven not only by a desire to obtain high-quality works through his best metropolitan sources, but also by a determination to popularise the gallery by choosing artists and subject matter that would be attractive to a wide audience. From the outset, the gallery had attracted criticism through both its associations with Walker and the costs that fell on the public purse. Even in the late 1880s there was still strong resentment at increasing expenditure on public museums and galleries. In 1887 the Liverpool Land and House Owners' Association successfully petitioned to prevent the library and art gallery committee from applying to Parliament for an extra halfpenny rate.[89] Changes in the method of collecting rates on compound property had reduced the local tax yield, and, without the flexibility to increase the rate beyond the statutory maximum of a penny, the committee was forced to cut its budget.[90] Despite protests from Rathbone, the library and art gallery committee's budget was cut by £500 for 1890, and the corporation made it clear that it would not allow the committee to increase its deficit.[91] Fortunately, by this time, Rathbone had already assembled a permanent collection that attracted considerable popular interest. The gallery could boast average daily visitor numbers of over 1,400, and over 60,000 people paid to visit the annual autumn exhibition.[92]

The Edwardian period saw a significant decline in the quality of works purchased by the corporation. E. R. Dibdin took over P. H. Rathbone's role as chief negotiator of acquisitions, and although he had previously assisted Rathbone in making new purchases, he did not continue Rathbone's policy of purchasing small numbers of high-quality works, preferring to acquire larger numbers of more modestly priced items. In 1907 Dibdin submitted details of over thirty works from the current autumn exhibition that he hoped his committee might consider purchasing. This approach annoyed many in the Liverpool art world, not least R. Rathbone Jnr, who was now himself a member of the library and art gallery committee.[93] A number of Liverpool artists issued a polemic against the corporation for allowing picture acquisitions to fall into the hands of 'the butcher, the baker, and candlestick maker'.[94] There was at least some truth in this charge. Although Liverpool had bought over seventy works between 1903 and 1909, few of them were thought to have lasting value. Manchester in contrast had been both more selective and more imaginative. Its acquisitions in this period included not only works by Ford Madox Brown, Millais, Watts and Rossetti, but also innovative and critically acclaimed works associated with the Impressionists, notably by Corot and d'Espagnat.[95] Dibdin was not an entirely conservative force in Liverpool. Most notably, he helped bring the work of French, Swedish and Danish artists to the Liverpool exhibition.[96] In 1914 he narrowly escaped internment after travelling to Germany shortly before the outbreak of war in order to bring the work of German artists before the Liverpool public.[97] However, after Rathbone's death, public criticism of the corporation's purchases grew, and few of Liverpool's Edwardian acquisitions stimulated the excitement of those of the previous generation.

The Walker gallery was born out of the failure of the municipality to persuade its public that art was anything more than a rich man's hobby. Ultimately, the art gallery question provided a local brewer with the opportunity to improve both his public reputation and his political standing. Some, such as Barrell, have suggested that the nineteenth century saw a decline in artistic narratives of civic humanism, with patrons increasingly consuming art in the domestic sphere and neglecting traditional public obligations.[98] Meanwhile, sociologists have tended to emphasise the way in which the middle class broke with aristocratic traditions by rejecting the conspicuous display of cultural consumption, preferring to consume cultural goods in private.[99] However, the widespread and extremely public nature of giving to cultural institutions suggests that this view needs to be treated with caution. Walker's philanthropy can be viewed as a form of public conspicuous consumption, informed by a civic humanism that placed high social value on the giving of public cultural goods. Nor is there any reason to suppose that Walker's actions were unusual. The 'benevolence' of Chantrey and Tate at national level is well known, and many industrial towns produced philanthropists who were prepared to endow public art galleries or provide for public collections. Manchester had Whitworth, Preston had Harris, and Oldham had the empire of the Platts.[100]

An examination of the gifting process inherent in public donation illustrates both the way in which the local state was dependent on the private sector for the initiation of key cultural goods and the limitations of private-sector philanthropy. The 'lumpy' nature of art gallery capital formation meant that municipalities often welcomed private donations to force their hands. Although the donation of a gallery implied ongoing financial commitment for a local authority, running costs were small in comparison to the initial capital provided by private donors. Thus an art gallery was a gift that could not be rejected.[101] However, the early years of the Walker gallery demonstrated that many were not willing to accept philanthropic gifts if they were from an individual associated with a morally dubious trade or from a civic leader acting out of partisan motivation. In order for an individual to reap the rewards of philanthropy, generous deeds had to be made public, but if this was done in a way that was too overt or extravagant, a hostile response was inevitable. The opening of the Walker gallery was met with overt resistance, not only from those with a Nonconformist conscience, but also from those who saw a great public cause being perverted for private benefit. Thus few galleries can have been met with the sort of ambivalent public response evident in the case of the Walker. Placards and billboards associating the gallery with prostitution, violence and drunkenness did little for A. B. Walker's reputation in Liverpool and little for the cause of art.

Rathbone realised from the outset that if the gallery was to be successful it had to be perceived as representing not the taste of one man but the artistic consciousness of a city. It was the approach of Roscoe almost a generation before, and there was much of the 'myth of Roscoe' in it. Although the parallels that Rathbone drew with the classical world were somewhat unrealistic, their democratic essence made him, and others, aware of the importance of making high art relevant to a mass and relatively uneducated public. Throughout his period on the art gallery committee the corporation was sensitive about the question of ratepayer expenditure on art. Even when tax yields dropped as a result of compounding reform, the corporation was unwilling to follow the example of other local authorities and seek parliamentary approval to raise rates beyond the statutory penny maximum. The gallery could meet these objections only if it continued to attract a large annual attendance and organise a successful modern exhibition. Consequently, it was largely due to the work of Rathbone that the Walker prospered, developing a collection of Victorian art that was both high in quality and popular to the visitor. Ultimately, Walker obtained the memorial that his philanthropy craved: a successful art institution housing one of the country's leading regional collections. Yet it was one of his political rivals, Rathbone, who secured Walker's reputation. Under Rathbone's careful management the gallery lost its associations with Walker's political vanities and became an important symbol of Liverpool's cultural identity.

NOTES

1 These expectations were, of course, rapidly changing in the second half of the nineteenth century. For background see J. Garrard, *Democratisation in Britain: Elites, Civil Society and Reform since 1800* (Basingstoke, 2002); P. Clarke, *Liberals and Social Democrats* (Cambridge, 1978).
2 B. Kirkman Gray, *A History of English Philanthropy* (London, 1905), vi–ix.
3 M. Curti, 'American Philanthropy and the National Character', *American Quarterly*, 10 (1958), 420–37, esp. 420–1.
4 R. L. Payton, 'Philanthropic Values', in R. Magat (ed.), *Philanthropic Giving: Studies in Values and Goals* (Oxford and New York, 1989), 29–45, esp. 33.
5 M. Cicero, *On Moral Obligation*, trans. J. Higginbotham (London, 1967), 54; also see Payton, 'Philanthropic Values', 32–3.
6 For example see C. Jones, 'Some Recent Trends in the History of Charity', in M. Daunton (ed.), *Charity, Self-Interest and Welfare in the English Past* (London, 1996), 51–63.
7 For background discussion see W. C. Lubenow, *The Politics of Government Growth* (Newton Abbot, 1971); W. H. Greenleaf, *The Rise of Collectivism*, vol. 1 (London, 1983).
8 M. Gorsky, *Patterns of Philanthropy: Charity and Society in Nineteenth Century Bristol* (Woodbridge, 1999), 1–12.
9 E. P. Thomson, *Customs in Common* (London, 1991); H. Perkin, *Origins of Modern English Society* (London, 1969).
10 M. Mauss, *The Gift*, trans. W. Halls (London, 1990), 65–8.
11 Mauss, *Gift*, 73–83.
12 R. J. Morris, 'Voluntary Societies and British Urban Elites, 1780–1850: An Analysis', *Historical Journal*, 26 (1983), 95–118.
13 B. Harrison, 'Philanthropy and the Victorians', *Victorian Studies*, 9 (1966), 353–74.
14 J. Vernon, *Politics and the People* (Cambridge, 1993); S. Gunn, *The Public Culture of the Victorian Middle Class: Ritual and Authority in the English Industrial City 1840–1914* (Manchester, 2000): P. Joyce, *The Rule of Freedom: Liberalism and the Modern City* (London, 2003).
15 For background see R. Morris and R Trainor (eds), *Governance in Towns and Cities* (Aldershot, 2000).

16 N. McCord, 'Aspects of the Relief of Poverty in Early Nineteenth-Century Britain', in R. Hartwell *et al.* (eds), *The Long Debate on Poverty* (London, 1972), 91–108, cited in Gorsky, *Patterns*, 9.

17 See, for example, J. Piliavin and H. Charng, 'Altruism: A Review of Recent Theory and Research', *Annual Review of Sociology*, 16 (1990), 27–65.

18 F. Ostrower, *Why the Wealthy Give: The Culture of Elite Philanthropy* (Princeton, 1995).

19 P. Shapely, 'Charity, Status and Leadership: Charitable Image and the Manchester Man', *Journal of Social History*, 32 (1998), 157–77.

20 For a recent discussion of the popular creation and transmission of personal narratives see P. Joyce, *Visions of the People* (Cambridge, 1991), esp. 27–55; P. Joyce, *Democratic Subjects* (Cambridge, 1994).

21 E. Morris, 'The Liverpool Academy and Other Art Exhibitions in Liverpool 1774–1867', introduction to E. Morris and E. Roberts (eds), *The Liverpool Academy and Other Exhibitions of Contemporary Art in Liverpool 1774–1867* (Liverpool, 1998), 10–15; M. Bennett, 'The Pre-Raphaelites and the Liverpool Prize', *Apollo*, 76 (1972), 748–53.

22 *Report on the History and Progress of the Libraries, Museum and Gallery of Arts* (Liverpool, 1887), 5–7.

23 Morris, 'Liverpool Academy', 14–15.

24 For details on Rathbone family see S. Marriner, *Rathbones of Liverpool* (Liverpool, 1861).

25 B. G. Orchard, *Liverpool's Legion of Honour* (Birkenhead, 1893), 577–9, 619–20.

26 *Daily Courier*, 6 August 1873.

27 *Liverpool Mercury*, 8 August 1873.

28 *Daily Courier*, 6 August 1873.

29 See comments of Minton, *Daily Courier*, 7 August 1873.

30 *Daily Courier*, 7 August 1873.

31 *Liverpool Leader*, 9 August 1873.

32 *Liberal Review*, 9 August 1873.

33 *Liverpool Leader*, 16 August 1873.

34 *Liverpool Courier*, 29 August 1873.

35 *Liverpool Mercury*, 30 August 1873,

36 J. A. Picton, letter, 30 August 1873, reproduced in *Liverpool Mercury*, 1 September 1873.

37 *Liverpool Mercury*, 1 September 1873; *Daily Courier*, 1 September 1873.

38 *Liverpool Mercury*, 1 September 1873.

39 *Liverpool Mercury*, 4 September 1873; *Daily Post*, 5 September 1873.

40 *Statement of the Works of Art Purchased or Presented to the Corporation of Liverpool* (Liverpool, 1875), in Liverpool Corporation (hereafter LC), Council Proceedings, 1874–75, 627, LRO.

41 *Liberal Review*, 6 September 1873.

42 *Liberal Review*, 6 September 1873.

43 *Daily Post*, 30 September 1873; *Liverpool Leader*, 4 October 1873.

44 Orchard, *Liverpool's Legion*, 687–9.

45 Orchard, *Liverpool's Legion*, 690.

46 'True Generosity', letter in *Liberal Review*, 6 September 1873.

47 *Liberal Review*, 15 November 1873.

48 *Daily Post*, 4 December 1873.

49 *Daily Post*, 4 December 1873.

50 *Liverpool Leader*, 6 December 1873.

51 *Illustrated London News*, 10 October 1874.

52 *Liverpool Mercury*, 2 April 1874.

53 *Liberal Review*, 26 September 1874.

54 *Statement of the Works of Art Purchased or Presented to the Corporation of Liverpool*, 627.

55 *Liberal Review*, 26 September 1874.

56 'Opening of the Walker Art Gallery', (leaflet), in Documents and Papers Connected with Laying the Foundation Stone, The Opening Ceremony etc, etc, of the Walker Art Gallery, Liverpool, 1877, LRO.

57 *Liverpool Mercury*, 22 August 1877; *Daily Post*, 24 August 1877.

58 'To the Orangemen of Liverpool' (leaflet), in Documents and Papers Connected with Laying the Foundation Stone.

59 *Daily Albion*, 22 August 1877.

60 *The Porcupine*, 18 August 1877.

61 'A Casket to Commemorate the Opening of the Potter's Field' (leaflet), in Documents and Papers Connected with Laying the Foundation Stone.

62 'A Casket to Commemorate the Opening of the Potter's Field').

63 'Walker Art Gallery' (historical notes), in Documents and Papers Connected with Laying the Foundation Stone.

64 Orchard, *Liverpool's Legion*, 690.

65 *Liberal Review*, 8 September 1877.

66 *Daily Post*, 4 February 1933.

67 *Daily Albion*, 6 September 1877.

68 *Statement of the Works of Art Purchased or Presented to the Corporation of Liverpool*, 627.

69 LC, Council Proceedings, 5 December 1877, 28.

70 LC, Council Proceedings, 16 January 1878, 79.

71 LC, Council Proceedings, 6 March 1878, 113.

72 LC, Council Proceedings, 1 May 1878, 130–2. Harvey was latterly resident in the Liverpool suburb of Walton.

73 B. H. Grindley, *Exhibitions of Pictures and Municipal Management* (Liverpool, 1875), 5.

74 P. H. Rathbone, *The Political Value of Art to the Municipal Life of a Nation* (Liverpool, 1875), 8.

75 Rathbone, *Political Value*, 45.

76 J. Mayer, *On the Art of Pottery* (Liverpool, 1871), 40–1; also see J. Mayer, *History of the Art of Pottery in Liverpool* (Liverpool, 1855).

77 P. H. Rathbone, *The English School of Impressionists as Illustrated in the Liverpool Autumn Exhibition* (Liverpool, 1883).

78 *Liverpool Mercury*, 6 September 1877.

79 *Twenty-Sixth Annual Report of the Committee of the Free Public Library, Museum and Walker Art Gallery of the Borough of Liverpool* (Liverpool, 1879), 22–6.

80 *Thirtieth Annual Report of the Committee of the Free Public Library, Museum and Walker Art Gallery of the Borough of Liverpool* (Liverpool, 1883), 29.

81 Orchard, *Liverpool's Legion*, 579.

82 *Twenty-Sixth Annual Report*, 26.

83 T. H. Hall Caine, *A Disquisition on Dante Gabriel Rossetti's Painting in Oil Entitled 'Dante's Dream'* (Liverpool, 1881).

84 E. R. Dibdin, 'The Liverpool Corporation Collection', *Magazine of Art*, 12 (1889), 50–6, esp. 50.

85 *Twenty-Fourth Annual Report of the Committee of the Free Public Library, Museum and Walker Art Gallery of the City of Liverpool* (Liverpool, 1877).

86 Dibdin, 'Liverpool Corporation', 55.

87 For more details see E. Morris, 'Philip Henry Rathbone and the Purchase of Contemporary Foreign Paintings for the Walker Art Gallery, Liverpool, 1871–1914', *Walker Art Gallery Annual Report and Bulletin*, 6 (1975–76), 59–67.

88 *Report of the Liverpool Royal Institution, 22 February 1905* (Liverpool, 1905), 14–15, in Royal Institution Reports 1897–1906, LRO.

89 LC, Council Proceedings, 26 October 1887.

90 *Report on the History and Progress of the Libraries, Museum and Gallery of Arts*, 7–9.

91 LC, Council Proceedings, 5 February 1890.

92 *Thirty-Eighth Annual Report of the Committee of the Free Public Library, Museum and Walker Art Gallery of the City of Liverpool* (Liverpool, 1891), 29–30.

93 *Liverpool Daily Post and Mercury* (undated cutting [December 1907]), in Newspaper Articles by E. R. Dibdin, LRO, HF 700 DIB, 3.

94 C. W. Sharpe (ed.), *The Sport of Civic Life or, Art and the Municipality* (Liverpool, 1909), 4.

95 Sharpe, *Sport*, 9–10.

96 *Morning Post*, 5 October 1912.

97 *The Scotsman*, 3 October 1914.

98 J. Barrell, *The Political Theory of Painting from Reynolds to Hazlitt* (London, 1986), esp. 1–13.

99 M. Savage, J. Barlow, P. Deickens and T. Fielding, *Property, Bureaucracy and Culture* (London, 1992), 36–57.

100 N. Atkinson, *Sir Joseph Whitworth* (Stroud, 1996); J. Moore, 'Periclean Preston, Public Art and the Classical Tradition in Late-Nineteenth-Century Lancashire', *Northern History*, 40 (2003), 299–323; B. Law, *Oldham, Brave Oldham* (Oldham, 1999), esp. 183.

101 Similar patterns can be seen in the American museum movement. See K. McCarthy, 'Creating the American Athens: Cities, Cultural Institutions, and the Arts, 1840–1939', *American Quarterly*, 37 (1985), 426–39.

7

A problem of scale and leadership? Manchester's municipal ambitions and the 'failure' of public spirit

The experience of Liverpool revealed that dependence on a single wealthy individual to finance art institutions could be controversial and problematic. Yet, as Manchester was soon to discover, without a major donor or strong leadership, it could be difficult to build public support or obtain municipal assistance for prestigious projects. Despite the city's grand ambitions, no major sponsor came forward to support municipal art in Manchester. By the early 1870s, even the prestigious RMI was struggling to funds its activities. Its annual sales exhibition, once the highlight of Manchester's cultural year, had long been in decline and generated little turnover to fund the RMI's other activities. The institution's membership was elderly, and subscriptions fell almost every year; it had barely enough funds to cover its running costs. The long-held dream of establishing a permanent central art gallery in Manchester looked lost, especially after the onset of the 'Great Depression' absorbed any surplus private capital that might otherwise have been available. Although the RMI had gradually built up the nucleus of a permanent collection since the 1830s, it had no way of competing with major municipal authorities, such as Liverpool, that were willing to spend several thousand pounds per year on public art. When the RMI did identity a major work worthy of purchase, there were often other pressing financial claims on the institution. Thomas Worthington was keen for the RMI to purchase Henrietta Brown's *Le Ducat* for the permanent collection in 1879, but it was decided instead to leave surpluses for future structural alterations to the building.[1] By this time Worthington and many senior members had become frustrated at the failure of Manchester patrons to support the RMI.[2] As early as 1877 enquiries had been made as to the ways in which the RMI could be brought under municipal control, and unofficial preliminary discussions were undertaken.[3] Finally, in March 1880, the RMI council issued a circular calling for a mandate to open formal negotiations for the transfer of its property to the corporation, noting, 'there is a manifest lack of appreciation and support on the part of the general public of the aims and purposes of the Institution'.[4] Municipalisation offered the promise of an exhibition and purchase fund supported by the rates. Yet if the public could not be persuaded to part with their money voluntarily in support of art, would they be enthusiastic about supporting what amounted to an art gallery rate? The RMI leadership also anticipated some objections from within its own membership as the proposal amounted to the municipalisation of the property of a private club. Somewhat ingeniously, the leaders of the RMI argued that the rules of the organisation precluded members obtaining any pecuniary advantage from the dissolution of the institute and that municipalisation would merely represent 'placing the Institution in accordance with the spirit of the age'.[5]

Unfortunately, the details of the private negotiations between the RMI authorities and the city council are not known. The city council had been interested in the development of a permanent gallery for some time and had been prepared to give limited support to a tentative 1860 initiative aiming to establish a privately funded public gallery in the city, a scheme that was prompted by the success of the 1857 Manchester Art Treasures Exhibition. In many respects, the council had shown a very forward-thinking approach to public art in commissioning Ford Madox Brown to paint a series of historical murals in the new town hall. Although one might query the choice of murals and their historical accuracy, they represented a major form of municipal art patronage.[6] The huge sums spent on the city's palatial town hall should make the historian cautious about condemning Manchester's city fathers for parsimony in their support of art. With the RMI already developing a permanent collection, albeit slowly, and overseeing a still significant annual exhibition of modern works, it was difficult for the city council to justify spending public money to develop a rival gallery. Public funding of a private institution would have been controversial and probably illegal. Museums and galleries legislation was primarily intended for support of the education of popular taste, a function that was already being partly fulfilled by the recently developed but very small Queen's Park Museum. The only way the city council could reasonably be expected to become involved in supporting the work of the RMI was for the RMI to pass its functions to the municipality. Even then some members of the council thought it unjust that 'the poorer classes' should be taxed to provide luxuries that it was thought they would never use.[7]

Negotiations over the transition did not go smoothly. Many RMI stalwarts opposed the outright dissolution of the institution, and this plan was soon dropped. The scheme that emerged at the end of 1881 allowed for the transfer of the RMI buildings to the corporation, but the continuation of the RMI as a private club with special privileges of access. However, there was still considerable opposition, and the plan failed to get its necessary three-quarters majority.[8] Part of the reason was that although the RMI was not generally well supported – only forty-three members voted on the issue of dissolution – it remained a prestigious private body which numbered among its members some of the most important merchants and industrialists in Manchester. Figures like Charles N. Rickards continued to give it active support, and in 1880, he provided a large part of his private collection for a G. F. Watts loan exhibition.[9] Richard Peacock, the railway engineering magnate and leading Liberal politician, gave a lavish banquet for the council and friends.[10] There was, therefore, considerable concern that municipalisation would bring about a fundamental change in the character of the institution and undermine its position as a fashionable social club. Negotiations continued. The major sticking points were the level of representation that RMI officials would have on the new governing body, the rights which RMI governors would have in the new institution, the level of financial support the city council would agree and the length of time for which this support would be guaranteed. Gradually progress was made. First, in April 1882, the city council agreed to a continuation of governors' privileges.[11] The issue of the constitution of the new art gallery committee was more controversial: the city council clearly wanted to limit the influence of outside bodies, while officials of the RMI wanted guaranteed seats not only for its own senior figures, but also for kindred bodies such as the school of art, Owens College, Manchester Grammar School and Manchester School Board.[12] Eventually, a compromise was reached giving the RMI seven representatives on the art gallery committee, almost a third of the total membership. The remaining stumbling block was the issue of the corporation endowment that was to be allocated to the purchase of public art. Although the figure of £2,000 per annum was agreed, the city council insisted on limiting the endowment to twenty years.[13] Despite other minor disagreements, the RMI endorsed the proposals on 1 May 1882, and the property of the RMI passed to the corporation through the Manchester Corporation Act of that year.[14]

The large purchase fund that was made available to the art gallery committee soon allowed for some major purchases for the permanent collection. The purchasing policy was largely similar to that adopted by the RMI authorities in that the emphasis continued to be on modern British painting, with famous London-based artists well to the fore. However, the very fact that £2,000 per annum was available for purchases now allowed the city to compete for some of the most important works of the season. Purchases were made from a variety of sources. Some were made directly from the artists concerned, such as that of Sir Frederick Leighton's *Last Watch of Hero* and *Captive Andromeda*. Others were made from major sales, such as Rickards's sale of 1887, where G. F. Watt's *Prayer* was obtained.[15] In some cases deputations were sent to London galleries, particularly fashionable ones, such as the New Gallery in Regent Street. In 1888 three major works were purchased from this source, including Alfred East's celebrated *Autumn*. Many pictures were purchased from the annual Manchester exhibition; municipal patronage of the exhibition was essential if the position of the exhibition was to be maintained. In 1888 the council obtained James Sant's oil *A Thorn Amidst the Roses* and William Eyre Walker's watercolour *Across the Forest, Hampshire*.[16] It purchased William Sadler's *In the Camp of the Amalekites* from the same source in 1889, and a year later George Sheffield's *A Hundred Years Ago*.[17] In contrast, the Manchester Academy exhibition received far less municipal patronage, partly because the overall quality was generally lower, but also because the exhibition attracted few of the popular London artists who seemed to have been most prized by the art gallery committee. The council did, however, purchase James Hey Davies's *Young Poachers* from this exhibition, illustrating that artists with Manchester connections were not entirely excluded from municipal support.[18]

Complaints continued that Manchester's well-to-do failed to support annual exhibitions and the work of the city art gallery committee, while others mocked the artistic ignorance of those who did attend.[19] Yet it does seem that the vigorous collecting policy of the new committee stimulated renewed interest in the institution. Rather than reducing private patronage, the use of public funds to support art actually encouraged more private donations for the permanent collection. Admittedly, some early gifts were relatively modest, such as C. P. Scott's gift of twenty-nine coloured plates of Italian ornament.[20] However, by the late 1880s, more significant contributions were being made. In 1888 the gallery received three major original works, C. R. Stanley's *View of Manchester from Kersel Moor*, given by William Houldsworth MP, W. J. Muckley's *Roses*, given by James Chadwick, and William Bradley's *Charles Swain*, given by Clara Swain Dickens.[21] In 1889 the art gallery received a further boost when a well-known Manchester collector, Roger Ross of Victoria Park, presented a major collection of fifty-eight watercolours to the corporation. The Ross pictures included important examples by Cox, Copley Fielding, De Wint, Prout and Varley and formed the basis of a new city watercolour collection.[22] Occasionally, private patrons donated works that the corporation could never have contemplated buying on grounds of costs, even with a £2,000 per annum budget. One such example was Holman Hunt's celebrated *Shadow of Death*, given by the Agnews, for which the artist received £10,500 – one of the largest sums ever paid at the time for a modern painting.[23] Sir Joseph Whitworth gave four Ettys, which complemented William Grant's donation of the famous *The Sirens and Ulysses*. James Braddock was perhaps the most prolific donor in the decade, contributing a dozen works, including old masters attributed to Rubens and Titian.[24]

With the city art gallery's permanent collection rapidly developing and Manchester's reputation as an art centre gradually being restored, thoughts naturally turned to the possibility of organising a major exhibition highlighting the progress that had been made. Ellis Lever, a coal merchant from Salford, was the somewhat unlikely figure responsible for promoting the idea of organis-ing such an event, an attempt to rekindle the memories of the Art Treasures Exhibition of 1857. In later years Lever was to develop a somewhat unsavoury reputation owing to his business practices,[25] but he was an important figure in convincing others that public art could be utilised not just for public educa-tion, but also to stimulate the local economy. While some were cautious about organising a major public event because of the state of trade, Lever argued that a major exhibition would do much to stimulate business and would 'attract millions to our city from all parts of the world'.[26] As 1887 was to be the year of the queen's jubilee, a celebratory exhibition was likely to capture the public mood. Rather like the Art Treasures Exhibition thirty years before, the Jubilee Exhibition proposal attracted many far beyond the city's usual art community, including the leading magnates of the day: Oliver Heywood, Daniel Adamson, W. H. Bailey, George Milner and William Holland.[27] Perhaps because of the rather imperialistic overtones of the exhibition, initial enthusiasm for the event came most strongly from senior Conservatives. The Conservative MP William Houldsworth made the connections between Manchester, industry and empire very explicit, declaring that there was nowhere 'where the connection between the prosperity of the nation and the public and private virtues of the Queen are more clearly understood'.[28] Liberals, thrown into some disarray by the Irish Home Rule question, were naturally less enthusiastic about encouraging an outbreak of imperialistic fervour that could be exploited by their opponents.

Oliver Heywood feared that the Home Rule crisis would draw the attention of public men away from involvement in such an exhibition, while William Mather shared similar sentiments and doubted whether an exhibition could be organised in such a short space of time.[29] There were other objections too. A recent 'Fisheries' exhibition in Liverpool had proved a financial disaster, losing £12,000, while some radicals feared that the exhibition was simply a scam by prominent citizens to attract royalty to the city and to promote themselves.[30] Others worried that the public was becoming somewhat jaded by annual exhibitions and that Manchester could be perceived as being 'actuated mainly by mere fussiness and vain childish rivalry' with Liverpool.[31] Despite these reservations, the project clearly captured the attention of many of the city's leading public men. On the suggestion of Houldsworth, a committee was formed consisting of the mayors and deputy mayors of Manchester and nearby towns, prominent industrialists, local MPs and those associated with the world of art and literature, such as Charles Rowley and N. C. Shou.

The exhibition had several objectives. At one level it was designed to commemorate and glorify the queen's jubilee. It also had the explicit goal of promoting Manchester's industries. Speakers at public meetings emphasised how major exhibitions in Edinburgh, London and Liverpool were often stocked with examples of Manchester industry, and therefore it was regarded as somewhat anomalous that Manchester had never organised a similar exhibition of its own.[32] The promotion of public art was something of a subsidiary function. Yet, from the outset, many were concerned to try to ensure that the exhibition left a lasting cultural legacy. William Mather tentatively suggested 'the establishment of a splendid institution for the teaching of the arts and sciences'.[33] The leading advocate of this approach was Ellis Lever, who felt that a 'People's Palace', modelled on that in the East End of London, should be included in the plans.[34] Unfortunately, after disagreements over the location of the exhibition, Ellis Lever's name was dropped from the committee, and thereafter there was little talk of trying to provide a permanent institution to commemorate the exhibition.[35]

The exhibition committee soon attracted considerable support. As the city authorities had no power to organise such an event, the Manchester jubilee committee adopted broadly the same procedure as that for the Art Treasures Exhibition. A guarantee fund was established on a private basis, with trustees held responsible for managing the exhibition. By 24 June 1886, the guarantee fund had reached £50,000. Yet this success hid political problems. There were ongoing complaints about the unrepresentative nature of the committee. Leaving the organisation of a major public exhibition to a committee of self-appointed plutocrats may have been acceptable to public opinion in 1857, but there was a growing sense that by the 1880s, bodies with important public functions should be more representative. Even the middle-class *Manchester City News* voiced its disquiet:

> Indeed it would have perhaps given greater popular satisfaction if the scheme had created a truly representative council of the city and neighbourhood. There is not much public spirit in men agreeing to become guarantors in order to have the whole control of the object they guarantee. In movements of this kind, care should be taken to command general confidence, to show that everybody is interested in them, and that the management is not exclusively in the hands of the wealthy.[36]

Linked to the issue of management of the exhibition was the question of what should be done with any surplus that was generated. No public discussion took place as to what would be done with any profits, although many clearly assumed that profits from the exhibition would be made available for public projects. This uncertainty was to cause much controversy after the exhibition closed.

The exhibition was widely recognised as a great success. The exhibition grounds utilised part of Trafford Park, very close to the location of the Art Treasures Exhibition of 1857. Responsibility for the various sections of the exhibition was divided between sub-committees. The fine art section was chaired by William Agnew, who was responsible for negotiating the loan of works, while the work of hanging was divided between T. O. Barlow, who took responsibility for deceased masters, and J. C. Horsley, who hung the work of living artists.[37] However, as this was the Jubilee Exhibition, a decision had been taken to limit exhibits to pieces 'produced in the United Kingdom during the reign of Her Majesty the Queen'.[38] This self-imposed limitation did not, of course, have any artistic or educational justification and attracted some adverse comment from Manchester art critics.[39] Yet the organisers' policy did mean that the exhibition had a strong modern and contemporary focus. Artists were given considerable influence in the tone of the exhibition. Selected artists, chosen by a committee, were each asked to nominate a work for exhibition that they thought to display best their own personal powers. These works were placed in a separate section from those of deceased masters.[40] A large number of British artists of the period were represented. The major oils included J. M. W. Turner's *Rain, Steam and Speed*, J. E. Millais's *The*

Escape of a Heretic, 1559, Ford Madox Brown's *Work*, Sir Edwin Landseer's *Scene in Braemar* and Sir Frederick Leighton's *Daphnephoria*. The watercolour section, occupying separate galleries, was equally impressive, with most of the major watercolourists of the second half of the century being represented. Works there included David Cox's *Calais Pier*, Copley Fielding's *Cader Idris* and Prout's *Hotel de Ville*. Major modern sculpture was also present, including Sir Fredrick Leighton's *The Python Slayer* from the Royal Academy.[41] What was particularly noticeable was the under-representation of the Pre-Raphaelites and particularly the work of their descendants. Burne-Jones had twelve exhibits, but Spencer Stanhope had only two, and others, such as Strudwick, were not represented at all.[42] The decision to limit the exhibition to work produced during the reign of Queen Victoria created somewhat perverse results for some collections. Landscape painting, which had historically been so popular at Manchester exhibitions, was particularly handicapped. Constable had died a few weeks before the accession of Queen Victoria, and Turner's most creative years were generally acknowledged to have passed by this point.[43] Perhaps those with most reason for complaint were the Manchester artists. Most of their pictures were badly hung, often in favour of works from the Royal Academy. Some critics clearly believed that this was a deliberate policy to curry favour among metropolitan artists. Once again, the now familiar plea to give more consideration to local painters was repeated. Although the marginalisation of Manchester artists may simply have occurred because the quality of the exhibition was very high, some local men seem to have been particularly unfortunate. While H. C. Whaite's pictures of Thirlmere were hung adequately, Anderson Hague's celebrated *Bracken Gatherers* was 'skied'.[44]

Although the Jubilee Exhibition was undoubtedly the most important art exhibition to be held in Manchester for thirty years, metropolitan critics were not wholly impressed.[45] Perhaps the most cutting criticism came in the *Magazine of Art*. William Agnew and his committee had set out not merely to organise a miscellaneous exhibition, but to arrange a hanging designed to illustrate the progress of British art during the Victorian period. Unfortunately, a significant number of major artists were simply not represented, including James Whistler, Alphonse Legros, William Windus and James Martin. Many were poorly repre-sented, from David Wilkie, who was active for just five years during Victoria's reign, to C. W. Cope, who had only recently retired.[46]

The promotion of fine art was only one aspect of the Jubilee Exhibition. Indeed, reports in exhibition catalogues and critical comment tended to perceive the object of the exhibition as promoting Britain and British manufactures in the general sense, rather than having any broad educational function. Some supposedly serious critics simply lapsed into complacent eulogies about the strength of British art. On visiting the galleries, foreigners would have to confess 'that this country [Britain] has produced a large proportion of the best pictorial works of the century'.[47] As British prosperity had increased rapidly, the last fifty years of British art had been 'progressive beyond all precedent'.[48] Comparisons were naturally made with the exhibition of 1857, as local and national patriotism was combined in a heady mix. Such events were 'brilliant epochs in the annals of Manchester, and will render the history of the city honourable in the records of European civilisation and progress'.[49] The jubilee committee had achieved its objectives in that it had organised a large celebratory exhibition which had attracted over 4.7 million visitors in just six months.[50] However, just how much the exhibition did in promoting a wider appreciation of art is somewhat questionable. Criticism of the exhibition suggests that the response to the fine art section was somewhat mixed. Once the exhibition was closed, the building was sold, and the land on which it took place was returned to Sir Humphrey de Trafford.

Once it was clear that the Jubilee Exhibition had made a substantial profit, debate turned to how the profit should be used. Ellis Lever re-entered the fray, arguing that sums should be dedicated to public works: open space, a technical college or an art gallery.[51] This prompted a series of letters to the local press from advocates of worthy causes, including those supporting local medical charities, 'People's Palaces' and art education.[52] Not everyone, however, had the same public-spirited view. Some argued that as the exhibition had been organised on a privately subscribed basis, then any surplus was the sole property of the guarantors of the exhibition and consequently any public discussion of how the surplus should be spent was, quite simply, 'next to an impertinence'.[53] By the time a celebratory dinner for the organisers of the exhibition was held at Manchester's Grand Hotel, it was clear that a significant minority of guarantors felt that the profits should remain in their own hands. While Sir George Haytor Chubb, the dinner's chair, emphasised that the guarantors had acted out of selfless motives, without any thought of reward, J. C. Lee, the chair of the executive committee, refused to be drawn but tellingly criticised those who had made suggestions for use of the profits but had failed to subscribe.[54] However, it was clear that public opinion was very critical of the suggestion that the profits were the sole property of the guarantors. The constitution of the jubilee committee had already come in for criticism for being unrepresentative, and now it seemed that some members of the committee were proposing to retain the profits for themselves. W. H. S. Watts accused the guarantors of dishonesty, pointing out that it was hardly likely that those patrons who had lent works of art would have done so gratuitously if they had known they were simply contributing to someone's private profit. As the movement had been begun by public petition for a public meeting, it seemed perverse that some individuals had sought to turn the project into an opportunity for private speculation.[55] Eventually the legatees of Sir Joseph Whitworth helped the jubilee committee out of its problem by proposing to work with it on the development of the Whitworth Institute.[56] Further talks ensued, and eventually the major part of the exhibition profits was used in the support of the school of art.

The Jubilee Exhibition demonstrated that Manchester was still an important centre of artistic patronage. Yet, in organising the exhibition, its senior public figures were motivated as much by national patriotism, civic pride and personal ambition as by artistic interests. Disputes over the use of the profits of the exhibition were indicative of a tension between public-spirited motives and the desire for private profit. However, the exhibition may have encouraged municipal leaders to take public art more seriously, at least for a time. The council was certainly more willing to pay large sums for individual pieces of work in the years that immediately followed. At a sale of D. G. Rossetti at Christie's in 1888, Charles J. Pooley, the art gallery committee's representative, was given 1,000 guineas to use at his discretion. Unfortunately, it is questionable how long this enthusiasm lasted. The following decade revealed increasing public reluctance to fund an expansion of the city's main gallery, and with it the limitations of public support for visual art.

The annual exhibition of modern paintings struggled to regain its former reputation during the 1880s, and while the permanent collection expanded, exhibition space contracted. It was decided in 1887, the year of the Jubilee Exhibition, to limit the annual exhibition to the purpose-built galleries alone. This necessitated a reduction in the number of works hung by about 30 per cent.[57] A year later the number of pictures fell still further – from 728 to 583 – making it the smallest annual exhibition for at least twenty-five years.[58] Shortly afterwards, the committee agreed to the remodelling of the interior, replacing the lecture theatre with a new central gallery.[59] Plans were composed for a new building on Deansgate, to be erected on council-owned land and to be dedicated primarily to the annual exhibition. Unfortunately objections, mainly on the grounds of cost, were raised in full council, and the proposal failed to gain approval.[60] Desperate to find extra space, the art gallery committee even considered converting downstairs side rooms for exhibition space, but it was decided that this plan would only cause more controversy. Works from the modern exhibition would effectively have to be juxtaposed with those from the permanent collection, potentially inviting unfavourable comparisons.[61] Fearing objections from artists, this plan was also dropped.

Although the transfer of the RMI building to the corporation and the enthusiasm surrounding the Jubilee Exhibition had boosted Manchester's position in the world of art, problems remained. The city council's £2,000 purchase fund had improved the permanent collection and had persuaded some private citizens to donate their own works for public display. Yet only a small proportion of the city's major art patrons made significant donations to the municipal gallery. C. J. Pooley noted with dismay that, despite all the wealth in Lancashire, the practice of making public donations was 'much less widely spread than it ought to be'.[62] Rarely were more than three or four significant works donated in any one year. This may have been partly because, by the early 1890s, it was well known that the city art gallery was chronically short of space and the city council seemed reluctant to build anew. The RMI had watched with growing alarm for some time until, in October 1891, it made public its frustration with the city authorities. The RMI favoured the construction of a new gallery behind the old one, arguing that this would be much more cost-effective than the building of an entirely separate gallery.[63]

The city's art gallery committee was caught in a difficult position. On the one hand, local artists and the RMI were angry at the failure of the corporation to meets its apparent 'obligations' towards the annual exhibition. On the other, it was clear that having agreed an annual endowment of £2,000, the corporation was reluctant to fund a new municipal gallery, especially as the Whitworth was being developed privately. Another short-term solution was proposed, namely structural alterations to the first floor, involving the removal of corridors and lavatories, to create more exhibition space. The proposal created discord in both the art gallery committee and the council generally. Several councillors talked about the alterations as a form of mutilation of what was widely regarded as a landmark building.[64] The officers of the RMI were appalled and issued a protest.[65] Charles Rowley, the most well-known art critic on the council, clashed with other art gallery committee members in the press, arguing that they were

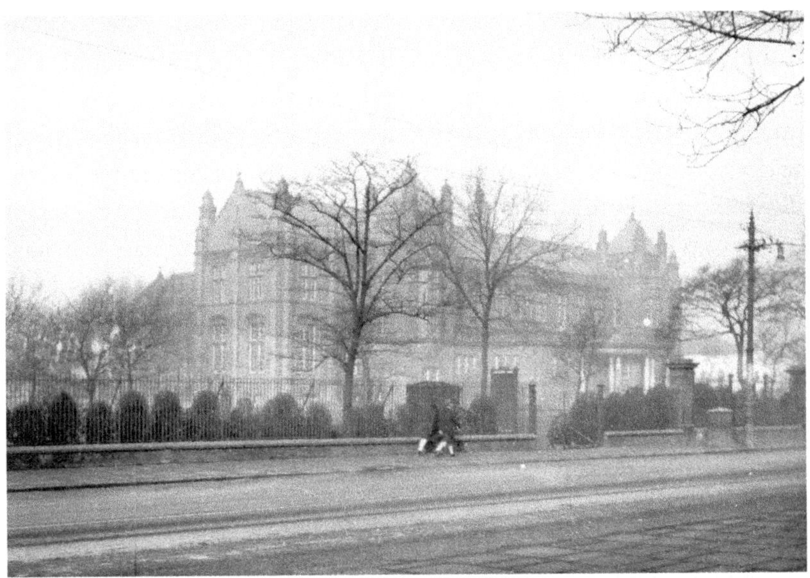

15 View of the Whitworth Art Gallery, showing its suburban parkland setting

'bent on obliterating one of the best pieces of art we have in Manchester'.[66] Despite the controversy the alterations were eventually agreed (Figure 15).[67]

The early 1890s were not entirely unproductive for the art gallery committee. In 1892 there was a review of purchasing policy, with a conscious attempt to move away from what C. J. Pooley termed 'miscellaneous buying, acted upon at the caprice of the moment' and give the officers of the committee more discretion to pursue purchases.[68] Although it is not entirely clear how this worked in practice, several important British works were obtained in the years that followed. Numerous works were obtained from the Allen sale of March 1893, including Stanhope Forbes's *The Lighthouse*, William Muller's *The Acropolis, Athens* and David Cox's *Driving Home the Flock*. Major works were also purchased by private contract directly from collectors, such as G. W. Fox of Manchester, who sold the corporation F. J. Shields's *Sisterly Help*, and James Leathart of Gateshead, who sold J. E. Millais's *Autumn Leaves*.[69] Millais was a favourite of the committee, and the following year his *Victory O Lord!* was purchased by private contract. The committee also exhibited a strong interest in Ford Madox Brown, acquiring his drawing *Work* in a similar manner.[70] Arguably, the corporation's most important Pre-Raphaelite works were obtained during this period.[71]

The mid-1890s brought a new sense of optimism to the art gallery committee. With the city council having recently completed large-scale engineering and sanitation work, it was widely thought that it would support the art gallery committee's attempts to develop a new city gallery.[72] Unfortunately, the overtures to the city council were largely ignored. The only ally the committee had was the middle-class press. Both Conservative and Liberal papers criticised the continuing lack of progress and began to look in desperation for private patrons. The *Manchester Courier* lamented that the city did not have a Walker as Liverpool did, for 'The best work of the year goes naturally to the place where it is best exhibited, and Liverpool and Glasgow are preferred to Manchester.'[73] Meanwhile, the *Manchester Guardian* observed a failure of public spirit. C. J. Pooley again went to the press, railing against 'a want of pride of citizenship in Manchester' and noting that it was 'a most extraordinary thing, having regard to the number of patrons in Manchester and the neighbourhood, that so little help had been afforded to the Art Gallery'.[74] The city council did little to encourage further private support with its own negative policies. Even proposals to appoint a professional art director were defeated on grounds of cost, provoking further criticism from the RMI and leading art patrons.[75]

The somewhat uneasy relationship between the RMI and the city council deteriorated further when it became clear that the council planned to abolish RMI representation on the art gallery committee when the city next put forward a private bill to Parliament. Under the new plans, power of appointment to the committee would rest solely with the council.[76] The constant criticism of the city council by the RMI was embarrassing, but to remove the RMI's right of representation was widely seen as breaking faith with the 1881 accord. J. E. Phythian was delegated by the RMI to attend a town's meeting in protest at the proposals and launched an outspoken attack on the 'discourteous action' and the 'objectionable manner' in which the proposals had been brought forward.[77] Fortunately, the RMI had a number of allies in the ranks of the city council; there was clearly a significant minority of municipal representatives who felt that corporation policy in relation to art was somewhat parsimonious. Even the chair of the art gallery committee, Alderman John Hopkinson, attempted to disassociate himself from those advocating the reform of the committee. The RMI hinted that if the proposals were put forward to Parliament they would be publicly opposed, as it had never intended the building to pass into the sole hands of the city council.[78] Following negotiations, RMI representation on the committee was reduced from seven to three, with the Whitworth Institute being given two representatives and Owens College two representatives. In practice, though, the personnel changed little, with the retiring RMI representatives J. D. Milne, Edward Salomans and J. E. Phythian gaining re-election as representatives of the Whitworth Institute and Owens College.[79] Simultaneously, the RMI reformed its membership structure with reduced share transfer fees and reduced annual subscriptions. The latter initiative was successful in doing much to revive the ailing institution, and by 1906, the RMI had attracted sixty additional annual governors.[80]

The reform of the city art gallery committee, making it more widely representative body, and the revival of the RMI helped to place the issue of a new municipal art gallery back on the political agenda. The annual modern exhibition was still struggling, and lack of space meant that the 1904 renewal was largely limited to oil paintings, although a separate watercolour exhibition had been held earlier in the year.[81] However, it was the purchase by the city council of the disused Manchester Royal Infirmary at Piccadilly that again raised hopes for the development of a new gallery. The site had primarily been purchased to effect street and public health improvement, but the library and art gallery committees saw the site as a possible location for future expansion (Figure 16).[82] From the start, members of Manchester's art community were divided on whether the dream of a magnificent new gallery at Piccadilly was a realistic option. The Manchester Academy, frustrated at the constant postponing of plans for a new gallery, was cautious and hoped that the city council would, in the first instance at least, find a way of constructing a temporary extension to the current gallery on Mosley Street.[83] The city art gallery committee established a special sub-committee to discuss various proposals. Eventually, it concluded that any extension of the present building could not satisfy future requirements and came out in strong support of the infirmary site, although it also recognised that this could only be a long-term project. In order to protect the annual exhibition, the committee agreed to investigate the construction of a temporary extension at the Mosley Street building on George Street.[84] Unfortunately, the city architect, Henry Price, was decidedly unimpressed by the sub-committee's proposals, arguing that they could not be implemented without interfering with the light of the neighbouring Athenaeum building and buildings on the other side of George Street. The proposed extension would also have been very expensive, particularly as it would have involved the construction of a tunnel over Back George Street.[85] Faced with such an unfavourable report, the sub-committee was forced to drop the extension proposals and concentrated instead on investigating

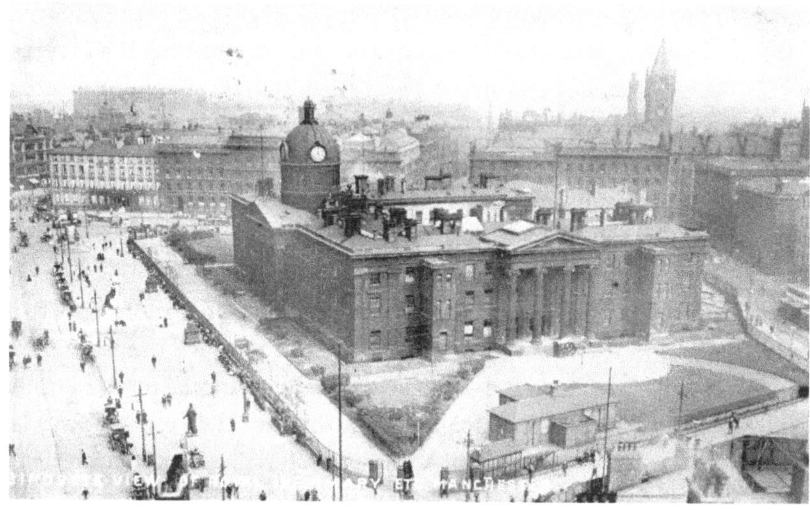

16 The Royal Infirmary, the proposed site of the new Manchester gallery

how the newly acquired Heaton Hall, in north Manchester, could be used as a temporary overflow gallery.[86]

Despite these setbacks, the art gallery committee was determined to pursue its interest in the infirmary site. As the library committee also favoured the infirmary site for expansion, thoughts naturally turned to how a completely new art gallery and central library could be jointly developed. The two committees came together in a powerful alliance to press for the redevelopment of the infirmary. In 1905 the members of the art gallery committee commenced what was in effect a grand tour of many of the major British and northern European art galleries, assembling a large amount of data for their own plans for a new Manchester gallery.[87] Their published report indicates just how ambitious the art gallery committee was: it intended to establish a gallery that could bear comparison with the best provincial galleries in Europe.[88] The committee's tour took in, among others, the Royal Museums of Painting and Sculpture in Brussels, the Royal Museum of Fine Arts and the Plantin-Moretus Museum in Antwerp and the Municipal Museum and Rijksmuseum in Amsterdam, together with the major museums and art galleries in Hamburg, Berlin, Dresden, Munich, Frankfurt, Cologne and Lille. The main conclusion from the tour was that Manchester's collecting policy was too parochial and narrowly focused.[89] No other gallery was found to have focused so much on one school of painting as Manchester, and it was recommended that picture collecting should no longer be confined to the modern British school, but instead to be unrestricted by period or nationality.[90] The Manchester deputation also compiled useful notes on the design aspects of any new gallery. There was a strong opposition among the committee to lofty rooms, with lower ceilings, such as those in the Kaiser-Friedrich-Museum at Berlin and the Kelvingrove galleries at Glasgow, now preferred. Great importance was attached to placing the gallery in an isolated location, to protect against fire and to ensure good light. Not all lessons from continental galleries were deemed to be relevant to Manchester. When German practice advised against the use of southern aspects to protect paintings from over-exposure, the delegation commented, somewhat facetiously, that it 'may be doubted whether the Manchester rooms will be troubled with too much sunlight'.[91]

Although the delegation's report was accepted, progress on the infirmary site was slow. The land in Piccadilly was commercially valuable and, once the street improvements had been completed, could have been re-sold for commercial use. The Manchester Exchange building, the city's commercial heart, was increasingly overcrowded, and some looked to the Piccadilly site as an excellent area for its re-location.[92] These competing claims on the site prompted a number of prominent art lovers to try to mobilise public support for the art gallery committee's proposals. A conference was called by members of the committee with the intention of starting a Society of Friends of Art, supposedly based on the models of the National Art Collections Fund and the Société des Amis du Louvre, although the body clearly had an explicitly political function. It was effectively a broad coalition of those interested in promoting public art, including J. D. Milne of the Whitworth, Elias Bancroft, honorary secretary of the Manchester Academy, Cllr T. Marr from the Ancoats Art Museum, E. W. Marshall from the RMI, and representatives from the Athenaeum Graphic Club.[93] Membership was thrown open to all, with a relatively low membership fee of five shillings per annum. Significantly, the radical Liberal councillor Walter Butterworth, the newly recruited chair of the art gallery committee, took on the chairmanship.[94] The society under Butterworth aimed to be 'a far more democratic organisation' than other art bodies and to include the 'mass of the people'.[95] Unfortunately, it succeeded in mobilising only limited support, attracting just 194 members. Subscriptions reached just £111, and this sum included one donation of £50. After just fifteen months of work Butterworth wound up the organisation, suggesting that members simply become governors of the RMI. Although the society had begun with great potential, the dream of forming a genuinely democratic body to press the cause of public art had disappeared in a wave of apathy.[96]

The RMI, however, continued to be a powerful voice in public art. Now strengthened with a growing membership, in the early months of 1907 it took the initiative and called upon the art gallery committee to organise a public meeting and begin a city-wide debate on the new gallery. The committee, somewhat embarrassed, declined.[97] The RMI refused to leave the matter there and instead went ahead and organised its own meeting, inviting representatives from all the major art bodies in Manchester. Supporters of a major new gallery, such as Professor Boyd Dawkins from the Victoria University, were keen to emphasise that the gallery plan was not a mere middle-class fad. Instead it was 'a democratic question' essential to promote the educational opportunities of the 'toilers and the workers'.[98] Similarly, social reformers such as T. C. Horsfall emphasised that it 'would enable them to do what was urgently necessary to raise the low level of life in the town' and in particular to provide alternative forms of recreation to gambling.[99] The meeting only highlighted the fact that public opinion was very divided on the project. F. W. Cooper, the city auditor, condemned the 'Apostles of Extravagance' who advocated expensive prestige projects simply so that the city could compete 'for the medal of importance'.[100] Even the vice chancellor of the university, Alfred Hopkinson, opposed the Piccadilly development, condemning the high rates as 'a dreadful burden on the most deserving class of people' and arguing that, in any case, open space was more valuable.[101]

Public debate revealed that there was a growing scepticism as to the didactic value of a new gallery. Although some social reformers, such as T. C. Horsfall, continued to view galleries as vital tools for social progress, others were becoming much more sceptical that heavy expenditure on art really was a very effective way of addressing Manchester's undoubted social problems. Even some of Horsfall's early supporters, such as the Rev. W. A. Connor, had grown sceptical about the efficacy of art in tackling ignorance and social injustice.[102] Similarly, the *Manchester City News*, widely regarded as the city's leading newspaper for artistic comment, was not convinced that didactic arguments held much weight:

> we require convincing that the rough of Angel Meadow [a slum area] is to be transmogrified into a creature of ethereal beauty by looking at an Art Palace, or, in some very remote instance, by being induced to enter it. Art has its educational and ameliorative influence and its elevating power, but Art does not stand alone, nor will men be redeemed by Art and nothing else.[103]

It was also questionable whether a city centre location would, in any case, be most suitable. Many felt that art should be brought closer to local communities. Branch libraries had been remarkably successful, and some advocated the development of more branch art galleries, or at least the use of public halls for temporary local exhibitions.[104] Horsfall's own Ancoats Art Museum demonstrated what could be achieved for relatively modest costs.[105] Ruskin's popular St George's Museum in nearby Sheffield followed a similar pattern, while also demonstrating the benefits of constructing an institution in healthier surroundings on the city's edge.[106] Manchester's smoggy city centre was not a particularly pleasant place to study art. Some went so far as to say that air pollution was so bad that major cultural institutions such as libraries and art galleries should not be located in city centres at all, but rather in open space in the suburbs.[107] The recent success of the Whitworth gallery and the new gallery in Heaton Park also suggested that the choice of a city centre location could be a backward step.

Even if the infirmary site was to be utilised, there was still the question as to whether the existing building should be adapted for library and art gallery use, or whether a completely new building should be constructed at greater cost. This issue became a central point of controversy in a local by-election in December 1907, highlighting just how sensitive the cost of the proposed new art gallery was.[108] The issue also divided the press. The *Manchester City News* did much to mobilise support the retention of the original building. In July it gave over many column inches to the proposals of Cllr T. Cook. Despite the fact that the corporation's architect opposed conversion, Cook drew up plans which appeared to show the building could be modified much more cheaply than developing an entirely new gallery. The infirmary would gain a new roof to allow for the top-lighting of the upper floor, which would become the art gallery. The lower level would then be adopted for library purposes. In all the scheme would have allowed for sixteen new galleries to be built, giving 2,865 yards of wall space, compared with 1,736 in the Mosley Street gallery,[109] and the individual galleries would have been between nineteen and thirty feet wide and around eighteen feet high.[110] While the *Manchester City News* was in favour of adapting the infirmary, the Liberal *Manchester Guardian* was outspoken in support of the construction of an entirely new gallery. This placed the newspaper in a very difficult situation when John Percy, a Liberal candidate for the local council in the leafy suburban ward of Rusholme, placed opposition to a new building in his election manifesto. In contrast, his Conservative opponent J. D. Chandler came out in support of an entirely new building.[111] The members of the Rusholme Liberal Association were appalled that *their* paper continued to campaign for a new art gallery and undermine the candidature of the otherwise progressive Percy. Yet C. P. Scott, the editor, refused to compromise, condemning Percy's 'perverse attitude on the Infirmary site question'.[112] The Liberal candidate was narrowly defeated, and while the result could not be interpreted as a rousing endorsement for a new building, the controversy demonstrated the strength of feeling that existed and how leading politicians even placed the issue above party loyalties.[113]

The art gallery committee's 'grand tour' of European art galleries may not have generated a great public yearning for a new Manchester gallery, but it did have an important influence on the collecting and exhibition policy of the council. Before the tour, the vast majority of art bought for Manchester represented the modern British school. After 1905, modern British art continued to be bought, including works from major figures such as W. H. Hunt, Ford Madox Brown, John Ruskin, G. F. Watts and Millais.[114] However, there was increasing interest in continental, and particularly French, works. In 1907 the art gallery committee organised a major exhibition of works by modern French painters, mainly from the Barbizon and Impressionist schools. The artists represented included Dupré, Millet, Corot, Boudin, Moret, Manet and Pissarro.[115] The success of this exhibition influenced future acquisitions: works purchased in 1908 included Camille Corot's *Sunset: Figures under Trees* and Gustave Loiseau's *The Seine near Port Marly*.[116] The committee also ventured into other Impressionists with the purchase of a d'Espagnat.[117] Works from the Barbizon and Impressionist schools were particularly accessible to the Manchester public as, since the 1870s, a number of leading Manchester artists had worked in France and had been influenced by these styles. When William Meredith, Houghton Hague and R. G. Somerset returned from their long spells in Pont Aven in Brittany with their French-influenced works, they came to lead a small movement of painters that became known as the 'Manchester school'.[118] Although the group stayed together for less than a decade, the prominence of this group in local art naturally prepared local taste for the modern French masters. French Impressionist painting continued to be influential throughout the Edwardian period, especially after Adolphe Valette took up a teaching position at the Manchester School of Art.[119]

While themed exhibitions, such as that of modern French painting, continued to be successful, the absence of exhibition space made organising a successful large-scale modern sales exhibition almost impossible. Critics regarded the 1907 exhibition as probably the worst in living memory – 'a shadow of its former self' – and criticised the sacrifice of the exhibition in favour of the permanent collection.[120] A year later the exhibition was even smaller and was condemned as 'half-hearted and mediocre', representing 'only the second-class work of painters, like the second pick of the season's novels at a circulating library'.[121] This criticism may have been a little harsh – the exhibition still attracted major celebrated artists such as Hubert von Herkomer, Sir Luke Fildes and Alfred East – but there was now no doubt that the Manchester modern exhibition had fallen a long way behind those of major municipalities. Following this vitriolic public criticism, the committee was forced to rethink its plans for the coming year. With no immediate prospect of more exhibition space, it was decided to abandon completely the open exhibition format. Instead, the committee chose to concentrate efforts on organising a small, well-hung exhibition of a select number of specially invited artists. This decision was practically forced upon it by lack of exhibition space but there were, in any case, increasing doubts as to whether large-scale general exhibitions – often watered-down replicas of the those in the Royal Academy – really achieved any useful purpose. Thus the 'huge bazaars' of the past were replaced by an exhibition of the works of just four modern artists.[122] Inevitably, not all were impressed by the change, and some accused the art gallery committee of simply becoming dealers, 'middlemen for the sale of a few London artists' second-rate works'.[123] The experiment was continued, although the following year eleven artists were invited to contribute works.[124] The most basic problem, though, remained. Exhibition space was limited and sales were disappointing. Falls in exhibition sales were not unique to Manchester and were, to some degree, a product of changing fashions. Experience showed that purchasing Royal Academy works from provincial exhibitions was not always a sound investment.[125] The new craze for the motor car inevitably ate up the leisure expenditure of the middle class, while taking families away from their homes and picture collections.[126] By this time, Manchester had obtained a particularly bad reputation as a market for pictures, the critic of the *Manchester City News* noting that the 'beggarly returns of sales from our public exhibitions is heartbreaking'.[127]

Members of the art gallery committee continued to believe that the only way to reverse the downward trend was to develop a completely new venue for exhibitions. Ongoing controversy over high rates made the construction of a completely new gallery politically impossible and so, by 1909, the committee turned its attention to plans for the reconstruction of the infirmary building.

The plans drawn up allowed for 3,800 square feet for the exhibition of pictures and 1,500 square feet for sculpture galleries, together with space for the display of prints, textiles, furniture and other miscellaneous works. There was also to be a library and a museum collection of antiquities, portraits and plans, formed in conjunction with the Lancashire and Cheshire Antiquarian Society. The basic design of the interior would follow that seen at Aberdeen, with a central sculpture court, arcaded with a balcony and surrounded by thematic galleries.[128] Unfortunately, the council was again concerned about the costs of the project and forced the committee to reduce the proposed gallery floor space by almost 10 per cent. This meant a significant reduction in space for textiles, furniture and library facilities and the elimination of separate space for the Egyptian, Assyrian and Mycenaean collection.[129]

If the cuts in the planned gallery were not enough, several councillors began to look to reduce the overall budget of the art gallery committee. It was reasoned that as the art gallery committee was continually complaining that it had insufficient exhibition space, it should not make any further picture purchases until a new gallery was completed. By this time, of course, the art gallery committee's legal obligation to spend £2,000 on pictures per annum had expired. Astonishingly, at a particularly rancorous meeting, a proposal to completely abolish the picture-purchasing budget was passed, albeit by only one vote. Walter Butterworth and the art gallery committee were naturally appalled and considered resigning, but fortunately agreed to stay and fight for the restoration of the grant.[130] The decision to cut the grant was, of course, potentially disastrous for public art in Manchester. Unless the corporation made purchases at its annual modern sales exhibitions, it was clear that private patronage would not sustain them, even in their much-reduced form. It was also clear that collectors would make donations to Manchester only if the city authorities were perceived to be taking public art seriously. Butterworth claimed that several collectors who had already contributed works threatened to cancel gifts or bequests unless the council changed its policy. The charge that pictures were being bought that would never be seen by the public was also somewhat unfair: in fact almost all of the permanent collection was on display in some form, at either the Queen's Park Museum, Heaton Hall, the school of art, branch libraries or other public institutions.[131] Standing orders of the council meant that the decision over the committee's budget could not be reconsidered for six months, effectively paralysing the committee. Fortunately, Butterworth's arguments were eventually accepted, and the grant restored, by a two-thirds majority.[132]

The art gallery committee continued to try to keep the new gallery development on the political agenda, but public opinion seemed, at best, largely indifferent. When a poll was taken in the local press on how to utilise the infirmary site, the most popular choice was to use it as a location for a new Royal Exchange, and the second most favoured option was open space, while the option of an art gallery and library was only the fifth most popular choice. The overall results seemed to suggest that the characterisation of Manchester as a city that placed commerce ahead of the arts was not entirely unfair.[133] It was, then, something of a surprise when in September 1910 the city council, after four hours' discussion, finally approved in principle the development of a new library and art gallery on the infirmary site. The decision seemed to take even the art gallery's supporters by surprise; the council that had earlier abolished the art gallery committee's picture purchases budget was now giving outline approval for a scheme that could cost £100,000.[134] Sadly, for the art gallery committee, the decision only seemed to spur on opponents of the new library and art gallery. The retail trading community launched an immediate protest. The traders in the main shopping area of Oldham Street and Market Street naturally wanted to see the Royal Exchange relocated to Piccadilly as it would undoubtedly have raised property values and brought members of the commercial middle class to their doors. Meanwhile, it was clear that a significant proportion of Manchester's commercial community not only wanted to see the development of a new exchange on Piccadilly, but were hostile to what were regarded 'luxurious schemes' at a time of increasing local and national taxation.[135] Faced with this disquiet, the city council backtracked and decided to appoint a committee of inquiry into future uses of the infirmary site.[136] Before the committee could report, a requisition was got up to force the mayor to call a public meeting on the question. The resultant chaotic meeting revealed just how divided public opinion was on the issue. First, the art gallery and library scheme was rejected, and then the plans for an exchange. Finally, it was decided that the site should remain open and unbuilt on for the following five years. Walter Butterworth accused opponents of packing the inquiry, but his own high-profile support for the new art gallery all but ended his political career.[137] In November 1912 he lost his seat on the city council after being rejected by his Newton Heath ward, a defeat in which the art gallery question was a significant factor.[138] This meant, of course, that he also lost not only the chairmanship of the art gallery committee, but his seat on it too. Such was Butterworth's standing that the Victoria University took the politically contentious step of nominating him as its own representative to the art gallery committee for the following year.[139] The art gallery committee even tried to elect him as its deputy chairman, despite his defeat at the polls, but Butterworth, anticipating criticism, declined to take this position.[140] The art gallery cause was effectively lost and its most passionate advocate politically humiliated.

In the half-century that followed the Manchester Art Treasures Exhibition, public art institutions seemed to be in a permanent struggle to maintain their status and to maintain Manchester's reputation as a leading art centre. By 1913 even art lovers admitted that the city's public had yet to develop a 'proper passion for art' and that it might take a further half-century before public opinion would countenance a the building of major new gallery.[141] In fact, it would not be until 2002 that a completely new municipal gallery would be opened, more than a century after the extension to the Mosley Street gallery was originally planned.[142] Although the Art Treasures Exhibition was a high-profile event, establishing Manchester as a leading cultural centre in the eyes of the world and encouraging private art patronage among Lancashire manufacturers, it is questionable whether it had a very significant impact on the development of public art institutions. After the buildings were sold and the paintings dispersed, the exhibition existed only as a memory of a mythical golden age of Manchester art. The plans for a new city art gallery in 1860 funded primarily by private capital came to nothing following the near economic collapse of the region during the cotton famine. After 1860 the RMI was never in a financial position to contemplate the development of a new gallery of its own, concentrating instead on developing a small permanent collection as soon as it could afford to do so. Another recession a decade later destroyed hopes that it would ever regain its former reputation, as Manchester's merchant princes struggled for economic survival. As Edgar Atkins noted, 'the first things a man involved in difficulties sold were his pictures'.[143] The turbulent nature of the Lancashire economy meant that few were immune from the perils of financial collapse. Even major Manchester collectors such as Henry McConnel and Sam Mendel suffered dramatic business failures and were forced to sell off their works of art.[144]

Competition from municipal galleries with large budgets from public funds effectively forced the RMI to hand over its operations to the city council. Although the development of the Whitworth Institute in the late 1880s demonstrated that private galleries could still be viable, it was clear that without a major private sponsor it could not compete successfully with municipal galleries. Despite

Manchester being the capital of probably the richest region of the country, the RMI failed to find such a sponsor. This may partly have been down to ill fortune; had Whitworth died a decade earlier his vast wealth might have been used to revive the RMI. It is likely, however, that there was a wide expectation that the city council would itself become a generous patron of art, especially after it agreed to an annual purchase fund of £2,000. This expectation was not realised. Part of the reason for Manchester's apparent parsimony was the growing annual rate bill brought about by major capital projects such as the Thirlmere water scheme.[145] Yet this can form only part of the explanation, as rising rates were a feature of most late nineteenth-century cities. It seems more plausible that the primary reason for Manchester City Council's apparent caution lay with the fear that expenditure on art was increasingly perceived as a luxury. The didactic argument for public art, so popular in the mid-nineteenth century, had been replaced by scepticism about what public art could actually achieve. While veteran social reformers such as T. C. Horsfall continued to believe in the regenerative value of public art, others were less convinced as the belief in 'art for art's sake' gained currency. If art did have a social reforming task, it was not at all clear that this was best achieved through the erection of lavish and expensive city-centre galleries to hold exhibitions which would be primarily be attended by the middle class. More small-scale community-based schemes, such as Horsfall's own Ancoats Art Museum or the Queen's Park Museum, seemed much more effective at attracting working-class visitors, especially when combined with programmes of elementary education.

Perhaps attitudes might have changed if wealthy art patrons in the Manchester region had themselves spoken out more strongly in favour of the development of a public gallery. However, this class was not known for its enthusiasm for the increasing taxation and public expenditure of the Edwardian era. This was the period when many of the upper urban middle class were believed to have finally abandoned Liberalism for the fiscal economy of Conservatism. It is also clear that only a small proportion of Manchester's economic elite ever patronised the RMI or the city art gallery beyond paying an annual subscription or attending an occasional exhibition. While it is true that Manchester's wealthier citizens were prepared to come forward with large sums to support prestigious events, such as the Manchester Art Treasures Exhibition and the Jubilee Exhibition, this was often done more because of personal ambition, civic pride and patriotic duty than because of a love of art. It is clear from the way in which some guarantors sought to pocket the profits from the Jubilee Exhibition that selfless motives did not always predominate. While prestigious activities easily attracted support, there was only limited private support available for the day-to-day operations of Manchester's major art institutions that represented the 'bread and butter' of artistic life in the city.

The reasons for the relative failure of Manchester's middle class to support the RMI and city gallery were clearly complex. Unlike that of Liverpool, Manchester's art scene lacked a single wealthy sponsor. Nor did the city have a politically influential and determined figure to articulate a collective civic vision. The scale of Manchester's commercial community and the fragmented nature of Manchester's civic leadership made it difficult for a single vision to become dominant. Manchester had no outstanding spokesman to speak out for art and the interests of artists in the second half of the century. Of the two most important members of the art gallery committee, Alderman Joseph Thompson was a relatively low-profile figure, and Walter Butterworth, although more dynamic, failed to convince the public of the need for a new gallery and came to be seen as a symbol of corporate extravagance. Robert Crozier and H. C. Whaite, successive presidents of the Manchester Academy, were universally respected as artists but were regarded as lacking the business tact and self-assertiveness necessary to represent the Manchester art community effectively.[146] R. D. Darbishire, the man widely credited for the success of the Whitworth gallery, rarely seemed to be on good terms with the municipal art authorities and, in any case, passed away before the issue of a new municipal galley became a serious prospect. Charles Rowley, an outspoken supporter of the social benefits of public art, left the council after it was claimed he had used his position on the council to secure contracts for his own picture-framing business. One might, of course, have expected some of the city's leading entrepreneurs to have taken a lead. However, it is clear that for many, ties with the city itself were lessening. The process of suburbanisation in Manchester began relatively early – with the development of private estates such as Victoria Park from the 1820s – and by the end of the century few leading Manchester businessmen lived close to the city centre. Even those who continued to patronise Manchester art often spent little time in the city. For some, such as William Agnew, business and political success took them increasingly to the capital. For others, such as J. E. Taylor, retirement meant a move to the south coast. T. C. Horsfall spent much of his life residing in Macclesfield. The fact that such figures continued to support Manchester art at all was, in itself, somewhat surprising.

By the outbreak of the First World War it was questionable whether Manchester could be said to be in the front rank of provincial cities in terms of public art provision. It had built up an impressive permanent collection of modern British painting, but had, until very recently, neglected continental schools almost completely. The city authorities had spent more than a decade discussing the development of a new city gallery, but disagreements in council and lukewarm, if not hostile, public opinion had seen ambitious new plans indefinitely postponed. Lack of gallery space undermined the annual commercial exhibition of modern paintings to the point where it was all but abandoned. The academy attracted 'the scantiest support from public bodies and private individuals' and was never very far from financial disaster.[147] Therefore, despite the success of high-profile national exhibitions and the reputation Lancashire had for being a vibrant market for modern works, public art institutions struggled to attract support. Art continued to be culturally fashionable, but, as leading contemporary art critics observed, it is questionable how many of those who professed to support art helped to advance its progress:

> Have our citizens, individually or in their corporate capacity, made any sacrifice of time or money or personal convenience for the sake of art? If they have they have succeeded with rare skill in covering up the traces of their good deeds. The provision of an adequate Art Gallery seems as far off as ever. The sales of works of art at our public exhibitions are heartbreaking in their meagreness. People pass the turnstiles of our free pictures shows in considerable numbers, and the authorities make some good parade of the large attendance. We wish we could believe that the majority of the comfortably-dressed people who are to be seen any evening at the Mosley-street Galleries were drawn thither by any genuine interest in art. How many of them, we wonder, go there because it is a quiet and comfortable place of meeting, where conversation, amatory or otherwise, can be carried on without interruption? How many of them who can well afford to pay for admission would be found there if the smallest charge were made?[148]

NOTES

1 RMI, Council Proceedings, 3 December 1879, MCL.
2 Worthington was president of the Manchester Society of Architects in 1875–77 and was influential in negotiating the transfer of the RMI to the corporation. See

A. J. Pass, 'Thomas Worthington', in J. H. G. Archer (ed.), *Art and Architecture in Victorian Manchester* (Manchester, 1985), 81–101, esp. 101.

3 See comments of Alfred Darbishire in 'Manchester as an Art Centre, March 19, 1877', *Manchester Literary Club*, 3 (1876–77), 211–17, esp. 212–13.

4 RMI, Council Proceedings, circular letter, 3 March 1880.

5 RMI, Council Proceedings, circular letter, 3 March 1880.

6 J. Treuherz, 'Ford Madox Brown and the Manchester Murals', in Archer (ed.), *Art and Architecture*, 162–207.

7 See, for example, the parallel debate on public libraries. J Partington, 'Manchester as an Art Centre', *Manchester Literary Club*, 3 (1876–77), 42–52, esp. 45–6.

8 RMI, Council General Meeting (hereafter CGM), 2 December 1881, MCL.

9 RMI, Council Proceedings, 7 July 1880.

10 RMI, Council Proceedings, 1 December 1880.

11 RMI, Council Proceedings, 24 April 1882

12 RMI, Council Proceedings, 13 March 1882.

13 RMI, CGM, 8 March 1882.

14 RMI, CGM, 1 May 1882.

15 RMI, CGM, 12 October 1887.

16 RMI, CGM, 6 May 1889.

17 RMI, CGM, 12 May 1890; 11 May 1891.

18 RMI, CGM, 6 May 1889.

19 See Nemo, letter, *Manchester City News*, 15 July 1882.

20 RMI, CGM, 12 October 1887.

21 RMI, CGM, 6 May 1889.

22 RMI, CGM, 11 May 1891.

23 *Magazine of Art*, 11 (1888), 211.

24 *Magazine of Art*, 11 (1888), 212.

25 J. Garrard, 'The Salford Gas Scandal of 1887', *Manchester Region History Review*, 2 (1988–89), 12–20.

26 *Manchester Guardian*, 9 June 1886.

27 For a detailed analysis of the event see J. Treuherz, 'The Manchester Royal Jubilee Exhibition of 1887', *Victorian Poetry*, 25 (1987), 192–222.

28 *Manchester City News*, 12 June 1886.

29 *Manchester City News*, 12 June 1886.

30 R.S., letter, *Manchester Guardian*, 11 June 1886.

31 M.A.N., letter, *Manchester Guardian*, 11 June 1886.

32 See comments of Alderman W. H. Bailey, *Manchester City News*, 12 June 1886.

33 *Manchester Guardian*, 12 June 1886.

34 Ellis Lever, letter, *Manchester Guardian*, 11 June 1886.

35 See 'Conversations with Ab-O'-Th'-Yate', *Manchester City News*, 7 August 1886.

36 *Manchester City News*, 24 July 1886.

37 *Magazine of Art*, 10 (1887), 281–2.

38 *Royal Jubilee Exhibition, Manchester 1887: Official Catalogue* (Manchester, 1887), 9.

39 *Manchester City News*, 24 June 1886.

40 *Critical Notes of the Picture and Water-Colour Drawings in the Royal Jubilee Exhibition, Manchester 1887* (Manchester, 1887), 3.

41 See *Official Catalogue*.

42 Walter Armstrong, *Fine Art at the Royal Jubilee Exhibition: Critical Notes* (Manchester, 1887), 5.

43 Armstrong, *Fine Art*, 9.

44 *Critical Notes of the Picture and Water-Colour Drawings*, 18.

45 *Art Journal*, July 1887, 249–51.

46 *Magazine of Art*, 10 (1887), 122–4.

47 *Critical Notes of the Picture and Water-Colour Drawings*, 3.

48 J. E. Hodgson, *Fifty Years of British Art* (Manchester, 1887), 99.

49 *Critical Notes of the Picture and Water-Colour Drawings*, 3.

50 *Manchester Guardian*, 11 November 1887.

51 Ellis Lever, letter, *Manchester Guardian*, 11 November 1887.

52 See correspondence in *Manchester Guardian*, 15–18 November 1887

53 White Rose, York, letter, *Manchester Guardian*, 23 November 1887.

54 *Manchester City News*, 2 December 1887.

55 W. H. S. Watts, letter, *Manchester Guardian*, 25 September 1887.

56 *Manchester City News*, 2 June 1888. For background on the Whitworth Institute see F. W. Hawcroft, 'The Whitworth Art Gallery', in Archer (ed.), *Art and Architecture*, 208–29.

57 RMI, CGM, 12 October 1887.

58 *Manchester City News*, 1 September 1888.

59 *Manchester City News*, 2 February 1889.

60 For discussion see *Manchester City News*, 22 February 1890; RMI, CGM, 12 May 1890.

61 RMI, CGM, 12 May 1890.

62 RMI, CGM, 26 October 1891.

63 RMI, CGM, 26 October 1891.

64 *Manchester City News*, 5 March 1892.

65 RMI, CGM, 2 May 1892.

66 *Manchester City News*, 9 April 1892.

67 *Manchester City News*, 16 April 1892.

68 RMI, CGM, 27 October 1892.

69 RMI, CGM, 25 October 1893.

70 RMI, CGM, 31 October 1894.

71 Other important Pre-Raphaelite works obtained before 1900 include Holman Hunt's *The Hireling Shepherd*, D. G. Rossetti's *Sibylla Delphica* and Charles Collins's *The Pedlar*. See E. Conran, 'Art Collections', in Archer (ed.), *Art and Architecture*, 65–80, esp. 79.

72 RMI, CGM, 31 October 1894.

73 *Manchester Courier*, 24 October 1895.

74 RMI, CGM, 23 October 1895; *Manchester Guardian* cutting, n.d.

75 RMI, CGM, 23 October 1895.

76 RMI, Council Proceedings, 12 October 1900.

77 RMI, Council Proceedings, 13 December 1900.

78 RMI, Council Proceedings, 13 December 1900.

79 RMI, Council Proceedings, 24 October 1902.

80 RMI, CGM, 31 May 1905; 30 April 1906.

81 *Manchester Evening News*, 26 September 1904.

82 Manchester City Council (hereafter MCC), Art Gallery Committee (hereafter AGC) Minutes, 14 November 1904, MCL.

83 *Manchester Guardian*, 15 February 1905.

84 MCC, AGC, 23 February 1905.

85 MCC, AGC, 30 March 1905.

86 MCC, AGC, 29 June 1905.

87 *Manchester City News*, 6 January 1906.

88 *Report to the City Council of Visits to Certain Art Galleries and Museums in Belgium, Holland, Germany and Great Britain* (Manchester, 1905), in MCC, AGC, 21 December 1905.

89 A view also shared by many later critics; see W. H. Brindley, *The Soul of Manchester* (Manchester, 1929), 166.

90 *Report to the City Council of Visits*, 16–17.

91 *Report to the City Council of Visits*, 16.

92 See comments of 'Merchant', *Manchester Guardian*, 3 December 1907.

93 *Manchester Courier*, 15 July 1906.

94 'Manchester and Salford Society of Friends of Art', circular in Manchester Academy of Fine Arts Cuttings Collection, vol. for 1904–12, MCL.

95 *Manchester City News*, 2 May 1908.

96 *Manchester City News*, 2 May 1908.

97 MCC, AGC, 30 May 1907.

98 *Manchester Guardian* cutting in RMI, Council Proceedings, 24 July 1907.

99 *Manchester Guardian* cutting in RMI, Council Proceedings, 24 July 1907.

100 *Manchester City News*, 20 July 1907.

101 *Manchester Guardian* cutting in RMI, Council Proceedings, 24 July 1907.

102 M. Harrison, 'Art and Philanthropy: T. C. Horsfall and the Manchester Art Museum', in A. Kidd and K. Roberts (eds), *City, Class and Culture: Cultural Production and Social Policy in Victorian Manchester* (Manchester, 1985), 140–1.

103 *Manchester City News*, 27 July 1907.

104 See, for example, Artisan, letter, *Manchester City News*, 14 March 1908.

105 M. Harrison, 'Art and Social Regeneration: The Ancoats Art Museum', *Manchester Region History Review*, 7 (1993), 63–4; Harrison, 'Art and Philanthropy', 120–47.

106 M. Waithe, 'The St. George's Museum', *Victorian Review*, 39 (2013), 35–40.

107 See comments of C. Rowley, *Manchester City News*, 3 August 1907.

108 *Manchester Guardian*, 16 December 1907.

109 *Manchester City News*, 6 July 1907.

110 *Manchester City News*, 13 July 1907.

111 *Manchester Guardian*, 12 December 1907.

112 See W. Bailey, letter, and editor's comment, *Manchester Guardian*, 16 December 1907.

113 The Liberal defeat was probably more due to a Catholic rebellion on the education question. See *Manchester Guardian*, 19 December 1907.

114 *Manchester City News*, 28 November 1908.

115 *Manchester Courier*, 23 November 1907.

116 *Manchester Courier*, 5 December 1908.

117 *Manchester City News*, 2 July 1910.

118 *Manchester City News*, 13 March 1909.

119 S. Martin, *Adolphe Valette: A French Influence in Manchester* (Manchester, 1994); C. Lyon, *Adolphe Valette* (London, 2006).

120 *Manchester City News*, 21 September 1907.

121 *Manchester Guardian*, 12 September 1908.

122 *Manchester Guardian*, 8 September 1909.

123 Art Lover, letter, *Manchester City News*, 30 October 1909.

124 *Manchester Guardian*, 9 September 1910.

125 *Manchester Guardian*, 6 September 1909.

126 See comments by Manchester Academy speaker, *Daily Despatch*, 20 February 1911.

127 *Manchester City News*, 16 February 1911.

128 MCC, AGC, 28 January 1909.

129 MCC, AGC, 27 January 1910.

130 *Manchester City News*, 2 July 1910.

131 MCC, AGC, 8 June 1910.

132 *Manchester City News*, 31 December 1910.

133 *Manchester City News*, 30 January 1909.

134 The precise net cost would have depended on the amount generated by the sale of land occupied by the reference library in King Street.

135 *Manchester City News*, 24 September 1910.

136 *Manchester Guardian*, 12 October 1911.

137 *Manchester City News*, 11 Nov ember1911.

138 *Daily Despatch*, 27 November 1912.

139 See Alfred A. Barlow, letter, *Daily Despatch*, 11 November 1912.

140 *Daily Despatch*, 18 November 1912.

141 See editorial comment, *Manchester City News*, 12 April 1913.

142 However, the city council did take over the former Manchester Athenaeum buildings for use as temporary gallery space.

143 See report of the debate at the Manchester Literary Club, 'Art and Citizenship', *Manchester Literary Club*, 32 (1906), 434–41, esp. 437–8.
144 Conran, 'Art Collections', 73.
145 The Thirlmere scheme almost bankrupted the corporation in the late 1870s.
146 *Manchester City News*, 22 February 1913.
147 *Manchester City News*, 22 February 1913.
148 *Manchester City News*, 20 February 1909.

8

Challenging 'the ocean of mediocrity and pretence'? The alternative visions of the Whitworth and Harris galleries

The availability of private investment through bequests, legacies or donations could change the direction of local art policies, empowering individuals or groups of collectors to develop galleries in very different directions. In the case of Liverpool, private donations were an inherently political act, with private finance being used as a strategy for direct social advancement. In the case of the Whitworth Art Gallery and the Harris Library, Museum and Art Gallery, the act of giving was less political contentious, but it did set in train important debates about the purpose of art galleries and local cultural priorities. In some respects, both of these galleries were outside the presumed 'spirit of the age', where local art policy was increasingly focused on the specific needs of local citizens and especially the education of the working class. The Whitworth and Harris were driven by a local cultural elite, in some respects in opposition to traditional municipal conventions and without the involvement of the wider community of elected local councillors. The two institutions serve to illustrate the plurality of local policy in relation to public art and the degree to which art galleries could be platforms for a range of divergent cultural agendas. Both institutions set themselves against the tendencies of 'commercialisation' and 'fashion' that they felt had invaded municipal galleries and municipal collecting policies, yet each sought different solutions to this perceived problem. Both institutions sought to embrace their local publics, but did so by offering somewhat elitist visions of what a socially inclusive gallery should look like. In contrast to the followers of Ruskin, these galleries offered a different message and one that emphasised the inadequacy of existing municipal and 'democratic' approaches to art, favouring a more paternalistic and politically conservative world view.

Manchester's Whitworth Art Gallery is now recognised as one of Britain's leading regional art institutions, but it had a problematic and controversial

221

birth. The Whitworth was an independent, privately financed public gallery built in an era when local authorities were increasingly taking responsibility for providing civic art galleries and museums.[1] State and municipal art galleries were not, of course, the only types of public art gallery to emerge in the half-century before the First World War. Although independent, privately funded art galleries were not as common in Britain as they were in the United States, the few that did emerge were often of considerable significance in the history of collecting.[2] Some, such as Lord Leverhulme's collection in the museum at Port Sunlight, were almost exclusively personal enterprises, with the Lady Lever Art Gallery built to house what was essentially an individually assembled private collection.[3] Other private art galleries saw themselves as promoters of broader civic culture, providing a public service where it was felt the state had failed or neglected to act. This was particularly the case for the Whitworth Art Gallery in Manchester, which was funded by a legacy from the engineering magnate Sir Joseph Whitworth. Whitworth's legatees inherited no collection, but merely a large sum of money and a direction to spend it on works of art and education for the public good. They had considerable freedom to build a gallery and to compile a collection that reflected their own cultural priorities and visions of public art. Yet because they claimed to be acting for the wider public good, they had to be responsive to criticism from public opinion, especially that from the press and leaders of the local art community. The result was that the Whitworth defined its collecting practice in opposition to the 'commercial' and 'fashionable' tendencies said to prevail in many municipal galleries. Partly through the ambition of its leadership and partly by accident, the Whitworth developed new and distinctive collecting activities. These in turn formed the vehicle for a new regional canon that highlighted the work of Manchester artists and the importance of watercolour in the history of British art.

The Whitworth Institute, the original name for the Whitworth Art Gallery, was conceived as a memorial to one of Manchester's leading industrialists. Sir Joseph Whitworth's career represented the classic nineteenth-century liberal ideal of the educated working man rising to great fortune. Although little is known of Whitworth's early life, he moved in 1824 to London to further his apprenticeship at the well-known engineering firm of Henry Maudslay. In 1832 he returned to Manchester to establish his own machine tool-making business, and by the time of the Great Exhibition of 1851 he had firmly established his international reputation as 'Britain's greatest mechanician'. Whitworth was a complex figure who combined an apparently progressive social outlook with a ruthless business mind.[4] While advocating industrial partnership and profit-sharing with his employees, he still demanded unquestioning obedience in matters of industrial relations.[5] He developed a reputation as one of Britain's greatest educational philanthropists and a patron of high culture, yet he was also a pioneering armaments manufacturer and perhaps the British Empire's most prominent arms trader.

Whitworth had long taken an active interest in technical and scientific education, although he had shown little interest in the visual arts. He was active in the development of Owens College, helping to create the first chair of engineering and endowing a series of Whitworth Scholarships for young engineers.[6] Whitworth gave long consideration to how his great wealth could be disposed; although married twice, he had no children. His initial plan was to leave his house in Manchester, The Firs, and his Derbyshire estate, Stancliffe Hall, to the nation for use as an engineering college and retirement home for academics. This plan suffered from legal complications, not the least of which was that gifts to the state were not then recognised by law. Whitworth's subsequent plan was to establish an educational foundation whereby young people from Stockport, Manchester and Salford would be enabled to receive artistic and technical instruction. However, before the technical instruction legislation of the 1890s, there was no means by which this scheme could be carried out, and on the advice of his friend and legal advisor Robert Dukinfield Darbishire, the scheme was withdrawn from his will.[7] Although discussions had taken place with Manchester Corporation on the possibilities of a joint funding scheme, changes to local government legislation would have been necessary for any such plan to go ahead. Consequently, despite all the thought Whitworth had put into the development of his own educational memorial, he eventually opted for the most straightforward of all options – to divide the residue of his estate between his trustees – R. D. Darbishire, R. C. Christie and his wife – unconditionally and without any formal direction as to how the funds should be spent.[8] This decision placed Whitworth's legatees in a very powerful position to influence the future development of art and technical education policy in Manchester. In the event, Darbishire led the development of the Whitworth Institute and is credited with much of the responsibility for its early development (Figure 17).[9]

Darbishire and fellow legatee Christie began by attempting to build a local consensus for the improvement of educational and art institutions. In particular, they sought co-operation with other parties to try to address the practical problems then facing Manchester's educational institutions, particularly the

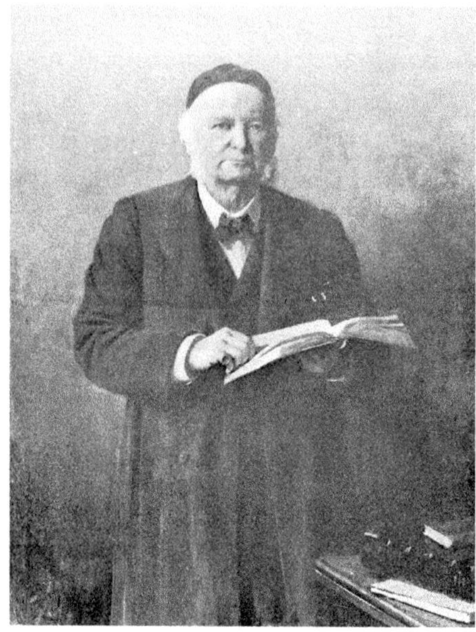

17 Robert Dukinfield Darbishire, solicitor, collector and a key figure behind the success of the Whitworth Art Gallery

technical school, which by 1887 was over £2,700 in debt and inadequate in size for the rapidly growing numbers of students.[10] The Whitworth legatees hoped to provide land and a limited subsidy in the hope that the corporation would take on responsibility for the development of the scheme. However, the corporation had recently taken over the buildings of the privately organised RMI, committing itself to spending £2,000 per annum on works of art, and was reluctant to commit itself to new initiatives.[11]

Despite these frustrations, the Whitworth legatees pressed ahead with plans for the art gallery.[12] The main site at Potter's Field was to be reserved for the 'Museum of Arts and Industries', which would be divided into departments – fine art; industrial art; mechanical, chemical and textile; commercial, raw products and samples – with a lecture hall and library.[13] Although Whitworth's own interests lay in technical education, the Museum of Arts and Industries would focus largely on the fine arts. Early plans for the museum show a large central gallery for the fine arts with two wings separated by a courtyard and corridor. The technical museum was to be located in the west wing and the commercial gallery in the east.[14] Committee members looked to the continent for inspiration, and especially to the new Musée Royal of Belgium, opened in 1887. This celebrated museum in Brussels, designed by Alphonse Balat, represented something of a benchmark in museum design, providing modern features within a simplified neo-classical form.[15]

The corporation's tardiness eventually persuaded the Whitworth committee to establish an independent private body to take the scheme forward. By March 1888, Darbishire's patience had run out when he spelled out the plans in blunt terms to Sir James Harwood, the city's leading Liberal alderman:

> The suggestion of founding the Institute immediately under the government of a widely representative body of [amendment] experienced [illegible] well qualified and interested men of course dispenses at once with the idea that we should wait till the Corporation and friends should undertake the erection and endowment of the proposed Buildings.[16]

Supporters of the Whitworth could draw upon the powerful connections of suburban Manchester's Liberal and educational elite, such as William Agnew, C. P. Scott of the *Manchester Guardian* and Sir Henry Roscoe, Liberal MP for South Manchester. It also had the support of many in the Manchester business community, to which Whitworth had so long been connected, most notably Thomas Ashton, Edward Donner, Oliver Heywood and William Mather.[17]

The constitution of the proposed new institute did little to encourage the corporation to look sympathetically on requests for public money. From the outset, the institute was tightly organised and based on a hierarchy inspired by that of the British Institution and the RMI. Members were concerned that the project should not be thrown off course by outside interference, stressing that the whole control of the Whitworth Institute should rest with the legatees until it was in full working order.[18] Although the charter did allow broader participation in the management of the institute, it had no pretensions to encourage popular involvement in its proceedings. The primary administration of the body was vested in a body of governors that included the legatees. Governors were partly elected and partly nominated by the city council, public bodies contributing to the funds of the institute, the technical school, the school of art and Owens College. Ordinary members could take part in general meetings, councils and special committees, but could not become senior officers.[19] High subscription fees limited membership to the wealthier middle classes.[20]

The Whitworth Institute charter went before the Privy Council in 1889, and during the same year the profits from the privately organised Manchester Jubilee Exhibition of 1887 – just over £43,000 – were placed in the hands of the institute. These funds were earmarked for the technical school, school of art and for the purchase of pictures for the proposed museum. The Whitworth Institute was inaugurated formally in the summer of 1890, with the opening of the newly landscaped Potter's Field, now called Whitworth Park, and a small fine art exhibition in Grove House, a building located within the park.[21] At the opening some supporters of the Whitworth could not resist the opportunity to criticise corporation policy towards the city's municipal galleries. Sir Charles Robinson was quite open in his belief 'that before many years had passed the works of art now hung in the dingy and lugubrious building in Mosley-street would find a Home in galleries in Whitworth Park'.[22] R. C. Christie was even more outspoken in his criticism of the corporation's care of its permanent collection, noting that 'Every great painting in the Royal Institution was gradually deteriorating, and that deterioration must continue ...'[23]

One might have expected the city art gallery committee to welcome the development of extra gallery space in Manchester, but the Whitworth's attack on the city gallery only served to antagonise the corporation authorities and some local art critics. From the outset, the *Manchester Guardian*'s art correspondent was critical of Whitworth policy, concerned that it would merely imitate the work of the corporation gallery, commenting caustically that 'we do not want two middling collections of middling contemporary pictures in Manchester'.[24] The Whitworth also attracted negative comment from those who felt that responsibility for public galleries should lie with the corporation as a matter of principle. Charles Rowley, the chairman of the school of art, deplored the creation of the Whitworth gallery and compared the decisions of the Whitworth legatees to those of the much-criticised trustees of the Chantrey bequest.[25]

While the corporation's plans for its own gallery extensions were quietly dropped, the Whitworth was determined to press ahead with its own museum and collection.[26] The first Whitworth Institute galleries were provided simply by converting a large domestic house located in the north-east corner of the park. The old conservatory was turned into a sculpture gallery and the bedrooms into top-lit picture galleries, while the downstairs rooms were converted into a caretaker's residence, and a second staircase was added to provide an exit from the building.[27] New legislation saw technical education made the responsibility of municipal corporations, and thus the technical school and the school of art, together with their Whitworth endowments, were transferred to the corporation in 1892, leaving the Whitworth legatees to concentrate on the art gallery. A new building committee, composed of the merchant Edward Donner, the leading watercolour collector Charles E. Lees and the art dealer William Agnew, concluded that new plans should concentrate on the development of galleries of fine art and illustrations of 'Mechanical and Industrial Arts and Manufactured Products'.[28] In early 1892, the Whitworth committee invited architects to submit preliminary drawings of proposed galleries.[29] The committee eventually obtained plans for two new galleries to be built around the existing Grove House, a north gallery of some 78 ft 6 in by 32 ft 6 in and a central gallery, perpendicular to the north, extending southwards and measuring 79 ft by 39 ft. The galleries were planned with a view to possible future extension, and their design was partly inspired by the temporary galleries of the recent Manchester Jubilee Exhibition. The trustees provided the finance through a further endowment of £50,000.[30] Manchester had an impressive new art institute built to modern standards, standing in stark contrast to the corporation's old RMI building. However, the gallery's collecting policy and activities were to be significantly different from those originally envisaged by its founders.

In response to public comment, the Whitworth gradually begin to articulate its own distinctive identity and collecting policy, partly in an attempt to differentiate itself from the city art gallery and partly as a consequence of the climate of opinion in the local art community. It was a long-standing complaint of Manchester artists that local patrons did little to support local art and artists.[31] During this period many Manchester artists had left the city to explore opportunities elsewhere, and some groups, such as the Royal Cambrian Academy in North Wales, had become dominated by former Manchester men.[32] Many artists were particularly angry that the RMI, founded to support Manchester's artists, had become moribund, while the corporation's display had become merely 'an exhibition of London artists' work'.[33] The Whitworth took advantage of this disillusionment and established itself as a platform for regional art and artists. One senior member of the Whitworth committee, T. C. Horsfall, was all too aware of local artists' complaints and donated £500 for the purchase of watercolour drawings of subjects within thirty miles of Manchester. He was determined to promote 'the custom which prevailed in ages when art influenced life deeply', and recommended that 'instead of buying pictures in London exhibitions and in studios, [patrons] shall ask the artist they think best able to do so to paint them pictures of prescribed subjects'.[34]

From very early on the Whitworth committee developed a particular interest in watercolour painting, partly because of the belief that this medium had been neglected by the municipal gallery in its desire to collect the 'oils of the season' from the Royal Academy. Shortly after Horsfall's donation, another Whitworth governor made an anonymous £500 donation for the development of the watercolour collection.[35] In 1891 the Whitworth organised a watercolour exhibition 'Illustrative of the Progress and Development of that Branch of the Fine Arts in Great Britain', by which time the purchase fund from the profits of the Jubilee Exhibition fund had already provided finance for the purchase of thirty-eight works; eventually fifty-four watercolours were purchased using this source.[36]

In 1892 the Whitworth received perhaps its most important bequest. John Edward Taylor, proprietor of the *Manchester Guardian*, presented 154 English drawings and watercolours from his own collection, a move that immediately gave the Whitworth one of the most important public watercolour collections and invariably shaped the future policy of the institute.[37] The nature of the gift suggests that Taylor was acting in support of an objective already identified by the Whitworth, namely to establish a collection illustrating the history of British watercolour painting. Taylor allowed selections to be made from his collection, and the choices made show a tendency towards the acquisition of works illustrating the development of particular artists.[38]

The expanded watercolour collection shaped future exhibition policy. The year 1903 saw a significant exhibition of watercolour works from the Roger Ross collection, loaned by the Manchester corporation.[39] Ross had been a prominent Manchester merchant who had formed a major private watercolour collection, including important examples by Cox, Copley Fielding, De Wint, Prout and Varley.[40] In 1912 there was another major visiting watercolour exhibition, mainly of deceased artists of the British school who were inadequately represented in the permanent collection. This included a number of important pictures by J. S. Cotman, lent by the well-known collector and entrepreneur R. J. Colman of Norwich.[41] The Whitworth's focus on watercolour was thus perpetuated, with donations and loans encouraged to fill perceived gaps in the existing collection. When supporters like J. E. Taylor Allen and Arthur Allen offered specific works by Turner, they did so in the knowledge that these would be pictures that the Whitworth authorities would be particularly pleased to receive.[42]

By the mid-1890s, the Whitworth had unequivocally decided to concentrate on the collection of fine art, leaving collections of art manufacture to be funded by the municipal art gallery.[43] It continued to receive donations of miscellaneous items and occasionally purchased oils, although these were outside its main area of interest.[44] The institution had effectively carved a specialist niche for itself as a high-quality non-commercial gallery, with loan exhibitions and a permanent collection that showed a significant bias towards watercolour painting and outstanding regional art. This degree of specialisation was somewhat unusual during this period and reflected the comparatively high level of private support visual art received from Manchester patrons. As it became clear that the Whitworth intended to complement rather than compete with the city gallery, relations between two generally improved.

In 1906 the corporation bought a long-term lease on Whitworth Park for a nominal sum. This released the Whitworth from its heavy annual expenditure on the park and allowed it to rearrange a large part of its endowment funds, releasing around £40,000 of capital for future development. Almost immediately plans were formed for a new central hall with a grand façade. The new facilities were to provide a new sculpture gallery on the ground floor and space for special exhibitions, offices and an improved library and reading rooms.[45] Plans were developed in consultation with Professor Percy Gardner of the University of Oxford and included a domed central entrance hall similar to that of the Tate Gallery in London.[46] The completed façade provided Manchester with one of the most imposing art gallery buildings in Lancashire, but one that privileged the needs of visitors over extensive ornamentation. The original plans for a dominant, but largely useless, central tower, modelled on that of the nearby Victoria University, never came to fruition.[47] Instead, the emphasis was on well-lit gallery space consistent with the contemporary aim of providing a location for serious study and contemplation.

The Whitworth depended on the endowments left to it by Whitworth or investments made by the Whitworth legatees. Unfortunately, a significant amount of income came from stocks and holdings whose market value was somewhat volatile. Many holdings came directly from the residuary estate of Whitworth, and the investments were of variable quality. Even R. D. Darbishire, on handing over certain stocks, noted diplomatically that they were 'not perhaps such an investment as the Council would select'.[48] In January 1909 the Whitworth found itself in particular difficulties with an accumulated debt to its bankers of £6,019, yet its railway shares had so depreciated in value as to make their sale unwise, with the result that it had either to call in other loans or to make a further arrangement for credit.[49]

The Whitworth did have access to miscellaneous sources of income that prevented the bankers from becoming too anxious, although even these did not yield altogether favourable results. The Whitworth's holdings included the

Grand Hotel, Conwy, which was a continual source of difficulty for the institute. In July 1910 the Whitworth finally thought it had disposed of the property on a mortgage for £4,000,[50] but within eighteen months the Grand had gone into liquidation, leaving the Whitworth's lawyers scrambling to protect their assets.[51] The institution's financial problems illustrated the difficulties inherent in trying to develop a major public gallery without secure long-term endowment or state sponsorship. Appeals for funds were concentrated directly on the wealthy elite of the city, although there were signs that they were less willing to make contributions than in the past. When, in 1911, it was decided to establish a picture purchase fund, efforts focused on 250 identified wealthy patrons of art in the area, although notices were also placed in the middle-class press. The appeal was only moderately successful. It attracted contributors from prominent Mancunians such as William Thorburn, Sir Alexander Porter and Alderman John Royle but generated annual subscriptions of little over £160.[52] There were already signs that the social composition of the Whitworth's patrons was changing. Death robbed the institution of many of its prominent supporters over a very short period of time. Thomas Ashton, the veteran Manchester collector who was one of the seven who initiated the Art Treasures Exhibition of 1857, died in 1898. During the next eight years most of the major figures associated with the early development of the Whitworth passed away, including R. C. Christie, John Hopkinson, J. E. Taylor, John Bowden and Herbert Philips. Few men of significant wealth came forward to replace then. The death of Darbishire in 1908 brought the final break with the past. The new chairman of the Whitworth council, Walter Butterworth, typified the new generation of men who replaced the old industrial plutocracy. Butterworth, although from a poor background, was a highly educated, cultured man and head of a firm of glass manufacturers in Newton Heath. He did not, however, have the immense wealth of his predecessors and, rather than developing a large personal art collection, spent his artistic energies in providing intellectual support and advice in developing the public art collections in the city.[53]

Although the Whitworth Institute was an oligarchic and elitist structure, it was an outward-looking body exercising its influence through its claim to be a public organisation. The very fact that a figure such as Butterworth could attain such a prominent position suggests that the Whitworth was a relatively open elite, and indeed it had to be in order to prosper. Although its membership fees were high, it was an oligarchy of intellect as much as of wealth. Whitworth's own desire to promote popular education meant that the legatees had to place education at the forefront of their own political agendas, even when the technical school was detached from the original plans. The local MP Sir Henry Roscoe hoped that the institute would be 'a source of perpetual gratification' but also that it would 'exert a permanent influence of the highest character in the direction of commercial and technical instruction and of the cultivation of taste and knowledge of the fine arts …'. William Mather stated explicitly that 'the Institute was not mainly intended to benefit the affluent classes' and pointed to Joseph Whitworth's own belief that 'mental culture should accompany manual proficiency'.[54]

Others noted that gradually the gallery was attracting more serious students – 'a not inconsiderable section who do appear to give great, and even minute attention to particular works or series of works'.[55] Many students from the school of art also used institute exhibitions for copying and drawing practice.[56] The opening of the Whitworth contributed to a particularly successful period in the school of art's history, most notably in the period before the First World War when the French impressionist Adolphe Valette was a permanent tutor at the school.[57]

The formation of the Whitworth Institute highlights the importance of cultural politics and institutional competition on collecting activity. It was a privately established institution, developed at a time when municipal authorities were increasingly taking responsibility for public art. It mimicked, in its organisation and political structure, the RMI, which just a few years earlier had become effectively moribund and handed its property over to the corporation. Indeed, had the city authorities acted more generously the Whitworth might have developed as a complementary branch of the city gallery. Unfortunately the cool response of the city council combined with the impatience of the Whitworth legatees meant that the Whitworth was forced to develop without the support of public funds, while the city council was not to get a new purpose-built gallery until the twenty-first century. It also meant that the prime institution for popular art education in the city was controlled not by the elected public authority but by a private, if benevolent, oligarchy (Figure 18).

The Whitworth Institute was built as a memorial to one of Britain's leading engineers, but it is questionable whether the galleries that emerged owed much to Whitworth's own visions, beyond that of his support for popular education. The institute was primarily shaped by the ideas of wealthy patrons on the council of the Whitworth and specialist advisors. Whereas the municipal gallery was handicapped by its existing infrastructure, outmoded buildings from the 1820s

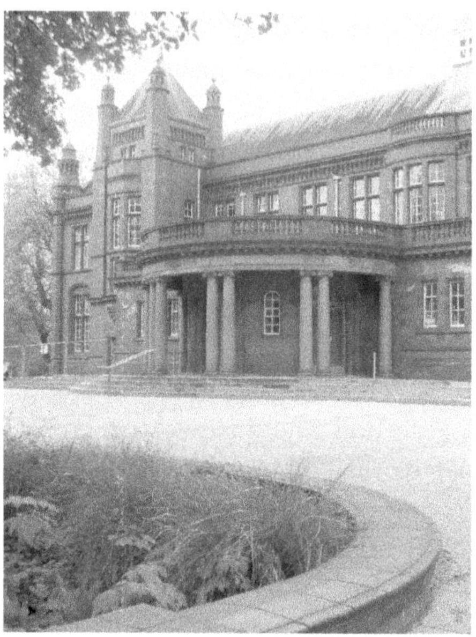

18 The Whitworth Art Gallery today

and heavy financial commitments, the Whitworth legatees were free to develop a gallery that was thematically organised and with rooms following modern curatorial practice. Borrowing ideas from as far afield as the Musée Royal in Brussels and the Tate Gallery in London, they could provide a more intimate space that would better show off watercolour collections. However, the steely determination of the founders to provide cultural leadership brought what was perhaps an inevitable conflict with the municipality and, in the long term, denied it the opportunity of state support.

Civic cultural institutions like the Whitworth were inherently weak unless they had secure forms of revenue funding, from either the public or the private sector. In Manchester the competition and rivalry between private and state art galleries shaped the nature of public collecting but, in some respects, enfeebled both institutions. The Whitworth Institute and its collection represented the high tide of nineteenth-century middle-class benevolence; but it was a tide that receded as the Victorian social group that created it disappeared.

Legacies and bequests did not always foster tensions with municipal authorities. Preston offers an example of a legacy investment being used to institutionalise the cultural authority of a town's civic leadership behind a very different but distinctive vision. The Harris Library, Museum and Art Gallery took the name of its benefactor, but was essentially the project of the town's municipal leader. The fact that one man, supported by a small group of political followers, could achieve such a dominant position says much about the cultural politics of smaller towns. It also highlights how capital availability was crucial for the ability of cultural visionaries to articulate a sustained and coherent policy towards art gallery development and collecting policy. In Preston, unlike many municipalities, most of the finance for the art gallery came from a single private source, unencumbered by restrictive covenants or the need to consult a wide range of interested parties. While the cultural policies of Manchester and Liverpool had to negotiate political rivalries and the demands for scrutiny over public expenditure, the fact that Preston's capital funds came from an unencumbered private gift from a dead individual allowed for the corporation's leadership to enjoy relative free rein over art gallery development.

The powerful influence of the philhellene Alderman James Hibbert meant that the Harris Library, Museum and Art Gallery was to be one of the last major neo-classical art galleries in England.[58] It was the physical manifestation of one man's views about the enduring importance of classical learning and its influence over modernity. Of course, during the early nineteenth-century classical revival, classically inspired buildings appeared in most major towns. Greek styles were particularly strong, with the influence of Stuart and Revett, and later Cockerell, seen in many public buildings of the period.[59] Yet by the mid-nineteenth century, classical forms were gradually being replaced by new fashions inspired by Gothic and Italianate work.[60] As most municipal art galleries were not developed until the second half of the century, few displayed strong classical influences.[61] The Preston gallery was perhaps the only truly classical public building of note erected in Lancashire since the opening of St George's Hall in Liverpool in 1855.

The classical style of Preston's gallery did not reflect a fashionable whim or an architect's fancy; rather it was to be a statement reaffirming the importance of classical knowledge and learning in the modern world.[62] At a time of civil unrest in Ireland, constitutional change and trade union militancy, the Harris was a classical and political essay on the dangers of 'popular' tyranny. The warnings of Thucydides on the excesses of democracy and personal rule found a strong echo in the present.[63] Indeed, the Harris represented something of a paradox. Museums are often seen as paradigms of modernity.[64] Yet the Harris stood as a monument to ancient ideals and the alleged cultural superiority of an ancient civilisation. The gallery rejected modernist trends of art and politics while, at the same time, offering a powerful critique of them. Arguably the outlook of the gallery was more forward-looking than that of many municipal galleries of modern art. While many local authorities, obsessed by imperialistic and nationalistic zeal, collected mainly works of the British school, the Harris looked beyond the confines of the national school to seek out works of excellence from all nations.[65] Although the Harris stood as a reactionary bulwark against modernism, it also stood as a monument to internationalism and humanism, in a world increasingly engulfed by imperialism and nationalist excess.

By the end of the century, the most prominent exhibitions at galleries such as Manchester were heavily influenced by commercial interests, and the galleries functioned little differently from private shops and studios. It was this model that Preston, like the Whitworth, explicitly rejected. With finance available from private sources and a visionary project architect, Preston railed against convention and set out to establish a historical gallery that would be an exemplar for its people. The Preston case demonstrates that although galleries were often represented as grand expressions of civic pride, they could, in reality, owe much to the creative expression of a single man and his desire to reassert classical cultural hegemony.

Many in Preston feared that the town's relative economic decline was being felt in the decay of its voluntary public institutions and cultural associations.[66] The vicious industrial conflicts of the 1870s were viewed as a symptom of this cultural decline and the failure of popular education.[67] In 1877 the dissolution of the literary and philosophical society threatened the existence of one of the town's most important literary collections.[68] Preston Corporation was faced with the choice of either purchasing the library from the society or allowing it to be dispersed. After setting up a special committee to examine alternatives, the corporation agreed to establish a new free public library. The library was financed partly by corporation funds and partly from money raised in connection with an earlier aborted scheme for a public library.[69] Combining the council's eighteenth-century Shepherd Library and that of the literary and philosophical society, the new institution opened in January 1879 in the town hall.

The new library was developed in the knowledge that there was a very good prospect of obtaining external funds for a new and much more extensive facility in the near future. Following the death of the local magnate Edmund Robert Harris on 27 May 1877, it became clear that very large sums were to be made available, through his trustees, for the patronage of educational and cultural institutions in Preston. Harris was a successful lawyer, although much of his wealth was inherited. As the last of a family line, he inherited wealth from his father, his uncles and his brother and sister, much of it derived from railway stock and real estate. When the Harris Art Gallery, Museum and Library opened in 1893, the amounts spent from the estate on educational and charitable purposes in Preston amounted to over £300,000.[70] Harris had been an important figure in attempts to establish a free public library in 1854, and it was inevitable, therefore, that the trustees, led by Charles Roger Jacson of Barton Hall, would make the building of a library a central priority.

The Harris trustees did not hand over the detailed management and planning of the new building to a committee of the corporation, but instead chose to establish their own committee to run the scheme directly. This may have been partly because of legal complexities in managing such an amount of money in trust: the scheme had to be presented to the Chancery division of the High Court for approval, and any major changes to the allocated budgets also required legal authorisation.[71] It may also have been because they wished to choose Alderman James Hibbert, the chairman of the corporation's free library committee, as the architect for the building. Had the corporation obtained any direct ownership of the project before its completion, Hibbert would have fallen foul of legislation prohibiting council officials from holding contracts with the local authority of which they were a member.[72] By contracting with the free library committee of the Harris trustees, Hibbert and the trustees had effectively found a loophole in the legislation, as it was always intended that the new building would become corporation property.

James Hibbert's ideas about the role and importance of art and classical scholarship are central to understanding the nature of the new library and art gallery, its early collecting policy and its educational activities. Hibbert, as planner, architect and chairman of the library and art gallery committee, effectively controlled the whole project, while Charles Jacson, who later gained much of the credit for the gallery, did little more than administer the project and its accounts. By the mid-1870s, Hibbert had established himself as a senior municipal figure and the town's leading architect. A local man, Hibbert trained in Manchester and London before returning to Preston in 1855 to practise in partnership with Nathan Rainford.[73] Over the next two decades, he completed some of the most notable buildings in Preston and Blackburn. His first important project was the new Baptist chapel in Fishergate, designed primarily in the Italian Romanesque style, but his general architectural approach combined a variety of influences.[74] His early works were all broadly inspired by classical or Romanesque approaches, but in 1866 he completed his first Gothic building, St Saviour's Church in Leeming Street. By the 1870s, his rather eclectic approach changed to one that favoured Gothic for ecclesiastical buildings and classical for public buildings.[75] Thus, the Harris was destined to be an essay in neo-classicalism, and the first important 'neo-Grec' building in England since the construction of St George's Hall in Liverpool forty years before.[76]

A sub-committee, headed by Hibbert, spent several months in 1878 touring public museums, libraries, and galleries throughout England, paying particular attention to those established by municipalities under the legislation of 1850, 1855 and 1866. The sub-committee reported in 1879, and it was clear from the outset that a very-large scale building was anticipated.

> A comprehensive permanent foundation for the encouragement of Learning, the cultivation of the Arts and Sciences, and the free diffusion of a varied literature … for the advancement of all classes in Preston, and its immediate neighbourhood.[77]

In 1881, the year of his mayoralty, Hibbert published his plans for the new institution. The building was to be an essay in classicism, heavily influenced by the eighteenth-century architectural textbooks of Stuart and Revett. The choice of Greek was not merely for aesthetic or decorative reasons; indeed, Hibbert was careful, in essays and speeches, to emphasise his reasons for the choice. For Hibbert, the ancient Greeks represented not so much the source of artistic, literary and cultural civilisation, but rather the peak of civilisation. The power of classical Greek culture was such that it stood above the fashions of the day and represented a simplicity and truthfulness of expression that would survive the judgement of time.

> The character of the design is academical, conceived the most appropriate. Influenced by studies of Ionic art, its chief features are simplicity and symmetry of plan, truthfulness of expression, and, in execution, refinement of detail. In the plastic arts, as in literature and geometrical science, the Hellenic race has reached the highest standard. If Greek architecture is to be retained in practical service, it is requisite, when opportunity affords, to present new combinations of its forms. For the purposes of a library and museum, – a repository of knowledge, of examples of the arts, and of specimens illustrative of the sciences, – its suitableness will be admitted. There are fashions in architecture, as in most artistic production of the time. A structure, however, that is fit for its

uses, subserves its distinctive functions, and is in harmony of expression with nature and quality of those functions, stands above the fluctuations of ephemeral taste.[78]

Hibbert sought to construct a building that would represent universal values underlying modern cultural achievement. The Harris was not to be a building for the nineteenth century or even one for the twentieth; rather it was envisaged as a permanent landmark. It was expected to last at least as long as the Greek temples that inspired it. When the Earl of Lathom laid the building's foundation stone in 1882, he expressed the wish that it would last 20,000 years and be a permanent inspiration to the townspeople.[79]

Hibbert's detailed plans for the layout of the new Harris Library, Museum and Art Gallery were nothing if not ambitious. Beyond the Ionic portico, inspired by the Erechtheion at Athens, and the entrance, the building was to feature a large central hall, which would contain the museum and art exhibitions. The hall would be surrounded by galleries and reading rooms, as appropriate. On the ground floor of the central hall there was to be a collection of models associated with industrial arts. The first floor, the principal floor, would be set aside for the reference library, but with the central hall laid out as a museum of casts and reproductions from the antique. All the upper floors were to be provided for museum and fine art purposes.[80] These galleries, 'for economy of wall-space and effective lighting', would be wholly lit from the top.[81] The central hall would be surmounted by a massive square lantern – not, strictly speaking, a purely Greek feature, but one which was used on other neo-classical buildings. It may have been inspired by the one superimposed on Charles Barry's design for the RMI.[82] For Hibbert, the key function of an art gallery was popular education. Consequently, he emphasised the importance of acquiring works that exhibited basic and fundamental principles of excellence, not merely those that were fashionable. Collections should avoid partisan preference for nation or school but instead appeal to higher principles.

> To fill a gallery with examples of one school or one nation is to lose sight of the fundamental principles which should guide those who have the conduct of the rapidly-increasing galleries of art in this country. The first aim and object of those concerned with these galleries is that they should be the means of educating and purifying the public taste ... Fashion should be carefully avoided, and modern works should only be chosen which exhibit the best elements of the modern school.[83]

In practice, Hibbert showed little interest in encouraging the purchase of any modern works. He felt that the priority was to compile a collection of reproductions, engravings and etchings which reflected the historical progress of art.[84] He was particularly influenced by an exhibition at the Walker gallery in Liverpool that contained a complete series of reproduction engravings of paintings in fresco by Italian and German masters, published by the Arundel Society, and he clearly envisaged a similar approach at Preston.[85] It was better to purchase autotypes of famous works from European galleries, and truly great domestic work, such as Turner's *Liber Studiorum*, 'than those mediocre specimens of the work of living artists which fom the greater part of our annual exhibitions'.[86]

For Hibbert, the library and art gallery should represent only excellence. This attitude was also represented in the detail of the exterior of the building and the sculptured pediment. The building was a self-conscious tribute to the Greek classical tradition and in particular to the age of Pericles, widely regarded as the apex of Greek civilisation. It represented and celebrated the 'prodigious superiority of the Greeks over every other nation, in all works of real taste and genius'.[87] Around the central lantern was inscribed Pericles' funeral oration by Thucydides, not in translation, but in the original Greek.

ΑΜΔΘΞΜ ΧΑΘ ΕΠΙΥΑΜΞΜ ΠΑΡΑ ΧΓ ΣΑΥΟΡ ϑΑΙ ΟΤ ΡΣΓΚΞΜ
ΛΟΜΟΜ ΕΜ ΣΓ ΟΙϑΕΙΑ ΡΓΛΑΙΜΕΙ ΕΠΙΧΘΑΥΓ ΑΚΚΑ ϑΑΙ ΕΜ ΣΓ
ΛΓ ΠΘΟΡΓϑΟΤΡΓ ΑΧΘΑΥΟΡ ΛΜΓΛΓ ΠΑΘ ΕϑΑΡΣΞ ΣΓΡ
ΧΜΞΛΓΡ ΛΑΚΚΟΜ Γ ΣΟΤ ΕΘΧΟΤ ΕΜΔΙΑΣΑΣΑΙ

For the whole earth is the sepulchre of illustrious men; not only are they commemorated by columns and inscriptions in their own country, but in foreign land there dwells also an unwritten memorial of them, graven, not upon stone, but in the hearts of men.[88]

The inscription was a recognition of the debt owed to classical civilisation, not merely for the style and beauty of the building, but for its contribution to modern learning. Beneath the lantern, the pedimental sculpture reflected the same theme, with Pericles in the centre surrounded by some of his most famous contemporaries associated with literature, poetry, philosophy and art. On the right-hand side Parmides, Zeno and Socrates discuss philosophy, while Thucydides contemplates history. At the centre is Pericles with Ictinus, the main architect of the Parthenon, and Ananxagoras. On the left are Pindar, Aeschylus,

Sophocles, Euripides and finally Herodotus with his completed books.[89] These men are further alluded to in the inscription below the pediment, appropriately enough in words written by Britain's most illustrious philhellene, Lord Byron.

> The dead, but sceptered Sovrans, who still rule
> Our spirits from their urns.[90]

Hibbert had taken a great deal of care with the design of the pedimental representations and inscriptions. The figures themselves were, of course, fashioned in the classical style to complement the building, and Hibbert was careful to explain the reasons for his choice of figures and inscriptions. He produced a *Memoir* explaining who each figure in his plans represented and extensive historical notes on the figures with a chronological table of key events in Athenian history.[91] The design for the pediment was completed by Edwin Roscoe Mullins, but at all stages Hibbert paid close attention to the progress of the work, assisted by a leading classical scholar, William Watkiss Lloyd. Lloyd made a number of observations, in particular advocating the transposition of Aristophanes and Pindar, feeling that Pindar had little connection with Athens.[92] Characteristically, Hibbert was disinclined to make changes.[93] The choice of figures reflected his own Conservative political values. Aeschylus was included not merely on literary grounds but because his writings represented a warning against the dangers of the excesses of democracy: 'the general fears attendant on an unbridled democracy, the ascendancy of which he feared was to come'.[94] Hibbert seems to have been considering turning over the entire pedimental inscription to verses warning against the dangers of anarchy and tyranny. Several options were considered. One suggestion was to include a reflective Aeschylus with the word 'Nemesis', but this was thought to be too remote an allegorical device for widespread understanding by Lloyd, who suggested instead the lines of the *Eumenides*:

> Nor Anarchy nor Tyrant's lawless rule
> Command I to many people's reverence; –
> Nor let them from their city banish Fear
> For who 'mong men uncurbed by Fear is just?
> Thus holding Awe in seemly reverence,
> A bulwark for our state shall ye possess
> A safeguard to protect your city-walls –[95]

The whole project became a reflection of contemporary Conservative political concerns. It was a reaction not only to artistic modernism, but also to political modernism. Uncomfortable with what he saw as the excesses of democracy, Hibbert looked to the age of Pericles to provide warnings against potential revolution. With citizenship came responsibility, and only vigilance and justice could protect democracy against anarchy and tyranny.[96] By reading classical texts, such as the *Eumenides*, Hibbert felt that 'the Democracy' – the people – could come to understand the reasons for the rise of Athens and avoid its failings and political collapse. Although Hibbert regarded the promotion of classical art as an important feature of the Harris gallery, he considered the promotion of classical literature to be equally important. Free public libraries represented a great opportunity to provide citizens with a constitutional education and to equip them for full political citizenship.

> Our Free Public Libraries are the machinery for disseminating, by means of translation, the spirit of the classical writers to every one who can read only his mother tongue. If the Democracy, which is to be, if it is not now already, the predominant power, could be made to understand by what means Athens rose to the summit of her unrivalled greatness, and what were the causes of the fall from her high estate – causes which lie upon the surface of her history, and which he who runs may read – one cannot but think that it would be better for the future of this country.[97]

Not everyone shared Hibbert's particular political preoccupations, and there are signs that he was aware that some of his colleagues were somewhat mystified by his classical obsession. The Victorian period was the age of Gothic revival, reflecting Romantic ideals and perceived economic and social values of medievalism.[98] Yet while many towns decorated public buildings with allusions to local craft industries, identity and heritage, Hibbert chose a classical design decorated with words in an ancient foreign language that few Prestonians could have comprehended. The suggestion of a local allegorical device in place of the pediment was put forward, but Hibbert was dismissive, declaring such devices to be 'trite and common'.[99] Rather than be narrowly nationalistic, Hibbert wanted the building to be 'more widely representative in embodying what is common in all civilised lands'.[100] The building was to be a statement of the universal inheritance and objective value of Greek civilisation, standing above 'the ocean of mediocrity and pretence that everywhere surrounds us'.[101]

Finally, in August 1893, the building was handed over to the corporation, together with over £15,000 held in trust for expenditure on developing the permanent collection.[102] Unfortunately, neither of the men closely associated with the development of the library and gallery were present at the formal handover. Charles Jacson, the chairman of the Harris free public library committee, had died just days before, while Hibbert was reportedly unable to attend through illness. Indeed, although Jacson was warmly praised by the mayor and others for his work in completing the project, Hibbert was barely mentioned during the proceedings, despite his position at the head of the free library committee.[103] It was clear that by this time Hibbert was already at odds with what he saw as the corporation's unenthusiastic policy in relation to art.

Hibbert continually pressed the committee to appoint a literary and art director. Many felt that Hibbert wanted to occupy the position himself, and one councillor even recalled a public discussion about whether it would be possible for Hibbert to keep his position as chairman and also take on the role of a paid official. Hibbert viewed the art directorship as essentially a temporary post, one that would not be required after the library and gallery had been established. He also felt that if the post could be paid for out of the Harris fund, his appointment would not break the law on municipal contracting.[104]

Hibbert's desire to take over the literary and art directorship was not an entirely selfish one; he had long harboured the view that many museums were managed in an amateurish way. As early as September 1893 he had published a pamphlet urging the free library committee to appoint a literary and art director and warned against the dangers of failing to take professional advice:

> Nothing was simpler, nothing was easier, than to buy a lot of books and call it a library, or to rake together from all quarters a heap of incongruous things, and to dignify the collection with the title of an Art Museum. Anybody who liked to have a finger in the pie could do this – there were plenty of instances of it – in fact, it worked automatically … If museums were to be created on this footing, they were not publicly worth either their cost or their maintenance. Such class of museums became, indeed, neither more nor less than evil centres and promulgators of vulgar taste and ignorant assumption.[105]

For some time it had been clear that 'friction and an unpleasant state of things existed on the Free Library Committee' and that some councillors 'appeared to regard the chairman as a sort of bogey man … continually at work in a Jesuitical fashion, springing mines upon the committee and taking advantage of the innocence of the members'.[106] By March 1895, Hibbert's relations with many in his committee had completely broken down, and, with the council refusing to endorse his proposals, he had little choice but to resign. The man who had fashioned the country's 'greatest provincial Athenaeum' was effectively banished from his own Athens. While the streets around the new library and art gallery were renamed in honour of Harris and Jacson, there was no memorialisation of Hibbert. Instead he was left to look on with dismay and bitterness at the gallery's amateurish forms of hanging and arrangement, writing to the press to complain that the 'galleries were intended to be something different from a sort of classical Madame Tussaud's' while expressing private disgust that his prized achievement had fallen into 'common hands'.[107] It took a considerable time for Preston Corporation to be persuaded to appoint an official art director. It was not until 1909 that W. B. Barton, the art instructor at the Harris Institute, was formally appointed as the first director of art.[108]

Hibbert may have been forced into a reluctant retirement but his approach to developing the permanent collection remained. His insistence that the art gallery should endeavour to obtain copies of the world's most notable works of art was the fundamental influence behind the first two decades of the Harris gallery's development. As early as the spring of 1890 the chairman of the Harris free public library committee, C. R. Jacson, began to purchase items for the developing institution.[109] Working with Jacson and the Harris trustees, Hibbert had obtained a £500 grant in aid from the Department of Science and Art in South Kensington to purchase reproductive works in plaster. Hibbert chose the reproductions himself. Some were Renaissance works, including reproductions of Michelangelo's *David and Moses*. Many of the purchases were, however, inspired by Hibbert's interest in the classical world. A whole series of casts of the eastern pediment of the Parthenon was ordered, including works representing the Houses of Helios, Theseus, Ceres and Proserpine, Iris, Nike and the Fates.[110] South Kensington was not entirely happy when it discovered that Preston did not have anywhere to exhibit the items it had purchased with its funds, but, after reassurances, a further £200 was provided for the following year.[111] Again Hibbert chose the items, although this time in conjunction with the advisor Fairfax Murray. Greco-Roman works continued to be particularly prominent, including a cast of the Hercules and Venus of Ostia.[112] Even after Hibbert left, the committee continued to acquire large amounts of classical art, including reproductions of items from Pompeii and Herculaneum, assisted by 50 per cent purchase grants from South Kensington.[113]

It would be wrong, however, to depict Hibbert as obsessed exclusively with the classical world. Hibbert believed that examples of excellence in art should be collected from wherever they could be obtained, and from any nation or period. In fact, he was responsible for obtaining some of the most important modern works in Preston's collection, namely the Newsham bequest pictures. Hibbert had shown his plans for the new gallery to a local art collector Richard Newsham, in a covert attempt to persuade him to leave his collection to the town.[114] It was a successful ploy, as following Newsham's death in December 1883, Preston acquired his very important collection of modern paintings, mainly of items from the British school. His collection, from his property in Winckley Square, was valued at around £40,000 and included works by many of Britain's most celebrated nineteenth-century artists, such as Sir Edwin Landseer, William Etty, W. P. Frith, R. Ansdell and J. M. W. Turner. The collection was strong in the landscape department, with important works by John Linnell, Thomas Creswick and John William Muller, while there were also a number of important works of still life by William Henry Hunt. Contemporary reviews of the collection gave prominence to the work of the most popular artists of the day. W. B. Barton's essay in the *Magazine of Art* gave special mention to David Cox's *The Way to the Hayfield* and *Lancaster Sands*, David Roberts's *Antwerp Cathedral*, E. M. Ward's *The Royal Family in the Temple* and J. F. Lewis's *The Bey's Garden*.[115] These five works, in particular, were of significant commercial value. Ward's picture of the French royal family probably represented one of the most valuable items in British municipal permanent collections at the time.[116]

Preston's ongoing interest in classicism influenced the Harris gallery's most important commission: the Athenian and Egyptian panels of John Somerscales. The art gallery committee, desiring a permanent historical decoration of the central galleries, sought to engage a number of internationally prominent mural painters for the work. After both Puvis de Chavannes and G. F. Watts declined, it awarded a commission to John Somerscales, younger brother of the better-known maritime painter Thomas, who had pictures exhibited at the Tate and the Walker.[117] The commission began with large monochrome paintings featuring the Athenian Acropolis, one representing the Parthenon and the Erechtheion and the other showing the Acropolis and the Temple of Theseus.[118] The following winter Somerscales completed four more important Greek works including one of the ruins of the temples at Aegina and Sunium.[119] By spring 1908, Somerscales's mural paintings had been carried round the whole of the walls of the central hall, with additional views of ruins in Asia Minor and Sicily.[120] Delighted by the results, the art gallery committee then extended the commission, sending Somerscales to Egypt to make colour studies of drawings of ancient temples and other representative historical features for mural decoration.[121]

For Hibbert, an art gallery's primary role was educational and improving; consequently only items of excellence could be included in a public museum. Picture price inflation meant that the very best original modern works were beyond Preston, and it had no interest in buying second-rate items. Consequently, unlike most other municipal galleries in Lancashire, Preston showed only limited interest in purchasing modern works or in organising commercial exhibitions for living artists. While municipalities such as Manchester, Liverpool, Southport and even Oldham fought to attract the unsold and often inferior pictures from the annual exhibition at the Royal Academy, Preston followed its own course. Classical copies were viewed by Hibbert as infinitely better than second-rate modern works, and thus Preston devoted almost all of its energy in that direction. Hibbert's departure saw no change in basic policy. The art gallery continued to see its central function as an educational one, presenting the most outstanding works of art from all periods to the public.

The examples of the Whitworth and Harris should make historians cautious about generalising about the trajectory of local cultural policies in Britain during the last two decades of the nineteenth century. While the ideas of John Ruskin may have become influential in some contexts, and while the growth of 'People's Palaces' of art may suggest a move towards increasing democratisation of cultural practices, in reality local art galleries had a range of origins, purposes and patterns of governance. The Whitworth's priorities reflected the interests of the circle of Whitworth legatees, a body of highly educated professional men who sought to challenge and supplant what they saw as the inadequate and ill-informed cultural policy of the municipality's elected leaders. The Harris's priorities reflected the views of the circle of a senior Conservative alderman, who felt that art should prepare the citizenry for liberal democracy through a somewhat paternalistic approach towards classical education. Both galleries sought to increase the visual literacy of the mass public, but neither took seriously the view that municipalities should encourage citizens to contribute to cultural policy. The one common feature of both institutions was a suspicion of elected municipal committees as custodians and promoters of 'high art'. During the two decades before the First World War, municipal art committees would increasingly come under attack from two sources. First, cultural elites would question the suitability of municipalities as engines for the promotion of art galleries and question their collecting choices and priorities. Secondly, local politicians, under pressure from local electorates, would increasingly question whether expenditure on art galleries really could bring about the social improvements that advocates of the art gallery movement so often claimed. The result was that the age of lavish local government expenditure on art institutions gradually receded, but not before municipal art galleries had spread to most industrial towns.

NOTES

Some of the material from this chapter has been previously published in the journal *Northern History*. J. Moore, 'Periclean Preston, Public Art and the Classical Tradition in Late-Nineteenth-Century Lancashire', *Northern History*, 40 (2003), 299–323.

1 The Whitworth Art Gallery remained independent until its absorption by the University of Manchester in 1958.

2 Unlike those in Britain, provincial art galleries and museums in the United States were often vested in independent trusts. See, for example, N. Harris, 'The Gilded Age Revisited: Boston and the Museum Movement', *American Quarterly*, 144 (1962), 545–66.

3 See special issue of *Journal of the History of Collections*, 4 (1992), especially introduction by E. Morris, 169–73; W. Leverhulme, *Viscount Leverhulme by his Son* (London, 1927); W. Jolly, *Lord Leverhulme* (London, 1976).

4 N. Atkinson, *Sir Joseph Whitworth* (Stroud, 1996), 298–9.

5 C. R. Dodwell, *Guide to the Whitworth Art Gallery* (Manchester, 1979), 5.

6 Dodwell, *Guide*, 5.

7 Atkinson, *Whitworth*, 289.

8 Atkinson, *Whitworth*, 301–2.

9 C. Nugent, *From View to Vision: British Watercolours from Sandby to Turner in the Whitworth Art Gallery* (Manchester, 1993), 4.

10 Manchester Technical School circular, Whitworth Committee Letters, University of Manchester Special Collections (hereafter UMSC).

11 S. MacDonald, 'The Royal Manchester Institution', in J. H G. Archer (ed.), *Art and Architecture in Victorian Manchester* (Manchester, 1985), 28–45.

12 Eventually it was determined that the Manchester Technical School should be located away from the park in Sackville Street – a less prestigious industrial location close to London Road railway station.

13 'Outline of a Scheme' (marked draft), February 1888, Whitworth Committee Documents, vol. 32, UMSC.

14 'Plan of Whitworth Park', n.d., Whitworth Committee Documents, vol. 32, UMSC.

15 Whitworth Committee, Galleries and Museums, 17 October 1888, Whitworth Committee Documents.

16 R. D. Darbishire, letter to J. J. Harwood, March 1888, Whitworth Committee Letters.

245

17 See circular from R. D. Darbishire, 30 April 1888, Whitworth Committee Documents, vol. 37.

18 LW. Mather, letter to R. D. Darbishire, 7 May 1888, Whitworth Committee Letters.

19 *The Manchester Whitworth Institute – Charter of Incorporation and Statutes* (Manchester, n.d.), MCL.

20 'Statutes Made by Governors at the First Meeting', 10 October 1890, UMSC.

21 *Manchester Guardian*, 18 July 1890.

22 *Manchester City News*, 19 July 1890.

23 *Manchester Guardian*, 18 July 1890.

24 *Manchester Guardian* cutting, n.d. (1890), in Whitworth Green Cuttings Book, UMSC.

25 *Manchester Guardian*, 15 July 1883, in Whitworth Blue Cuttings Book, UMSC.

26 *Manchester City News*, 5 March 1892; *Manchester City News*, 9 April 1892.

27 *Manchester Examiner*, 12 July 1890, in Whitworth Blue Cuttings Book.

28 Report of the Council to the Governors, February 1895, 4–5, in Whitworth Art Gallery Annual Reports 1893–1906 (incomplete), MCL, 708.273 W2.

29 *Manchester Guardian*, 17 February 1892, *Manchester Courier*, 16 February 1892, in Whitworth Blue Cuttings Book.

30 Report of the Council to the Governors, February 1895, 4–5.

31 For a recent popular account of Manchester's Victorian artists see S. Thomson, *Manchester's Victorian Art Scene and its Unrecognised Artists* (Warrington, 2007).

32 Royal Cambrian Academy Minutes, book 1, 12 November 1881, Royal Cambrian Academy Archives, Conwy.

33 See, for example, 'A Local Artist', letter, *Manchester City News*, 18 October 1890.

34 *Manchester Examiner*, 6 August 1890, in Whitworth Green Cuttings Book.

35 Report of the Council to the Governors, February 1895, in Whitworth Art Gallery Annual Reports 1893–1906 (incomplete), MCL, 708.273 W2.

36 Nugent, *View*, 4.

37 Dodwell, *Guide*, 8.

38 For example, sixteen of the twenty-five Turners were dated to before 1802, relatively early in his career. I am indebted to Charles Nugent for noting this point.

39 Report of the Council to the Governors, June 1904, 8, in Whitworth Art Gallery Annual Reports 1893–1906, MCL, 708.273 W2.

40 F. S. Stancliffe, *John Shaw's Club* (Manchester, 1938), 337–8, 405; RMI, Council General Meeting Minutes, 11 May 1891, MCL, M6/1.

41 Report of the Council to the Governors, 1912–13, in Whitworth Institute Annual Reports, 1890–1923, UMSC.

42 Minutes of Council, vol. C, 31 July 1912, 187–8, Whitworth Art Gallery, UMSC.

43 Report of the Council to the Governors, Whitworth Institute Annual Reports, June 1904, 8, MCL, 708.273 W2.

44 Report of the Council to the Governors, Whitworth Institute Annual Reports, June 1904, 8, MCL, 708.273 W2.

45 Report of the Council to the Governors, July 1906, 8–9, in Whitworth Art Gallery Annual Reports 1893–1906, MCL, 708.273 W2.

46 P. Gardner, letter to R. D. Darbishire, 20 October 1904 (copy), in Whitworth Institute Annual Reports 1890–1923, UMSC.

47 E. Wood and T. Taylor, 'Gallery of Fine Art', n.d., MCL, m58971/122614.

48 R. D. Darbishire, letter to J. D. Milne, 24 February 1897 (loose leaf), in Minutes of Council, vol. B, 62 (copy), Whitworth Art Gallery, UMSC.

49 Minutes of Council, vol. C, 26 January 1909, 84, Whitworth Art Gallery, UMSC.

50 Minutes of Council, vol. C, 10 June 1910, Whitworth Art Gallery, UMSC.

51 Minutes of Council, vol. C, 27 November 1912, Whitworth Art Gallery, UMSC.

52 Minutes of Council, vol. C, 31 January 1912, 178, Whitworth Art Gallery, UMSC.

53 *Manchester Guardian*, 2 September 1935.

54 *Manchester Guardian*, 18 July 1890.

55 Report of the Council to the Governors, July 1897, 6, in Whitworth Art Gallery Annual Reports 1893–1906, MCL, 708.273 W2.

56 Report of the Council to the Governors, May 1898, 18, in Whitworth Art Gallery Annual Reports 1893–1906, MCL, 708.273 W2.

57 S. Martin, *Adolphe Valette: A French Influence in Manchester* (Manchester, 1994); C. Lyon, *Adolphe Valette* (London, 2006).

58 For further background and illustrations see S. Sartin, *The People and Places of Historic Preston* (Preston, 1988); J. Convey, *The Harris Free Public Library and Museum, Preston, 1893–1993* (Preston, 1993).

59 J. M. Crook, *The Greek Revival* (London, 1972); D. Stillman, *English Neo-Classical Architecture*, 2 vols (London, 1988); D. Watkin, *Athenian Stuart: Pioneer of the Greek Revival* (London, 1982); D. Watkin, *The Life and Work of C. R. Cockerell* (London, 1974); R. Stoneman, *Land of Lost Gods* (London, 1987), esp. 11–35.

60 J. Macaulay, *The Gothic Revival, 1745–1845* (Glasgow, 1975); C. Brooks, *The Gothic Revival* (London, 1999), esp. 223–58, 291–340.

61 Except where municipalities took over existing buildings, such as the RMI building in Mosley Street, Manchester. MacDonald, 'Royal Manchester Institution', 28–45.

62 Despite changing fashions Victorians continued to enjoy a close and complex relationship with classical Greece. See R. Jenkyns, *The Victorians and Ancient Greece* (Oxford, 1980); H. Lloyd-Jones, *Blood for the Ghosts: Classical Influences in the Nineteenth and Twentieth Centuries* (London, 1982); R. M. Ogilvie, *Latin and Greek: A History of the Influence of the Classics on English Life from 1600 to 1918* (London, 1964), esp. 91–133; F. M. Turner, *The Greek Heritage in Victorian Britain* (London, 1981).

63 Ogilvie, *Latin and Greek*, 110, and see below.

64 For a recent exploration of this issue see N. Prior, *Museums and Modernity: Art Galleries and the Making of Modern Culture* (Oxford, 2002).

65 Even large cities like Manchester tended to concentrate on collecting modern British works. See *Report to the City Council of Visits to Certain Art Galleries and Museums in Belgium, Holland, Germany and Great Britain* (Manchester, 1905) and W. H. Brindley, *The Soul of Manchester* (Manchester, 1929), 166.

66 For problems of the public library movement see A. Hewitson, *A History of Preston* (Preston, 1883); J. Hibbert (ed.), *Notes on Free Public Libraries and Museums* (Preston, 1881).

67 A. Berry, *Proud Preston's Story* (Preston, 1928), 285.

68 C. McDougal, 'Library Growth in Preston 1694–1893: The Development of the Harris Free Public Library and Museum', BA thesis, St John's College, York, n.d., 15.

69 Or at least as much money from the 1854 scheme that could be located. Some, apparently, went missing. See Hewitson, *History*, 288.

70 Convey, *Harris*, 12–13.

71 McDougal, 'Library Growth', 20.

72 The 1835 Municipal Corporations Act maintained the restriction imposed by previous anti-corruption legislation by disqualifying those who held 'any Office or Place of Profit, other than that of Mayor, in the Gift or Disposal of the Council of such Borough, or during such time as he shall have directly or indirectly, by himself or his Partner, any Share or Interest in any contract or Employment with, by, or on behalf of such Council'. See A. Doig, *Corruption and Misconduct in Contemporary British Politics* (Harmondsworth, 1984), 65.

73 M. Bowe, 'James Hibbert of Preston', BA. thesis, University of Manchester, 1958.

74 Convey, *Harris*, 18.

75 Bowe, 'James Hibbert'.

76 R. S. Dixon, 'The Harris Free Library and Museum, Preston', *Architects' and Builders' Journal*, 20 August 1913, 179. Dixon, although recognising Hibbert's Gothic work, considered him to be 'by predilection a Classicist' (180).

77 Report to the Free Library Committee, 12 February 1879, in Hibbert, *Notes*, ix.

78 *The Builder*, 9 September 1882, cutting in Harris Cuttings, vol. 2, Harris Collection, PLS, T25 PRE.

79 *Preston Chronicle*, Guild Supplement, 9 September 1882.

80 *The Builder*, 26 August 1882.

81 J. Hibbert, *A Report to Accompany the Design of the Harris Free Public Library and Museum, July 1882* (Preston, 1882), 4.

82 A suggestion made by Bowe. See Bowe, 'James Hibbert'.

83 Hibbert, *Notes*, 100.

84 *The Builder*, 9 September 1882; Hibbert, *Notes*, 101.

85 Hibbert, *Notes*, 102.

86 Hibbert, *Report*, 7.

87 J. Hibbert, *Memoir to Accompany the Design for the Sculptured Pediment, July 1885* (Preston, 1885).

88 Cited in Convey, *Harris*, 31.

89 Hibbert, *Memoir*.

90 Taken from Byron's *Manfred*.

91 Hibbert, *Memoir*.

92 W. W. Lloyd, letter to J. Hibbert, 26 March 1886, Hibbert Correspondence Collection, PLS, P920 B LLO, 50/11737.

93 J. Hibbert, letter to W. W. Lloyd, 8 April 1886, Hibbert Correspondence Collection.

94 J. Hibbert, letter to W. W. Lloyd, 8 April 1886.

95 Quoted in W. W. Lloyd, letter to J. Hibbert, 19 November 1886, Hibbert Correspondence Collection. The lines quoted in the original Greek are 696–702.

96 To some modern scholars this is somewhat ironic as many view Pericles as a tyrannical imperialist and demagogue. See, for example, P. Green, *The Shadow of the Parthenon* (Oakland, Calif., 1972), 24–32.

97 J. Hibbert, 'The Proposed Sculptured Pediment', 19 September (Preston, 1885 (copy)).

98 The classic histories of the Gothic Revival are C. L. Eastlake, *A History of the Gothic Revival* (London, 1872): K. Clark, *The Gothic Revival* (London, 1928).

99 Hibbert, 'The Proposed Sculptured Pediment'.

100 Hibbert, 'The Proposed Sculptured Pediment'.

101 Hibbert, *Notes*, 107.

102 Preston Free Public Library Committee, vol. 2, 18 August 1893, PLS.

103 *Preston Guardian*, 19 August 1893.

104 *Preston Guardian*, 1 December 1894.

105 'Alderman Hibbert on the Formation of the Harris Reference Library and Art Museum', September 1893, in Harris Cuttings – Building and Opening, vol. 1, Harris Collection, PLS, T25 PRE.

106 Remarks of Cllr Thompson, *Preston Guardian*, 1 December 1894.

107 Letter to the *Preston Herald*, n.d., private memorandum cited in Bowe, 'James Hibbert'.

108 *Preston Council Proceedings 1909–10, 31st Annual Report* (Preston, 1910) (year ending 31 March 1910).

109 Preston Free Public Library Committee, vol. 2, 3 March 1890, PLS.

110 Preston Free Public Library Committee, vol. 2, 6 October 1890, PLS.

111 *Preston Council Proceedings 1891–2, 13th Annual Report* (Preston, 1892) (year ending 31 March 1891).

112 *Preston Council Proceedings 1892–3, 14th Annual Report* (Preston, 1893) (year ending 31 March 1892).

113 *Preston Council Proceedings 1899–1900, 21st Annual Report* (Preston, 1900) (year ending 31 March 1900).

114 *History of the Harris Free Public Library and Museum* (Preston, n.d [1976]) (pamphlet), 6.'

115 W. B Barton, 'The Harris Library and Museum, Preston: A Record', *Magazine of Art*, 25 (1900–1), 49–56.

116 Hibbert, *Catalogue*, 19–20.

117 *Preston Guardian*, 10 February 1910.

118 *Preston Council Proceedings 1905–6, 27th Annual Report* (Preston, 1906) (year ending 31 March 1906).

119 *Preston Council Proceedings 1906–7, 28th Annual Report* (Preston, 1907) (year ending 31 March 1907).
120 *Preston Council Proceedings 1907–8, 29th Annual Report* (Preston, 1908) (year ending 31 March 1908).
121 *Preston Council Proceedings 1908–9, 30th Annual Report* (Preston, 1909) (year ending 31 March 1909); Convey, *Harris*, 61.

9

The rise and fall of the municipal art gallery movement? The public and private dimensions of local civic art

By the First World War, most Lancashire towns had established some form of art gallery, supported in part by the local municipal exchequer. Art galleries were no longer limited to the large industrial centres; smaller towns had embraced the movement, often with great enthusiasm. Exploring this development is complex as the local art gallery movement was driven by a variety of visions, narratives and objectives. While many earlier municipal galleries, often based on the 'Salford model', tended to be driven by the desire to promote popular education and improve the 'taste' and visual literacy of the industrial population, the factors influencing the creation of later galleries were often more complex. Some public authorities, such as Preston, continued to use galleries to express an explicit and specific cultural and political agenda, but often the reasons for developing galleries were more complicated and diffuse. Supporters of local art galleries ranged from those who saw art galleries as a vehicle for local pride and civic reputation to those who saw cultural institutions as creating educated liberal citizens, and places where the corrosive forces of mass commercial culture and 'modernity' could be contained.[1]

From the start, local art gallery movements, like those in the major cities, had an uneasy relationship with the more commercial aspects of art. Yet it was private art collecting, a product of the new consumer society, that helped drive demand for local public galleries. In some cases the relationship was explicit, with art galleries deriving much of their authority from their ability to act as commercial exhibition places and sites of public consumption. The growth of the regional art market ensured that galleries often looked to develop com-mercial relationships with dealers and artists in order to enhance their cultural status and media profile. Southport and Oldham were two towns which hosted high-profile commercial exhibitions that brought to the town many of the

London 'pictures of the season' from the major metropolitan galleries and, in particular, unsold pictures from the Royal Academy. While the Royal Academy was sometimes seen to represent an over-commercialisation of local galleries, Lancashire artists also contributed to the commercialisation of municipal art galleries. Members of the Royal Cambrian Academy were particularly successful at using local exhibitions to raise their profile. The capital for the municipal gallery at Blackpool was effectively provided by a member of the academy, and the academy and Blackpool Corporation enjoyed a close relationship right up to the Great War.

As this book has shown, art gallery development was often dependent on the pecuniary support of a small nexus of private individuals, usually material consumers of art, who could be driven by interest linked to, but sometimes tangential to, broader civic agendas. Because of the high costs of building and equipping galleries, most local authorities looked to private sponsors to initiate art institutions. Sponsors were rewarded with personalised permanent monuments to their generosity, as in the case of the Walker gallery (Liverpool), the Atkinson gallery (Southport) and the Grundy gallery (Blackpool). Within the confines of the gallery the importance of private patronage in shaping the development of cultural policy was even more evident. Major private donations often provided the core of permanent collections for many years and shaped future collecting activities. The Newsham collection dominated Preston's Harris gallery, the Lees collection that of Oldham and the Grundy collection that of Blackpool. Very few significant municipal collections in industrial towns were developed primarily by public expenditure or through a specific purchasing policy. In their forma-tion, construction, exhibitions and activity, art galleries relied upon essentially private consumer decisions, mediated by shared conceptions of public welfare and value.

It is, therefore, important to recognise that consumerism and 'private' taste did not invade civic culture; rather, individual consumer preferences were an important agent of local civic cultures, helping to explain their plurality and diversity. Social anthropology has highlighted how the physical consumption of material objects is only part of the 'service' provided by goods. Much of the value in the experience of consuming is in the sharing of names, experiences and interpretations, whether this be in reviewing the performance of a local football team or the performance of a Royal Academician. It was the sharing of experience, based on common consumption, that proved judgements and ultimately shaped and reshaped contemporary canons of taste. In order to control and regulate the veracity of their interpretations, cultural agents attempted to control the processes by which these judgements were made.[2] In short, art galleries were places of cultural verification where the boundaries of 'high culture' could be policed, standards maintained and existing canons protected.[3] Art galleries protected shared cultural values and, in so doing, the commercial values of private collections whose worth had been proven in the public sphere.

Private interest in local galleries facilitated their growth and helped them to overcome the practical and legal constraints they faced. The municipal gallery operated within important practical and political restraints, especially when compared with regional galleries in France and Germany. Local authorities were responsible for the management of galleries, and very few had among their membership significant major collectors or people with specialist artistic knowledge. Collaboration with wider civic society was, therefore, essential, especially in view of the financial constraints upon smaller galleries. The nature of municipal fiscal policy was the most obvious formal constraint on local cultural policy and gallery development. All municipal corporations were subject to a statutorily limited rate of a penny in the pound for library and art gallery expenditure. As the demands for comprehensive public library provision grew in the 1860s and 1870s, many municipal authorities found it difficult to provide sufficient resources for libraries, let alone finance public museums and galleries. With the acceleration of suburbanisation the demand for branch libraries made the fiscal problem even worse. Very large cities suffered from particular fiscal difficulties because processes of suburbanisation meant that large numbers of non-ratepaying residents lived outside city boundaries, drawing upon municipal services but not paying directly to use them. Smaller towns also suffered because their tax base was small in comparison to the considerable fixed costs of providing library and museum facilities. It is, then, perhaps not surprising that the most active and dynamic art galleries were often those in independent medium-sized industrial towns, outside the immediate hinterlands of the major cities, such as Preston, Blackburn, Southport, Bolton and Oldham. One solution to the fiscal problem was to promote private parliamentary legislation to allow a local authority to set a higher rate than the national statutory limit. By 1903, thirty corporations had successfully applied for permission for an increased library and museum rate.[4] Predictably, it was the very large cities, such as Manchester, Liverpool, Birmingham and Sheffield, and smaller towns, including Ashton, Hyde, Warrington and Wigan, that were represented most numerously in this list. Some medium-sized towns with major art galleries also petitioned to have the limit raised or abolished, including Oldham, Preston and Salford.[5]

Statutory restrictions, then, were an irritant, but not a serious constraint on the financing of cultural projects. Corporations which needed these restrictions to be relaxed found it relatively easy to promote the necessary legislation. However, they still had to raise popular support for new expenditure, which was not always easy at a time of rising local tax burdens.[6] Free library provision was popular and was seen as an essential piece of cultural infrastructure, especially after the passing of Forster's Education Act in 1870. Art galleries, however, never fell into the same category. Unlike libraries, art galleries could not provide their citizens with an individual physical product that could be enjoyed in the private home. They provided a service of shared experience, a cultural forum in which discussion and judgements could be made and canons defended. As the local art gallery movement spread, it often appeared to become more elitist. By the 1870s the mass popular appeal of museums appeared to be on the wane. This was partly due to the rise of alternative forms of leisure, including mass spectator sport and commercial entertainment; however, the nature of galleries was also changing. Some, such as Warrington and Salford, increasingly saw themselves as promoters of contemporary art, providing a rather elite educational service to a visually literate public. This had important implications for the future rate support of galleries. While the reformers of the 1840s were optimistic about the mass educational value of art galleries, by the Edwardian period both Liberals and socialists questioned the efficacy of the 'traditional' gallery. Plans for a new gallery in Manchester fell foul of precisely this concern. By the turn of the century it was not at all clear that the types of work collected by municipal galleries could do much to educate the rising *fin de siècle* generation. Art galleries stuffed full of haphazardly collected mid-Victorian British paintings could seem out of date when faced by the modern fashions for the Barbizon school, the *plein air* movement or even rising Scandinavian artists. British galleries began to look insular at a time when British political and economic imperialism was at its zenith. As the canons changed, galleries which had invested heavily in expensive modern fashions soon found that their investments had suffered significant depreciation.

For an art gallery movement to be successful, the municipality had to overcome popular resistance to an ever-rising rate burden and persuade its population that visual art, like literature, was an essential component of cultural infrastructure. Complex strategies were used and differed depending on local circumstances and the structure of local politics. Much depended on the articulation of a 'civic gospel' that combined local civic pride, classless collective endeavour and the desire for personal 'improvement'.[7] The difficulty for advocates of public art was that rhetoric and reality were often mismatched. The intensity of civic competition made it difficult and extremely expensive for a town to construct an 'art palace' that would be significantly more attractive than its neighbour, particularly if its neighbour had enjoyed the benefit of private capital investment in its construction. The most prestigious events in the art gallery calendar, the annual exhibitions, were often anything but classless events. The need to provide a congenial atmosphere for wealthy patrons and buyers meant that ticket prices were often set to exclude those from the working class on the opening days, when local media coverage was most extensive. Moreover, as commercial interests gained ground, the explicitly educational agenda was lost. This undermined the claim that art galleries were an essential part of the local cultural infrastructure. In some places, of course, the mismatch between rhetoric and perception was less evident. Even in Birmingham, a city nationally famous for promoting the civic gospel, politicians had to balance expensive public improvement programmes with the need to keep local taxation down. Small retailers and shopkeepers, in particular, feared the reduction in disposable income that rate rises could bring, and special attempts had to be made to persuade this group that civic cultural investment would yield long-term benefits to their trades.[8] Although Hennock's famous depiction of nineteenth-century local government political conflict largely revolving around the battle between 'improvers' and 'economists' may be an oversimplification, public improvement schemes had to articulate an economic, educational or other social rationale if they were to attract wider public support.[9] If they failed to do so, their future was rendered uncertain.

The civic gospel was an attractive integrative force because it could be seen to resolve some of the emerging tensions in late nineteenth-century urban governance. By the beginning of the 1860s, the 'flight to the suburbs' had begun in earnest, creating more fragmented middle-class households which were more isolated from their immediate neighbours, and producing the conditions in which associational life became increasingly important.[10] Associations and public educational institutions could provide not only a wider rationalised social life for the middle classes, but also a unifying set of purposes which reached beyond the constant conflicts engendered by party political associations, pressure groups and sectarian rivalries. Museums and galleries could be particularly useful symbols of local unity and united educational purpose. Loaded with symbolism, they often comprised collections and displays explicitly designed to foster social unity, highlight shared historical origins, reduce conflict and ensure stability and continuity.[11] Thorstein Veblen saw middle-class patronage of the arts as reflections of conspicuous consumption and the middle-class ego; this helps to explain the power of this form of patronage over the middle class.[12] Art galleries, once again, can be seen as an outgrowth of consumerism, where a whole class establishes a network to create judgement and values or an information system to secure and make 'rational' a specific cultural synthesis. This anthropological approach to understanding galleries supports a Veblenesque world view in which culture, to make any sense, must be conspicuous. These interpretations can offer an important psychological insight into the competitive, materialist and ultimately fragmented collective identity of the middle class, and an important explanation for its tolerance of expensive cultural endeavours.[13]

As noted throughout this work, civic pride was often the central component of the civic gospel, offering an overarching vision of a community united behind a material, cultural and artistic endeavour. This too can be read as a form of collective conspicuous consumption, offering an abstract unifying social force through the development of spectacular town halls, public lecture rooms, libraries, galleries and museums – buildings that were 'proof of the success of the town's economy and the good taste of its citizens'.[14] Civic pride, however, was a complex concept that varied in character over time and space. It is difficult to escape the conclusion that the mid-Victorian period saw a spectacularly new form of civic pride emerge, fostered by the need for the new local authorities, established in the wake of the 1835 Municipal Corporations Act, to establish a new identity and legitimacy. Where incorporation did not immediately follow the 1835 Act, as in Oldham, the old regime invested heavily in symbolism to reinforce the sense of continuity and historical legitimacy of 'unreformed' local government. In Oldham this meant the construction of a spectacular town hall in the classical style which, in its stained glass windows, celebrated the town's Anglican and aristocratic past.[15] Later, when the town became an incorporated borough, the new regime invented its own civic traditions, replacing corporation plate and introducing new robes, chains and symbols of office.[16]

Civic pride cannot simply be read as the independent expression of a town's municipal elite or understood in isolation from its region. Emulation was an important feature in the development of civic pride and, consequently, in the development of public facilities such as baths, museums and galleries. Pressure for emulation increased in the later nineteenth century, partly fostered by the establishment in 1872 of the Association of Municipal Corporations, which encouraged the development of municipal networks outside the metropolitan area.[17] Oldham's economic links to Manchester naturally encouraged an awareness of civic progress in that city, but there was also considerable competition between smaller neighbouring towns. In the West Riding, for example, economic and political competition between Wakefield and Halifax, Dewsbury and Batley, and Keighley and Bingley shaped local identities, civic pride and the pattern of urban improvement.[18] Evidence from the study of art galleries suggests that north and east Lancashire towns exhibited very similar patterns of competition between localities.

Although the public municipal art gallery had, by 1914, become a universal feature of the industrial town, the profile, function and public acclaim afforded to galleries varied considerably. Gallery histories tend to celebrate the private innovators and financiers responsible and, while these are important, they do not necessarily explain either the motivations of the private supporters or the constraints they imposed. In some respects the association of Walker with the Liverpool gallery actually damaged its reputation, and the subsequent management of the Walker attempted to partly disengage itself from the gallery's 'creation myths' that celebrated Walker's benefaction. Although the patronage of private individuals was important in the development of almost all major galleries, it was rarely enough to sustain a successful and vibrant art institution in the long term. The failure of the Stockport gallery demonstrated that even the high-profile support of a local MP could not provide the necessary preconditions for success if there was not an educational rationale, civic gospel or cultural infrastructure in place to provide an intellectual profile. Individual agency may be essential to understand the world of consumption that created the need for the universal art gallery, but this agency was itself shaped by a broader materialism in which a group, the urban middle class, sought to regulate both itself and wider categories of culture.

Why then did the civic art gallery become a universal feature of the fragmented, consumer-driven industrial town? To understand the dynamics of civic culture it is necessary to move beyond a conceptual model to the specifics of local cultural formation. In particular, what were the factors that created local cultural life? Although conceptual models make close links between the rise of a 'consumer society' and the emergence of cultural institutions, the absolute level of consumer spending appears to be less important that the consumer networks which exist and the tensions that operate across them. These tensions and disputes can sometimes help to explain why cultural institutions became a prominent part of urban life. The first major cultural institution in Manchester, the Manchester Literary and Philosophical Society, deliberately avoided issues of politics and religion in order to provide a social nexus in which all of Manchester's elite could meet. A century later the development of Liverpool's Walker Art Gallery was undermined because of its partisan associations, and it really thrived only when they were removed. Therefore, in order to understand the emergence of cultural facilities, it is essential to know something of the social nexus within towns, the pre-existing cultural infrastructure and the sense of shared local identities. To explore these factors it is important to appreciate the variety of north-west industrial towns and the nature of their individual endeavours.

The industrial towns of Lancashire developed art galleries at different times and at different rates. In general, the larger industrial towns tended to develop galleries in the period 1870–85, often when their library facilities were being expanded or when new libraries were being built. Towns such as Oldham, Bolton and Blackburn fitted into this particular category. However, it is important to recognise that a town's size, or perhaps more accurately the size of its local tax base, was only one factor influencing the timing of art gallery construction. Rochdale was almost as large as Oldham and had a history of somewhat lavish expenditure on prestige municipal projects, dedicating £155,000 to its new town hall – a fantastic sum for the period.[19] Yet Rochdale did not develop an art gallery until the twentieth century. Similarly, Blackpool was a rapidly developing holiday town with an economy geared to the leisure interests of Lancashire population, yet it did not develop a gallery until the Edwardian era, and then only at the behest of well-known local artists. In order to understand the development, form and function of the local art gallery movement one needs to look beyond explanations that simply focus on the wealth and surplus capital available in a town. Galleries were the product of a combination of consumer forces, perhaps most notably the nature of local elite networks, pre-existing cultural infrastructure, local civic gospels and narratives and, sometimes, local political competition.

Although few mid- and late Victorian galleries were tied to specific narratives of educational improvement, the nature of local educational infrastructure often played a part in mobilising support for the formation of an art gallery. Sometimes the almost complete lack of educational infrastructure precipitated public alarm sufficient to mobilise local government into action. Blackburn Corporation feared in 1869 that without an adequate museum, a school of art or a mechanics' institute the town would suffer greatly in competition with other towns and with 'scientifically trained capitalists and artisans of other parts of the world'.[20] Over the next six years, this alarm was enough to persuade the local authority to support a major 'Art and General Exhibition' that ultimately helped pay for the construction of an art gallery as an adjunct to the existing museum.[21] Often, however, art gallery movements grew out of an existing cultural nexus focused on a particular educational institution. The early development of art in Oldham owed much to the establishment of the Oldham Lyceum and its associated school of art. The Lyceum was not a mechanics' institute in the true sense but rather something akin to a literary and philosophical society, composed, as far as it is possible to tell, of the lower middle class.[22] The Lyceum and its associated art school not only provided a location for occasional small exhibitions of visual art but gradually began to provide high-quality elementary training for artists who would eventually progress to the Manchester Academy and later to professional careers within the region, in London and, in some cases, overseas. By the 1870s the Lyceum was fostering the development of a new generation of Oldham artists who would rise to prominence by the end of the century, often by going on to study at the Manchester School of Art. Among the artists to follow this route were F. W. 'Lancashire' Jackson and G. H. Wimpenny.[23] The presence of a successful art school and a successful body of professional artists provided a powerful stimulus for both public and private enthusiasm for art gallery formation. However, sometimes new art galleries were simply formed around the networks of particular artists or patrons. The initiation of the Grundy gallery at Blackpool came mainly through the action the Grundy family, or more precisely a pair of artist brothers, who organised a public exhibition and donated the displayed collection to the local council.[24] In some cases, the local authority played little part in the development or encouragement of the local cultural nexus. In the case of Blackpool, the local sketching society had petitioned for the development of a local art gallery, but the corporation had failed to act.[25] It was only when local professional artists, supported by colleagues from the prestigious Royal Cambrian Academy, took concrete action that the local authority took an interest. Even then the work began only after the Grundy brothers offered £2,000 to part-finance the project, and ultimately they were required to find more than £3,000 to meet higher-than-expected costs.[26] In most cases, gallery schemes were supported by groups of local art enthusiasts who tried to encourage their local corporation to be more ambitious in their plans or provide for future extensions. The local industrialist James Ogden was keen to support the expansion of Rochdale's local free library and was surprised to find that his generosity in offering to finance a lecture room and assembly hall was rejected. Although Ogden was offended that the corporation had 'condemned me unheard', he offered £1,000 to the corporation, to be spent on pictures if no library extension could be agreed.[27] Despite the corporation's reluctance, Rochdale's art gallery scheme went ahead with support and donations, not only from Ogden, but also from a number of local collectors, including Robert Taylor Heape, Colonel Henry Fishwick, Colonel Royds MP and W. Wiles.[28] Bodies of subscribers and supporters were often crucial factors in the development of local gallery schemes. Even in small towns such as Carlisle, a network of collectors and art enthusiasts was instrumental in the development of the town gallery. Here, in August 1890, a body of subscribers handed over a building for the development of not only an art gallery, but also a new art school.[29] In all these cases a body of visually literate art supporters, often private collectors, were present to mobilise support for a gallery: a place where art could be consumed, where artistic passions could be shared and where private interests could be validated by the public endorsement of the local corporation – the embodiment of local political authority. Whereas major galleries such as the Walker, the Harris and the Whitworth were conceived as donor memorials, many of the smaller galleries did not receive large sums from a single source or were not influenced by a specific legacy. Thus, somewhat paradoxically, these could sometimes be more representative of local art communities than the larger, more prestigious, donor galleries. Some of the more high-profile and active smaller municipal galleries of the period – Oldham, Southport and Warrington – appear to have acquired their status because of the high level of identification they enjoyed with elements of the local community. So was this identification simply the product of pre-existing cultural networks and educational concerns, or were the supporters of galleries able to articulate new civic agendas to support the institutionalisation of public art displays?

Although there is evidence to suggest that, in some towns, a nexus of art collectors existed before the creation of a public gallery, it is clear that proposals to create public galleries and art schools served to create new circles of art enthusiasts. These in turn engaged with a broader public to articulate a civic gospel which highlighted the benefits of art to the wider community. Mobilisation of support for galleries was a public act that had to engage the support of the press and the electorate as much as members of the local corporation. Just as the political conditions in the towns differed, so did the specificities of the local civic gospel. Yet there were common features. Some civic narratives were derived from the conditions of existing civic identity, some from inter-urban competition and some from an agenda of social reform or social 'improvement'. All emphasised the capacity of art to promote specific and essential collective objectives. The success of the art gallery movement lay precisely in its ability to morph itself into a variety of public agendas, from the Arnoldian defence of high culture or the protection of classical values to the promotion of popular rational recreation and the vanities of civic pride. Yet this catholic message often fragmented art policy and made it difficult to direct art collecting policies towards a specific objective.

Oldham is an interesting case of a town that promoted an art gallery as an agent of 'public improvement' in order to satisfy a number of local policy objectives. Ten years after the opening of the town's art gallery, James Orrock RI described Oldham as, for its size, 'the most prominent town in art in the kingdom'.[30] It had an important watercolour collection provided by Charles E. Lees and the most high-profile regional exhibition of modern painting outside Liverpool and Manchester. Oldham was by no means an obvious place for a public art movement to take root. The area's rapid industrial expansion had produced a town with a reputation for being crowded, smoky and somewhat unruly. Regional newspapers made sarcastic references to 'beautiful Oldham',[31] and it was viewed as 'typical of the aesthetic barrenness which a busy trade centre is blighted'.[32] Prominent municipal leaders were embarrassed by Oldham's reputation, but recognised that it was at least partly deserved. Some, such as Alfred Emmott, felt that art and the development of artistic taste were not only important to the economic health of the district, but were an essential component in future social progress. For Emmott, practical legislation needed to be combined with artistic education to ensure that in future 'great industrial communities might be planted in surroundings which were not so unutterably hideous as many of our great towns were to-day'.[33]

This insecurity about Oldham's identity did much to rally supporters of a municipal art gallery and to shape attitudes towards collecting art. Several contemporary commentators were to argue that the very 'ugliness' of Oldham as an industrial town did much to stimulate the growth of both private and public art collections. In 1890 the collector and patron Elliot Lees commented that no part of Britain possessed better collections than south-east Lancashire and that this was a direct consequence of the industrial surroundings:

> Oldham people did not live under a cloudless sky, and did not enjoy most magnificent scenery at their front door ... it was owing to that fact that the richer men of Oldham had made the inside of their homes, or at any rate the walls of their houses, as beautiful as the walls of the houses in any other part of the country.[34]

This was a view that was shared by local press commentators when noting the surprising success of municipal exhibitions:

> Perhaps one reason we in Oldham are so fond of pictures, of scenery, and of flowers, is that we are surrounded by so few natural objects of beauty. Our forest is mill chimneys, our lakes are mill lodges, our music is the sound of the loom and the spindle and rattle of machinery. These are essential to our lives, and are ever before us, but it is pleasant at times to turn away our eyes and let them rest on something less vivid, and less realistic.[35]

These attitudes became evident in local corporation acquisitions policies. Rural landscapes, particularly of North Wales, came to dominate, with very few works based on the depiction of the town of Oldham itself.[36] This is not to suggest, however, that there was no local pride, but merely that in an industrial town, rural scenery was attractive in educating tastes to the country that existed beyond the urban, and in providing exemplars of how rural beauty could be incorporated into the urban landscape. Sometimes this intention was quite explicit. Sarah Lees, the widow of Charles E. Lees, Oldham's most prominent collector of watercolours and landscapes, became a prominent member of the 'Beautiful Oldham' movement, which dedicated itself to planting bulbs, opening public gardens and tackling the urban smoke nuisance.[37] The collecting of rural landscapes had become part of a much broader movement aiming to improve urban taste and the urban civic landscape.[38] Growing civic pride and public demand for education facilities, combined with insecurities about Oldham's identity, provided a public environment in which advocates of free libraries, museums and art galleries could be heard.

A similar concern with local civic reputation could be seen in nearby Rochdale. Rochdale had invested heavily in civic facilities in the last two decades of the nineteenth century, transforming the area around the imposing town hall and constructing a fashionable esplanade over the rather polluted local river. In

Rochdale the construction of an art gallery was conceived as a way of completing the local civic infrastructure, the new building being located directly opposite the slopes of the park and setting off the western portion of the esplanade. The local press boasted proudly of the civic – and aesthetic – achievement:

> Few manufacturing towns anywhere, and certainly none in Lancashire, with the possible exception of Preston, can boast of a more pleasing view in their centre than Rochdale possesses here … It seems, indeed, as if art had combined with nature to make a most charming view, the Town Hall and the Slopes on the left, the Manor House and Free Library on the right with the Presbyterian Church in the distance all uniting to complete a picture as we have indicated, it would be difficult to equal in any manufacturing town. And the picture, we venture to assert, is as pleasing from the other end of the Esplanade, – the Presbyterian Church end – and to a stranger seeing it for the first time must present itself in the nature of an aesthetic revelation.[39]

The gallery was conceived as an aesthetic advertisement for the town. James Ogden, the donor who had done so much to persuade the council to adopt an art gallery scheme, rejected the first set of plans on the grounds that they were 'not sufficiently comprehensive for a town of the importance of Rochdale' and then persuaded the authority to adopt a more extensive plan.[40] Ornamentation was important too, with local council members coming forward to pay for carved panels on the front of the building.[41] Again, the major object was to change the image of Rochdale and, according to Ogden, provide the type of cultural facilities 'too often neglected in a manufacturing town'.[42] The gallery's major opening exhibitions were advertised in the regional press and on billboards at railway stations across east Lancashire, including Oldham Mumps, Manchester, Bury, Bolton, Todmorden and Bacup.[43] The Rochdale authorities were also keen to organise temporary picture exchanges with other local galleries in order to promote the Rochdale gallery and the town as a centre of high culture.[44]

This concern for civic reputation was not limited to Lancashire's industrial districts. It could also be seen in the leisure and retirement towns of Blackpool and Southport. In Blackpool, in particular, there was a long-running concern to protect the social tone of the resort. Despite its modern reputation, Blackpool was never an exclusively working-class resort, and it depended on significant numbers of middle-class visitors.[45] South Shore and parts of 'the North' probably had more in common with nearby Lytham St Annes than with the popular entertainments of the world-famous Blackpool Tower and Raikes Hall gardens. Covenants restricting development and tolls were among the many devices used to maintain the 'social tone' of these areas.[46] Famously, North Shore hoteliers fought hard to keep out amusements and popular attractions likely to attract working-class visitors.[47] Even in the marketing of Blackpool, there was more than a hint that town officials were particularly concerned to attract middle-class visitors. Blackpool guide books, although attempting to appeal broadly, seem to have been aimed at a largely middle-class market; indeed the guide books after 1898 seem to have become particularly concerned with appealing to middle-class sensibilities. Rather than adopting unpretentious accessible language, they focused on promoting Blackpool as a respectable resort, emphasising the opportunities for rational recreation and relaxation rather than popular and raucous indoor entertainment.[48] When, in the Edwardian period, Blackpool redesigned its main railway publicity poster, it chose an artistic portrait of a child on a beach rather than a humorous cartoon. There was some alarm in the Liberal press when the local council suggested dropping this poster in favour of one that was much bolder or racier. The *Blackpool Times* remarked somewhat sniffily that the choice depended on 'which class of visitor it is deemed most necessary to cultivate'.[49] Thus when the Grundy brothers offered to organise an exhibition of modern painting, including a number of well-known artists associated with the Royal Cambrian Academy, the local authority was enthusiastic about an attraction that it believed would cultivate a better class of visitor.[50] Although the leisure-based economy of Blackpool was very different from the economies of the cotton towns, the town was still often perceived as a ruthlessly commercial place whose leadership had little interest in art or culture. This view was reinforced when only around twenty of the eighty prominent local men invited to the first exhibition of 1903 bothered to respond.[51] A local art critic mused that there was much truth in the claim that Blackpool men had 'no appreciation of the higher things of life' and that 'money-making is the summon'.[52] The local press demanded that the town prove its civility and improve its reputation by supporting art exhibitions. An exhibition of seascapes and coastal landscapes was opened by the chairman of the corporation library committee with a challenge to Blackpool to reject its near obsession with 'material pursuits and material enterprises'.[53] This was a challenge that was widely picked up by the local middle class, who went on to engage in an enthusiastic debate about where the proposed new art gallery should be located and the place it should have in the town's cultural landscape.[54]

Even in predominantly middle-class leisure resorts, such as Southport, the issue of civic reputation was important. In the last two decades of the nineteenth century, Southport was increasingly developing a reputation as a retirement town for Lancashire industrialists. It was therefore appropriate that a Manchester cotton manufacturer, William Atkinson, was the initiator of the town's art gallery movement. Atkinson provided around £13,500 for the construction costs of a new library and art gallery, and the gallery was named in his honour. However, the success of the gallery lay in its ability to mobilise the support of the town's increasingly affluent population. The gallery opened in 1878 with a loan exhibition. Works were mainly provided by local collectors, and over 1,000 items were included in the final display.[55] The gallery's exhibition cemented the town's cultural reputation and encouraged the development of a regular sale exhibition of modern paintings. Although sales were patchy, the social profile of Southport made it relatively easy to attract the work of celebrated artists and a significant number of wealthy and retired potential buyers, many of whom had only recently moved to the coastal districts.

Local art galleries were not, however, conceived merely as ways as improving the physical appearance of a town or changing external perceptions. In many cases galleries were seen as active agents that could transform the behaviour of those who came into contact with them. The creation of art galleries was associated with the creation of liberal citizens. Although explicitly educational agendas were less prevalent in late Victorian art galleries than in those inspired by the earlier Salford model, there was still a widespread belief that public galleries could shape personal character and conduct. Sometimes this belief was articulated explicitly in the political and civic rationale for public galleries. This was particularly the case in Oldham, where fear of the 'rougher' element was central to discourses of public civility. 'Boomtown Oldham' had attracted hardened labourers from around the British Isles whose social habits were not always regarded as especially desirable. Oldham's weavers and millhands were often caricatured within the region as uncouth and uneducated, with a disposition to rebel against their economic and social superiors. 'Owdham Fellys' (Oldham Fellows) were viewed in local folklore as 'a rough and independent lot' who 'thoroughly believed in the adage that "Jack was as good as his master"'.[56] The phrase 'Oldham Roughhead' was still in common currency at the end of the century and was used by those who pointed to the importance of art education in encouraging younger scholars to develop more cultured taste.[57] The organisers of early industrial exhibitions in Oldham were clearly nervous of public behaviour at exhibitions and were 'extremely gratified' – and somewhat surprised – when no significant exhibits were damaged or destroyed by visitors.[58]

Fear of the Oldham roughhead dominated the thoughts of those responsible for managing the municipal gallery. Detailed and extensive by-laws were drawn up to regulate behaviour. In addition to the usual restrictions on unclean and intoxicated persons, sleeping was banned, and children could be admitted only with an adult, with each adult being allowed to take a maximum of two children into the building.[59]

The use of art gallery rules and regulations to regulate and soften behaviour was common to most galleries and museums. However, it took on particular significance in rapidly expanding towns with transient populations, such as the industrial towns of Lancashire. For a gallery to express its influence and authority, it had to be a welcoming space for the visitor. This emphasis on accessibility opened the public gallery to the ill-educated and illiterate, whom one might not otherwise expect to find in libraries or newsrooms. Severe punishments were dealt out to those breaking the rules. The standard disciplinary procedure was illustrated in the case of a young boy, George Owen, charged with mutilating one of the books in the Rochdale Reference Library. Owen was called up before the municipal committee, admonished by the chairman and forced to pay for a placard, to be displayed around the town, by way of a public apology.[60] A large notice appeared at the entrance to the art gallery demanding that parents keep their children under proper control and prevent them from touching pictures.[61] Almost all galleries adopted lengthy series of rules and regulations policing public behaviour, which were usually published not only on noticeboards but also in exhibition catalogues, handbooks and other publicity material. Many art gallery committees clearly either copied the regulations of the National Gallery or British Museum or adopted those from a nearby town. As galleries were promoted as places of relaxation and leisure, some citizens clearly expected a certain licence to behave as they would at home or in a public house. Regulations aimed at the creation of a genteel atmosphere where picnicking, drinking, sleeping and noise were to be strictly forbidden.[62] Traditional private cultural facilities, such as subscription libraries and newsrooms, were often informal spaces of relaxation. The Greaves Street room in Oldham was essentially a 'tea room' for the retired middle class where, according to a newspaper correspondent, more than a dozen elderly gentlemen could be seen snoozing and making a 'good chorus … with their nasal organs'.[63] Art gallery committees demanded a more formal space where culture could be celebrated in an appropriately decorous fashion.

Should one, then, see local museums as a product of the disciplinary society and the growth of urban governmentality?[64] Some, notably Bennett, have attempted to apply Foucauldian notions of visibility and mutual regulation to argue that museums and galleries were designed to regulate the social behaviour within them. Like prisons and shopping arcades, grand galleries were created to form an architecturally planned space in which all citizens were on display and all were regulated by their mutual visibility.[65] While this argument may have some purchase in relation to the major, purpose-built national galleries, smaller town museums tended to be much more intimate and were often built after models of domestic architecture. The precise size and shape of a gallery usually depended on the amount of available capital and the availability of space available after the needs of the local library had been taken into account. In a number of cases, municipalities were required to utilise existing domestic buildings in the core of their plans. The Salford gallery and the Stockport gallery each utilised a domestic property that was extended as needs required and finances allowed. Even the Whitworth gallery in Manchester began life as a domestic residence that was then gradually extended in a piecemeal fashion. From the 1870s, there was a tendency for town councils to develop entirely new buildings wherever possible, but when suitable domestic properties were available, they were usually utilised in some form. The Tullie House museum in Carlisle was adapted from a large townhouse.[66] Even into the twentieth century, aristocratic estates were popular with corporations as museum venues, although experience showed that such out-of-town locations found it difficult to attract working-class visitors. Burnley Corporation took over the property of the Townley family, Townley Hall, while Manchester adopted Heaton Hall as an 'overflow' gallery. Even when local councils decided to opt for a new build, the galleries that emerged were rarely of the grand arcaded type suitable for the processes of visual self-government and self-regulation.

In most cases the buildings occupied by galleries were shared with public libraries, with an enclosed ground floor used by the library services and an upper floor used for art exhibitions. In some towns, such as Rochdale and Blackpool, the art gallery was a later extension constructed at the same level as the library. The precise layouts of purpose-built town galleries were as diverse as their architectural form. A few, such as Southport, adopted free neo-classical styles with imposing balconies and lofty rooms. The most common style was neo-Gothic with some classical influence. The galleries of Oldham, Blackburn, Bolton and Rochdale all fall into this category. External decoration varied too. Preston's Periclean temple was unusual in having specific classical dedications. Southport's was similar, having pedimentary figures representing art, science and literature, with a central figure representing inspiration. These were matched with low reliefs on the façade depicting Aeschylus, Apelles, Homer, Ictinus and Phidias. In general, however, classical representation and allegories formed only a limited part of the iconography of town museums. The sculptor of the Southport reliefs, G. W. Searle, was also responsible for the reliefs of the Blackburn art gallery, yet here the panels represented agriculture, iron manufacture, cotton manufacture and commerce, as well as science and literature. These depictions were not apparently the product of collective deliberation by the art gallery committee, but rather the outcome of private business sponsoring the iconography of the new cultural centre. The cotton manufacturer John Fish paid for the dedication to cotton, while members of the Dugdale family, engineers, machinists and cotton spinners, paid for the dedication to commerce. The iconography of other galleries was often a combination of classical allegories of the arts and more modern representations of crafts and industries. This approach can be seen in Bury, where the sculptured reliefs include representations of not only the nine Muses, but also building, crafts, modelling, heraldry, design and wood-carving. The iconography of galleries tended to focus on the bringing together of timeless artistic virtues while celebrating the triumph of modern commerce and industry. Far from modern commerce and art being in conflict in the way Ruskin described, art and culture were seen in gallery iconography as the product of commercial and industrial endeavour. For the Oldham art curator E. R. Dibdin, the nature of industrial society simply quickened 'our understanding of the need of humanity for beautiful things'.[67] The presence of the local municipal gallery was proof that high art and tall chimneys were not incompatible. Art galleries performed an ever-present visual proof of the triumph of a new urban culture.

Yet the iconography of individual buildings was, arguably, less significant as a cultural signifier than the civic rituals and public performance associated with art gallery activity. The civic gospel was promoted as much through the activities surrounding the gallery as through its physical shape and form. The major public events surrounding the openings of new exhibitions, new exhibits or extensions rendered the gallery visible to a wider public, celebrating collective achievements and distinctive didactic values. The early municipal galleries celebrated their openings with lavish ceremony. Salford was able to attract Queen Victoria to the rededication of Peel Park and its museum, while Stockport turned the opening of the Vernon museum into a public festival involving all the public and voluntary organisations of the town. By the 1870s, public art galleries were less of a novelty, but individual towns still marked their commissioning and opening with public performances of civic authority. Although the details of the ceremonies varied, they typically included a parade of civic dignitaries from the town hall to the new building, watched by an assembled mass of townsfolk. Within the parade the various sections of official society would be organised. The mayor of the host town would typically lead the way with an entourage of mayors from neighbouring areas. These would be followed by aldermen and then councillors, usually in order of seniority. Behind them would often come the representatives of local civic society, the chamber of trade and professional organisations, local church groups and then, finally, trade societies and working men's organisations. Often the parades would be accompanied by volunteer battalions and representatives of the police, usually in full dress uniform. Parades were thus a celebration of civic authority: a celebration that centred on the mayoralty and corporation, but included representatives of the whole town.[68] The power of the civic art gallery parade was in its ability to focus attention of the civic elite while being inclusive of all classes of citizenry. The ceremonies of public opening were similarly symbols of public unity. Platforms were often constructed to accommodate the various civic leaders and their guests, with those of all parties coming together to celebrate the civic gospel and enact the ritualism of a community united by art.

The civic performance was one designed to reward and celebrate the munificence and taste of those associated with the art gallery project. In many cases there was a 'presentation of the keys' in which a senior member of the art gallery committee was rewarded with the act of opening the building. The honour was always to be accepted in a mild and modest way. In Rochdale it fell to Colonel Fishwick, chairman of the committee, who declared that the honour was 'entirely unexpected' and emphasised the collective effort involved in the success of the project.[69] In order to avoid the accusation of conceit, local authorities had to be careful not to be seen to be rewarding the work of any single individual too greatly. It was important that a town was not seen to be using the occasion merely for self-promotion or self-aggrandisement. Careful attempts were made to include civic leaders from neighbouring authorities in the feastings and collective celebrations, a process which also made them aware of the towns' success. During the laying of the foundation stones for the Oldham gallery, the mayors of nearby Ashton, Stalybridge and Bury joined with the Oldham civic leaders at the head of the ceremonies.[70] The opening of the Blackpool gallery was marked with a loan exhibition of paintings from the civic collections of all the major surrounding towns. The length of the guest list meant that the subsequent celebrations were so large that a nearby church had to be borrowed to house all the local civic leaders.[71] The power of the public performance came not simply through its ability to mobilise the civic elite but from its success in stimulating broader public enthusiasm. Thousands turned out to view the parades of civic authority, and businesses along the routes of the parades made special efforts to include themselves in the collective endeavour. Flags, banners and symbols of local patriotism were often seen to line the route, wishing success to the new venture and commemorating the local achievement of the town.

Of course, this public performance was not merely for the benefit of those assembled in the parade or in the crowd. It was, at least in part, a performance for the regional press and for distinguished guests. The press played a key role in promoting the achievements of the new gallery and, by implication, the view of the town as a centre of culture and progress. By the 1880s, the local press expected there to be a public performance whenever a significant civic event took place. When the performance was too low-key it could be heard to complain. Visitors witnessing the laying of the foundation stone for the Oldham gallery were said to be 'awfully disappointed at the meagre show', especially those from the suburbs, who had clearly expected a more lavish event.[72] The local press was keen to report the civic ritualism and expected major spectacles. Almost every gallery opening was received by verbatim reports in the local papers detailing the order of activities, the dignitaries involved and, often, the 'reception' of the festivities among the ordinary population. The public performance was a celebration of the town and its culture, but it could also be a celebration of a town's commercial interests. Coverage of the festivities in Oldham included detailed discussion of the businesses which had decorated their shops for the occasion, emphasising the role of each in the local economy and remarking on their civic patriotism. In contrast, those who had failed to engage with the spirit of the civic gospel received only terse comment and sometimes mild censure.[73]

The verbatim newspaper reports reflected the sense of occasion and the belief that the creation of a local art gallery was a landmark in the cultural progress of a town. Wherever possible, reporters sought to highlight the efforts and local craftsmen behind the gallery's success. In some cases this was easy. The Rochdale gallery was designed by the local architect Jesse Horsfall of Todmorden and Manchester, and the major contractors and project workers were from Rochdale.[74] However, the usual process of anonymous architectural competition for gallery designs and competitive tendering for construction work meant that the construction of an art gallery was rarely the exclusive product of local labour. The regional nature of architectural work and the limited number of art gallery commissions meant that very few architectural practices could be said to specialise in art gallery design. Even those architects associated with high-profile galleries, such as James Hibbert of Preston, rarely sought commissions for other art institutions. Consequently, although the iconography of buildings could sometimes represent local trades, commerce and histories, it was rare for architects or contractors to be celebrated as emblematic of local cultural achievement as often they had few local connections. Instead, it was the local art gallery committees that tended to be celebrated. Although they often had only a limited role in the detail of planning and design, it was they who were commemorated in the local press and in local art publications of the time. Specially commissioned commemorative publications often provided the basis of press reports, providing as they did details of the gallery specifications, the key elements of internal and external decoration and, of course, biographies of the key individuals on the municipal art gallery committee. Sometimes these publications could be particularly elaborate. The opening of the Blackpool gallery was marked with a programme that included a floor plan, photographs of the key architectural features and portraits and biographies of all the civic worthies associated with the project.[75]

The celebration of the art gallery committee was not, of course, limited to commemorative programmes. Almost all exhibition catalogues featured detailed listings of those responsible for the arrangement of the exhibition. In many cases, the numbers listed were far in excess of those needed for the efficient administration and hanging of works of art. The Blackburn Art and General Exhibition of 1874 boasted thirty-three members on its fine art committee, many of whom appear to have played only a very limited role in the conduct of the exhibition.[76] A long list of supporters provided an exhibition with credibility and encouraged less publicly visible collectors to come forward and either lend works or offer financial support. It also celebrated and promoted a town's civic elite. Unlike other corporation committees, art gallery committees tended to co-opt significant number of lay members, usually men known locally as collectors or those with a reputation for literary or artistic interests. Lay men could have their status as men of culture validated by the local state, while councillors and aldermen could bask in the glory of the knowledge and culture of others. This glory was only enhanced when senior guests could be persuaded to attend opening ceremonies. In many cases opening ceremonies were deliberately reserved for local dignitaries, but occasionally, and especially when towns sought wider publicity and validation, the task was passed to leading national public figures. Sir John Lubbock was called upon to open the inaugural Oldham exhibition in 1883, while no less a figure than the Earl of Derby cut the opening ribbons of the new gallery at Bury in 1901.[77]

Almost all municipal galleries issued annual reports detailing their proceedings, acquisitions and exhibitions. This culture of annual reporting was a reflection of the practice of voluntary and subscription organisations, all of which typically issued an annual report before an annual general meeting or before seeking re-election. Although art gallery committees did not face annual general meetings, and their re-election by full council was usually a formality, the annual reports represented an important interface between the committee and the public. In many cases the reports of council committees were not simply designed for the consumption of other councillors and public officials. The reports of art gallery committees were aimed at a much wider audience and were printed as separate pamphlets and circulated among local collectors and sponsors. It is not clear which galleries initiated this practice, although the Salford museum issued reports in this way from its inception and most later municipal galleries adopted a similar approach. Reports were similar and formulaic. They tended to begin with a list of the committee and sometimes a photograph of its most eminent members. There was then a short statement by the committee chairman, reflecting on the triumphs and occasionally frustrations of the year, followed, often, by a detailed statistical analysis of the year's activities. Typically, this included the numbers of people going through the turnstiles for each exhibition, the numbers attending lectures or educational events and, of course, a statement of balances which highlighted the museum's success in attracting voluntary contributions. This was then concluded with a list of donations to the museum, with details of the subscribers and something on the provenance of each item donated. The annual report was a tool for subjecting the art gallery committee to public scrutiny at a time when concern about the rising cost of rates was provoking increasing questions about the cost of galleries. Sensitivities about public funding meant that the report tended to highlight the contribution of the private donor and the degree to which private investment was generating new exhibitions and activity. By demonstrating a sometimes absurd attention to detail, galleries could persuade their publics that they were anything but profligate. If a gallery like Bury could faithfully record that it had taken charge of 11,617 visitors' umbrellas at a charge of a penny each, the public could be persuaded that purse strings were being guarded safely.[78] The promotion of the civic gospel meant the creation of an image of a cultured civic leadership, engaged with broader intellectual culture, and one that was accountable to the highest standards of public probity.

The emphasis on visibility, accountability and transparency was, of course, central to the liberal civic agenda. Commemorative programmes, catalogues, annual reports and press coverage celebrated cultural leadership while exposing it to public scrutiny. They made a town's cultural leaders visible and offered acknowledgement and rewards to suitably qualified men who were prepared to support the gallery's activities. The involvement of local connoisseurs and private collectors was, of course, essential if a gallery was to offer relevant, innovative and rotating exhibits for its local public. Few of the smaller galleries had the substantial funds available to the larger cities, such as the Manchester City Art Gallery committee, which was contractually required to set aside £2,000 per year for acquisitions of works of art. Some galleries benefited from the success of inaugural commercial exhibitions, which often attracted large attendances and created surpluses which then could be dedicated to later purchase funds. Blackburn, for example, was left with over £700 profit from its exhibition fund, even after the purchase of models from busts and specimens for local art students.[79] Oldham also benefited from the success of a commercial exhibition, although in practice few of the profits were made available for the purchase of works of art, partly because the capital costs of the gallery were substantially more than predicted.[80] In any case, the rising costs of contemporary art meant that it was impossible for smaller galleries to compete for major original works, the 'pictures of the day' from the Royal Academy. The cost of major new works by Alma Tadema at the Royal Academy was often more than the entire annual budget of an art gallery committee. Bury's entire annual rate for library and art gallery purposes in 1904–5 raised just £3,300. More than £1,200 was accounted for annually in servicing the mortgage costs, while salaries and wages alone accounted for more than £600.[81] The art acquisitions budget was rarely more than a few hundred pounds. Consequently, most art gallery committees were heavily dependent on local private supporters.

One way in which an art gallery could engage with its community was by attracting loans and donations of local portraiture. By placing portraits in a magnificent new gallery, local families were being encouraged not merely to take part in an activity of civic patriotism but to have their status confirmed in a place of public veneration and worship. This type of portraiture was viewed as a historical artefact, recording the service of the citizen to the polis. Robert Ashcroft of Oldham likened the municipal collecting of portraiture to the Roman practice of putting tablets into a city wall to record the honourable service of citizens to the state.[82] While not every family could enjoy a grand statue in the market square, most bourgeois families had portraits they could donate to celebrate the contribution of their ancestors to the tribunate of their local town. Often exhibitions of portraiture were linked to great public events. In Rochdale the town's jubilee was marked with an exhibition to record the contribution of 'many of the men who had been foremost in bringing Rochdale to its present state'.[83] Portraiture was being used as civic exemplar. It was there, according to the mayor of Rochdale, for 'the burgesses to reflect upon the character of men whose foresight and zeal had secured to them the benefits of the best form of local government known'.[84] Yet despite this civic hyperbole, some were uncomfortable with the idea of galleries becoming a mere celebration of the public ostentation of a civic elite. Bury art gallery committee was much more circumspect about the uses of civic portraiture. For it, portraiture filled a useful gap in the exhibition programme during winter, but it was not allowed to distort the direction of the gallery's programme of artistic education. Instead, Bury concentrated on attracting loans of high-quality modern pictures from local collectors.[85] This was the strategy adopted by many of the smaller galleries, especially in those areas such as Southport, Bolton and Blackburn where there were active bodies of modern collectors prepared to loan works. Although local loan exhibitions from private sources were often of a miscellaneous character, they frequently brought to public attention important local collectors who were not otherwise engaged in local art committees. Even very small galleries, such as Blackpool, were able to attract significant pictures from private collections. A general exhibition of loan works in 1913 uncovered a number of surprises, including a work attributed to Anthony Van Dyck, *Abraham's Offering*, and others said to be by Peter Paul Rubens and Giacopo Bassano. Some of these old master attributions may be questionable, but the quality of modern painting only served to underline the network of collectors who existed in the area. Significantly, the resident gentry now appeared to be sharing the passion for modern British works, with the Clifton family providing Richard Ansdell's *A Disputed Way* and J. F. Herring's *A Strawyard in Winter*.[86] Regular loan exhibitions made private collections visible, fostered new networks between collectors and allowed towns to demonstrate the depth of their local cultural resources.

Of course, not all loan exhibitions relied upon private sources. In the last two decades of the nineteenth century local authorities fought a series of successful campaigns to persuade so-called 'national' collections to make their works available for loan to the major regional galleries. Regional galleries had a history of being in dispute with the trustees of so-called 'national' collections based in London, which were often seen to be unwilling to release material for loan to galleries with supposedly inadequate facilities. In 1877, Birmingham Corporation organised a conference of local authorities with the aim of urging the government to encourage the British Museum and other national bodies to provide loan collections to regional institutions. The initiative was largely fruitless, but 1880 brought a change of government and the prospect of a new arts policy. Birmingham Corporation again used its network of local authorities to organise a further lobby of local authorities. This lobby, which included Oldham and other north-west towns, eventually led to the National Gallery Loan Act of 1883 and the provision of finance to South Kensington for the distribution of museum collection grants to all local authorities.[87]

The 1883 Act came at an ideal time for galleries such as Oldham, which obtained several items from the National Gallery collection, including two minor works of Turner: *Sandbank with Gypsies* and *Phyrne Going to the Bath at Venus*. The latter piece was regarded by Ruskin as the best-preserved piece of post-1820 work by Turner in the national collection.[88] There was also J. Ward's work of some regional interest *Lake and Tower in De Tabley Park*, depicting an attractive country estate in Cheshire.[89] Unfortunately, the lack of electric lighting in the Oldham gallery alarmed the keeper of the National Gallery, who pointedly asked if the gallery when kept open after dark was lit by gas, and the Oldham committee was forced to close the gallery at dusk.[90] This was the beginning of a rather uneasy relationship with the National Gallery, which showed little interest in securing wider regional circulation of its loaned collections. In December 1886, the directors of the National Gallery made it clear that they were not prepared to entertain requests for annual exchanges of paintings – a move that stimulated the Oldham authorities to contact other municipal galleries with national loan collection pictures to ascertain whether they would be prepared to offer direct exchanges.[91] Further requests to the National Gallery almost two years later produced a similar response, with the directors making it quite clear that they would not permit the exchange of collections between 'provincial institutions'.[92] Ultimately, the Oldham authorities lost patience with the National Gallery and approached the local MPs for assistance. Questions were asked in the Commons, and the Oldham members asked for an improvement in the number and names of artists offered for regional exhibition.[93] Eventually, following a meeting with no less a person than the Chancellor of the Exchequer, Oldham's Elliot Lees extracted a promise from the government that it would try to persuade the National Gallery trustees to exchange pictures as requested.[94] With a change in government policy, other national institutions gradually became more co-operative, with the South Kensington museum exchanging its collections with regional galleries on an annual basis. These collections, however, tended to contain its less prestigious works and focused more on applied arts rather than on original painting or sculpture.[95] By the end of the century, most local galleries tended to receive more loans of fine art from neighbouring local galleries than from the national collections. The larger regional galleries appear to have been happy to encourage this practice. The curator of the Walker Art Gallery in Liverpool assisted with loan exhibitions in both Blackburn and Blackpool, by which time the regular loaning of municipal collections was common practice.[96] Loan exhibitions allowed galleries to offer more sophisticated interpretations and syntheses of particular schools or artists. The organisation of an exhibition of modern Scottish painting at Blackpool in 1912 was an excellent example of the collaborative effort of the Lancashire regional galleries. With the assistance of E R. Dibdin, curator of the Walker, the gallery was able to assemble a collection of 'Scotch moderns' that would have been impossible just a few years earlier.[97] Yet, of course, the willingness of corporations to loan works was not simply the product of benevolence. Corporation pictures were cultural ambassadors for a town, a fact that was often made explicit in the reporting and interpretation of exhibitions. The Rochdale gallery's opening exhibition included works from a series of neighbouring towns including Oldham, Preston and Bury. The press was to freely admit that the Rochdale loans served 'the dual purpose of ministering to the enjoyment of the people of Rochdale and of advertising in a populous centre the Galleries to which they belong'.[98] Material exchange was representative of local civic cultural authority.

The individual collecting policy of galleries was important not only in establishing the educational and cultural orientation of individual institutions but also in determining the relationships of individual institutions within a broader regional nexus. As most small galleries had only limited purchase funds, many of their most important acquisitions came through donations and bequests. These often set the tone for the institution's broader collecting policy. Although one might expect the larger towns to be more successful in attracting donations because of their broader cultural hinterland, smaller galleries often benefited too. Bury, for example, was particularly fortunate in acquiring the collection of the well-known paper manufacturer Thomas Wrigley. The items in the collections were acquired with the assistance of Agnew and represented a wide-ranging selection of British nineteenth-century painting. They included Turner's celebrated 'everyday' scene *Calais Sands at Low Water* as well as the famous Landseer hunting scene *The Random Shot*, often interpreted as an indictment of the cruelties of aristocratic sports.[99] Later Victorian paintings reflected Wrigley's interest in historical subject matter, with works such as Frederick Goodall's *An Episode in the Happier Days of Charles I* and E. M Ward's *The Fall of Clarendon*. It is tempting to suggest that Wrigley's most important pieces reflected his staunch Liberal and Nonconformist view on ethics, politics and history. Wrigley's children, who gave these pieces to the municipality, could be seen to be attempting to institutionalise these values within the civic aesthetic, memorialising the private tastes of their father by placing the valued items of his material world in public views. However, Wrigley's collection actually covered a broad range of themes, including a range of more modest landscapes that reflected somewhat more conservative values. In practice, it was rare for a municipal gallery to be dominated by the works from one collection. Bury was unusual in that its gallery was constructed to house the collection of a single private collector. Even then the gallery was never exclusively dedicated to Wrigley, as many fellow manufacturers followed the example of the Wrigley family and donated works in support of the municipal project. James Kenyon provided important works such as E. W. Cooke's *A Modern St Francis* and Edwin Long's *A Girl of Trinidad*, while others donated landscape works, mainly traditional fishing and mountain scenes from North Wales.[100]

Other smaller art galleries received significant collections, through either donations or bequests, but they tended to vary in quality and importance. When many of the major regional galleries were established in the final quarter of the nineteenth century, the prices at auction for modern British painting remained high, and it would be some years before the values of many more modest early and mid-Victorian paintings were revised downwards. This may explain the apparent reluctance of donors to provide wholesale collections to the municipalities. Often such collections represented considerable personal investments that, at a time of the 'Great Depression' and increasing economic uncertainty in the Lancashire economy, could not be disposed of lightly. The collections that galleries received tended to be modest or to consist of items of a lower commercial value, such as watercolour collections. Southport, for example, received thirty-nine paintings and watercolours from a hitherto unknown collector, Miss Ball. The works were mainly of the British landscape school and, while useful items of study for art students, hardly matched the magnificence interior of Southport's new gallery. Preston received the well-known Newsham bequest of watercolours, which, while being of considerable interest, looked ill at ease with the powerful didactic neo-classical values that the Harris art gallery was deemed to represent. Oldham also benefited from the donation of part of the watercolour collection of Charles E. Lees. This was a more significant collection and could, with some justification, claim to be illustrative of the development of watercolour painting since the eighteenth century.[101] Unfortunately, however, a large portion of the collection ended up in the more prestigious surrounding of the new Whitworth gallery in Manchester. Lees's Oldham pictures did, at least, have a disciplinary rationale in that they were able to illustrate the historical emergence of the British watercolour school. Other collections, assembled in a less systematic way, provided galleries with strategic difficulties. Usually major donors to art galleries expected to see their pictures hung together in one room, as a collection representing their taste and public generosity. Some donors even added restrictive covenants to their donations, preventing them from being hung elsewhere. James Ogden's donation to Rochdale, for example, came with a series of conditions. Ogden insisted on a dedicatory plaque recording the purpose of the donation and a covenant preventing his pictures from being exhibited more than three-quarters of a mile from the town hall.[102] Even when such formal restrictions were not in place, art gallery committees often felt uncomfortable about breaking up collections for historical or disciplinary reasons. Donor collections, such as the Newsham collection at Preston, were invariably hung together and were often provided with an exclusive, labelled room dedicated to the 'munificence' of the donor. In this atmosphere of donor memorialisation, it was very difficult for curatorial practice to break these bonds and provide hangs that drew together disciplines, schools and subject matter or provided innovative interpretations of existing collections.

The donation of an entire collection to a municipal gallery was, however, somewhat rare. It was much more usual for leading collectors to donate a small number of 'choice' works that could be seen to be representative of their taste or interests. Blackburn, despite being a town of considerable size, never attracted the donation of a major collection, although it received a number of significant individual items. These included John Collier's *Hetty Sorrel*, donated by A. C. Boulter, H. C. Whaite's *The Convent Garden*, provided by the local magistrate James Kenyon, and, perhaps most famously of all, Edwin Long's *Diana or Christ?* The latter, which became one of the most renowned Victorian paintings after achieving a world record price at auction in 1882, was presented by John Edmondson in 1919 to commemorate the town's war sacrifices. In many cases, of course, works donated reflected fairly traditional Victorian tastes. As the donation of works was a specifically public act, exposing the taste of the donor to critical public glare, it is not surprising that collectors tended to donate their more mainstream or uncontroversial works. There were, however, exceptions to this general tendency. Blackburn received Fred Hall's adventurous work *A Golden Evening* from the collection of J. W. Clayton. This was an important piece and one of the first major works of the Newlyn school to be exhibited in Lancashire. E. A. Hornel's *The Butterfly Chase*, donated to the gallery in 1912, was also an unconventional work. Hornel, a member of the Glasgow school, became known as a follower of Post-Impressionism and, like Manchester's Adolphe Valette, incorporated contemporary Japanese influences into his work.[103] By the time these works were donated the canons of British art were changing, with collectors moving away from the early and mid-Victorian landscape and genre painting that had been the mainstay of the first public galleries. The donations of works by Hall and Hornel suggested that at least some municipal galleries were catching up with contemporary trends.

During the Edwardian period local civic galleries were in a somewhat awkward position. Those that had been established in the 1870s and 1880s had acquired collections often dominated by lesser Victorian artists, which, in recent years, had borne the brunt of criticism and had often fallen in commercial value. Recently established galleries often found that they were being offered just these pictures that were now increasingly regarded as being out of fashion. For example, in 1902 Robert Taylor Heape offered a number of Victorian history and genre paintings to the Rochdale gallery. These included works such as F. W. Topham's *The Story of Ruth and Boaz*, R. F. Pickersgill's *Ferdinand and Miranda* and Mrs E. M. Ward's *The Princes in the Tower*.[104] Twenty years earlier these would have been regarded as works of didactic, even high art, most suitable for the educational work of a municipal gallery. By the Edwardian age, they were dated and out of fashion. However, a municipal gallery, faced with the offer of pictures by a well-known artist from the collection of a well-known local businessman, had little choice but to accept the donor's 'munificence'. The scope for innovation was limited when art gallery committees were largely dependent on contributions from individual donors, some of whom were simply offloading dated or unfashionable items from their private collections. James Hibbert, the architect of the Preston gallery, had warned, back in the early 1880s, about the dangers of municipal galleries following fashion too closely and collecting items that would not endure the verdict of posterity.[105] While local galleries did receive many outstanding works from private sources, the codes of obligation that bound galleries to their publics made it difficult for them to reject unsuitable exhibits. A gallery conceived to reflect the taste of its citizens could scarcely reject the donations of their most significant leaders. There was the ever-present danger that an exhibition would indeed become 'a heap of incongruous things' rather than a systematic display promoting a distinctive civic message.[106] Indeed, because galleries were viewed, at least in part, as didactic institutions, collectors could dispose of unfashionable history and genre painting without this necessarily reflecting too adversely on their own artistic judgement. While such pictures may have had little commercial value, they could still play a public didactic role while, at the same time, advertising the benevolence of their owners. Kept in the home, such pictures marked their owners as outmoded and lacking in judgement. In the public gallery, they could be seen as 'historical' items, promoting the public good and memorialising the benevolence of their owners. The danger was, of course, that local galleries would become museums to the values of the Victorian age rather than dynamic centres of contemporary thought and modern art.

Much depended on the ability of art gallery committees to construct innovative exhibitions and to buy new works with judgement and discrimination. The individual art gallery committees were usually given a free hand to purchase works that they regarded as the most desirable, within a budget agreed by the whole corporation. Only rarely did full council play a role in selecting works for purchase. In most cases, it was the chairmen and vice chairmen of the art gallery committees who, in effect, made the appropriate recommendations and enacted the purchases. They often had very limited access to specialist advice. In some cases, they could draw upon the expertise of the curators of the major regional galleries, such as E. R. Dibdin, who assisted Blackburn and Blackpool. In general, however, they relied on the advice of local artists, collectors and, on some occasions, their own museum curators and librarians. The corporation museum curator or librarian was usually a non-specialist with little academic training in art curatorship. Even in large galleries, such as Preston, it was often difficult to persuade the local authority to appoint specialist art and literary directors. Preston Corporation's refusal to appoint a specialist to care for the collection led to James Hibbert, the art gallery committee's inspirational chairman, leaving the committee in disgust.[107] Oldham also failed to provide a dedicated member of staff to look after its art collection. Charles E. Lees not only donated a large portion of his watercolour collection to Oldham, he effectively acted as unofficial curator for his collection, providing advice on hanging and collecting practice.[108] T. W. Hand, head of the gallery between 1885 and 1898, was officially employed as the librarian and showed little specialist knowledge of museum practice. The Lees watercolour collection suffered particular neglect, with dust collecting between mountings and glass, minute fungi growing inside the frames and discolouration caused by damp.[109] The Lees family complained, but the art gallery committee, no doubt embarrassed by the discoveries, was reluctant to admit there was a problem. After publicly declaring that the complaints were unfounded, it proceeded to instruct Hand to clean and restore the collection![110]

Art gallery committees tended, instead, to buy in specialist help when they felt it was needed. Agnew and Sons were, of course, the major Lancashire dealers, and most municipal art committees used them, either to give advice on maintaining collections or to provide suggestions for purchases. Although art gallery committees were nominally free to make purchases from any source, they were often governed by broader civic considerations. Those galleries that held an annual sales exhibition of modern paintings were required to use at least some of their annual purchase budget to support the exhibition. This effectively meant that the corporation had to buy works from the annual exhibition, especially in the years when the number of private buyers was small. The Oldham annual sales exhibition was, perhaps, the most successful regular sales exhibition in the region outside Liverpool and Manchester. However, the Oldham authorities were constantly alarmed at the low level of private sales. Alderman Emmott warned in 1889 of the consequences of failure to support the exhibition; put quite simply, 'artists would not send pictures if they could not sell them'.[111] Only a very small number of pictures were sold at the exhibition, and in many cases it was either the corporation, or corporation members acting privately, who made the bulk of the large purchases. In 1892, only three pictures were recorded as having being sold at the exhibition, and the only one bought by a private purchaser fetched just £8 8s.[112] By 1896, there were more private buyers, but even then only eleven private purchases were made.[113] Few private collectors outspent the corporation, and none came close to matching the £500 spent by the Oldham committee on S. Melton Fisher's *Dreams* in 1902.[114] The maintenance of an annual exhibition in a town such as Oldham may have been a commercial absurdity, but it was essential if the town's artistic reputation was to be maintained. Consequently, art gallery committees were required to spend substantial sums on works at these exhibitions, even if more appropriate or significant works were available elsewhere. The distorting effects of exhibitions on purchasing policy may account for some of the rather unusual choices. Southport chose Alice Havers's *The Belle of the Village* as one of the first items it acquired for its permanent collection. This was a bizarrely titillating work with overt sexual overtones, far removed from the didactic and educational agendas prevalent in the purchases of many civic collections. Rochdale's first significant purchases also came from sales exhibitions, and here the decision about purchases seems to have been left in the hands of the town's major. If specialist advice was sought it was not recorded.[115]

Within the constraints of tight municipal budgets and the need to patronise local sales exhibitions, some galleries did develop expansive ambitious purchasing policies. Despite the generosity of the Grundy brothers, Blackpool Corporation was reluctant to provide an annual purchase fund, although it did occasionally set aside specific sums for new acquisitions.[116] When a significant collection of thirty-seven paintings, owned by Alderman William Smith of Brighouse, came on the market the Blackpool committee acted quickly. Rowland Hill, the borough librarian, initially approached Smith in the hope of obtaining loan works, but after an exchange of letters, Blackpool decided to purchase the entire collection – a collection which included celebrated works such as Sir Edward Landseer's *Highland Cattle*, William Gale's *Hosanna* and G. E. Hicks's *The Happy Mother*. Although somewhat eclectic, it did offer nationally important representative examples of historical and landscape painting, notably William Linnell's *The Introduction of Christianity into Wales* and John Linnell's *The Woodcutters*.[117] The acquisition of this collection meant that the pictures in Blackpool's permanent collection now numbered about 100 and that the collection contained not merely local works, or works obtained through the Grundys' own network at the Royal Cambrian Academy, but significant exhibits from some of Britain's leading artists.

Blackburn was another civic gallery which, despite limited resources, bought adventurously and outside the confines of the traditional canons of Victorian regional galleries. Its acquisition of Albert Moore's *The Loves of the Winds and the Seasons* from the McCulloch sale in 1913 was particularly notable. A number of other leading civic galleries, including Manchester, had been interested in this work, but Blackburn managed to acquire it for just £456. For many commentators, this was Moore's most important work and a landmark in British symbolist painting. This acquisition was the culmination of a purchasing policy that had provided Blackburn with a collection representing some of the key developments of art in the period. There was the mysticism of Edward Stott's *The Watering Place, Evening* and the aestheticism of Frederick Leighton's *Mother and Child (Cherries)*. In sculpture, there was Alfred Drury's marble *Age of Innocence*, a key example of the 'New Sculpture', and the influential sentimentalism of Marcus Stone in *Two's Company, Three's None*. It is difficult to measure the relationship between the willingness of a corporation to buy ambitiously and the willingness of the surrounding art community to support by bequest or donations the artistic activities of the gallery. However, in the case of Blackburn there is significant evidence that a dynamic art committee, committed to purchasing challenging new works, generated a profile for civic art which encouraged private donors to support the development of the permanent collection. In 1905, for example, the Blackburn committee received a bequest that included works by Sir Thomas Lawrence and Sir Joshua Reynolds: a remarkable gift, given that by then eighteenth-century portraiture was reaching hitherto unseen prices at auction.[118] While some of the larger and longer-established galleries, such as Salford, were struggling to attract donated works, Blackburn continued to attract significant modern works right up to the First World War, including, in 1914, a collection of British and continental paintings from the Harrison collection.[119] However, it would be misleading to suggest that the collecting activities of the smaller municipal galleries conformed to specific standards or canons. The nuances and dynamics of civic culture made it difficult for an art committee to decline any works offered to it by prominent members of the community. To do so would have compromised the gallery's – and the corporation's – claim to be representative of that community.

Art galleries were an expression of a process of urban cultural formation that depended on specific activities, places and technologies for their role as agents of community. They needed to be places of consumption, creating a common location that could command the attention of local elites and where values and ideas could be exchanged. They had to reflect the interests of a network of art consumers, while playing a fundamental role in producing and reproducing the social links and bonds within that network. They were promoters of standards and values, not only for works of art, but also for notions of liberal citizenship. Finally, in order to fully realise these roles, they required forms of projection to validate and objectify their public claims, whether through civic ritualism, architectural form, exhibition practice or mass literary culture. Art galleries, as processes of urban cultural formation, prospered in so far as their claims to the promotion of a broader public good were seen to be representative of valuable and achievable civic goals. Although they may have been run by small committees, and sometimes by a single enthusiastic individual, their power lay in their collective claim over the civic consciousness. For an art committee to adopt an exclusive interpretation of how that civic consciousness could be promoted would have destroyed its power. Innovation had to be tempered with an awareness of consumer taste. Art galleries had to be relatively open spaces in which liberal citizens could assemble freely and take part in activities of collective consumption. Without guidance, however, this could lead to the triumph of conservative tastes or the fashions of the seasons, with sometimes overtly reactionary or commercial priorities shaping local civic canons of art. Much depended on the manner in which the art gallery committee, the critic, the press and the visitor moulded these private expressions into a broader narrative or ritual that had worthwhile meaning for local citizens.

While it was relatively easy to construct a narrative or ritual meaning around a new gallery – an empty building with a specific purpose – it was more difficult to do this with a fragmented collection, often delivered to a town as much by historical accident and private inclinations as by a collective purpose. While larger galleries often attracted major single donations, had substantial purchase funds and could extend their function to meet changing demands, smaller galleries were inevitably less well funded and less able to access the resources needed to fashion the local art community. Outside Liverpool and Manchester patrons and donors were rarely large in number, and few of them provided sustained support to local galleries. When a smaller gallery did try to mobilise the local art community behind a specific modernist agenda by organising an annual sales exhibition, this could prompt criticism of commercialisation. Without permanent specialist advice there was a danger that gallery committees would be swept along by the fashions of the time, purchasing mediocre history and genre paintings whose currency was inevitably limited. As these paintings fell out of fashion in the auction room they became more likely to turn up in bequests and donations. While such items may now be regarded as items of significant historical interest, they endangered the contemporary relevance of the modern gallery and raised fundamental questions about the purpose of local art institutions. The civic art gallery was in danger of becoming a museum of outmoded Victorian taste rather than an exemplar of the contemporary movements sweeping across and through the Edwardian art world.

NOTES

1 For background see on the search for liberal stability see S. Gunn, *The Public Culture of the Victorian Middle Class: Ritual and Authority in the English Industrial City 1840–1914* (Manchester, 2000) and S. Gunn, 'The Public Sphere, Modernity and Consumption New Perspectives on the History of the English Middle Class', in A. Kidd and D. Nicholls (eds), *Gender, Civic Culture and Consumerism* (Manchester, 1999), 12–30. For an examination of Manchester see M. Hewitt, *The Emergence of Stability in the Industrial City: Manchester 1832–65* (Aldershot, 1996); A. Kidd and K. Roberts (eds), *City, Class and Culture: Cultural Production and Social Policy in Victorian Manchester* (Manchester, 1985).

2 For an exploration of these issues, see M. Douglas and B. Isherwood, *The World of Goods: Towards an Anthropology of Consumption* (London, 1979), 75–8.

3 The classic account of the emergence of consumer society is to be found in N. McKendrick, J. Brewer and J. H. Plumb, *The Birth of a Consumer Society: The Commercialization of Eighteenth-Century England* (London, 1982). The complexities of the debate about modern consumerism can be appreciated in J. Benson, *The Rise of Consumer Society in Britain, 1880–1980* (London, 1994) and M. J. Lee, *The Consumer Society Reader* (Oxford, 2000).

4 *Municipal Journal*, 12 (4 September 1903), 796.

5 *Municipal Journal*, 12 (23 January 1903), 66.

6 M. J. Daunton, *Trusting Leviathan: The Politics of Taxation in Britain 1799–1914* (Cambridge, 2001), ch. 9; P. J. Waller, *Town, City and Nation: England 1850–1950* (Oxford, 1983), esp. 298–316.

7 'Civic promotion' was often an explicit and organised activity. See R. Rodger, 'The Common Good and Civic Promotion: Edinburgh 1860–1914', in R. Colls and R. Rodger (eds), *Cities of Ideas: Civil Society and Governance in British Cities* (Aldershot, 2003), 144–77.

8 E. P. Hennock, *Fit and Proper Persons: Ideal and Reality in Nineteenth Century Urban Government* (London, 1973), 127–8.

9 E. P. Hennock, 'Finance and Politics', *Historical Journal*, 6 (1963), 212–15.

10 P. Bailey, *Leisure and Class in Victorian England: Rational Recreation and the Contest for Control, 1830–1885* (London, 1978), 76–9.

11 F. E. S. Kaplan, *Museums and the Making of 'Ourselves'* (Leicester, 1994), 1–5. For recent discussions of the politics of collections see E. Hooper-Greenhill, *Museums and the Shaping of Knowledge* (London, 1992); G. Kavanagh (ed.), *Museum Languages: Objects and Texts* (Leicester, 1991); R. Lumley (ed.), *The Museum Time Machine* (London, 1988); S. Pearce, *Museums, Objects and Collections* (Leicester, 1989).

12 T. Veblen, *The Theory of the Leisure Class* (New York, 1899).

285

13 D. Riesman, *Thorstein Veblen: A Critical Interpretation* (New York, 1953); T. Goodale and G. Godbey, *The Evolution of Leisure: Historical and Philosophical Perspectives* (London. 1998), 101–2.

14 R. Sweet, *The English Town, 1680–1840* (Harlow, 1998), 263.

15 J. Vernon, *Politics and the People: A Study in English Political Culture, c.1815–1867* (Cambridge, 1993), 51–4.

16 Vernon, *Politics and the People*, 103.

17 W. H. Fraser, 'From Civic Gospel to Municipal Socialism', in D. Fraser (ed.), *Cities, Class and Communities: Essays in Honour of Asa Briggs* (Hemel Hempstead, 1990), 70.

18 A. Briggs, *Victorian Cities* (London, 1963, reprint 1990), 150–3.

19 B. Law, *Oldham, Brave Oldham* (Oldham, 1999), 157–8.

20 Blackburn Corporation, Annual Report of the Blackburn Free Public Library and Museum, March 1869 (Blackburn, 1869), 2.

21 *Blackburn Art and General Exhibition: Official Catalogue* (Blackburn, 1874).

22 P. Lord, 'History of Education in Oldham', MEd thesis, University of Manchester, 1938, 124.

23 W.B., 'Oldham Art and Artists', *Oldham Chronicle*, 3 October 1936, in Oldham Newspaper Cuttings: Art Gallery and Museum, vol. 4, 1935–46, Oldham Record Office (hereafter ORO).

24 *Blackpool Gazette*, 24 April 1903.

25 Blackpool Corporation Proceedings, 18 February 1902, 85, Blackpool Public Library.

26 Blackpool Corporation Proceedings, 23 March 1909; 23 March 1910, 102.

27 Rochdale Council Proceedings, 1 August 1901; 20 January 1902, Rochdale Local Studies Library.

28 *Bury Times*, 4 April 1903.

29 Carlisle Public Library, Museum, Art Gallery and School of Science and Art, Annual Report, 25 March 1895, Carlisle Public Library.

30 Oldham Newspaper Cuttings: Art Gallery and Museum Committee, vol. 1, 1890–1907, 27, ORO; *Manchester Guardian*, 2 February 1893.

31 'Oldham and Oldham Men' (cuttings book), ORO, FP53.

32 *Manchester Examiner*, 8 February 1889, in Oldham Newspaper Cuttings: Art Gallery and Museum Committee, vol. 1, 1890–1907, 8.

33 *Oldham Chronicle*, 7 February 1899.

34 *Oldham Advertiser*, 7 March 1890.

35 *Oldham Standard*, 7 February 1899, in Oldham Newspaper Cuttings: Art Gallery and Museum, vol. 1, 1890–1907, 74.

36 T. Coombs, *Rising from Reality. Art in Oldham from 1820 to 1890* (Oldham, 1990), 5.

37 Law, *Oldham*, 211–12.

38 The relationship between urban culture and landscape painting is, of course, a long and complex one. For recent overviews and assessments see A. Hemingway, *Landscape Imagery and Urban Culture in Early Nineteenth-Century Britain* (Cambridge, 1992) and M. Rosenthal, C. Payne and S. Wilcox (eds), *Prospects for the Nation: Recent Essays in British Landscape 1750–1880* (New Haven, 1997).

39 *Rochdale Times*, 4 April 1903.

40 Rochdale Council Proceedings, 30 December 1901, 20 January 1902.

41 Rochdale Council Proceedings, 19 November 1902.

42 Inscription of the Ogden donation, recorded in Rochdale Council Proceedings, 18 March 1903.

43 Rochdale Council Proceedings, 13 March 1903.

44 *Bury Times*, 4 April 1903.

45 J. Walton, *The Blackpool Landlady* (Manchester, 1978), ix.

46 H. J. Perkin, 'The "Social Tone" of Victorian Seaside Resorts in the North West', *Northern History*, 11 (1975), 181–94, esp. 186–8.

47 Walton, *Blackpool Landlady*, 156.

48 D. Shaw, *Selling an Urban Image: Blackpool at the Turn of the Century*, Department of Geography, University of Birmingham: Working Papers, 54 (Birmingham,1990), 16–19.

49 *Blackpool Times*, 21 December 1912.

50 *Blackpool Gazette*, 24 April 1903.

51 *Blackpool Gazette*, 9 June 1903.

52 *Blackpool Gazette*, 9 June 1903.

53 *Blackpool Gazette*, 1 November 1904.

54 Blackpool Corporation Proceedings, 6 August 1907; *Blackpool Times*, 11 September 1907.

55 E. Morris, *Public Art Collections in North-West England* (Liverpool, 2001), 168–9.

56 J. F. L. Sandbach, 'Bury Muffs', *Lancashire Review* (1899), 338.

57 *Oldham Chronicle*, 11 September 1880. The term 'Oldham Roughheads' was later adopted as a moniker for the local rugby league football team.

58 A. Tait, *History of the Oldham Lyceum* (Oldham, 1897), 33.

59 Oldham Corporation Free Library and Museum (hereafter FLM) Committee Book 2, 22 July 1885, ORO, CBO/20/1/1/2.

60 Rochdale Council Proceedings, 4 February 1903.

61 Rochdale Council Proceedings, 15 April 1903.

62 'No person who is in a state of intoxication, or is uncleanly in person or dress, or who is suffering from an infectious or offensive disease, shall be admitted or allowed to remain in the Library, museum or Art Gallery. No person shall be allowed to lie on the benches or chairs, or to sleep in the building, or to interfere with the arrangements for conducting it, or of the comfort of the readers therein, or to use the same for any purpose for which it is not intended. No conversation shall be permitted in the Reading Rooms. No person shall partake of refreshments, or smoke, spit, or strike matches, or bring a dog into the building.' FLM Committee Book 2, 22 July 1885, CBO/20/1/2/.

63 'A Lover of Truth', letter, *Oldham Standard*, 2 March 1888.

64 For discussion of the development of this concept see J. O'Neill, 'The Disciplinary Society: From Weber to Foucault', *British Journal of Sociology*, 37 (1986), 42–60.

65 T. Bennett, *The Birth of the Museum: History, Theory, Politics* (London, 1995); E. Hooper-Greenhill, 'The Museum in the Disciplinary Society', in S. Pearce (ed.), *Museum Studies in Material Culture* (Leicester, 1989), 61–72.

66 Carlisle Public Library, Museum, Art Gallery and School of Science and Art, Annual Report, 25 March 1895.

67 E. R. Dibdin, 'The Pictures in the Oldham Art Gallery', *Windsor Magazine* (1910), in Oldham Catalogues, Oldham Library, PXS.

68 Sometimes the original opening day parades were replicated on subsequent anniversaries. *Stockport Advertiser*, 25 September 1906.

69 *Rochdale Times*, 4 April 1903.

70 *Oldham Evening Express*, 8 May 1882.

71 Blackpool Corporation Proceedings, 31 October 1911, 643–6.

72 *Oldham Evening Express*, 8 May 1882.

73 *Oldham Chronicle*, 2 August 1883.

74 *Oldham Chronicle*, 4 April 1903.

75 *Grundy Art Gallery Programme and Souvenir*, 26 October 1911 (Blackpool, 1911).

76 *Blackburn Art and General Exhibition: Official Catalogue.*

77 *Oldham Evening Chronicle*, 2 August 1883; Bury Public Library and Art Gallery Committee, Annual Reports, First Annual Report 1901–2, Bury Public Library.

78 Bury Public Library and Art Gallery Committee, Second Annual Report 1902–3, 12.

79 Blackburn Corporation, Annual Report of the Blackburn Free Public Library and Museum, 17th Annual Report, February 1879 (Blackburn, 1879), 14.

80 The original estimate was £8,000; the final cost exceeded £20,000 exclusive of miscellaneous litigation costs. Oldham Corporation Free Library and Museum Committee Book 2, 4 February 1885, 15 April 1885.

81 Bury Public Library and Art Gallery Committee, Fourth Annual Report 1904–5, 16.

82 *Oldham Chronicle*, 18 December 1897.

83 *Rochdale Times*, 8 September 1903.

84 *Rochdale Times*, 8 September 1903.

85 Bury Public Library and Art Gallery Committee, Fifth Annual Report 1905–6, 10.

86 *Blackpool Gazette*, 14 February 1913.

87 Oldham Corporation Book 4, 23 January 1882 – 16 March 1882, ORO, CBO/24/4.

88 *Oldham Standard*, 8 August 1885.

89 FLM Committee Book 1, 12 November 1884.

90 FLM Committee Book 2, 12 August 1885.

91 FLM Committee Book 2, 29 December 1886.

92 FLM Committee Book 2, 19 September 1888.

93 FLM Committee Book 2, 8 July 1891.

94 FLM Committee Book 2, 5 August 1891.

95 FLM Committee Book 2, 28 December 1891.

96 Blackburn Corporation, Report of the Committee of the Blackburn Free Library, Museum and Art Gallery, 1 August 1901–31 July 1907.

97 *Blackpool Times*, 10 February 1912.

98 *Bury Times*, 4 April 1903.

99 Morris, *Public Art Collections*, 49–51.

100 Bury Public Library and Art Gallery Committee, First Annual Report, 1901–2, 10–11.

101 Berry, *Oldham*, 26.

102 Rochdale Council Proceedings, 18 March 1903.

103 S. Martin, *Adolphe Valette: A French Influence in Manchester* (Manchester, 1994).

104 Rochdale Council Proceedings, 3 December 1902.

105 J. Hibbert (ed.), *Notes on Free Public Libraries and Museums* (Preston, 1881), 100.

106 'Alderman Hibbert on the Formation of the Harris Reference Library and Art Museum', September 1893, in Harris Cuttings – Building and Opening, vol. 1.

107 *Preston Guardian*, 2 March 1895.

108 FLM Committee Minute Book 2, 2 May 1888.

109 *Oldham Chronicle*, 18 February 1896.

110 *Oldham Chronicle*, 11 July 1896, 11 August 1896.

111 *Oldham Evening Express*, 7 February 1889.

112 Exhibition Ledger 1886–1936, 37–40, ORO, CBO/20/2/3/11.

113 Exhibition Ledger 1886–1936, 48–53.

114 Exhibition Ledger 1886–1936, 94–102.

115 Rochdale Corporation Council Proceedings, 18 April 1904, 1 March 1905.

116 In 1911, for example, it set aside a sum of £300 for the purchase of works of art. *Blackpool Times*, 16 October 1912.

117 *Blackpool Gazette*, 25 July 1913, 8 August 1913.

118 Annual Report of the Blackburn Free Public Library and Museum, 1 August 1904–31 July 1905 (Blackburn, 1905).

119 Annual Report of the Blackburn Free Public Library and Museum, 1 August 1913–31 July 1914 (Blackburn, 1914).

BIBLIOGRAPHY

PRIMARY SOURCES

Manuscript material (including annotated material)

Broadside Collection, Warrington Public Library Local Studies, W352.921.

Corporation of Salford Museum and Library Committee, Minutes, 5 July 1849, Salford Royal Museum and Library.

Documents and Papers Connected with Laying the Foundation Stone, the Opening Ceremony etc, etc, of the Walker Art Gallery, Liverpool, 1877, Liverpool Record Office.

Ford, W., 'Characters of the Different Picture Collectors, in, and about Manchester', c.1827), Manchester Central Library, MS 827.79, fol. 43.

Harris Collection, Preston Local Studies Library, T25 PRE.

Hibbert Correspondence Collection, Preston Local Studies Library, P920 B LLO, 50.

'Historical Manchester, Famous Manchester Men' (cuttings book), Manchester Central Library, 920.042 73 Sw1.

Manchester Academy of Art Cuttings Collection (annotated vols), Manchester City Art Gallery.

Manchester City Council, Art Gallery Committee Minutes, various, Manchester Central Library.

Manchester Cuttings Collection, Manchester Central Library, F942.7 M10, vol. 12.

Manchester Cuttings Book, Manchester Central Library, F942.7389 Sc4.

Minutes of Council,, Whitworth Art Gallery, UMSC.

Newspaper Articles by E. R. Dibdin, Liverpool Record Office, HF 700 DIB, 3.

Oldham Corporation Free Library and Museum Committee Books and Exhibition Ledger, Oldham Record Office, CBO/20/1/1–2, CBO/24/4, CBO/20/2/3/11.

'Oldham and Oldham Men' (cuttings book), Oldham Record Office, FP53.

Oldham Newspaper Cuttings: Art Gallery and Museum Committee, various, Oldham Record Office.

Royal Cambrian Academy Minutes, Royal Cambrian Academy Archives, Conwy Library.

Royal Manchester Institution, Association for the Patronage of the Fine Arts Minutes, Manchester Central Library, M6/1/6.

Royal Manchester Institution, Council General Meeting Minutes, Manchester Central Library, M6/1.

Royal Manchester Institution, Council Minute Book, Society of Artists Meetings 1823, Manchester Central Library, M6/1/1/1.

Royal Manchester Institution, Council Proceedings, Council and General Meetings Volume, Manchester Central Library.

Salford Corporation, Proceedings of Council, Salford Library Local Studies Centre.

Salford Royal Museum and Library Committee Minutes and Report Books, Salford Library Local Studies Centre.

'Statutes Made by Governors at the First Meeting', 10 October 1890, University of Manchester Special Collections.

Stockport Borough Manorial Tolls Committee Minute Book, Stockport Reference Library.

Stockport Borough Parks Committee Proceedings, Stockport Reference Library.

Stockport Reference Library Miscellaneous Cuttings Collection, Stockport Reference Library, S C 71.

Swindells, T., 'A Merchant Prince, The Romantic Career of Sam Mendel' (cutting), in 'Historical Manchester, Famous Manchester Men' (cuttings book), Manchester Central Library, 920.042 73 Sw1.

Warrington Council Minutes, Warrington Public Library Local Studies.

Whitworth Blue Cuttings Book, University of Manchester Special Collections.

Whitworth Committee Document Volumes, University of Manchester Special Collections.

Whitworth Committee Letters, University of Manchester Special Collections.

Whitworth Green Cuttings Book, University of Manchester Special Collections.

Printed reports and catalogues

Advertisement for *Catalogue of the Loan Collection of Pictures, Jubilee Exhibition 1894*, Manchester Central Library, L 708.273 SALa.

An Act for Encouraging the Establishment of Museums in Large Towns, 21 July 1845, 8 and 9 Vic. c. 43.

Art and Citizenship', *Manchester Literary Club*, 32 (1906), 434–41.

Blackburn Art and General Exhibition: Official Catalogue (Blackburn, 1874).

Blackburn Corporation, Annual Report of the Blackburn Free Public Library and Museum, various.

Blackpool Corporation Proceedings, various, Blackpool Public Library.

Bury Public Library and Art Gallery Committee, Annual Reports, various, Bury Public Library.

Carlisle Public Library, Museum, Art Gallery and School of Science and Art, Annual Report, various, Carlisle Public Library.

Catalogue of the Art Treasures of the United Kingdom Collected at Manchester (London, 1857).

Catalogue of the Exhibition Held at the Opening of the Art Gallery (Warrington, n.d.), Warrington Public Library Local Studies, P.S. 20.

Catalogue of the Exhibition of Pictures by Living British Artists in the Gallery, No. 83 Market-Street – the First (Manchester, 1827), Manchester Central Library, S&A 378.

A Catalogue of the Manchester Exhibition of Paintings by Various Masters of the Italian, Flemish, Dutch, German and English Schools (Manchester, 1811), Manchester Central Library, S&A 378.

A Catalogue of the Valuable Amateur Topographical and Illustrative Prints, English and Foreign Portraits being a Part of the Stock in Trade of Mr Wm. Ford Smith, Bookseller (Manchester, 1816), Manchester Central Library, 769 9 F1.

Catalogue of the Valuable Collection of Paintings and Drawings, Prints and Etchings, Cabinets of Insects etc (Manchester, 1814), Manchester Central Library, 708 2733 Cal.

City of Liverpool Education Committee, Proceedings and Appendix to Proceedings of the Education Committee, 1903–4, Liverpool Record Office, H370 EDU.

Collectanea Relating to Manchester and its Neighbourhood', *Chetham Society*, 68 (1866), 240–58.

Craig, W. M., circular letter, 1 December 1802, Manchester Central Library, H910.

Critical Notes of the Picture and Water-Colour Drawings in the Royal Jubilee Exhibition, Manchester 1887 (Manchester, 1887).

The Exhibition of the Society for Promoting Painting and Design, in Liverpool, September 1784 (Liverpool, 1784) (copy).

The Exhibition of the Society for Promoting Painting and Design, in Liverpool, September 1787 (Liverpool, 1787) (copy).

Grundy Art Gallery Programme and Souvenir, 26 October 1911 (Blackpool, 1911).

The Guide to Manchester and Salford (Edinburgh, 1877).

Handbook to the Technical and Art School and Colleges of the United Kingdom (London, 1909).

Lancashire Pamphlet Collections, vols 13 and 14, British Library, 1866 e7.

The Laws and By Laws of the Roscoe Club (Liverpool, 1847).

Laws and Regulations of the Manchester Academy for Drawing and designing (Manchester, 1805), Manchester Central Library, H910.

Laws and Regulations of the School of Design, Manchester' (Manchester, 1839), in Manchester School of Design etc, Manchester Central Library, 707.0942 M2.

Liverpool Corporation Council Proceedings, various, Liverpool Record Office.

Liverpool Institute, Annual Reports of the Directors, Liverpool Record Office.

Liverpool Institute Mount Street, Established 1825 (Liverpool, 1861), Liverpool Record Office.

Liverpool Mechanics' Institution School of Arts, Addresses, in Lancashire Pamphlet Collections, British Library, 1866 e7.

Liverpool Royal Institution Reports 1897–1906, Liverpool Record Office.

Liverpool School of Art, *44th Annual Report of the Directors*, 20 January 1869 (Liverpool, 1869), Liverpool Record Office.

Manchester: A Catalogue of Books etc. (Manchester, n.d.) (property of John Leigh Philips), Manchester Central Library, M84/3/8/1.

Manchester School of Art, Annual Reports, various from 1854, Manchester Central Library.

Manchester School of Design, Annual Reports, various to 1853, Manchester Central Library.

Manchester School of Design: A Report, 15 January 1844 (Manchester, 1844), Manchester Central Library.

Manchester School of Design: A Report, 13 January 1845 (Manchester, 1845), Manchester Central Library.

Manchester School of Design, 24 February 1846 (Manchester, 1846), Manchester Central Library.

Manchester School of Design etc, Manchester Central Library, 707.0942 M2.

The Manchester Whitworth Institute – Charter of Incorporation and Statutes (Manchester, n.d.).

Memorial Exhibition of the Art of John Finnie, RE, RCA (Liverpool, 1907).

Minutes of Evidence Taken before the Select Committee on Public Libraries, vol. 1 (London, 1849).

Oldham Lyceum, Reports of the Directors of the Oldham Lyceum, various from 1863, British Library.

Philips, J. L., Library Catalogue, 1805, Manchester Central Library, M84/3/7.

Preliminary Prospectus – Grand Art Union (Manchester, 1881).

Preston Council Proceedings, various (Preston, 1891–1914).

Preston Free Public Library Committee, Preston Local Studies Library.

Prospectus of the Course of Instruction, Terms and Regulations of the School Attached to the Liverpool Mechanics' Institution (Liverpool, 1837).

Report from the Select Committee on the School of Design, 14 May 1849, in *Reports from Committees*, vol. 18 (1849).

Report of the Academy of Art, Liverpool Royal Institution Report 1828 (Liverpool, 1828).

Report of the Committee of the Blackburn Free Library, Museum and Art Gallery [Blackburn], 1 August 1901–31 July 1907 (Blackburn, 1907).

Report of the Directors of the Liverpool Mechanics' Institution, 4 March 1835, Liverpool Record Office.

Report of the Directors of the Liverpool Mechanics' Institution, 8 March 1843 (Liverpool, 1843).

Report of the Libraries and Museums Committee (Stockport) (Stockport, 1876).

Report of the Select Committee on Schools of Art (London, 1863), Appendix 13: 'Schools of Art Established, Changed or Closed since 1852'; Appendix 14: 'Table of Local Subscriptions, Fees, Government Aid, Donations and Local Expenses'; Appendix 16.

Report on the History and Progress of the Libraries, Museum and Gallery of Arts (Liverpool, 1887).

Report to the City Council of Visits to Certain Art Galleries and Museums in Belgium, Holland, Germany and Great Britain (Manchester, 1905).

Rochdale Council Proceedings, various, Rochdale Local Studies Library.

Royal Jubilee Exhibition, Manchester 1887: Official Catalogue (Manchester, 1887).

Salford Royal Museum and Library Annual Reports, various, Salford Library Local Studies Centre.

Statement of the Works of Art Purchased or Presented to the Corporation of Liverpool (Liverpool, 1875).

The Stranger in Liverpool; or An Historical and Descriptive View of the Town of Liverpool and its Environs (Liverpool, 1823).

Technical Instruction Committee of the City Council of Manchester, Annual Reports, various.

Thirtieth Annual Report of the Committee of the Free Public Library, Museum and Walker Art Gallery of the Borough of Liverpool (Liverpool, 1883).

Thirty-Eighth Annual Report of the Committee of the Free Public Library, Museum and Walker Art Gallery of the City of Liverpool (Liverpool, 1891).

Tracts on the Arts etc. (Manchester, 1838).

Twenty-Fourth Annual Report of the Committee of the Free Public Library, Museum and Walker Art Gallery of the City of Liverpool (Liverpool, 1877).

Twenty-Sixth Annual Report of the Committee of the Free Public Library, Museum and Walker Art Gallery of the Borough of Liverpool (Liverpool, 1879).

Warrington Museum Committee Annual Reports, various, Warrington Public Library Local Studies.

What to See & Where to See it or the Visitor's Guide to the Opening Exhibition, Manchester School of Art (Manchester, 1881).

Whitworth Art Gallery Annual Reports 1893–1906 (incomplete), Manchester Central Library, 708.273 W2.

Whitworth Institute Annual Reports 1890–1923, University of Manchester Special Collections.

Published materials

Armstrong, W., *Fine Art at the Royal Jubilee Exhibition: Critical Notes* (Manchester, 1887).

Arnold, M., *Culture and Anarchy* (London, 1869).

Aspinall, J., *Roscoe's Library* (London and Liverpool, 1853).

Axon, W. E. A., *Lancashire Gleanings* (Manchester, n.d.[1882?]).

Baines, T., *The Liverpool Tribute to Roscoe* (London, 1853).

Barton, W. B., 'The Harris Library and Museum, Preston: A Record', *Magazine of Art*, 25 (1900–1), 49–56.

Blackwell, T., *An Enquiry into the Life and Writings of Homer* (London, 1735).

Blundell, H., *An Account of the Statues, Busts, Bass-Relieves, Cinery Urns, and Other Ancient Marbles, and Paintings, at Ince, Collected by H.B.* (Liverpool, 1803).

Brierley, B., *Irkdale* (Manchester, 1868).

Bright, H. A., *Address Delivered to the Annual Meeting of the Proprietors of the Liverpool Royal Institution* (Liverpool, 1873).

Brooke, R., *Liverpool as it Was during the Last Quarter of the Eighteenth Century, 1775 to 1800* (Liverpool, 1853).

Cicero, M., *On Moral Obligation*, trans. J.Higginbotham (London, 1967).

Darbishire, A., 'Manchester as an Art Centre, March 19, 1877', *Manchester Literary Club*, 3 (1876–77), 211–17.

Dibdin, E. R., 'The Liverpool Corporation Collection', *Magazine of Art*, 12 (1889), 50–6.

Dibdin, E. R., 'The Pictures in the Oldham Art Gallery', *Windsor Magazine* (1910), in Oldham Catalogues, Oldham Library, PXS.

Dickens, C., *Hard Times* (London, 1854; Penguin edn 1985).

Dixon, R. S., 'The Harris Free Library and Museum, Preston', *Architects' and Builders' Journal*, 20 August 1913, 179.

Dobkin, M., 'Mendel of Manley Hall', *Jackson's Row Newsletter* (Manchester), 5:6 (1890), 8–9.

Duguid, T., *Address Delivered at the Annual Meeting of the Proprietors of the Liverpool Royal Institution* (Liverpool, 1861).

Eastlake, C. L., *A History of the Gothic Revival* (London, 1872).

Edwards, E., *Lives of the Founders of the British Museum* (London, 1870).

Ellis, H., *The Townley Gallery of Classical Sculpture in the British Museum* (London, 1846).

Espinasse, F., *Lancashire Worthies*, 2nd series (London, 1877).

Fairbairn, W., *Observations on Improvements of the Town of Manchester* (Manchester, 1836).

Ferguson, A., *An Essay on the History of Civil Society*, 5th edn (London, 1782).

Fishwick, H. (ed.), *Works of John Collier (Tim Bobbin)* (Rochdale, 1904).

Gibbon, E., *History of the Decline and Fall of the Roman Empire* (London, 1766–88).

Grindley, B. H., *Exhibitions of Pictures and Municipal Management* (Liverpool, 1875).

Grindley, B. H., *History and Work of the Liverpool Academy of Arts* (Liverpool, 1875).

Grindon, L. H., *Manchester Banks and Bankers* (Manchester, 1878).

Hall Caine, T. H., *A Disquisition on Dante Gabriel Rossetti's Painting in Oil Entitled 'Dante's Dream'* (Liverpool, 1881).

Heartwell, H., 'Characteristics of Manchester V', *North of England Magazine*, 1 (1842), 564.

Hewitson, A., *A History of Preston* (Preston, 1883).

Hewitt, E., 'Stockport Museum: Its History and Aims', Conference of the Museums Association, 25 April 1912.

Hibbert, J., *A Report to Accompany the Design of the Harris Free Public Library and Museum, July 1882* (Preston, 1882).

Hibbert, J., *Memoir to Accompany the Design for the Sculptured Pediment, July 1885* (Preston, 1885).

Hibbert, J. (ed.), *Notes on Free Public Libraries and Museums* (Preston, 1881).

Hird, F., *Lancashire Stories* (London, 1911).

Hodgson, J. E., *Fifty Years of British Art* (Manchester, 1887).

Irving, W., *A Sketch of William Roscoe* (Liverpool, 1853).

Jackson, G., 'On the Means of Improving Public Taste' (Manchester, 1844), in Manchester School of Design etc, Manchester Central Library, 707.0942 M2.

Jackson, G., 'Two Essays on a School of Design for the Useful Arts, Delivered at the Mechanics Institute' (Manchester, 1837), in *Tracts on the Arts etc*, Manchester Central Library, 751 243 Ku1.

Kirkman Gray, B., *A History of English Philanthropy* (London, 1905).

Leech, B., *History of the Manchester Ship Canal*, 2 vols (Manchester, 1907).

Lithgow, R. A. D., *The Life of John Critchley Prince* (Manchester, 1880).

Lyttelton, G., *Dialogues of the Dead* (London, 1760).

MacColl, D., *The Administration of the Chantrey Bequest: Articles Reprinted from 'The Saturday Review', with Additional Matter, Including the Text of Chantrey's Will and a List of Purchases* (London, 1904).

Marillier, H. C., *The Liverpool School of Painters* (London, 1904).

Marriner, S., *Rathbones of Liverpool* (Liverpool, 1861).

Mayer, J., *History of the Art of Pottery in Liverpool* (Liverpool, 1855).

Mayer, J., *On the Art of Pottery* (Liverpool, 1871).

Mayer, J., *Roscoe and the Influence of his Writings on the Fine Arts* (London, 1853).

Milner, G. (ed.), *Poems and Songs of Edwin Waugh* (London, n.d.).

Mitford, W., *The History of Greece* (London, 1784–1810).

Muir, R., *The History of Liverpool* (Liverpool, 1907).

Mullen, B., *The Royal Museum and Libraries, Salford* (Salford, 1899).

Murgatroyd, J., *Remarks Concerning the Manchester School of Art and Schools of Art Generally* (Manchester, 1881).

Orchard, B. G., *Liverpool's Legion of Honour* (Birkenhead, 1893).

Ostrogorsky, M., *Democracy and the Organization of Political Parties*, 2 vols (London, 1902).

Partington, J., 'Manchester as an Art Centre', *Manchester Literary Club*, 3 (1876–77), 42–52.

Pollard, W., *The Stanleys of Knowsley: A History* (London, 1869).

Rathbone, P. H., *The English School of Impressionists as Illustrated in the Liverpool Autumn Exhibition* (Liverpool, 1883).

Rathbone, P. H., *The Political Value of Art to the Municipal Life of a Nation* (Liverpool, 1875).

Rathbone, T., *Descriptive and Historical Catalogue of the Pictures, Drawings, and Casts in the Gallery of Art of the Royal Institution* (Liverpool, 1859).

Richardson, J. Snr, and Richardson, J. Jnr, *An Account of Some of the Statues, Bas-Reliefs, Drawings and Pictures in Italy, &c with Remarks* (London, 1722).

Roscoe, H., *An Ode on the Institution of a Society in Liverpool for the Encouragement of Designing, Drawing, Painting …* (Liverpool, 1774).

Roscoe, H., *The Life of William Roscoe*, 2 vols (London, 1833).

Roscoe, W., *The Life and Pontificate of Leo X*, 2nd edn, vol. 1 (Liverpool, 1806).

Roscoe, W., 'On the Comparative Excellence of the Science and Arts, by Mr William Roscoe. Communicated', *Memoirs of the Society at Manchester*, 3 (1787), 244–59.

Roscoe, W., *On the Origin and Vicissitudes of Literature, Science and Art, and their Influence on the Present State of Society* (Liverpool, 1817).

Ross, D., *Sketch of the History of the House of Stanley, and the House of Sefton* (London, 1848).

Rowley, C., *Fifty Years of Work without Wages* (London, n.d.[1913?]).

Scharf, G., 'On the Manchester Art Treasures Exhibition, 1857', *Transactions of the Historic Society of Lancashire and Cheshire*, 10 (1857–58), 269–331.

Sharpe, C. W. (ed.), *The Sport of Civic Life or, Art and the Municipality* (Liverpool, 1909).

Stuart, J., andN.Revett, *Antiquities of Athens*, 4 vols (1762–1816).

Swindells, T., *Manchester Streets and Manchester Men*, 1st series (Manchester, 1906).

Swindells, T., *Manchester Streets and Manchester Men*, 2nd series (Manchester, 1907).

Swindells, T., *Manchester Streets and Manchester Men*, 4th series (Manchester, 1908).

Tait, A., *History of the Oldham Lyceum* (Oldham, 1897).

Townley, R. (ed.), *The Miscellaneous Works of Tim Bobbin* (London, 1806).

Traill, T. S., *Address Delivered February, 1827 at the General Meeting of Proprietors of the Liverpool Royal Institution* (Liverpool, 1827).

Traill, T. S., *Address Delivered February, 1828 at the General Meeting of Proprietors of the Liverpool Royal Institution* (Liverpool, 1828).

Traill, T. S., *Address Delivered February, 1829 at the General Meeting of Proprietors of the Liverpool Royal Institution* (Liverpool, 1829).

Traill, T. S., 'Memoir of William Roscoe', *Edinburgh New Philosophical Journal*, 26 (Edinburgh, c.1832), 193–221.

Tuckerman, H. J., *Characteristics of Literature: the philanthropist William Roscoe* (London, 1849).

Veblen, T., *The Theory of the Leisure Class: An Economic Study of Institutions* (New York, 1899).

Walford, C., *The Commercial Greatness of Liverpool* (London, 1883).

Winstanley, T., *Catalogue of the Pictures, Casts from the Antique, &c in the Liverpool Royal Institution, June 1836* (Liverpool, 1836).

Bibliography

Wood, E., and T. Taylor, 'Gallery of Fine Art', n.d., MCL, m58971/122614.
Wood, R., *An Essay on the Original Genius and Writings of Homer* (London, 1775).

Newspapers and periodicals

Architects' and Builders' Journal
Art Journal
Art Union
Blackpool Gazette
Blackpool Times
The Builder
Bury Times
Daily Albion
Daily Courier (Liverpool)
Daily Despatch
Daily Post (Liverpool)
Gentleman's Magazine
Illustrated London News
Lancashire Review
Liberal Review (Liverpool)
Liverpool Courier
Liverpool Leader
Liverpool Mercury
Magazine of Art
Manchester and Salford Advertiser
Manchester City News
Manchester Courier
Manchester Evening News
Manchester Examiner
Manchester Guardian
Manchester Literary Club
Manchester Mercury
Morning Post
Municipal Journal
North of England Magazine
Oldham Advertiser
Oldham Chronicle
Oldham Evening Express
Oldham Standard
The Porcupine (Liverpool)
Preston Chronicle
Preston Guardian
Preston Herald

Rochdale Times
Roscoe Magazine
Salford Weekly News
The Scotsman
South Manchester Gazette
Stockport Advertiser
StockportChronicle
Warrington Guardian
Windsor Magazine

SECONDARY SOURCES

Books

Allthorpe-Guyton, M., and J. Stevens, *A Happy Eye: A School of Art for Norwich 1845–1982* (Norwich, 1982).
Anstey, R., *Liverpool, the African Slave Trade, and Abolition* (Liverpool, 1989).
Archer, J. H. G. (ed.), *Art and Architecture in Victorian Manchester* (Manchester, 1985).
Ashwin, C. (ed.), *Art Education Documents and Policies 1768–1975* (London, 1975).
Atkinson, N., *Sir Joseph Whitworth* (Stroud, 1996).
Bailey, P., *Leisure and Class in Victorian England: Rational Recreation and the Contest for Control, 1830–1885* (London, 1978).
Ballantyne, A., *Architecture, Landscape and Liberty: Richard Payne Knight and the Picturesque* (Cambridge, 1997).
Barrell, J., *The Political Theory of Painting from Reynolds to Hazlitt* (London, 1986).
Barlow, P., and C. Trodd (eds), *Governing Cultures: Art Institutions in Victorian London* (Aldershot, 2000).
Bate, W. J., *From Classic to Romantic: Premises of Taste in Eighteenth-Century England* (Cambridge, Mass., 1946).
Bell, Q., *The Schools of Design* (London, 1963).
Bennett, M., *The Art Sheds 1894–1905* (Liverpool, 1991).
Bennett, T., *The Birth of the Museum: History, Theory, Politics* (London, 1995).
Benson, J., *The Rise of Consumer Society in Britain, 1880–1980* (London, 1994).
Bergin, T., D. Pearce and S. Shaw, *Salford: A City and its Past* (Salford, 1974).
Bermingham, A., and J. Brewer (eds), *The Consumption of Culture 1600–1800* (London, 1995).
Berry, A., *Proud Preston's Story* (Preston, 1928).
Borsay, P., *The English Urban Renaissance* (Oxford, 1989).
Bottomore, T., and R. Nisbet (eds), *A History of Sociological Analysis* (London, 1979).
Bourdieu, P., and H. Haacke, *Free Exchange* (Cambridge, 1995).
Brewer, J., *The Pleasures of the Imagination: English Culture in the Eighteenth Century* (Chicago, 1997).
Brewer, J., and J. Plumb (eds), *The Birth of a Consumer Society* (London, 1982).

Briggs, A., *Victorian Cities* (London, 1963, reprint 1990).

Brindley, W. H., *The Soul of Manchester* (Manchester, 1929).

Brooks, A., and B. Haworth, *Boomtown Manchester 1800–1850: The Portico Connection* (Manchester, 1993).

Brooks, A., and B. Haworth, *Portico Library: A History* (Lancaster, 2000).

Brooks, C., *The Gothic Revival* (London, 1999).

Bruton, F. A., *A Short History of Manchester and Salford* (Manchester, 1927).

Burton, A., *Vision and Accident: The Story of the Victoria and Albert Museum* (London, 1999).

Burton, V. (ed.), *Liverpool Shipping, Trade and Industry: Essays on the Maritime History of Merseyside 1780–1860* (Liverpool, 1989).

Bury, J. B., *The Idea of Progress: An Inquiry into its Origin and Growth* (London, 1928).

Cameron, G., *Liverpool: Capital of the Slave Trade* (Birkenhead, 1992).

Cammack, P., *New Institutionalist Approaches to Macro-Social Analysis* (Manchester, 1989).

Campbell, C., *The Romantic Ethic and the Spirit of Modern Consumerism* (Oxford, 1987).

Cannadine, D. (ed.), *Patricians, Power and Politics in Nineteenth Century Towns* (Leicester, 1982).

Cardwell, D. S. L. (ed.), *Artisan to Graduate* (Manchester, 1974).

Carline, R., *Draw They Must: A History of the Teaching and Examining of Art* (London, 1968).

Chambers, C., *Reasonable Democracy: Jürgen Habermas and the Politics of Discourse* (London, 1996).

Chandler, G., *Liverpool* (London, 1957).

Chandler, G., *William Roscoe of Liverpool 1753–1831* (London, 1953).

Clark, K., *The Gothic Revival* (London, 1928).

Clark, P., *British Clubs and Societies, 1580–1800* (Oxford, 2000).

Clarke, M. L., *Classical Education in Britain, 1500–1900* (Cambridge, 1959).

Clarke, P., *Lancashire and the New Liberalism* (Cambridge, 1971).

Clarke, P., *Liberals and Social Democrats* (Cambridge, 1978).

Cleveland, S. D., *The Royal Manchester Institution* (Manchester, 1931).

Coleman, D. C., *Myth, History and the Industrial Revolution* (London, 1992).

Colls, R., and R. Rodger (eds), *Cities of Ideas: Civil Society and Governance in British Cities* (Aldershot, 2003).

Convey, J., *The Harris Free Public Library and Museum, Preston, 1893–1993* (Preston, 1993).

Cooke, M., *Language and Reason: A Study of Habermas's Pragmatics* (London, 1994).

Coombs, T., *Rising from Reality. Art in Oldham from 1820 to 1890* (Oldham, 1990).

Crafts, N., *British Economic Growth during the Industrial Revolution* (Oxford, 1985).

Crane, S. (ed.), *Museums and Memory* (Stanford, 2000).

Crook, J. M., *The Greek Revival* (London, 1972).

Crouch, C., *Design Culture in Liverpool* (Liverpool, 2002).

Dakin, D., *British and American Philhellenes* (Thessaloniki, 1955).

Darcy, C. P., *The Encouragement of the Fine Arts in Lancashire, 1760–1860* (Manchester, 1976).

Daunton, M. (ed.), *Charity, Self-Interest and Welfare in the English Past* (London, 1996).

Daunton, M. (ed.), *The Cambridge Urban History of Britain*, vol. 3: 1840–1950 (Cambridge, 2001).

Daunton, M. J., *Trusting Leviathan: The Politics of Taxation in Britain 1799–1914* (Cambridge, 2001).

Dodwell, C. R., *Guide to the Whitworth Art Gallery* (Manchester, 1979).

Doig, A., *Corruption and Misconduct in Contemporary British Politics* (Harmondsworth, 1984).

Douglas, M., and B. Isherwood, *The World of Goods: Towards an Anthropology of Consumption* (London, 1979).

Duncan, C., *Civilizing Rituals: Inside Public Art Museums* (London, 1995).

Dyos, H. J., and M. Wolff (eds), *The Victorian City: Images and Reality* (London, 1978).

Englander, D., *Landlord and Tenant in Urban Britain 1838–1914* (Oxford, 1983).

Fancy, H., *A History of Stockport Museum* (Stockport, 1971).

Farnie, D., *The English Cotton Industry and the World Market, 1815–1896* (Oxford, 1979).

Farnie, D., *The Manchester Ship Canal and the Rise of the Port of Manchester, 1894–1975* (Manchester, 1980).

Feather, J., *The Provincial Book Trade in Eighteenth-Century England* (Cambridge, 1985).

Fejfer, J., and E. Southworth, *The Ince Blundell Collection of Classical Sculpture*, 2 vols (London, 1991–97).

Fielding, S., *Class and Ethnicity: Irish Catholics in England, 1880–1939* (Buckingham, 1993).

Flint, K., *Impressionism in England: The Critical Reception* (London, 1984).

Fraser, D., *Urban Politics in Victorian England* (Leicester, 1976).

Fraser, D. (ed.), *Cities, Class and Communities: Essays in Honour of Asa Briggs*(Hemel Hempstead, 1990).

Garrard, J., *Democratisation in Britain: Elites, Civil Society and Reform since 1800* (Basingstoke, 2002).

Garrard, J., *Leadership and Power in Victorian Industrial Towns* (Manchester, 1983).

Gilbert, P., *The Victorian Painter's World* (Gloucester, 1990).

Gold, J., and M. Gold, *Cities of Culture* (Aldershot, 2005).

Goodale, T., and G. Godbey, *The Evolution of Leisure: Historical and Philosophical Perspectives* (London, 1998).

Gorsky, M., *Patterns of Philanthropy: Charity and Society in Nineteenth Century Bristol* (Woodbridge, 1999).

Green, P., *The Shadow of the Parthenon* (Oakland, Calif., 1972).

Greenleaf, W. H., *The Rise of Collectivism*, vol. 1 (London, 1983).

Gunn, S., *The Public Culture of the Victorian Middle Class: Ritual and Authority in the English Industrial City 1840–1914* (Manchester, 2000).

Habermas, J., *The Structural Transformation of the Public Sphere* (Cambridge, 1989).

Harford, I., *Manchester and its Ship Canal Movement* (Keele, 1994).

Harris, J. R., *Liverpool and Merseyside: Essays in the Economic and Social History of the Port and its Hinterland* (London, 1969).

Hartwell, R., *et al.* (eds), *The Long Debate on Poverty* (London, 1972).

Haskell, F., *The Ephemeral Museum: Old Master Paintings and the Rise of the Art Exhibition* (New Haven, 2000).

Hayes, C. (ed.), *Stories and Tales of Old Manchester* (Manchester, 1991).

Hemingway, A., *Landscape Imagery and Urban Culture in Early Nineteenth-Century Britain* (Cambridge, 1992).

Hennock, E. P., *Fit and Proper Persons: Ideal and Reality in Nineteenth Century Urban Government* (London, 1973).

Hewitt, M., *The Emergence of Stability in the Industrial City: Manchester 1832–65* (Aldershot, 1996).

Hill, K., *Culture and Class in English Public Museums, 1850–1914* (Aldershot, 2005).

History of the Harris Free Public Library and Museum (pamphlet) (Preston, n.d. [1976]).

Hodgson, M., *The Evolution of Institutional Economics* (London, 2004).

Hooper-Greenhill, E., *Museums and the Shaping of Knowledge* (London, 1992).

Howe, A., *The Cotton Masters 1830–1860* (Oxford, 1984).

Hyde, F., *Liverpool and the Mersey: An Economic History of a Port 1700–1970* (Newton Abbot, 1971).

Hyde, F. E., B. B. Parkinson and S. Marriner, *The Nature and Profitability of the Liverpool Slave Trade* (London, 1953).

Jenkyns, R., *The Victorians and Ancient Greece* (Oxford, 1980).

Jeremiah, D., *A Hundred Years and More* (Manchester, 1980).

Jolly, W., *Lord Leverhulme* (London, 1976).

Jones, A., *The Modalities of European Union Governance: New Institutionalist Explanations* (Oxford, 2001).

Jones, R. F., *Ancients and Moderns* (London, 1936).

Joyce, P., *Democratic Subjects* (Cambridge, 1994).

Joyce, P., *The Rule of Freedom: Liberalism and the Modern City* (London, 2003).

Joyce, P., *Visions of the People: Industrial England and the Question of Class, 1848–1914* (Cambridge, 1991).

Kaplan, F. E. S., *Museums and the Making of 'Ourselves'* (Leicester, 1994).

Kavanagh, G. (ed.), *Museum Languages: Objects and Texts* (Leicester, 1991).

Khandwalla, P., *The Design of Organizations* (New York, 1977).

Kidd, A., *Manchester* (Manchester, 1996).

Kidd, A., and D. Nicholls (eds), *Gender, Civic Culture, Consumerism* (Manchester, 1999).

Kidd, A., and K. Roberts (eds), *City, Class and Culture: Cultural Production and Social Policy in Victorian Manchester* (Manchester, 1985).

Kirk, N. (ed.), *Northern Identities Historical Interpretations of 'the North' and Northernness* (Aldershot, 2000).

Law, B., *Oldham, Brave Oldham* (Oldham, 1999).

Lawrence, J., *Speaking for the People: Party, Language and Popular Politics in England, 1867–1914* (Cambridge, 2002).

Lee, M. J., *The Consumer Society Reader* (Oxford, 2000).

Lenman, B., *Integration, Enlightenment and Industrialisation: Scotland 1745–1832* (London, 1981).

Leverhulme, W., *Viscount Leverhulme by his Son* (London, 1927).

Lloyd-Jones, H., *Blood for the Ghosts: Classical Influences in the Nineteenth and Twentieth Centuries* (London, 1982).

Lubenow, W., *The Politics of Government Growth* (Newton Abbot, 1971).

Lumley, R. (ed.), *The Museum Time Machine* (London, 1988).

Lyon, C., *Adolphe Valette* (London, 2006).

Macaulay, J., *The Gothic Revival, 1745–1845* (Glasgow, 1975).

Macdonald, S., *The History and Philosophy of Art Education* (London, 1970).

Macleod, D. S., *Art and the Victorian Middle Class: Money and the Making of Cultural Identity* (Cambridge, 1996).

Magat, R. (ed.), *Philanthropic Giving: Studies in Values and Goals* (Oxford and New York, 1989).

Martin, S., *Adolphe Valette: A French Influence in Manchester* (Manchester, 1994).

Mathias, P., and J. Davis, *The First Industrial Revolutions* (Oxford, 1989).

Matthews, G., *William Roscoe: A Memoir* (London, 1931).

Mauss, M., *The Gift*, trans. W.Halls (London, 1990).

McCord, N., *The Anti-Corn Law League 1838–1846* (London, 1958).

McKendrick, N., J. Brewer and J. H. Plumb, *The Birth of a Consumer Society: The Commercialization of Eighteenth-Century England* (London, 1982).

Morris, E., *Public Art Collections in North-West England* (Liverpool, 2001).

Morris, E., and E. Roberts (eds), *The Liverpool Academy and Other Exhibitions of Contemporary Art in Liverpool 1774–1867* (Liverpool, 1998).

Morris, R., and R. Rodger (eds), *The Victorian City, 1820–1914* (Harlow, 1993).

Morris, R., and R. Trainor (eds), *Governance in Towns and Cities* (Aldershot, 2000).

Neal, F., *Sectarian Violence: The Liverpool Experience, 1819–1914* (Manchester, 1988).

Nugent, C., *From View to Vision: British Watercolours from Sandby to Turner in the Whitworth Art Gallery* (Manchester, 1993).

O'Brien, E., *Eminent Salfordians*, vol. 1 (Salford, 1982).

O'Brien, P., *Warrington Academy 1757–86* (Wigan, 1989).

Offer, A., *Property and Politics 1870–1914* (Cambridge, 1981).

Ogden, H. W., *The Geographical Basis of the Lancashire Cotton Industry* (Manchester, 1928).

Ogilvie, R. M., *Latin and Greek: A History of the Influence of the Classics on English Life from 1600 to 1918* (London, 1964).

O'Gorman, F., *The Long Eighteenth Century: British Political and Social History 1688–1832* (London, 1997).

Ormerod, H. A., *The Liverpool Royal Institution: A Record and a Retrospect* (Liverpool, 1953).

Ostrower, F., *Why the Wealthy Give: The Culture of Elite Philanthropy* (Princeton, 1995).

Outhwaite, W., *Habermas: A Critical Introduction* (Cambridge, 1994).

Paul, C. (ed.), *The First Modern Museums of Art* (Los Angeles, 2012).

Pearce, S., *Museums, Objects and Collections* (Leicester, 1989).

Pearce, S. (ed.), *Museum Studies in Material Culture* (Leicester, 1989).

Pearce, S. (ed.), *Objects of Knowledge* (London, 1990).

Pears, I., *The Discovery of Painting: The Growth of Interest in the Arts in England, 1680–1768* (London, 1988).

Perkin, H., *Origins of Modern English Society* (London, 1969).

Peters, B. G., *Institutional Theory in Political Science* (London, 1999).

Pickering, P., *The People's Bread: A History of the Anti-Corn Law League* (Leicester, 2000).

Pratt, T., *The Portico Library: Its History and Associations* (Manchester, 1922).

Pressly, N. L., *The Fuseli Circle in Rome: Early Romantic Art of the 1770s* (New Haven, 1979).

Prior, N., *Museums and Modernity: Art Galleries and the Making of Modern Culture* (Oxford, 2002).

Rees Leahy, H. (ed.), *Art, City, Spectacle: The 1857 Manchester Art Treasures Exhibition Revisited* (Manchester, 2009).

Rendall, J., *The Origins of the Scottish Enlightenment 1707–1776* (London, 1978).

Riesman, D., *Thorstein Veblen: A Critical Interpretation* (New York, 1953).

Robins, R. S., *Political Institutionalisation and the Integration of Elites* (London, 1976).

Roderick, G. W., and M. D. Stephens, *Education and Industry in the Nineteenth Century: The English Disease?* (London, 1978).

Rosenthal, M., C. Payne and S. Wilcox (eds), *Prospects for the Nation: Recent Essays in British Landscape 1750–1880* (New Haven, 1997).

Roth, R. (ed.), *Who Ran the Cities: Elite and Urban Power Structures in Europe, 1700–2000* (Frankfurt, 2007).

Rubinstein, W. D., *Elites and the Wealthy in Modern British History* (London, 1988).

Rutherford, M., *Institutions in Economics: The Old and the New Institutionalism* (Cambridge, 1994).

Rykwert, J., *The Idea of a Town* (Princeton, 1976).

St Clair, W., *That Greece Might Still Be Free: The Philhellenes in the War of Independence* (Oxford, 1972).

Sandberg, L., *Lancashire in Decline: A Study in Entrepreneurship, Technology, and International Trade* (Columbus, 1974).

Sartin, S., *The People and Places of Historic Preston* (Preston, 1988).

Savage, M., J. Barlow, P. Deickens and T. Fielding, *Property, Bureaucracy and Culture* (London, 1992).

Seckler, D., *Thorstein Veblen and the Institutionalists* (London, 1979).

Sellers, I., *Early Modern Warrington 1520–1847* (Lampeter, 1998).

Shaw, D., *Selling an Urban Image: Blackpool at the Turn of the Century*, Department of Geography, University of Birmingham: Working Papers, 54 (Birmingham, 1990).

Simonsuuri, K., *Homer's Original Genius: Eighteenth-Century Notions of the Early Greek Epic* (Cambridge, 1979).

Singleton, J., *Lancashire on the Scrapheap: The Cotton Industry 1945–1970* (Oxford, 1991).

Skipp, V., *The Making of Victorian Birmingham* (Birmingham, 1983).

Smith, E., *Reform or Revolution? A Diary of Reform in England, 1830–2* (Stroud, 1992).

Solkin, D., *Painting for Money: The Visual Arts and the Public Sphere in Eighteenth Century England* (New Haven, 1992).

Speirs, M., *Victoria Park, Manchester* (Manchester, 1976).

Stamp, G., *Alexander 'Greek' Thompson* (Glasgow, 1999).

Stancliffe, F. S., *John Shaw's Club* (Manchester, 1938).

Stephens, W. B., *Adult Education and Society in an Industrial Town: Warrington 1800–1900* (Exeter, 1980).

Stevens, T. (ed.), *James Hamilton Hay* (Liverpool, 1973).

Stewart, C., *Regional College of Art, Manchester – a Short History* (Manchester, n.d.).

Stillman, D., *English Neo-Classical Architecture*, 2 vols (London, 1988).

Stobart, J., *The First Industrial Region: North-West England, c.1700–60* (Manchester, 2004).

Stockport Libraries: A Century of Service (Stockport, 1975).

Stoneman, R., *Land of Lost Gods* (London, 1987).

Stray, C. (ed.), *Classics in 19th and 20th Century Cambridge* (Cambridge, 1999).

Sutton, G., *Artisan or Artist? A History of the Teaching of Arts and Crafts in English Schools* (London, 1967).

Swedenberg, H. T., *The Theory of the Epic in England, 1650–1800* (New York, 1972).

Sweet, R., *The English Town, 1680–1840* (Harlow, 1998).

Swift, J., *Changing Fortunes: The Birmingham School of Art Building 1880–1995* (Birmingham, 1996).

Taylor, B., *Art for the Nation* (Manchester, 1999).

Thomson, E. P., *Customs in Common* (London, 1991).

Thomson, S., *Manchester's Victorian Art Scene and its Unrecognised Artists* (Warrington, 2007).

Tiffin, H. J., *A History of the Liverpool Institute Schools* (Liverpool, 1935).

Timmins, G., *Made in Lancashire: A History of Regional Industrialisation* (Manchester, 1998).

Trevelyan, G., *British History in the Nineteenth Century and After* (London, 1922).

Turner, F. M., *The Greek Heritage in Victorian Britain* (London, 1981).

Vernon, J., *Politics and the People: A Study in English Political Culture, c.1815–1867* (Cambridge, 1993).

Walcott, F., *The Origins of 'Culture and Anarchy': Matthew Arnold and Popular Education* (Toronto, 1970).

Waller, P. J., *Town, City and Nation: England 1850–1914* (Oxford, 1983).

Walton, J., *The Blackpool Landlady* (Manchester, 1978).

Walton, J., *Lancashire: A Social History, 1558–1939* (Manchester, 1987).

Waterfield, G., *The People's Galleries: Art Museums and Exhibitions in Britain, 1800–1914* (London, 2015).

Watkin, D., *Athenian Stuart, Pioneer of the Greek Revival* (London, 1982).

Watkin, D., *The Life and Work of C. R. Cockerell* (London, 1974).

Wiener, M., *English Culture and the Decline of the Industrial Spirit, 1850–1980* (Cambridge, 1981).

Willett, J., *Art in a City* (London, 1967).

Woodson-Boulton, A., *Transformative Beauty: Art Museums in Industrial Britain* (Stanford, 2012).

Woodward, C., *In Ruins* (London, 2002).

Wolff, J., and J. Seed (eds), *The Culture of Capital: Art, Power and the Nineteenth Century Middle Class* (Manchester, 1988).

Articles

Balfour, K., 'A. "Petty" Professor of Modern History: William Smythe (1765–1849)', *Cambridge Historical Journal*, 9 (1948), 217–38.

Beckett, J., and C. Smith, 'Urban Renaissance and Consumer Culture in Nottingham, 1688–1750', *Urban History*, 27 (2000), 31–50.

Ben Israel, H., 'William Smythe, Historian of the French Revolution', *Journal of the History of Ideas*, 21 (1960), 571–85.

Bennett, M., 'A Check List of Pre-Raphaelite Pictures Exhibited at Liverpool 1846–67, and Some of their Northern Collectors', *Burlington Magazine*, 105 (1963), 477–95.

Bennett, M., 'The Pre-Raphaelites and the Liverpool Prize', *Apollo*, 76 (1972), 748–53.

Bermingham, A., 'Introduction: The Consumption of Culture: Image, Object, Text', in A. Bermingham and J. Brewer (eds), *The Consumption of Culture 1600–1800* (London, 1995), 1–20.

Berry, H., 'Promoting Taste in the Provincial Press: National and Local Culture in Eighteenth-Century Newcastle upon Tyne', *British Journal for Eighteenth-Century Studies*, 25 (2002), 1–18.

Bock, K., 'Theories of Progress, Development, Evolution', in T. Bottomore and R. Nisbet (eds), *A History of Sociological Analysis* (London, 1979), 55–7.

Borsay, P., 'The English Urban Renaissance: The Development of Provincial Urban Culture c1680–c1760', *Social History*, 2 (1977), 581–603.

Bud, R. F., 'The Royal Manchester Institution', in D. S. L. Cardwell (ed.), *Artisan to Graduate* (Manchester, 1974), 119–33.

Cain, P., and A. Hopkins, 'Gentlemanly Capitalism and British Expansion Overseas, I: The Old Colonial System, 1688–1850', *Economic History Review*, 39 (1986), 501–25.

Chalkin, C., 'Capital Expenditure on Building for Cultural Purposes in Provincial England, 1730–1830', *Business History*, 22 (1980), 51–70.

Checkland, S. G., 'Economic Attitudes in Liverpool, 1793–1807', *Economic History Review*, 5 (1952), 58–75.

Chun, D., 'Patriotism on Display: Sir John Fleming Leicester's Patronage of British Art', *British Art Journal*, 4 (2003), 23–8.

Conran, E., 'Art Collections', in J. H. G. Archer (ed.), *Art and Architecture in Victorian Manchester* (Manchester, 1985), 65–80.

Cook, B. F., 'Townley, Charles (1737–1805)', *Oxford Dictionary of National Biography* (Oxford, 2004), online edn, September 2014, www.oxforddnb.com/view/article/27601, accessed 7 August 2017.

Cowan, J. S., 'Joseph Brotherton and the Public Library Movement', *Library Association Record*, 59 (1957), 156–9.

Curti, M., 'American Philanthropy and the National Character', *American Quarterly*, 10 (1958), 420–37.

Daunton, M., '"Gentlemanly Capitalism" and British Industry 1820–1914', *Past and Present*, 122 (1989), 119–58.

Dellheim, C., 'Imagining England: Victorian Views of the North', *Northern History*, 22 (1986), 216–31.

Diamond, P., 'Joseph Wright of Derby (1734–1797): The Importance of a Local Museum in the Formation of An Artist's Reputation', *British Art Journal*, 14 (2013), 18–23.

Doyle, B. M., 'The Changing Function of Urban Government: Councillors, Officials and Pressure Groups', in M. Daunton (ed.), *The Cambridge Urban History of Britain*, vol. 3: 1840–1950 (Cambridge, 2001), 287–313.

Fine, B., and E. Leopold, 'Consumerism and the Industrial Revolution', *Social History*, 15 (1990), 151–7.

Finke, U., 'The Art Treasures Exhibition', in J. H. G. Archer (ed.), *Art and Architecture in Victorian Manchester*(Manchester, 1985), 102–26.

Finlay, M. I., 'The Ancient City: From Fustel de Coulanges to Max Weber and Beyond', *Comparative Studies in History and Society*, 19 (1977), 305–27.

Fraser, W. H., 'From Civic Gospel to Municipal Socialism', in D. Fraser (ed.), *Cities, Class and Communities: Essays in Honour of Asa Briggs* (Hemel Hempstead, 1990), 58–80.

Garrard, J., 'The Salford Gas Scandal of 1887', *Manchester Region History Review*, 2 (1988–89), 12–20.

Goodwin, M., 'Objects, Belief and Power in Mid-Victorian England: The Origins of the Victoria and Albert Museum', in S. Pearce (ed.), *Objects of Knowledge* (London, 1990), 9–49.

Gunn, S., 'The Middle Class, Modernity and the Provincial City: Manchester c.1840–80', in A. Kidd and D. Nicholls (eds), *Gender, Civic Culture and Consumerism* (Manchester, 1999), 112–27.

Gunn, S., 'The Public Sphere, Modernity and Consumption: New Perspectives on the History of the English Middle Class', in A. Kidd and D. Nicholls (eds), *Gender, Civic Culture and Consumerism* (Manchester, 1999), 12–30.

Hakala, T., 'A Great Man in Clogs: Performing Authenticity in Victorian Lancashire', *Victorian Studies*, 52 (2010), 387–412.

Harris, N., 'The Gilded Age Revisited: Boston and the Museum Movement', *American Quarterly*, 14 (1962), 545–66.

Harrison, B., 'Philanthropy and the Victorians', *Victorian Studies*, 9 (1966), 353–74.

Harrison, M., 'Art and Social Regeneration: The Ancoats Art Museum', *Manchester Region History Review*, 7 (1993), 63–4.

Harrison, M., 'Art and Philanthropy: T. C. Horsfall and the Manchester Art Museum', in A. Kidd and K. Roberts (eds), *City, Class and Culture: Cultural Production and Social Policy in Victorian Manchester* (Manchester, 1985), 120–47.

Hawcroft, F. W., 'The Whitworth Art Gallery', in J. H. G. Archer (ed.), *Art and Architecture in Victorian Manchester* (Manchester, 1985), 208–29.

Hennock, E. P., 'Finance and Politics', *Historical Journal*, 6 (1963), 212–15.

Hewitt, M., and R. Poole, 'Samuel Bamford and Northern Identity', in N. Kirk (ed.), *Northern Identities: Historical Interpretations of 'the North' and Northernness* (Aldershot, 2000), 111–32.

Hoock, H., '"Struggling against a Vulgar Prejudice": Patriotism and the Collecting of British Art at the Turn of the Nineteenth Century', *Journal of British Studies*, 49 (2010), 566–91.

Hooper-Greenhill, E., 'The Museum in the Disciplinary Society', in S. Pearce (ed.), *Museum Studies in Material Culture* (Leicester, 1989), 61–72.

Hopkinson, M., 'The Print Market in Liverpool in the Late Eighteenth Century', *Print Quarterly*, 24 (2007), 107–15.

Jones, C., 'Some Recent Trends in the History of Charity', in M. Daunton (ed.), *Charity, Self-Interest and Welfare in the English Past* (London, 1996), 51–63.

Journal of the History of Collections, 4 (1992) (special issue).

Klein, R., 'Art and Authority in Antebellum New York City: The Rise and Fall of the American Art-Union', *Journal of American History*, 81 (1995), 1534–61.

Langton, J., 'The Industrial Revolution and the Regional Geography of England', *Transactions of the Institute of British Geographers*, 9:2 (1984), 145–67.

Lee, R., 'Ut Pictura Poesis: The Humanistic Theory of Painting', *Art Bulletin*, 22 (1940), 197–269.

Macandrew, H., 'Henry Fuseli and William Roscoe', *Liverpool Bulletin*, 8 (1959–60), 5–52.

MacDonald, S., 'The Royal Manchester Institution', in J. H. G. Archer (ed.), *Art and Architecture in Victorian Manchester*(Manchester, 1985), 28–45.

MacLeod, D., 'Homosociality and Middle-Class Identity in Early Victorian Patronage of the Arts', in A. Kidd and D. Nicholls (eds), *Gender, Civic Culture and Consumerism* (Manchester, 1999), 65–80.

Marchand, S., 'The Quarrel of the Ancients and Moderns in the German Museums', in S. Crane (ed.), *Museums and Memory* (Stanford, 2000), 170–85.

McCarthy, K., 'Creating the American Athens: Cities, Cultural Institutions, and the Arts, 1840–1939', *American Quarterly*, 37 (1985), 426–39.

McCord, N., 'Aspects of the Relief of Poverty in Early Nineteenth-Century Britain', in R. Hartwell *et al.* (eds), *The Long Debate on Poverty* (London, 1972), 91–108.

McInnes, A., 'The Emergence of a Leisure Town: Shrewsbury 1660–1760', *Past and Present*, 120 (1988), 53–87.

McKendrick, N., 'The Consumer Revolution of the Eighteenth-Century England', in N. McKendrick, J. Brewer and J. Plumb (eds), *The Birth of a Consumer Society* (London, 1982), 9–33.

Millward, R., 'The Political Economy of Urban Utilities', in M. Daunton (ed.), *The Cambridge Urban History of Britain*, vol. 3: 1840–1950 (Cambridge, 2001), 315–49.

Monod, P., 'Painters and Party Politics in England, 1714–1760', *Eighteenth Century Studies*, 26 (1993), 367–98.

Moore, J., 'Periclean Preston, Public Art and the Classical Tradition in Late-Nineteenth-Century Lancashire', *Northern History*, 40 (2003), 299–323.

Moore, J., 'Progressive Pioneers: Manchester Liberalism, the Independent Labour Party, and Local Politics in the 1890s', *Historical Journal*, 44 (2001), 989–1013.

Moore, J., 'Urban Space and Civic Identity in Manchester 1780–1914', *Transactions of the Historic Society of Lancashire and Cheshire*, 153 (2004), 87–123.

Moore, J., and R. Rodger, 'Municipal Knowledge and Policy Networks in British Local Government, 1832–1914', *Yearbook of European Administrative History*, 15 (2003), 29–58.

Moore, J., and R. Rodger, 'Who Really Ran the Cities?', in R. Roth (ed.), *Who Ran the Cities: Elite and Urban Power Structures in Europe, 1700–2000* (Frankfurt, 2007), 33–70.

Morris, E., 'The Formation of the Gallery of Art in the Liverpool Royal Institution, 1816–1819', *Transactions of the Historic Society of Lancashire and Cheshire*, 142 (1992), 87–98.

Morris, E., 'The Liverpool Academy and Other Art Exhibitions in Liverpool 1774–1867', introduction to *The Liverpool Academy and Other Exhibitions of Contemporary Art in Liverpool 1774–1867* (Liverpool, 1998).

Morris, E., 'Philip Henry Rathbone and the Purchase of Contemporary Foreign Paintings for the Walker Art Gallery, Liverpool, 1871–1914', *Walker Art Gallery Annual Report and Bulletin*, 6 (1975–76), 59–67.

Morris, R. J., 'Voluntary Societies and British Urban Elites, 1780–1850: An Analysis', *Historical Journal*, 26 (1983), 95–118.

O'Gorman, F., 'The Instability of Britain (1688–1832)', unpublished paper, British Society for Eighteenth Century Studies conference, Manchester, 2002.

O'Gorman, F., 'Party Politics in the Early Nineteenth Century', *English Historical Review*, 102 (1987), 63–84.

O'Neill, J., 'The Disciplinary Society: From Weber to Foucault', *British Journal of Sociology*, 37 (1986), 42–60.

Pass, A. J., 'Thomas Worthington', in J. H. G. Archer (ed.), *Art and Architecture in Victorian Manchester* (Manchester, 1985), 81–101.

Payton, R. L., 'Philanthropic Values', in R. Magat (ed.), *Philanthropic Giving: Studies in Values and Goals* (Oxford and New York, 1989), 29–45.

Perkin, H. J., 'The "Social Tone" of Victorian Seaside Resorts in the North West', *Northern History*, 11 (1975), 181–94.

Phillips, J., and C. Wetherell, 'The Great Reform Act of 1832 and the Political Modernization of England', *American Historical Review*, 100 (1995), 411–36.

Piliavin, J., and H. Charng, 'Altruism: A Review of Recent Theory and Research', *Annual Review of Sociology*, 16 (1990), 27–65.

Pointon, M., 'W. E. Gladstone as an Art Patron and Collector', *Victorian Studies*, 19 (1975), 73–98.

Roberts, E., 'The Liverpool Academy as a Teaching Institution', in E. Morris and E. Roberts (eds), *The Liverpool Academy and Other Exhibitions of Contemporary Art in Liverpool, 1774–1867* (Liverpool, 1998), 21–34.

Rodger, R., 'The Common Good and Civic Promotion: Edinburgh 1860–1914', in R. Colls and R. Rodger (eds), *Cities of Ideas: Civil Society and Governance in British Cities* (Aldershot, 2003), 144–77.

Roeder, C., 'William Green, the Lake Artist', *Transactions of the Lancashire and Cheshire Antiquarian Society*, 14 (1896), 100–30.

Rose, R. B., 'The Jacobins of Liverpool', *Liverpool Bulletin*, 9 (1960–61), 35–49.

Rubinstein, W. D., '"Gentlemanly Capitalism" and British Industry 1820–1914', *Past and Present*, 132 (1991), 150–70.

Saumarez Smith, C., 'The Institutionalisation of Art in Early Victorian England', *Transactions of the Royal Historical Society*, 20 (2010), 113–25.

Seed, J., 'Commerce and the Liberal Arts: The Political Economy of Art in Manchester, 1775–1860', in J. Wolff and J. Seed (eds), *The Culture of Capital: Art, Power and the Nineteenth Century Middle Class* (Manchester, 1988), 45–81.

Sellers, I., 'William Roscoe, the Roscoe Circle and Radical Politics in Liverpool 1787–1807', *Transactions of the Historic Society and Lancashire and Cheshire*, 120 (1968), 45–62.

Shapely, P., 'Charity, Status and Leadership: Charitable Image and the Manchester Man', *Journal of Social History*, 32 (1998), 157–77.

Smith, C., 'The Institutionalisation of Art in Early Victorian England', *Transactions of the Royal Historical Society*, 20 (2010), 113–25.

Smith, J., 'Urban Elites c.1830–1930 and Urban History', *Urban History*, 27 (2000), 255–75.

Stobart, J., 'Building an Urban Identity. Cultural Space and Civic Boosterism in a "New" Industrial Town. Burslem, 1761–1911', *Social History*, 29 (2004), 485–98.

Tite, C., 'Sensation, Danger and New Protagonists of Taste in Mid-Eighteenth Century Britain', *Anglia – Zeitschrift für englische Philologie*, 123 (2005), 26–44.

Trepp, J., 'The Liverpool Movement for the Abolition of the English Slave Trade', *Journal of Negro History*, 13 (1928), 265–85.

Treuherz, J., 'Ford Madox Brown and the Manchester Murals', in J. H. G. Archer (ed.), *Art and Architecture in Victorian Manchester* (Manchester, 1985), 162–207.

Treuherz, J., 'The Manchester Royal Jubilee Exhibition of 1887', *Victorian Poetry*, 25 (1987), 192–222.

Trodd, C., 'The Authority of Art: Cultural Criticism and the Idea of the Royal Academy in Mid-Victorian Britain', *Art History*, 20 (1997), 3–22.

Trodd, C., 'Representing the Victorian Royal Academy: The Properties of Culture and the Promotion of Art', in P. Barlow and C. Trodd (eds), *Governing Cultures: Art Institutions in Victorian London* (Aldershot, 2000), 56–68.

Velema, W., 'Ancient and Modern Virtue Compared: De Beaufort and Van Effen on Republican Citizenship', *Eighteenth-Century Studies*, 30 (1997), 437–43.

Wach, H. M., 'Culture and the Middle Classes: Popular Knowledge in Industrial Manchester', *Journal of British Studies*, 27 (1988), 375–404.

Wach, H. M., 'A "Still, Small Voice" from the Pulpit: Religion and the Creation of Social Morality in Manchester, 1820–1850', *Journal of Modern History*, 63 (1991), 425–56.

Waithe, M., 'The St. George's Museum', *Victorian Review*, 39 (2013), 35–40.

Weisinger, H., 'The English Origins of the Sociological Interpretation of the Renaissance', *Journal of the History of Ideas*, 11 (1950), 321–38.

When Napoleon was Attacked in the Park …', *Stockport Heritage Magazine*, 3:6 (Summer 1995).

Wilson, A., 'Cultural Identity of Liverpool, 1790–1850: The Early Learned Societies', *Transactions of the Historic Society of Lancashire and Cheshire*, 147 (1997), 55–80.

Wilson, A., '"The Florence of the North"? The Civic Culture of Liverpool in the Early Nineteenth Century', in A. Kidd and D. Nicholls (eds), *Gender, Civic Culture, Consumerism* (Manchester, 1999), 34–46.

Wohl, A., '"Gold and Mud": Capitalism and Culture in Victorian Britain', *Albion*, 23 (1991), 275–81.

Unpublished theses

Bowe, M., 'James Hibbert of Preston', BA thesis, University of Manchester, 1958.

Carter, G., 'William Beaumont (1797–1889) and the Town of Warrington in the 19th Century', diploma thesis, University of Liverpool, 1983.

Chun, D., 'A History of the Leicester Family, Tabley House, and its Collection of Paintings', PhD thesis, University of Manchester, 2000.

Heydari, S., 'Manchester School of Art', BA thesis, Manchester Metropolitan University, n.d.

Lord, P., 'History of Education in Oldham', MEd thesis, University of Manchester, 1938.

McDougal, C., 'Library Growth in Preston 1694–1893: The Development of the Harris Free Public Library and Museum', BA thesis, St John's College, York, n.d.

Morris, C., 'History of the Liverpool Regional College of Art 1825–70', MPhil thesis, Liverpool Polytechnic, 1985.

Regan, G., 'Art Education in an Industrial Town: Warrington School of Art 1853–93', BA thesis, Manchester Metropolitan University, 1982.

Whitfield, V., 'A Lottery for Art: The Manchester Art Union 1840–1850', BA thesis, University of Manchester, 1997.

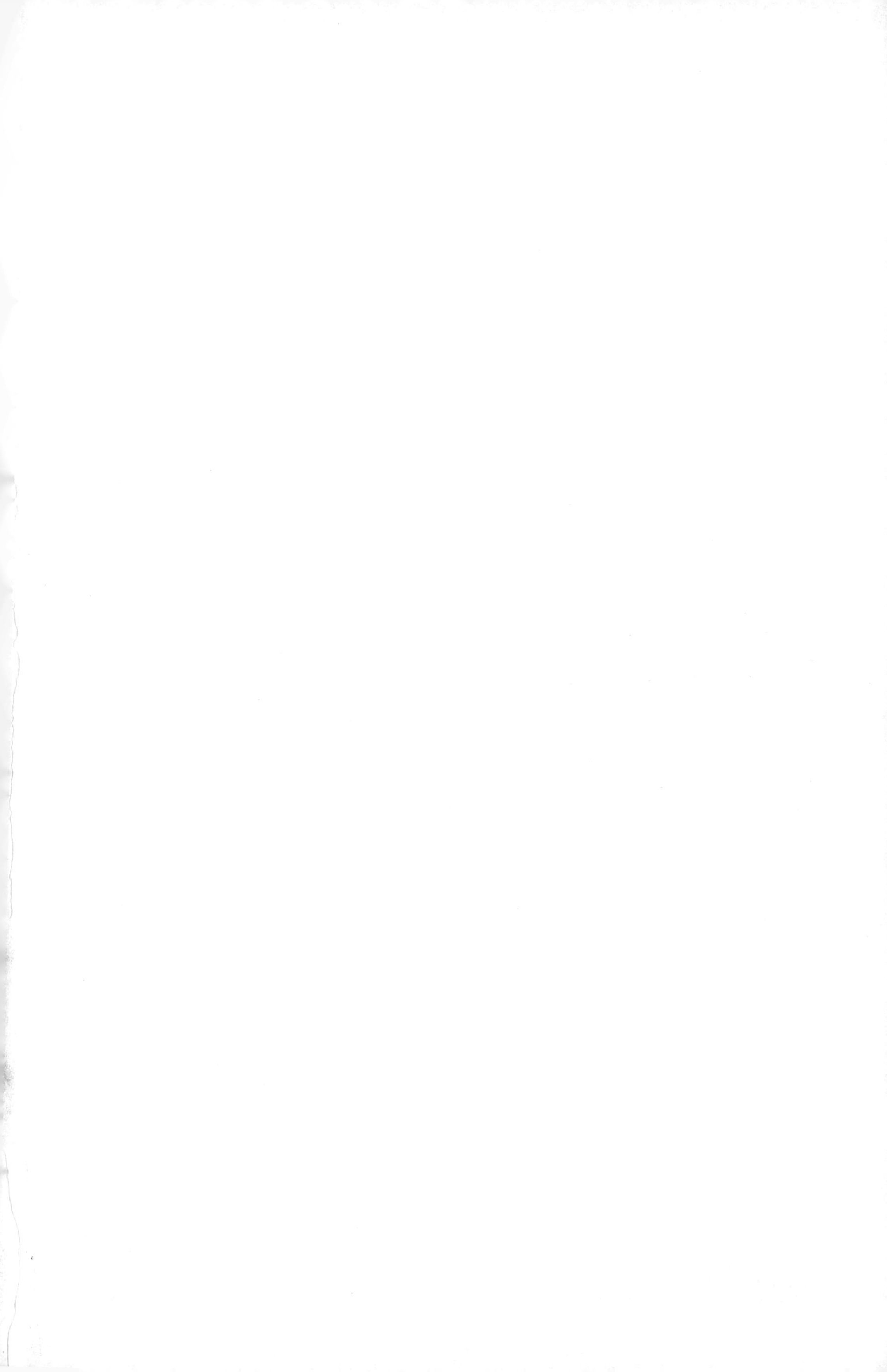